Asian American Drama:

9 plays from the Multiethnic Landscape

Play Anthologies from Applause

NATIONAL BLACK DRAMA ANTHOLOGY
edited by Woodie King

BLACK HEROES edited by Errol Hill

PLAYS BY AMERICAN WOMEN 1900-1930
edited by Judith Barlow

PLAYS BY AMERICAN WOMEN 1930-1960
edited by Judith Barlow

WOMEN ON THE VERGE edited by Rosette Lamont

WOMENSWORK edited by Julia Miles

WOMEN HEROES edited by Julia Miles

**HERE TO STAY: FIVE PLAYS FROM
THE WOMEN'S PROJECT** edited by Julia Miles

AMAZON ALL-STARS edited by Rosemary Keefe Curb

CLASSICAL TRAGEDY edited by Robert Corrigan

CLASSICAL COMEDY edited by Robert Corrigan

MEDIEVAL & TUDOR DRAMA edited by John Gassner

ELIZABETHAN DRAMA edited by John Gassner and
William Green

**THE SERVANT OF TWO MASTERS AND OTHER
ITALIAN CLASSICS** edited by Eric Bentley

**THE MISANTHROPE AND OTHER FRENCH
CLASSICS** edited by Eric Bentley

LIFE IS A DREAM AND OTHER SPANISH CLASSICS
edited by Eric Bentley

Asian American Drama:

9 plays from the Multiethnic Landscape

edited by Brian Nelson

APPLAUSE
NEW YORK • LONDON

AN APPLAUSE ORIGINAL
Asian American Drama: Nine Plays from the Multiethnic Landscape
edited by Brian Nelson
Anthology format and notes © 1997 Brian Nelson
Forward © 1997 David Henry Hwang
Introduction © Dorinne Kondo

Library of Congress Cataloging–in–Publication Data:
Asian American drama : 9 plays from the multiethnic landscape / edited
by Brian Nelson
    p.   cm.
  "An Applause original"--T.p. verso
  Contents: Foreword / David Henry Hwang -- Introduction / Dorinne
Kondo -- Day standing on its head / Philip Kan Gotanda --Tokyo
bound / Amy Hill -- As sometimes in a dead man's face / Velina Hasu
Houston -- Bondage / David Henry Hwang -- The gate of heaven / Lane
Nishikawa and Victor Talmadge -- S.A.M. I am / Garrett H. Omata --
The rainy season / Dwight Okita -- The art of waiting / Rob Shin --
Hiro / Denise Uyehara.
  ISBN 1-55783-314-1
  1. American drama --Asian American authors. 2. American
drama--20th century. 3. Asian Americans--Drama. I. Nelson, Brian.
PS 628.A85A88 1997
812'.54080895--DC21   97-27054
                                  CIP

British Cataloging–in–Publication Data:
A catalogue record of this book is available from the British Library

Applause Theatre Book Publishers   **A&C Black**
1841 Broadway   Howard Road, Eaton Socon
New York, NY 10023   Huntingdon Cambs PE19 3EZ
(212) 765–7880   0171 242 0946
FAX   (212) 765–7875   FAX: 0171 831–8478

CONTENTS

ACKNOWLEDGMENTS

The editor wishes to thank the playwrights whose talent and generosity made this volume possible, as well as the following people whose advice or time assisted in one way or another in the completion of this anthology: Doris Baizley, Luisa Cariaga, Jay Chan, Patricia Chu, Paula Cizmar, William Craver, Tim Dang, Mitch Douglas, Kenny Fries, Naomi Iizuka, Steve Kaplan, Dave King, Dorinne Kondo, Benjamin Lum, Jaime Meyer, Julia Miles, Barbara Payne, Rob Narasaki, Alysa Shwedel, Stephen Weeks, Jill Westmoreland, Jerry Whiddon, Tom Whitaker, Elizabeth Wong, Wakako Yamauchi, and Chay Yew.

Special thanks, as always, go to Barbara Calvi for her unwavering support, and to Nobu McCarthy and Tom Donaldson for giving me a chance.

This volume is dedicated to the memory of Garrett Omata.

THE MYTH OF IMMUTABLE CULTURAL IDENTITY

As I approach the end of my second decade in the American theatre, I am struck by a profound shift in works by Asian/Pacific
American playwrights. The most heated debates among Asian/Pacifics
have traditionally centered around the issue of cultural authenticity.
The most common criticism any Asian/Pacific author hears is that his
or her work "reinforces stereotypes." I criticized the Broadway musical *Miss Saigon* for reinforcing the stereotype of Asian women as submissive to white men. My own play *M. Butterfly* was criticized for
reinforcing the stereotype of Asian men as effeminate. Amy Tan's *The
Joy Luck Club* has been criticized for portraying Asian men as undesirable. Maxine Hong Kingston's *The Woman Warrior* was criticized for
inauthentic uses for Chinese mythology. Frank Chin's play *The
Chicken Coop Chinaman* was criticized for reinforcing stereotypes of
broken–English–speaking Chinatown tour guides.

While no author enjoys bearing the brunt of criticism, these con-
troversies have been largely constructive, for they have enabled
Asian/Pacific audiences to define their own experience, by either embracing or rejecting the vision of a particular artist. Certainly, we have
all endured for too long images of Asian/Pacifics that are clearly inauthentic, two–dimensional caricatures void of humanity, from the
heartlessly evil (Fu Manchu) to the heartlessly good (Charlie Chan).
Yet the question of what constitutes an "authentic" vision is much
more complex. What if the voice of a particular Asian/Pacific writer
does not ring true to my ears? Is that work therefore false, its author
brainwashed by the pervasive force of white racism? Is my experience
more authentic than yours?

For several decades, those on various sides of such arguments have
shared a powerful underlying assumption: that a single Asian/Pacific
perspective can lay claim to the mantle of authenticity. Groups and individuals have fought bitterly over this Holy Grail. Yet the premise
that an immutable cultural identity actually exists has gone largely un-
challenged. In theory, such a perspective lives separate from the corrupting influences of white America. The authors of such work would
have escaped the abyss of the American melting pot; having remained
unassimilatable, they would speak as guardians of Asian/Pacific
American purity.

Taken together, the plays in this volume seriously challenge notions of cultural purity and racial isolationism; indeed, they explode

the very myth of an immutable cultural identity. Written largely by younger, or "Third Wave" Asian/Pacific playwrights, these works acknowledge the fluidity of culture itself, declaring it a living thing, born of ever–changing experience and therefore subject to continual reinterpretation. We may be victims of racism but we may also be its perpetrators, as in Rob Shin's *The Art of Waiting*. Racial background may play only one part in our identities, as in Denise Uyehara's *Hiro*. Philip Kan Gotanda's *Day Standing on its Head* suggests that political perspectives which once seemed sufficient for self–definition may grow old and wither with time. Perhaps most revolutionary is the recognition that our identities as Asian/Pacifics cannot be separated from the other cultures which have also become part of our personal histories, whether these be Jewish, gay, or the natural result of a mixed–race heritage. In these plays, a Japanese American male can become the literary voice of angry white men, or a man and woman can mutate together from one ethnic identity to another, in search of common connection and higher love.

In their rejection of cultural fundamentalism, the plays in this volume illuminate a path which may lead Asian/Pacifics, indeed all Americans, into the coming century. These authors accept the search for identity as a lifelong journey, riddled with winding paths and strange detours, a set of questions to be asked over and over again, but perhaps never to be definitively answered.

David Henry Hwang
New York City, 1996

INTRODUCTION

The plays in Brian Nelson's anthology mark the emergence of a vibrant moment in the history of American theatre. Deploying various aesthetic strategies and speaking in multiple voices, the playwrights here delineate the complexities of our lives in an increasingly diverse and complicated racial landscape. These complications, including new forms of political and cultural possibility and the articulation of contradiction and tension, are particularly evident in states such as California, where there soon will be no single racial majority, and where racial issues — immigration, affirmative action, multiculturalism, and in theatre, "non-traditional" casting — bristle with significance. The plays in this volume eloquently voice these dilemmas of our times in tones that are at once lyrical, funny, fantastic, serious — and always, always provocative.

Thus, the publication of *Asian American Drama: Nine Plays from the Multiethnic Landscape* occurs within a shifting racial matrix in which conventional definitions of race are being challenged, proliferated, and transformed, even as race continues to have powerful, often oppressive, effects in the world. Perhaps most crucially, the collection begins to take account of the significant continuities and changes in the very articulation of what it means to be "Asian American." A term formed in the 1960s as — in part — a replacement for the exoticizing, imperializing epithet "Oriental," "Asian American" is a historically specific, coalitional identity that embraces peoples of Asian origin, and with the increasing use of the term "Asian Pacific American," peoples from the Pacific Islands. "Asian Pacific Americans" come from nations of origins often with rivalrous, sometimes even mutually hostile, relations; it is the shared historical horizon of racism in this country that creates a common struggle and political solidarity. Thus, "Asian American" is a strategic alliance, not an inert, monolithic category. And like any collective identity, it is in turn crosscut by other forces, including gender, class and sexuality. Above all, "Asian American" and "Asian Pacific American" call forth new kinds of racialized subjects and perform new kinds of racial identities.

This identity is always in process. In the 1960s "Asian American" reflected the general demographics of the Asian diaspora in the United States. Since the earliest waves of Asian immigration primarily comprised workers from China and Japan, with lesser numbers from the Philippines, Korea and India, so the definition of "Asian American" seemed largely East Asian in origin. The passage of the

1965 Immigration Act removed quotas based on national origin, thus removing barriers to Asian immigration in the U.S. 1965 thus constitutes a watershed in the historical formation of Asian American identities, as post–1965 immigrants from Korea, Vietnam, Cambodia, Laos, the Philippines, India and the Pacific Islands continue to change the face of Asian America.

The plays in this anthology chart these continuities and transformations, speaking in part to such differences in immigration histories. The major "ethnic" theatres — for example, East West Players in Los Angeles, Asian American Theatre Company in San Francisco, Pan Asian Repertory in New York, and Northwest Asian American Theatre Company in Seattle — were founded primarily by Chinese American and Japanese American artists as alternatives to mainstream–dominated venues. The ethnic composition of the artists reflected the demographics of the Asian American population, as well as class background and duration of residence in the United States. Accordingly, the themes treated in Asian American dramas tended to emphasize historical experiences common to these groups: Chinese immigration and labor histories, such as work on the railroads, and the Japanese American internment camps of World War II. Indeed, the naturalistic "camp play" came to embody "Asian American theatre" of this period. As the generations shift, plays by Chinese American and Japanese American playwrights deploy ever more various narrative strategies and themes, as the plays in this anthology demonstrate. And with post–1965 immigration, we are continuing to see the emergence of new playwrights from newer Asian Pacific communities, including the vibrant and exciting work of young playwrights and performance artists such as Rob Shin, Han Ong, Linda Faigao–Hall, Sung Rno and others.

Here, it is crucial to underline the highly significant mediating role played by theatres such as East West Players as sites for the performance and creation of what it means to be "Asian American." Training actors and offering them opportunities to perform in plays that would be closed to them in mainstream theatre, and fostering new playwrights in workshops such as the David Henry Hwang Writers' Institute (which nurtured the work of two playwrights represented here as well as this author), are invaluable contributions to American theatre and to the continuing creation and re–creation of Asian American identities and communities. Here, teachers such as playwrights R.A. Shiomi, David Henry Hwang, Paula Cizmar and Brian

Nelson, among others, provided and continue to provide critical instruction and encouragement indispensable to the development of new artists. This pedagogical function can be combined with equally significant curatorial roles, such as Chiori Miyagawa's untiring efforts in New York to develop the work of Asian American playwrights, and Roberta Uno's New WORLD Theater at the University of Massachusetts, Amherst, and her work documenting and archiving plays written by Asian American women. Development of this kind provides invaluably rich resources for artists "on the margins" who might otherwise never come to voice, never dare to dream that they, too, could write a play, act or direct. In addition to the pathbreaking efforts of theatres devoted to the work of artists of color, the discourses of multiculturalism have opened doors in mainstream regional theatres. We have recently witnessed this increasing receptivity in Los Angeles, for example, through the Asian Theatre Workshop, the Latino Theatre Initiative, and Blacksmyths at the Mark Taper Forum; and in New York, the sponsorship of the work of performance art and plays by artists of color, through the efforts of artistic director George Wolfe at Joseph Papp Public Theatre/New York Shakespeare Festival.

In similar fashion, the appearance of published work—anthologies like this one—writes new forms of Asian American/Asian Pacific American identity into existence. The anthological text is a medium particularly well-suited to the contradiction and multiplicities of Asian American identity. The different voices, narrative strategies, aesthetic and thematic preoccupations of the various playwrights enact this multiplicity. The anthology itself exemplifies—performs—the strategies of alliance, collectivity, and coalition embodied in the very term "Asian American." Certainly, as one who teaches Asian American theatre, the appearance of new work such as this, collecting the creative output of many playwrights, is welcome indeed in a world in which only three other anthologies exist: Misha Berson's *Between Worlds*, Velina Hasu Houston's *The Politics of Life*, and Roberta Uno's *Unbroken Thread*. Along with the collected works of noted playwrights David Henry Hwang and Philip Kan Gotanda, and shortly, that of Chay Yew and Sandra Tsing Loh, collections such as this volume claim a space for Asian American theatre artists as they write and enact the contradictions, possibilities, tensions and joys of our multiracial society, continuing to move this fresh, vital new work from the wings onto the center stage of American theatre.

Indeed, this anthology actively participates in the process of shap-

ing new forms of racial and ethnic identities. Racial multiplicities occur on many levels, as the Asian American protagonists of these plays
make their lives within a complex, multiracial landscape where
cross–racial alliances and identifications can arise. Shared oppressions
as well as racial and historical differences emerge as meaningful
themes. For example, Lane Nishikawa and Victor Talmadge excavate
buried histories, as they describe the little–known interrelations, in-
tersections and historical parallels among Japanese Americans and
Jews. Their play details the relationship between a Japanese American
soldier in World War II and a Jewish concentration camp survivor liberated by Nisei (second generation Japanese American) soldiers.
Following the friendship over many years, Nishikawa and Talmadge
dramatize the tenderness and love possible among men and stage for
us one aspect of these little–known historical relations, particularly the
parallels between the situation of Japanese Americans in the U.S. and
Jews in Nazi Germany. The differential racial positionings of Japanese
Americans and Jews are highlighted in the historical ironies faced by
Sam, the Nisei soldier: participating in the liberation of Dachau while
his own family was still imprisoned in a relocation camp in the U.S.,
and the continuing discrimination that he must fight on the job as he
is passed over again and again for promotion. Dwight Okita writes a
different tale of relationships of men and the erotics of race in his
sweet, funny and poignant *The Rainy Season*. The protagonist Harry
exoticizes and idealizes his Brazilian object of desire, Antonio, while
Antonio also displays racialized desire/ambivalence when he uses
"Japanese" as a name for Harry. Okita's play is also a classic narrative
of the ambivalent journey of separation from mother and family, exploring the different registers of love. The play concludes with a
sobering, inspiring moment when Harry's mother, who has attempted
to keep her son with her during much of the play, steps outside into
the rain, out into the world. Mature love, Okita seems to say, means
allowing others their separate subjectivities.

The position of Asian American men and of other people of color
in a society where whiteness still indexes a site of privilege come
poignantly to the fore in the work of David Henry Hwang, Rob Shin
and Garrett Omata, who detail the effects of racism on the articulation
of Asian American masculinities, especially as it bears on the erotics of
race. For all three, racism produces a desire to transcend racial marking. In Hwang's case, this desire assumes the form of fantasy play with
racial and gender roles; with Omata and Shin, racial marking produces
the desire to become white, if only for a time. Their work speaks elo-

quently of the way power relations can produce what could be called a colonization of consciousness, and shows us in witty, sometimes playful yet deadly serious fashion the toll it takes to be visibly "different" and part of a historically denigrated "minority."

At another level, Nelson's collection of stage works addresses the contradictions and tensions within any collective identity, including "Asian American" itself, or even more obviously, within the broader rubric "people of color." Rob Shin offers insights into these dilemmas in his humorous and innovative *The Art of Waiting*. He describes tensions among people of different races, as mutual stereotyping occurs among the Asian American waiters and their African American and white customers. Equally notable is Shin's ironic commentary on intra–ethnic differences among Asian Americans, as he wryly observes the contradictions of his own situation—a Korean American stand–up comic waiting tables in a Chinese restaurant. Velina Hasu Houston's multiracial family lives out their tensions and loves passionately, murderously, tenderly, possessively, cruelly, in ways that seem fresh and startling in the history of Asian American theatre. Similarly, Amy Hill's gently humorous characterizations of her life growing up as part Finnish, part Japanese in South Dakota, her experiences in Japan, and her poignant coming–to–terms with her mother's life history, articulate the contradictions and wonder of this multiracial, multicultural heritage.

Other playwrights open up and proliferate conventional definitions of a single racialized identity. Philip Kan Gotanda renders an unusual portrayal of third–generation Japanese American (Sansei) activists from the Asian American movement. The existential dilemmas of midlife crisis and guilt/atonement for a transgression committed long ago animate this lyrical, literate work. Cream, Magritte, radical politics, Peggy Lee, the legal establishment and the university become features in a dreamlike landscape, in a play that writes the complex historical formations of Sansei identity—and for this Sansei, does so in a voice familiar and recognizable, that writes "us" into existence. Denise Uyehara, in her inspiring fantasy *Hiro*, proliferates racial complexity in another sense: race, here, is merely an incidental feature of the landscape. Though the characters all happen to be Japanese Americam, race is never thematized explicitly in the play, marking a different moment in the contemporary scene. Indeed, it is the situation for which the protagonists in the plays by Hwang, Shin and Omata yearn, where race no longer really matters.

Here, differences in narrative strategies and style also perform the multiplicity of Asian American identities. The fantastic and/or the psychologically macabre, for example, emerge as key strategies in the surreal landscape of Gotanda's *Day Standing on its Head*, the matter–of–fact magic realism in *Hiro*, and Velina Hasu Houston's long–lost brother/ghost come–back–to–life in *As Sometimes in a Dead Man's Face*. Omata and Shin entertain us with lively, comic voices that impart a serious message, while David Henry Hwang uses his incisive wit in a theatrically compelling dialogue set in an unusual venue: an SM parlor. Naturalism, too, has its place: Nishikawa and Talmadge deploy it to move us profoundly, while Amy Hill's vibrant performative style shows us how effective realism in performance art can be. In short, there is no single voice, theme or aesthetic form that unifies "Asian American performance," for it is above all various, multiple and resistant to uniformity.

Finally, let me end by underlining the importance of Asian American drama as an intervention that refigures our contemporary notions of race. Dominant racial ideologies define race in terms of a black–white polarity, hierarchically aligned. Latinos and Asian Americans are often erased from this picture, or if included, are conceived in terms of monolithic groups again hierarchically arranged — Asian Americans more toward the white pole, Latinos more toward the black, while Native Americans continue to be erased. The plays in this anthology write an "Asian American" identity that is complex, contradictory and multiple, and that refuses to be encapsulated by the black–white binary. Equally, and in various ways, the playwrights challenge stereotypes that constrain and limit the lives of Asian Americans and other people of color. Whether it is a woman who can fly; people who can don and remove racial and gender identities like items of clothing; young men who yearn to be white and then realize in the process the enormity of racism's toll; multiracial families, midlife crisis and the role of the Asian American movement; or alliances and friendships across race and ethnicity: the themes and characters of these plays show us the complexities, joys and challenges — the many colors of language — that animate life in our late twentieth century worlds.

Dorinne Kondo
Professor, Anthropology; American Studies and Ethnicity;
Director, Asian American Studies,
University of Southern California

Philip Kan Gotanda

DAY STANDING ON ITS HEAD

Day Standing on its Head was produced by the Asian American Theatre Company (Diane Takei, Artistic Director; Pamela A. Wu, Executive Director) in San Francisco, California, on March 29, 1994, with the following cast:

NINA	Bonnie Akimoto
MOM	Juliette Chen
FISHERMAN	David Furumoto
SAM	William Ellis Hammond
JEFF	Michael Chih Ming Hornbuckle
JOE	Michael Edo Keane
HARRY	Ken Narasaki
LILLIAN	Diana C. Weng
LISA	Jennie S. Yee

Directed by Marya Mazor and Philip Kan Gotanda. Set Design by Wing Lee; Costume Design by Karen Lim; Lighting Design by Wilbur Obata; Composer, Dan Kuramoto; Sound Design by Jeff Mockus; Dance Consultant, Naomi Goldberg.

An earlier draft was produced by Manhattan Theatre Club (Lynne Meadow, Artistic Director; Barry Grove, Managing Director) in New York City, in January 1994, with the following cast:

HARRY KITAMURA	Keone Young
LILLIAN	Kira Ann Joyce
JOE OZU	Stan Egi
LISA	Liana Pai
NINA	Tamlyn Tomita
MOTHER	Kati Kuroda
FISHERMAN	Glenn Kubota
SAM	Zar Acayan

Directed by Oskar Eustis. Associate Director, Naomi Goldberg; Set Design by David Jon Hoffman; Costume Design by Lydia Tanji; Lighting Design by Christopher Akerlind; Composer, Dan Kuramoto; Sound Design by John Kilgore; Production Stage Manager, Ed Fitzgerald.

AUTHOR'S NOTES

Gotanda offers the following authorial notes on producing the play:

"Set should be elemental, spare. For the most part empty. Perhaps a raised stage area with a scrim. Feeling of the world should be that of a German Expressionist film — moody, black and white. The score, however, is more eclectic and for the most part indicated. Costuming should have an ambiguity of eras — 90s with a comfortable 30s retro quality.

"In the production directed by Marya Mazor and myself, the set was on a steep rake, with a counter rake built in the center with one lone chair. This level playing area was Harry's world. A trap door provided for Harry's "Sinking-into-his-Chair" scene and for an entrance for Cream. Upstage was a level playing area that was about 4 feet deep and ran the entire length of the stage where the Man-walking-the-Dog and other actions took place.

The look was a loose interpretation of Magritte. Large checkerboard patterns on the floor, the upstage wall adorned with columns and drapes and a painted blue sky full of billowy clouds. Above the stage hung a large, ornately framed picture of an anatomically drawn dog.

Also the costumes hinted at Magritte, with everyone dressed in the same outfit -- black cutaway suits, Homburgs and black high-top tennis shoes. No costume changes but for Peggy Lee's blonde wig, fur wrap and dark glasses. Though the costume design hinted at Magritte, the original impulse was a picture of my grandfather, newly arrived in America from Japan, posing in his "western" garb. Also, because of the raked stage, movement became integral to the production. Naomi Goldberg created the choreographed scenes in both productions."

EDITOR'S NOTES

Perhaps no other Asian American writer (except Ping Chong?) makes as much use of the theatrical resources available to him as Philip Kan Gotanda. The number of sound cues for a Gotanda production can number in the hundreds, and the interplay of sound, light, movement and poetry calls for a stage crew with pinpoint timing and a special openness to the nuance of the immediate moment.

But while Chong has only recently begun to explore his ethnic background (*Chinoiserie*), Gotanda's heritage is inextricably woven into nearly all of his work. The combination of family memories and theatrical invention make a Gotanda play comparable to a latter-day *Ghost Sonata* — the past visibly invades the present of Gotanda's characters, while the author weaves a distinctly theatrical spell around them.

A mix of imagery, music, and innovative use of space marks many Gotanda plays — a giant puppet of Godzilla destroys part of the set of *Yankee Dawg You Die*, while visions of a tranquil Nisei fisherman juxtaposed with white men savagely attacking his son form part of the core of *Fish Head Soup*. And both of those plays feature arguments between men with differing visions of how (or even if) Asian Americans should fight to be a part of America. But in *Day Standing on its Head*, Gotanda takes the argument one step further.

The radical leaders of a generation ago have lost a great deal of prominence; in one of his wryest lines, Gotanda writes that Joan Baez is still doing "exactly the same thing, I think." And in the Asian American community, Frank Chin is as likely to be heard criticizing Amy Tan as he is attacking the white power structure. The characters of *Day Standing on its Head* are facing the fallout of infighting among Asian American political factions — either they're caught refighting the old battles, or they've lost their political drive as trhey become stockbrokers. Gotanda suggests that the real battle should not be against other Asian factions, or even the larger white society, but rather, inside oneself. The bliss that Harry Kitamura finds by standing his life on its head is the true victory.

Day Standing on its Head locates itself within a multiethnic landscape in intriguing ways. Most obviously, Gotanda avidly makes use of cultural references spanning three continents. From Japanese soap operas to the music of Cream to the paintings of Rene Magritte, *Day* is a postmodern feast. Second, Gotanda's characters live against a backdrop of interracial controversy that continues every day. References to the Vincent Chin case — in which Detroit autoworkers beat an Asian man they mistakenly believed to be as Japanese as the makers of Toyotas — and the Latasha Harlins case — in which an Asian woman shopkeeper received a shockingly light sentence for shooting a black teenage shoplifter—remind an audience that the issues lurking on stage may face them at home tonight.

But even more interestingly for those who focus on the living stage, Gotanda asks his Asian cast to play a wide range of white characters, from the college president to Miss Peggy Lee. In order to present such characters realistically, the actors must set aside any internal issues about playing a person from the "majority culture." (Actors in a 1991 production of Vernon Takeshita's *The Rising Tide of Color*, when asked to play white racists in 1920, spoke to me about their reluctance to find the oppressor in themselves.) By having all characters, no matter their race, played by Asians, does Gotanda highlight the different ethnic issues in his world, or does he suggest that race doesn't matter as much as one's inner heart? As with the best theatre, it's up to an audience to decide.

As an aside, Gotanda's fascination with the magical properties of nighttime was also explored in a performance piece he developed while also writing *Day Standing on its Head*. *In the Dominion of Night* as performed by Gotanda himself and composer Dan Kuramoto (of the fusion band Hiroshima), featured Joe Ozu as one of its characters, and took its audiences on a nocturnal odyssey which recalled both the Beat poets and Leopold Bloom in Nighttown. Gotanda recognizes, I think, that a theatre audience is uniquely ready for a call to explore the nightscape.

TIME AND PLACE: *The present. City.*

HARRY KITAMURA *in pool of light. Glasses, intellectual looking.*

HARRY: I awoke from a deep sleep... I had the strangest feeling. That my arm was disappearing. Becoming invisible... I wasn't dreaming, I was awake, or at least I believed so. I turned to my wife... She must have been having a dream because when I touched her arm she whispered a name I had never heard before...

LILLIAN: [*Standing, eyes closed.*] "Raoul"... [*As she fades to black, opens eyes.*]

HARRY: The feeling left. I went back to sleep. [*Lights dip to black, then up again.*] The incident was soon forgotten as I was quite busy researching a new paper I was starting to write. However, a week later I had a dream. In this dream, I felt like my arm was disappearing again. Just like I had experienced earlier when I was awake. Only this time, in the dream, a Man appeared... [MAN #1 *appears. Seedy, dangerous looking.*] He didn't say a word. But he knew what was happening to me, my arm. And though he made no move to speak or even acknowledge me, I knew he was somehow connected to this whole affair. That is, what was happening to my arm. But how? Was he going to show me how to get my arm back?

[AN OLD MAN *moves very, very slowly across upstage. Using a cane, he can barely move — moves forward only in minute increments. He is walking a* DOG, *played by an actor. This should be done in a non-literal way. Fade to black.*]

[HARRY *getting dressed in front of mirror, adjusting tie.*]

HARRY: I'm a law professor at a local institution. It's not one of the more well known ones and to tell the truth I'd been a little embarrassed about it. However, I'd recently submitted an idea for an article to a prestigious law journal and they had accepted it. In the early 70s I was part of one of the seminal strikes of the Asian American movement. I hadn't thought about it for a long time. But for some reason I decided to write about it.

[LILLIAN *enters, finishing touches on dressing, earrings. Conservative, business look.*]

LILLIAN: If it bothers you that much just go ahead and color it. Look, you can hardly notice it, I've told you that, Harry.

HARRY: I first met my wife during the struggle. When a rival group seized power and co-opted the strike we all scattered. We lost contact. Years later we met again.

LILLIAN: [*Trying earrings on.*] Do these look better or the other ones? Besides, white hair's better than no hair, believe me...

HARRY: I'd also just turned 40 and was having some difficulty accepting it...

LILLIAN: I have to work late tonight. The commission wants the report by next week. I'm feeling very insecure about this one... [*Noticing* HARRY'S *reaction.*] I don't have to. I can tell Raymond we can do the work over the weekend. You sure? Okay. I'll call you from the office. [LILLIAN *exits.* HARRY *watches her.* HARRY *shifts into lecturing his class.*]

HARRY: — campus unrest was spreading throughout the country, especially among the Third World students. Within the Asian American group there were two competing factions vying for power. The pro-Maoist Yellow Guard of which I was a founding member and the more middle of the road Asian Americans For Action, known as AAFA. It was well known at the time that AAFA was merely an instrument for the Administration while the Yellow Guard truly represented a revolutionary point of view. Infiltration by administration spies and ideological differences eventually led to the Yellow Guard's disbanding...

[A STUDENT *appears. Played by same actor as* MAN #1.]

STUDENT: Professor Kitamura?

HARRY: Yes, Mr... Mr. Jozu?

STUDENT: It's fine to tell old war stories about your days as an Asian American radical but what does this have to do with us? I mean, to students right now, in the 90s. Isn't your idea of a Third World Student Movement a bit of a dinosaur given the trend toward anti-Asian violence in African American and Latino communities?

HARRY: [*Flustered.*] Well. What I thought was. My feeling is that by describing, in some way, in anecdotal form, earlier political activities, it might lay the foundation —

STUDENT: I think we're all aware that the LA Uprisings shattered any remnant of your 60s political model and I quite frankly find your lecture outdated and irrelevant to our discussion here on "current" political Asian American trends and the legal system. My Aunt was also a member of the Yellow Guard. Julie Hong, maybe you remember her? She claims that the group didn't disband because of ideological differences or whatever but because of some stupid boyish prank the male leaders pulled. How do you respond to that, Professor Kitamura? Professor?

[STUDENT *fades to black. Shaken,* HARRY *removes his glasses, cleans them, puts them back on. Then, puts on a Homburg.*]

HARRY: My wife and I were leaving a popular restaurant that had just opened. I didn't think we could get a reservation but my wife knows a lot of people because of her work and managed to get us all in. I normally refuse to go out but this evening I chose to go. I found the place too noisy and her friends obnoxious. My wife wanted to stay longer but I insisted we leave. [LILLIAN *enters and they leave.*] My wife always says...

LILLIAN: — all you ever want to do is stay at home. What's your problem, Harry? Why can't you just relax and enjoy yourself once in a while. There's a world out there, you know, let's have some fun once in a while.

HARRY: I have a headache. I have to go home and work on the new piece. I'm having a difficult time getting started —

LILLIAN: Now? These are my friends, Harry. This is embarrassing having you do this all the time.

HARRY: No, I don't...

LILLIAN: Yes, yes, you do — we're somewhere and suddenly you decide you don't want to be there and it's like if we don't just get up and leave you start pouting like a little boy or something...

HARRY: I'm not feeling good, okay, the place was getting to me, I'm sorry, it's just the way I am.

LILLIAN: Where's your heart, Harry? Open up. Let go. Live a little, huh? [*Pause.*] All right, all right, I'm sorry. Harry? It's okay...

HARRY: You stay. Really, you stay and I'll catch a taxi home.

LILLIAN: No, Harry, I don't mind, let's go home.

HARRY: I want to be alone.

LILLIAN: Look, I said I don't mind —

HARRY: I want to be alone, it's okay.

LILLIAN: [*After a beat.*] All right, okay, but you take the car. I'll have Liz give me a ride home.

[LILLIAN *exits. Upstage a night sky slowly evolves. Unusual. Deep bluish, black hue.*]

HARRY: Instead of driving right home from the restaurant like I told Lillian I was going to do, I decided to take a walk. [*A comet streaks across the horizon. In the distance we hear its faint sound.*] I noticed two young women talking to a man. [*Two* WOMEN *and a* MAN *appear. This is* MAN #1, *the same man who appeared in* HARRY'S *dream. Night sky fades to black.*] They seemed to be engaged in a lively conversation that quickly turned into a heated argument. It appeared that the man wanted one of the women to go with him and that she did not want to. I thought it might turn violent when the man abruptly left. As the two women turned and began walking my way, I recognized one of them as a student I had had the semester before. Her name was Lisa.

[*Music: classical, melancholic romanticism.*]

LISA: Hello Professor.

HARRY: She was quite beautiful and I had occasionally fantasized about her.

LISA: This is my friend . . .

[FRIEND *ignores* HARRY, *seemingly preoccupied.*]

HARRY: I noticed you were having some trouble over there. [LISA *stares uncomprehending. The other woman looks momentarily, noncommittally, at* HARRY, *then turns away. Her face is not visible to* HARRY.] With the young man?

LISA: Excuse me?

HARRY: I found it odd that neither seemed to know or want to acknowledge what I was talking about but I quickly recovered and the conversation with Lisa became quite pleasant. [HARRY *moves away; the others remain in their own light.*] I could tell Lisa was attracted to me. She had made it rather obvious during the course of the year but I had managed to be good about the whole thing.

MAN #1: [*Appearing in shadows.*] Didn't you want to make love to her?

HARRY: [*Caught off guard.*] I remember once she had come by the office . . . [LISA *approaches.*] We were sitting rather close to each other discussing a difficult legal point when I felt her leg push against mine. For a moment I wasn't sure what to do . . . She then moved her face so close to mine I could feel her breath on my face. It was sweet, like the smell of fresh peaches . . . [LISA'S *face is quite close to* HARRY'S. *He steps away.* MAN #1 *dims to darkness, motioning disgustedly to* HARRY.] As I said, Lisa is quite stunning but oddly during the encounter I found myself drawn to the other woman . . . [HARRY *moves down toward her. She is framed with light.*] She was not that pretty and in a particular light the severity of her features made her appear almost ugly. I could sense a childlike vulnerability that she covered with an air of sullenness. She was quite unfriendly in my presence and seemed to disapprove of Lisa's flirting with me.

LISA: Would you like to join us for a drink?

HARRY: She never looked directly at me. She always had her face turned slightly away. [*Noticing.*] She had — [*Pin light on neck of woman. We hear* NINA'S *musical theme.*] — the most beautiful nape. I had never really noticed this part of a woman before. Something about the way her hair was pulled up so the back of her neck was exposed. Her nape, the soft hairs, the way they... It was as if I were looking at some intimate part of a woman, a woman I did not even know. I found myself compelled to stare...

WOMAN: We have to meet him. Lisa? I promised him...

LISA: Oh, yes.

WOMAN: You know how he can be...

LISA: [*Looking back at* HARRY.] Well...

HARRY: [*As they turn and exit.*] I watched them leave... [*We hear moaning. As* HARRY *speaks, lights rise on* LILLIAN *and* MAN #2 *making love. She stands against a wall, dress pushed up, one of her legs wrapped around* MAN #2'S *torso.*] That night when Lillian returned from the restaurant we made love several times. We hadn't had sex in several weeks so it was rather an unusual event. [*Beat.*] She had an affair a couple of years earlier. [*Beat.*] I found out in a rather interesting way... [LILLIAN *pulls away from* MAN #2 *and joins* HARRY. *They enact the events as he describes them.* MAN #2 *participates also.*] We were going to her colleague's house for dinner. I remember the one time I met him I was struck by the ease with which he was able to get women to like him. Even Lillian seemed to hang on his every word, laugh at his seemingly insipid jokes. I remember not liking him, yet feeling, against my will, envious of him. That he somehow understood something about women which had eluded me. Lillian said she had never been to his house before and we had gone through an elaborate discussion of how to get there, with Lillian even looking at a map before we left. I rang the doorbell. There was a screen door I pulled on to open, only it was stuck. Lillian, without thinking, reached in, pushed the handle in a peculiar fashion and the screen door popped loose. [LILLIAN *and* HARRY *exchange looks. Then* HARRY *looks at* MAN #2. MAN #2 *and* LILLIAN *exchange looks. He reaches out to touch her face but she pulls away.* HARRY *watches them.*] We've worked it out. It wasn't easy. That was a while ago. [HARRY *and* LILLIAN *look out from separate pools of light.*] I'm a bit of a cerebral person. On more than one occasion Lillian has accused me of being...

LILLIAN:...cold. Sometimes you seem to have no feeling. No heart.

HARRY: I believe too much feeling is a waste of time, gets in the way of logical thinking...

LILLIAN: Once when I was in Big Sur I looked up into the night sky and saw moving lights...

HARRY: And that at its worst it can make you unsure of yourself, confuse you...

LILLIAN: [*Staring as* MAN #2 *appears in half light.*] He had these extraordinary eyes...

HARRY: Make you do things you wish you hadn't...

LILLIAN:...Eyes that always said "yes"...

HARRY: [*As* MAN #2 *fades to black.*] Things you'd rather forget.

[*Lights change. They turn back towards each other.*]

LILLIAN: I'm sorry. I apologize. It will never happen again.

HARRY: It's my fault, too. I realize I'm not the most...well, attentive husband.

[*Pause. They stare at each other. We hear classical music. They fade to black.*]
[*Upstage, the* OLD MAN *and his* DOG *move very slowly, now around the middle of the stage. While this action goes on upstage,* HARRY *and* LILLIAN *appear. A quiet Sunday afternoon. The music continues.* LILLIAN *reads a book,* HARRY *sits in a chair watching tv.* HARRY *slowly begins to sink into the seat of the chair.* LILLIAN *laughs quietly to herself over a passage she's just read.*]
[*Life is pleasant, the day peaceful, the sun moves across the sky and begins to set. Lights slowly fade as* HARRY *continues to sink. We sense* HARRY *is becoming aware of his situation yet is helpless to do anything about it. He begins to struggle, his middle body being swallowed up into the seat. Terrified, trying to signal* LILLIAN.]
[HARRY'S *legs are now sticking out, disappearing into the chair.* LILLIAN *takes no notice, turns the page. The music swells. A dog's head, suspended in the air above the stage, is flashed up briefly. At an odd angle.* HARRY *and* LILLIAN *fade to black.*]
[*The* DOG *and* OLD MAN *continue their very slow walk.* OLD MAN *and* DOG *fade to black.* HARRY *appears.*]

HARRY: I'd begun to feel a little out of sorts. I couldn't write — every time

I sat down and tried to recall the events of the strike... I decided to visit my mother. She lived alone in a nearby town that I had grown up in ... [MOTHER *appears watching a video movie on the tv.* HARRY *puts on his Homburg and sits down with her. We hear the sounds of Japanese voices from the tv.*] She loves to watch Japanese movies...

[*Japanese samurai movie comes to life. Two* SAMURAI WARRIORS *appear in battle. Loud, brutal.*]

WARRIOR #1: INU O KOROSHITA! [You killed the dog!]

[*He attacks and slashes the other's arm. It is violent and not pretty.*]

WARRIOR #2: AHHH!...

[MOTHER *switches off the video with her remote. The* WARRIORS *disappear.* MOTHER *shakes her head and gets up to switch the videotape.*]

MOTHER: Too much violence these days...

HARRY: Hi mom.

MOTHER: Hi Harry.

HARRY: You been okay?

MOTHER: Uh-huh.

HARRY: What'd the doctor say?

MOTHER: Said it was nothing. [*Beat.*] Richard brought more tapes for me. You staying for dinner, I'm cooking a roast? You know how Daddy likes his roast beef. I keep telling him so much red meat's not good for him. "I eat what I want, do what I want"... I give up.

[*As* HARRY *watches, she settles back next to him and switches on the video. A Japanese soap opera comes on.* MAN *and* WOMAN *appear enacting the video, speaking in Japanese. It's the actress who plays* NINA *and* MAN #1 *from his dream.*]

WOMAN: Atashi o tsuketeru no desu ka? [You've been watching me, haven't you?]

MAN: Eh? [What?]

HARRY: I don't speak Japanese, but there were subtitles so I could follow the story...

[*The characters shift from Japanese to English.*]

WOMAN: You've been staring at me.

MAN: Excuse me?

WOMAN: I saw you.

MAN: I'm sorry, you must be mistaking me for someone else. I don't know —

WOMAN: Who are you? What do you want from me?

MAN: Really, I don't know what you're talking about . . .

WOMAN: If you don't tell me I'm going to call the police.

MAN: [*Starting to back away.*] I don't think you need to do —

WOMAN: You try and run I'll scream.

MAN: Yes, but I'm not doing —

WOMAN: I'll scream, I will. I'll scream and you'll be found out. Thrown in jail. Disgraced. A common criminal.

MAN: What do you want?

[WOMAN *turns and now begins to address* HARRY *as if he were the* MAN. *The* MAN *now watches the action.*]

WOMAN: What do "I" want? You're the one, mister. You've been following me. Watching me. Staring at my . . . [*Beat.*] My neck. [*Realizing.*] Yes . . . That's it, isn't it? You like the back of my neck. [*She stares at him for a bit. Looks at the* MAN, *then back to* HARRY. *Slowly turns and lifts up her hair for him.*] Go ahead. Touch it. [*Lights dim. Pin light on her nape.* HARRY *hesitates. Looks at his* MOTHER, *the* MAN, *then back to the* WOMAN. *Slowly raises his arm reaching out . . . then stops.*]

MAN: What's wrong?

[SAMURAI #1 *strolls in before* HARRY, *wearing trench coat, dark glasses and hat. Looks Mafioso. We hear a musical tag similar to the theme from "The Godfather."*]

ITALIAN SAMURAI: [*Italian accent.*] A gift from the Don . . .

HARRY: What? Excuse me? . . .

ITALIAN SMAURAI: [*Pulls a shotgun from beneath his coat.*] You killed the dog. Ciao Harry . . .

[*Blackout. Crack of thunder. The sound of rain.* LILLIAN *appears in black funeral dress, holding a black umbrella.*]

LILLIAN: Why don't you like to visit your mother?

HARRY: [*Appearing.*] It's not so much her as . . . Something about going back home. Returning to memories . . .

[LILLIAN *fades to black. Sound cue ends.* MOTHER *appears, watching a Japanese video movie.*]

MOTHER: I should start the rice. Daddy's going to be home soon.

HARRY: Mama? Mama? Listen to me carefully. Dad's dead. He passed away 10 years ago. Okay?

MOTHER: [*Stares, then pats him on the head.*] Harry? It's all right. It is. You'll be all right.

HARRY: I needed to clear my head out... [HARRY *puts on his Homburg, goes for a walk.* MOTHER *fades to black as fog begins to roll in.*] It was very foggy. I could barely see. I began to remember things... [*We hear Sutra chanting. Casket appears.*] My father's funeral. I remember riding in a limousine with my mother and younger brother to the church. It was very hot and the sunlight so bright you had to squint to look outside the windows. This squinting made the outside world shimmer and sparkle. Sitting there with my mother and brother, on the way to Dad's funeral, I suddenly felt like a little boy again passing through some fantastical world... [FISHERMAN *gradually appears in half light trudging across a river. Same actor who plays the* OLD MAN.] I began to remember how he would take me fishing every week. How he knew a secret fishing spot that he would share only with me.

FISHERMAN: Want a ride?

HARRY: How he would pick me up and let me ride on his back. And we'd forge across the river's current to get to the other side to that special place. At those moments he was huge in my eyes, the bravest of warriors and I would do anything to make him proud of me.

FISHERMAN: [*Waves, laughing.*] Harry...

[BUDDHIST REVEREND *enters and begins to Sutra chant.* FISHERMAN *fades to black.*]

HARRY: It was a Buddhist service. The opulence of gold everywhere, hypnotic chanting and overpowering smells of burning incense filling your head. And amidst it all a minister wrapped in peculiarly restrained black robes. [MOTHER, UNCLE *and* AUNT *appear before the casket. Black suits, somber.*] I sat with my mother's side of the family. They are all very proper. No one yells, no one ever misbehaves, and they all have professional careers...

UNCLE: I'm a pharmacist...

AUNT: [*Trying to top each other.*] I'm a dentist...

UNCLE: My son's a pediatrician...

AUNT: My daughter's a brain surgeon...

HARRY: Lillian says we're all repressed. [MOTHER *and two* UNCLES *look at each other curiously. Two of* FATHER'S RELATIVES *enter. Hawai'ian shirts, zoris.*] On the other side sat my father's family. They're all Hawai'ian — they gamble, they drink...

HAWAI'IAN #1: [*Arguing loudly in thick pidgin.*] I pay dis time...

HAWAI'IAN #2: What you mean? I pay. You went pay last time. You all da time pay.

HAWAI'IAN #1: Hey bull lie, my turn for pay brudda...

HAWAI'IAN #2: No, no, no...

HAWAI'IAN #1: [*Overlapping.*] Yeah, yeah, yeah...

HARRY: ...they shout at life, embrace it with their souls. [*Beat.*] Lillian wanted to sit with them but I ushered her to our side... The service was moving along without a hitch when —

[*A* MAN *bolts past* HARRY, *wails mournfully over the casket.*]

UNCLE ARTY: Willie, Willie, I should have gone before you. You were so good to us, I'll miss you Willie, I'll miss you... I love you, I love you ...

HARRY: It was Uncle Arty, Dad's older brother. My mother's side of the family was mortified at his lack of decorum, his raw, unrestrained expression of grief and despair...

[ARTY'S *wailing grows; he's now stretched over the casket sobbing. The* REVEREND *takes no notice, continues to chant.*]

UNCLE ARTY: DON'T GO, DON'T GO WILLIE... LET ME GO IN YOUR PLACE, I'LL GO, I'M THE OLDER BROTHER, I SHOULD HAVE GONE BEFORE YOU...

HARRY: I found myself feeling a strange mixture of emotions. I was at once shocked, painfully uncomfortable at his overt calling attention to ourselves, the event. And at the very same moment, wanting to join him, to wail, to sob unabashedly, to let a flood of complex feelings pour out of me. [*Beat.*] But instead... [LILLIAN *and the two* HAWAI'IAN RELATIVES *escort* UNCLE ARTY *away.* MOTHER, UNCLE, AUNT *and* REVEREND *follow them.* HARRY *stands alone staring at the casket. He starts to approach it. It fades to black. Sutra chanting stops.*] I decided to head back to my mother's house. The fog was getting to me and I started to feel very cold...

[HARRY *approached by a shadowy* STREET PERSON. *Filthy. Hat, face is covered with a tattered muffler. Played by the same actor who played* MAN #2.]

STREET PERSON: Excuse me sir? Excuse me? [HARRY *tries to avoid him, but he keeps getting in front of* HARRY. *There's a sense of danger about him, violence just beneath the surface.*] Excuse me sir but I need some money to eat. I haven't eaten in days and I could sure use some money. [HARRY *fumbles through his pockets.*] You're not from here are you? Life's been good to you, I can see that. Not me though. You try and serve the people. You do what's right and see what happens. Betrayal, friends abandon you, the world cuts off your legs and leaves you to rot half a man. Who said "A foolish old man can move a mountain?" Huh? Who said? Better to keep your mouth shut. Go along with everybody else. Then you can have your pretty, pretty wife. Nice, fat job at the university. Big fancy house full of fancy wines and expensive jewelry. [*As* HARRY *hands him some change.*] What's this? Fucking Chinamens, fucking Chinamenjaps — the cheapest motherfuckers on the face of the earth! YOU GOT — [*Gets right in front of* HARRY'S *face.*] — ALL THE MONEY AND YOU'RE THE CHEAPEST MOTHERFUCKERS, NEVER GIVE ANY MONEY, TRY TO PRETEND LIKE I'M NOT HERE, LIKE I DON'T EXIST, I'M HERE, I'M HERE, I'M HERE!!!

[*Blackout on* STREET PERSON. HARRY *composes himself.*]

HARRY: That night I couldn't sleep. The incident with the street person along with the strange images that had begun to invade my mind at my mother's house had left me rattled and confused. I tossed and turned, alternately sweating and feeling icy cold. Finally I passed into a fitful sleep . . .

[HARRY *lies down in a pool of light.* MOTHER *and* NAPE WOMAN *stroll backward through the edges of the light.*]

LILLIAN: [*Appearing, eyes closed.*] I love you Harry. I love you with all my heart.

[LILLIAN *fades to black. Sound of birds chirping. Dawn.* FISHERMAN *appears, listening to the birds. Mimes pole.* HARRY *looking out. Dreamscape.*]

FISHERMAN: Beautiful, huh? I was thinking. Maybe if you recorded the birds. Then put the sounds of their chirping down as musical notes. Don't you think it'd make a wonderful song?

HARRY: Sometimes I don't recognize myself anymore. I find myself feeling things I never felt before. Thinking the oddest thoughts.

FISHERMAN: I do the same thing. I look in the mirror. Who is this person? I feel like a young man inside, like I could still dive deep, catch fish in my mouth, dance the hula with the wahinis all night long. Then I see this wrinkled, old man staring back at me.

HARRY: Is that what happened? I mean, I always wondered. They just found your boat, nothing disturbed. Everyone assumed it was an accident, but... [*Beat.*]

FISHERMAN: We all die, Harry. That's a given. But you don't have to grow old...

[*Blackout. Lights up on* HARRY. *He has only one arm.* HARRY *stares at his missing arm.*]

HARRY: Then the dream changed... [*Loud music. Wild, dangerous.* HARRY *moves through an urban night. Music shifts into background, coming from inside a nearby club.*] I find myself wandering through a rough part of town... [MAN #1 *and the* NAPE WOMAN *appear at a table.*] I walk into a club and see this person who looks like the man who appeared in my dream. He is sitting with a woman whose back is to me but I instantly know it's the same woman who was with Lisa. The back of her neck... [NINA'S *theme music plays.*]... I find that I can't help myself. That I have to look. The man notices and seems angry. He glares threateningly at me and I know I should avert my eyes but I am beyond myself, being pulled along by something I do not recognize. I must watch her, her nape, the way the hairs on her neck... [*The* MAN *gets up violently, knocking the chair over. At that instant, three* EXOTIC DANCERS — *two* MEN, *one* WOMAN — *appear upstage in silhouette. Music very loud. Wild sexual dance.* MAN *strides towards* HARRY, *stands over him, pulls out a knife. Then notices* HARRY *has only one arm. Slowly lowers his knife. Dancers fade to black, music dips.*]

MAN: Come on. [*As* HARRY *hesitates.*] Come on, come on over here. I said come on... [*He drags* HARRY *to the table, presents him to the* WOMAN *who's drinking vodka. A bottle sits in front of her.*] Look who's here, Nina. Your friend. [*He tosses the knife on the table in front of her. The woman glances at them, then goes back to drinking.*] She likes you. You're the man with the disappearing arm.

WOMAN: He's not my friend.

MAN: Ahh, but you're always thinking about him. He's always on your mind. Talks about you in her sleep, says your name —

WOMAN: Why do you do this to me, huh? He's not my friend, I've told you that over and over. He's not my friend, I don't think about him. He's old, he's not sexual, and most of all — [*She grabs the knife and suddenly drives it into* HARRY'S *chest. Music cuts away. Lights shift to isolate them.* HARRY *stares aghast at the knife sticking out of him.*] ... he has no heart. No heart. How could I ever be interested in a man who has no feelings, no passion, no fire. The man has no heart. He's already dead and he doesn't even know it.

[MAN *pulls knife out of* HARRY'S *chest.* HARRY'S *still in shock. Back to previous lighting.*]

MAN: Nina, Nina, you're such a ... tough woman. That's why I love you so much ... [*Touches her cheek, she knocks his hand away.*] Allow me to introduce myself. Joe. Joe Ozu. And this is Nina. Nina, the Gorgeous. And in a certain light, Nina the Ugly. But. And always. Nina with the mysterious nape, huh? Don't worry. You can't bleed if you got no heart, Harry. Besides, this is just a dream, right? [*Holds out a pill.*] A magic pill. Go ahead. Take it. Don't be afraid. If you want to dance you gotta pay the band, Harry.

NINA: Don't.

HARRY: What does it do?

JOE: [*Puts pill in* HARRY'S *hand, leans into* HARRY'S *ear.*] It makes you dumb. You're too clever, Harry ...

NINA: [*Into* HARRY'S *other ear.*] Go home. Back to your quiet, suffocating, inconsequential life, Harry ...

JOE: You need to have a heart attack. Explode something inside your head. Die. And then live again ...

NINA: It's safe. No risks. You don't have to worry about someone like me. You don't have to bleed ...

JOE: Go ahead. Trust me, Harry. You have absolutely everything to lose ...

NINA: You'll live and die and it will all pass like a quiet Sunday afternoon ...

JOE: And that's what you want, isn't it?

NINA: Your wife reading, you watching TV, sinking, sinking ... [*Beat.*] Who cares about some dumb paper?

JOE: Who cares about some dumb strike?

NINA: Just keep it all locked up deep down inside ...

JOE: And the tiny scream inside your head?

NINA: Just tell it to shut up ...

[JOE *and* NINA *begin barking and howling like dogs. Dancers brought up.*

Loud music. HARRY, *disoriented, stares at the pill in his hand. Fade to black.*]

[*Lights rise on* HARRY *nervously adjusting a tape recorder. A man wanders around, looking at things. He has the feeling of an ex-hippie who never quite left the era. This is* JEFF *from* HARRY'S *college days. Continuously whacking a pack of cigarettes against his palm in a gesture to pack the tobacco.* HARRY *notices* JEFF *pulling out a cigarette.*]

HARRY: Jeff? I would appreciate it if you wouldn't smoke inside? Lillian doesn't like it. [*A beat, as* JEFF *stares, puts the cigarette away.*] Actually I was about to abandon the idea altogether. The Strike. Writing about it. So when you called out of the blue I was a little —

JEFF: I heard you. [*Points to his head.*] In here...

[*Beat.*]

HARRY: Now as I explained I'm doing research on this paper. In particular I'm interested in the factionalism in the Asian American groups, politically what each group stood for...

JEFF: [*Whispering, overlapping.*] Chuckie...

HARRY: [*Distracted but continuing.*]See if we can trace their roots back to early pre-war Asian communities, to any political, lefty leanings that might have even been brought over from the old countries...

JEFF: [*Giggling.*] Chuckie...

HARRY: And then trace those movements into the present to see how they've impacted present day activism, court litigations —things like the Korematsu case, Vincent Chin, the Soon Ja Du-Latasha Harlins case...

JEFF: [*Overlapping.*] Chuckie, Chuckie...

HARRY: That's not my name, Jeff. It's Harry.

JEFF: Chuckie, Chuckie...

HARRY: [*Switches off recorder.*] Is there a problem here, Jeff?

JEFF: It's not over.

HARRY: What?

JEFF: [*Taking out a cigarette again.*] You may think it is. But nothing's forgotten. Everything's remembered. You notice how the music is coming back? I always think about Sam. You heard from him?

HARRY: No, no, I haven't...

JEFF: Remember how Sam always used to quote Mao? That parable about the "foolish old man?" I heard a rumor he went underground and was hiding out with the Weathermen. That he was in the Patty Hearst house and got out just before the big shootout. When I was in —

HARRY [*Overlapping.*] No actually, other than Lillian you're the first person I've contacted...

JEFF: — South America I heard he went to Cuba on one of those Venceremos Brigades, stayed on and became one of Fidel's inner circle. [*Beat.*] Remember how our group was having trouble with that other group, AAFA? During the strike? As to who should represent the Asian component in the negotiations? I mean, we were all fighting the Administration but there was all this infighting going on —

HARRY: Jeff, Jeff, actually I'm not so much interested in anecdotal material as I am in a critical analysis of the social structures of that time and their relationship to present day legal —

JEFF: Asian Americans for Action? AAFA? Remember?

HARRY: Well, yeah, of course I remember them but —

JEFF: No, no, this was a big thing, this was a big thing...

HARRY: I wouldn't go that far, it wasn't that big of —

JEFF: Chuckie, Chuckie, how you going to write this paper if you don't remember right? It was a big thing. It was like the war, our group against theirs. People doing things, ugly things to each other...

HARRY: [*Watching as* JEFF *lights a cigarette.*] I remember one time I stayed up all night helping Sam write that speech. The one he gave on the steps of the Student Union. He had guts. And I sent that fake memo so they'd set up the microphone for us...

JEFF: You disappeared. Where'd you go?

HARRY: My father got sick. I had to go back home...

JEFF: You didn't.

HARRY: What?

JEFF: I helped Sam write that speech. You didn't.

HARRY: I did too, Jeff.

JEFF: I sent the memo, you didn't.

HARRY: I didn't say I did it alone, I meant we —

[OLD MAN *and* DOG *appear upstage, continuing their walk.*]

JEFF: [*Interrupts.*] Lillian took your place after you left. Sam and she worked together but things weren't quite the same with the group. Everything fell apart, people accusing each other of being spies for the administration... [*Beat.*] Wasn't there this thing about a dog? Remember that? The campus police and some kind of dog incident?

[*The main stage goes to half light.* DOG's *head lit above.* JEFF *exits.*]
[OLD MAN *becomes the* SCHOOL PRESIDENT *and enters the scene with* HARRY. *He leads* HARRY *to his chair and sits him down. Looks at him for a beat.* PRESIDENT *then moves to edge of the scene and watches. A* YOUNG SAM *and* JEFF *enter.* SAM *played by same actor who played* MAN #1 *and* STREET PERSON. *Both carry copies of Mao's* Little Red Book. *In the offices of the Yellow Guard. Early 70s.*]

SAM: The administration has arranged a meeting with Asian Americans for Action to discuss their position on the strike. But if they don't show up, the administration pigs will have to come to us to negotiate. That's why we need you to do this...

[HARRY *is silent.*]

JEFF: Chuckie?

[*No response.*]

SAM: You know why we call you that? Chuckie? Jeff named you that. Because you never say anything. You're like this worker bee, buzzing around the office—doing this, doing that but you never talk.

JEFF: Like Charlie Chaplin in one of those silent movies.

HARRY: But why do I have to—

SAM: You have to stop fighting us. The Yellow Guard wants you to be part of the family... [*Watching* HARRY.] They like people like you. You're just like your parents. My parents. We always do what we're told. We do. It's in our blood. Quiet, hardworking, successful—the model minority. Engineers, accountants, maybe even marry Donna Reed. They love saying to our Black and Brown brothers and sisters, "Hey, the Orientals made it on their own, why can't you people?" And secretly our chests swell up. Another crumb tossed our way and we lap it up—"Yeah, we raised ourselves up by our bootstraps, why can't they?" The "model minority." It's all bullshit. So they accept us for now but at what price? To live like a cowardly mouse, never making a peep 'cause we're afraid they'll take it away? Always wearing this silent frozen mask of middle class propriety while inside you want to rage, scream at the injustices all around you? Look at who's getting slaughtered in Southeast Asia, then look in the mirror. It don't lie. One day we'll get too good at what we do. We'll make a little too much money, figure out the game a little too well and then we'll see middle class America's real face. They'll hate us, they'll hunt us down, kill us in the streets...

HARRY: [*After a pause, quietly.*] But AAFA's got a lot more members than we do...

SAM: Even a Foolish Old Man can move a mountain, Harry. [*Beat.*] We have to do something that will let AAFA know we mean business. So they'll get out of the way. So the President will have to come to us. He'll hate that. Having to deal with the Yellow Guard. These are desperate times, Harry.

JEFF: The Panthers being systematically executed. Chicano farm workers being exploited by our very own kind...

SAM: My Lai...

JEFF: William Calley...

SAM: Cambodia...

JEFF: Plain of Jars...

SAM: It's the end of the world and the beginning of the world and we're here to usher it in. [*Quickly opening the* Red Book *to a dog-eared passage.*] Mao says, "Political power grows from the barrel of a gun." It must be a statement so single-mindedly committed, so terrifyingly beautiful, AAFA will wilt under the weight of its deed... [*Beat.*] The Yellow Guard wants you to do something for us. Can you, Harry? [*Beat.*] Or is it Chuckie?

HARRY: You've been like. Family to me. Here. With you. I feel. Finally. Like I'm in my house. I can breathe. Finally breathe. Just be who I am.

[*We hear music similar to "The Godfather" theme.*]

SAM: We went to see a movie...

[SAM *and* JEFF *withdraw.* PRESIDENT *enters, before* HARRY.]

PRESIDENT: As the School President I have to ask you these things. [*Beat.*] Harry? [*Threateningly, as* HARRY *resists.*] Harry?

HARRY: [*Relenting, quietly.*] Sam. [*Beat.*] The Yellow Guard...

[PRESIDENT *nods, withdraws — and goes back to being the* OLD MAN *walking the* DOG. *They continue slowly across upstage. The older* JEFF *returns. Back in the present.*]

JEFF: Wasn't there this thing about a dog? The campus police and some kind of dog —

HARRY: [*Interrupts.*] There was no dog. [*Noticing.*] I said not to smoke, Jeff, Jesus. [*Muttering to himself.*] What the hell's wrong with you, can't remember anything. You take too many drugs or something?...

JEFF: I'm not crazy, Harry. I get the feeling you want me to be but I'm not. I remember everything. Nothing's forgotten. [*Beat.*] Chuckie...

[JEFF *withdraws.* HARRY *turns upstage and watches the* OLD MAN *and his* DOG *for a beat. Then, approaches them. The* OLD MAN *stops and turns away to wipe his forehead with his handkerchief, admiring the view.*]
[*As he does,* HARRY *reaches in, attempting to snatch the* DOG. *The* DOG *resists, knocking his hand away at each attempt, curious but wary of* HARRY'S *advances. Then* HARRY *grabs its leg.* DOG *is puzzled, then struggles to get away.* HARRY *is pulling on the* DOG's *leg.* DOG *is trying to signal the* OLD MAN *who is preoccupied, blowing his nose. Fade to black.*]
[LILLIAN *appears, just finished packing bags.*]

LILLIAN: I'm leaving you, Harry.

HARRY: But I'm just not ready for that kind of responsibility...

LILLIAN: It's not just the baby thing, it's —

HARRY: I can't make that kind of commitment right now...

LILLIAN: You don't want a baby, that's fine, I can accept that. It's just... You're 40 years old, Harry, what do you mean, "I can't make that kind of commitment RIGHT NOW"? [HARRY *can't respond.*] I have to go ...

HARRY: I'll change, I promise. [*Beat.*]

LILLIAN: You live on the surface of your life. And you think if you just touch another person's skin, that's living.

HARRY: Is it Raoul?

LILLIAN: [*Stroking his cheek.*] You're pathetic, Harry. I love you.

[HARRY *watches* LILLIAN *leaves.* FISHERMAN *appears fishing with a mimed pole. Wears a Homburg. No shoes, bare feet. Creel sits beside him.* HARRY *approaches.*]

HARRY: Catch anything?

FISHERMAN: A son's duty is to be greater than his father. [*Beat.*]

HARRY: I don't fish anymore. It's not that I don't like it. It's just... You have to get everything ready the night before — tackle, poles, reels, prepare food, get your clothes out. Then get up and the sun's not even out yet and pack it all in the car, then drive all the way up there. Then when you're done, you gotta pack it all back in the car again, drive all the way back, unload the car, throw away all the garbage, wash off all your gear, put your dirty clothes in the hamper, then after all that you still gotta clean all the damn fish. It just seems like too much work, you know. What's the point, huh? What's the point?

[FISHERMAN *reaches into his creel and pulls out a live flapping fish.*]

FISHERMAN: You're my hope, Harry. [*Beat.*]

HARRY: [*Remorseful.*] I'm sorry. I failed you.

[FISHERMAN *fades to black.* HARRY *looks down at his hand. There's a pill. He pops it into his mouth. Blackout.*]
[*Lights up on* JOE. *He has earphones on and is drumming the air with a pair of drumsticks. He has swimmer's eye goggles pushed up on his forehead. He wears a small parachute pack. Another pack sits on the ground.* HARRY *stands next to him.*]

JOE: Here, put these on. [JOE *hands him swimmer's eye goggles with dark lenses.* HARRY *hesitates.*] What's wrong?

HARRY: It's night time.

JOE: [*Can't hear, louder.*] I said, "What's wrong?"

HARRY: It's dark.

JOE: So?

HARRY: Well, then I can't see . . .

JOE: [*Putting them on him.*] Whoa, Mr. Uncool. We're talking style here. If you're going to go, you want to go with style, right?

HARRY: Where am I going?

JOE: Trust me, I know what I'm doing. What? You don't know what I do?

HARRY: Hey, I just got this tape. Amazing. You ever heard of Ginger Baker? [*Louder.*] Ginger Baker? Cream? I'd never heard of him. Picked this up in an oldies bin. This guy's nuts. I mean "really" nuts. I can't believe this — Everybody thinks he's making music but he's really just going off the deep end, schizo. You can feel his confusion, pain. He's working out his inner torment, trying to organize it so it's manageable but he can't. It's out of control, breaking apart, bits and pieces of his soul flying out through his hands, into the sticks, onto the skins . . . [*We hear music similar to a Ginger Baker solo from his "Cream" days over the house speakers played loudly. Talking over the sound:*] . . . we get to hear his psychosis. The rhythm of his madness.

People paid money for this stuff. Crazy, huh? [*Loud drumming continues. They speak over the sound.*] I arrange things. What I do? I arrange things for people. Services. Actually a very special service. In fact, you could say it's a one of a kind service, to be performed only one time. [*Waiting.*] Don't you want to ask me something? [*As* HARRY *stares.*] Like what kind of service this is?

HARRY: What kind of service?

JOE: Funny you should ask. I arrange for people's deaths. Most people find planning their own demise a rather distasteful task. Why I'll never know. I think there's a sort of built-in survival mechanism that just resists the idea of killing oneself — [*Putting the parachute pack on his back*] — off even when a big change is in the best interests of all parties involved. So it means not only must I have steely determination but also be tricky and manipulative to get the desired results...

HARRY: What are you doing?

JOE: [*Grabs his arm.*] We're going for a little swim...

[*They go to the lip of the stage and jump. Lighting transition. We hear the sound of rushing air. Ginger Baker fades away. They're leaning out at a 60 degree angle, held by cables from behind. Air blown into their faces. A little smoke to simulate clouds. Bright light shooting up from below at them illuminating their bodies. Darkness all around them.* JOE *has his arms spread out and is negotiating the air.* HARRY *flails about. Upstage a night sky.*]

HARRY: Swimming? Swimming?

JOE: I lied! Spread your arms out! Spread your arms out! Like this! like this! That's right, that's right. Great, huh? I like to jump at night. That way, you can't tell how far you are from the ground. More of a thrill. Just joking, joking, I can tell by my watch. We have 90 seconds left to pull our rip cords or it's boom. Custard pie.

HARRY: [*Searching.*] Where is it? Where's the rip cord?

JOE: These are special chutes, no rip cords. The chute opens only when you give the right answer. It hears the right answer and poof, they open up like beautiful, fluffy clouds.

HARRY: Right answer to what? To what?

JOE: Oh–oh, 55 seconds. You better hurry up, Harry.

HARRY: To what?! To what, what's the question?!

JOE: Show me your face.

HARRY: What?

JOE: Oh-oh, 25 seconds!

HARRY: Show you my face?

JOE: Yes, show me your face!

HARRY: WHAT KIND OF FUCKING QUESTION IS THAT!!!

JOE: 10 seconds!

HARRY: UH, UH—I DON'T KNOW WHAT IT MEANS! WHAT DOES THE QUESTION—HOW'S—

JOE: [Overlapping.] 5! 4! 3!

HARRY: [Overlapping, making weird funny facial expressions.] THIS! HOW'S THIS ONE?! HOW ABOUT THIS ONE?!

JOE: —2! 1!...

HARRY: AHHHHH!!!

[Blackout. Wind cuts away to silence. JOE and HARRY appear, parachutes gone. JOE stares to HARRY.]

JOE: Funny. [Feeling him.] You didn't break apart. Hmmm. You're so tight. I figured the pressure of impending death would force you beyond the threshold, to the other side. Make my work easy. You got tighter and tighter, more and more conflicted but you didn't break. I figured at least the force of the crash would shatter you, make you see beyond yourself... But you're a hard nut, Harry. [Beat; JOE thinks.] Something with more flare, more theatricality, more high drama...

[We hear a song similar to Peggy Lee's "Is That All There Is?" Upstage a JAPANESE WOMAN appears, lip-synching the song, wearing a blonde wig, slinky dress, imitating Peggy Lee. Played by actress who plays Lisa. A strikingly handsome WAITER walks by with a tray of martinis. JOE takes one, then kisses the waiter on the lips, a long, wet one.]

JOE: Would you like one, too?

[HARRY quickly shakes his head. JOE looks at the WAITER and shrugs.]

WAITER: Pity...

JOE: [As WAITER exits.] Your song, Harry. Peggy's singing your song. Gosh, you're lucky. It never happens for me. You must be born under a special star. And look. Look who's here...

HARRY: Isn't that...That's Angela Davis, isn't it?

JOE: Uh-huh...

HARRY: And there's, there's, what's his name, what's his name...

JOE: Mario Savio...

HARRY: Mario Savio, I'd forgotten all about him. What happened to him? [JOE *shrugs*.] And there's Joan Baez, what's she doing now?

JOE: Exactly the same thing, I think.

HARRY: Oh my God — S.I. Hayakawa? With his Tam O'Shanter no less.

JOE: Yes, yes, and look who else is here...

[JOE *withdraws*. NINA *appears, beautiful and coolly reserved. She directs* HARRY *to a bench where they sit. Night sky is filled with stars. They look out.*]

NINA: I don't want to be here, Harry. I don't.

HARRY: We don't seem to have much choice in the matter. I'm sorry.

NINA: Please don't apologize. It spoils the illusion.

HARRY: I'm sorry...

[*He catches himself.* NINA *pulls out a bottle of champagne and pours two glasses.*]

NINA: I know there is more here than meets the eye. Please don't waste my time, Harry. Especially time taken against my will. Show me your face.

HARRY: What is this face business? I don't know what everyone is talking about...

NINA: [*Hands him a glass.*] Here, maybe this will help you... [*Downing a glass, pouring herself another.*] By the way, how's your arm?

HARRY: What?

NINA: Drink, drink... There you go... Obviously you refuse to tell me the truth about your face, your arm... Drink, go ahead and drink. It'll help the mood.

[*They both drink, she pours more, both begin to loosen up.*]

HARRY: There are so many things I want to tell you...

NINA: Then tell me, Harry. We haven't much time. The pill? The effects wear off. [*Downs another glass, notices something in the sky.*] Look, that star. It's moving...

HARRY: I don't know where to begin.

NINA: You wrote a poem for me. [HARRY *doesn't know what she's talking*

about. She reaches into his pocket, pulls out a sheet and gives it to HARRY.]
I'm all ears, Harry. I'm all eyes. I'm all mouth and we're waiting...

[HARRY *looks at the poem, hesitant. She watches him while sipping. He begins to read.*]

HARRY: "In this night. In this night of flight. I hover above your city...

NINA: Yes, let it go...

HARRY: "A web of tears and tiny fires buoyed up on soft hands... "

NINA: I like it.

HARRY: "...soft hands of wind. I am like a moth, struggling against my nature. Do I willingly die in your mysterious fire? Allow myself to be swallowed up in eyes, so drunken and wild with fearless wanting that I am as a little child in the face of new knowledge? How will I make my way home?

NINA: My hands will guide you...

HARRY: "If I were to offer you a rose. Lush, combustible, its fragrance an angel's scent. Would your eyes say yes? So that I may dream and dream and dream.

NINA: Good Harry...

HARRY: "I long to fall into your breath. Inhale me, deep into your body. I will ignite, rapturous and howling, I will surrender everything and more to you... "

[*Too much for* HARRY. *He stops, feeling his chest, breathing with difficulty.*]

NINA: Harry?

HARRY: I can't take this. It's too much...

NINA: I know.

HARRY: I'm afraid I will die.

NINA: That's what love is about.

[*Beat. She turns and offers her nape to him. He bends forward, about to kiss her. Out of nowhere the* STREET PERSON *appears, in the same state of agitation, pushing his face between them.*]

STREET PERSON: Excuse me, excuse me, but I haven't eaten for days, I could sure use some money...

HARRY: Look, last time I gave you change you yelled and said some very insulting things —

[OLD MAN *appears, walking the* DOG, *happy, whistling.* NINA *looks at him.*]

NINA: Don't you recognize him?

STREET PERSON: Don't you know me, Harry? Don't you remember me?

[*He takes off his hat and muffler and reveals who he is.*]

HARRY: Sam?

NINA: Our father.

OLD MAN: Hi, Nina.

HARRY: What?

NINA: You see, I'd been having visions. Of a Man with a bleeding heart. A Man rising into the air. So I decided to enter a convent ...

SAM: [*To* HARRY.] You mean run away.

NINA: But who would take care of my dog Raymond?

SAM: Ahh, the dog...

OLD MAN: [*As* DOG *barks playfully.*] I'll take care of him. Down Raoul, down boy.

SAM: You ruined my life, Harry. You're responsible for my fate.

HARRY: What are you talking about? You took advantage of me. I believed in you so much and then you asked me to do that thing to the Old Man's dog...

SAM: Aren't you going to do it?

[OLD MAN *becomes the* SCHOOL PRESIDENT.]

PRESIDENT: You have a bright future, Mr. Kitamura...

SAM: You have to prove your loyalty...

PRESIDENT: Law school, medical school...

SAM: What are you waiting for?

PRESIDENT: I'd hate to see all that ruined...

NINA: Who are you going to listen to? Whose voice are you going to obey?

SAM: Then you ran away like a coward. Abandoned me. What's a leader with no followers?

PRESIDENT: Your father will have to hide his face when other fathers brag about their sons.

SAM: Even Lillian lost confidence in me after that.

PRESIDENT: Bow his head in shame, whisper your name like a dirty word.

SAM: How do you think she ended up with you?

PRESIDENT: Maybe even kill himself...

[*The* PRESIDENT *becomes the* OLD MAN *walking his* DOG *again, and exits.*]

HARRY: No, don't say that...

SAM: I ended up dying before my time.

HARRY: What, what—you, too?

NINA: Harry?

SAM: I drowned. Didn't you hear the rumor? I sank beneath the surface, the victim of neglect and loveless air.

NINA: What did you do?

[*Lights shift. Back to the 70s Yellow Guard scene. We hear music similar to "The Godfather" theme.* DOG's *head lit.*]

SAM: We saw this movie. They were trying to make this point to this Hollywood producer and he was being stubborn so they delivered the head of his favorite horse to him. Just the head. [*Beat.*] We'll do the dirty work, Harry. We know how much you prefer to keep your hands clean. We'll do that part. But you get us the dog.

HARRY: What?

SAM: You get the dog. We need a dog. We know an old man who has this mangy mutt.

HARRY: I can't do that...

SAM: AAFA needs to know we mean business.

HARRY: Yeah, but ...

[JEFF *drags the dog in.* SAM *looks at* HARRY.]

SAM: Good, Harry. You did good.

[*Sam pulls out a knife, holds it above the dog. Then he stops, looks at* HARRY, *holds the knife out to him.*]

HARRY: What?

SAM: Harry.

HARRY: I delivered the dog. That's all you said I had to—

SAM: There's been some talk about you. Rumors. About your... trustworthiness. Harry? [*Beat.*] What are you waiting for? Harry? [*Blackout. Beat.* HARRY *appears.*]

HARRY: I began to lose myself. What was happening to me. My mind was raging with so many conflicting thoughts. And at night, as soon as I'd close my eyes, all I could see was Nina — [NINA *appears, walking the* DOG.] — her face, her eyes, the way she smelled . . . I tried to maintain some semblance of normalcy in my life . . .

[LILLIAN *enters with his Homburg and scarf. As she puts them on him,* NINA *fades to black.*]

LILLIAN: Have a good day. I'm working late again. I'll call you from the office. [*Under her breath.*] You selfish asshole.

HARRY: What?

LILLIAN: Nothing, nothing dear . . .

[*They kiss. As she turns, her* ATTORNEY *appears, carrying a briefcase.* LILLIAN *joins him.*]

LILLIAN'S ATTORNEY: As your attorney I have to ask you these things. [LILLIAN *nods to proceed, putting her arm through his.*] I understand you wanted a baby and he didn't?

LILLIAN: I wanted to give birth to a child but not marry one . . .

[LILLIAN *and her* ATTORNEY *exit arm in arm.* HARRY *puts his glasses on, opens his notes. He's in the midst of a lecture.*]

HARRY: — thus, the Supreme Court is ultimately not truly free, an objective, unbiased body as we would like to believe. But rather, it is subject to the same cultural and racial biases that the rest of this society . . . [*Stops, looks out anxiously.*] I was in the middle of a lecture to one of my classes when my mind blanked out . . . I couldn't remember anything. What had I just said? What was I going to say next? Excuse me, I'm not feeling well. That's all for today . . . I had to put an end to this, find her one way or another. I hurried back to my office and locked the door. I had an idea . . . [*Picks up a phone and dials.*] I decided to call Lisa. Maybe she would know how to get in touch with her.

LISA: [*Appearing on phone.*] Who?

HARRY: It's Harry. Professor Kitamura? Harry Kitamura?

[*Beat.*]

LISA: Oh, yeah . . . What do you want? I'm kind of in a hurry.

HARRY: This will only take a moment. Remember when I ran into you the other day. You were with this woman. This was, oh, about three weeks ago? The two of you were arguing with this man. You asked me if I wanted to join you for drinks. But the woman said —

LISA: I'm sorry I don't remember this. When was this?

HARRY: About three weeks ago? The woman, your friend said —

LISA: My friend? What was her name?

HARRY: I don't know, that's why I'm calling you. I wonder if you might know how to —

LISA: I don't remember being with any woman. Look, I have to go now. Sorry I can't help you...

HARRY: No, no, wait ...

[LISA *hangs up. Blackout.*]

[*Lights up on* HARRY *and a well-dressed* YOUNG MAN. *He's from the Law Review Committee. The* YOUNG MAN *is nervous, looking around.*]

HARRY: I don't understand. I thought it was all decided. You said you wanted it for next year's Law Review —

LAW STUDENT: Some things came up. I'm not at liberty to say.

HARRY: What kinds of things?

LAW STUDENT: I can't tell you, they asked me not to say.

HARRY: No, no, I want to know — what kinds of things came up?

LAW STUDENT: Look, we all felt it would have been a very good article. Obviously, I mean, we had planned to publish it —

HARRY: [*Grabbing him.*] What kinds of things, tell me...

[HARRY'S *got him by the collar.* STUDENT *is unsure whether to divulge the information. He looks around, lowers voice.*]

LAW STUDENT: Let's just say the article would have been given the okay except for some indiscretions on your part in your college days ... [*Pushing* HARRY'S *hands away.*] Now excuse me, I've said enough already. If you'd like to resubmit the outline or even the article to next year's selection panel, I'm sure they would be happy to consider it again.

[STUDENT *looks around, then hurriedly turns and exits.* HARRY *watches him leave, then pulls out a phone and dials.* LISA *appears at phone.*]

LISA: I told you I don't know who you're talking about. Now would you please leave me alone.

[LISA *turns and starts walking.*]

HARRY: I followed her after one of her classes... [*Starts to follow her.*] Maybe, just maybe she could lead me —

[LISA *abruptly turns and confronts* HARRY. *This first part should echo the earlier Japanese soap opera scene.*]

LISA: Why are you following me? What do you want from me?

HARRY: Eh? I'm not following —

LISA: Yes, yes you are. I don't know anything about this woman, all right?

HARRY: But I met her with you. If you could just tell me how —

LISA: You keep harassing me I'm going to tell the school officials on you.

HARRY: You don't understand, it's —

LISA: [*Overlapping.*] I'm going to tell my boyfriend — I'LL SCREAM, I'LL SCREAM AND YOU'LL BE IN BIG TROUBLE, NOW —

HARRY: [*Overlapping.*] — not you, it's the other woman I've got to see . . .

LISA: [*Overlapping.*] — LEAVE ME ALONE!

HARRY: All right, all right . . .

[HARRY *backs away as* LISA *runs off.* HARRY'S ATTORNEY *grabs him by the arm, pulling him along to the divorce hearing.* JUDGE *appears with* LILLIAN *and* LILLIAN'S ATTORNEY.]

LILLIAN'S ATTORNEY: . . . the house, her BMW, Harry's Saab, the CD player, the televisions, all the furniture, the IRAs, the T-bills, the stocks and bonds . . .

HARRY: [*Overlapping, to* LILLIAN.] Why are you doing this?

[LILLIAN *refuses to talk.*]

LILLIAN'S ATTORNEY: [*Droning on.*] — and most of all, she wants custody of their child Harry . . .

HARRY: [*Whispering to his* ATTORNEY.] We don't have a child . . .

LILLIAN'S ATTORNEY: . . . by the other woman.

HARRY'S ATTORNEY: [*To a confused* HARRY.] Don't lie to your attorney. Lying to your own attorney is like lying to your god.

JUDGE: Attorney for Harry, what is your response?

HARRY'S ATTORNEY: [*To* HARRY.] Jesus, now I'll have to lie, too . . .

[*She's about to answer the* JUDGE *when a phone rings. The* WAITER *from the Dream Club walks in with a remote phone on a drink tray. We hear a hint of the Club music.*]

WAITER: Phone call for Harry! Phone call for Harry!

HARRY: [*To his* ATTORNEY.] Wait, wait... [*To the* JUDGE.] Excuse me, your Honor, I just need to...

[*As* HARRY *takes the phone, the* WAITER *grabs him and kisses him hard — then pulls back smiling. A* UNIVERSITY OFFICIAL *appears on a phone, with his back to* HARRY. LISA *stands next to the* OFFICIAL, *glaring at* HARRY, *who is still dazed by the kiss.* LISA *points at* HARRY.]

LISA: There he is!

OFFICIAL: [*German accent.*] These are very serious charges, Herr Kitamura. Normally you would be put on indefinite suspension until this could be investigated fully... However, since you are a professor of good standing and it is her word against yours, we will overlook it this time.

LISA: Pigs...

[LISA *leaves in disgust.* HARRY *stands confused. Blackout on everyone but* HARRY.]

HARRY: I began walking home...

YOUNG MAN: [*Appearing.*] Harry? Harry the Law Professor?

HARRY: Yes?

YOUNG MAN: I'm Lisa's boyfriend...

[*He suddenly strikes* HARRY *in the face, punches him in the stomach;* HARRY *falls to the ground. The* MAN *begins to kick* HARRY *savagely, over and over. Slow fade to black as* HARRY *is repeatedly kicked, violently, relentlessly.*]
[*Lights rise slowly on* HARRY, *badly beaten, mumbling deliriously.*]

HARRY: Nina... Nina? What? My arm? Yes? Nina? Nina the gorgeous... Nina the ugly... Nina the nape woman... Nina the dog lady...

[*Music similar to a Ginger Baker drum solo fades up.* HARRY *lies down in a half light, continuing to moan and babble in the dark.*]
[*A door opens and a gush of bright light pours through. Drumming increasing in volume. Three dark figures wearing long lab coats enter with flashlights, and with lights attached to their foreheads like miners, looking for something. They speak with working class British accents.*]

MR. BRUCE: Dr. Baker, Dr. Baker there he is!

DR. BAKER: Hurry, check his rhythm, Mr. Bruce.

MR. BRUCE: [*Checking his pulse.*] My god...

DR. BAKER: What?

MR. BRUCE: It's all out of whack. He's beating out a 7/4 over a 13/8 . . . What do you think, Mr. Clapton?

MR. CLAPTON [*Feeling pulse.*] Extraordinary, bloody extraordinary . . .

MR. BRUCE: What shall we do, Dr. Baker?

DR. BAKER: Mr. Bruce, Mr. Clapton, get him up. Get him up and walking . . .

MR. CLAPTON: He seems too weak . . .

DR. BAKER: Harry? Harry, can you hear me? Can you get up?

HARRY [*Blinded by the flashlights.*] What? Who? Nina? Nina?

DR. BAKER: It looks bad, boys. We'll have to carry him . . .

[*They pick him up and carry him above their heads.*]

MR. BRUCE:: Dr. Baker, are we going to have to . . .

DR. BAKER: I'm afraid so, Mr. Bruce.

MR. CLAPTON: Poor bloke, I'd hate to be in his shoes . . .

[*They set him down on an operating table. An operation room light descends. Figures still remain shadowy. They pull out small red saws.*]

HARRY: Wait, wait, what's going on here?

DR. BAKER: We're going to have to amputate, Harry . . .

HARRY: Why?

DR. BAKER: It's starting to rot. . . .

HARRY: My arm?

DR. BAKER: Lack of use . . .

HARRY: Say, aren't you Eric —

MR. BRUCE: . . . It's wasting away.

HARRY: Yeah, but I might need it to —

MR. CLAPTON: We have to cut it off . . .

MR. BRUCE: . . . before it infects . . .

DR. BAKER: . . . the rest of your soul . . .

[*They grab him, hold him down; he struggles for his life.*]

HARRY: Give me a chance! Wait! Please! DON'T, DON'T, I NEED MY ARM! AHHHH!!!! . . .

[HARRY *disappears beneath the* MEN *and their red saws. We hear him screaming in pain. Drumming increases in volume.* NINA *appears in a shaft of light, watching. Blackout.*]

[*Silence. We hear the distant strains of a song similar to "Is That All There Is?"* PEGGY LEE *appears silhouetted upstage. Lights rise on center stage. One should get the sense of a new landscape, a shift in reality.* HARRY *stands, dressed in a trenchcoat, hat, dark glasses. Unmoving. He appears a broken man.*]

[NINA *stands next to him, staring. She takes off his trenchcoat and hat. His one arm hangs limply at his side. She moves carefully so as not to awaken him, as if a sudden shock might prove fatal. She delicately removes his dark glasses. His eyes are closed. She watches him as he slowly, wearily opens his eyes.*]

HARRY: Nina?

NINA: Yes, Harry, it's me.

HARRY: Nina, I'm lost.

NINA: I know.

HARRY: I'm lost in this dream of you.

NINA: And I in yours. I've been waiting for you.

HARRY: Is there some reason for all of this, why I met you? Or, or, are you just...Who are you? What's happening to me? I've given —

NINA: [*Overlapping.*] Harry?

HARRY: [*Overlapping.*] — up everything — career, my standing in the community, personal life...It's all gone, taken, ripped from me, destroyed. All I can see is you. All I can think about is being with you. What's happening to me? I'm lost, lost...I'm nothing...I no longer exist...

NINA: Harry? Harry? [*He stops and listens.*] I think you're ready now. [*She takes out a pill.*] You want to get to know me, don't you, Harry? Really know me. You can. But there's a price. A terrible, wondrous, excruciating price that most sane people would never dare to pay. [*He reaches for the pill. She withdraws it, shaking her head.*] Tonight you're on your own. [*She takes it.*] Even a dream needs a little help now and then... You keep thinking I'm not letting you in. Harry, you're not letting yourself in. In the face of truth I'm always open. It's that simple. You have to live the truth. Be the truth. Every instant of every heartbeat, the truth. Are you ready to do that, Harry? Live the truth, be the truth? If you are, then you're also ready to cross the line. Cross the line, Harry? If the moment calls for it, demands it, who will you listen to, whose voice will you obey? What society wants you to do? Or your own? No matter what it says? No matter where it takes you? Are you ready to cross the line? [*Noticing*] Look, look, it's the time in between. Two moons and a rogue comet grace the sky. Is it dawn or dusk? Is the sun setting or rising on your life? Your call, Harry. The best kept secrets are always right in front of your nose. Whose scent do you smell? Are you ready, Harry? Are you ready to take the plunge? To hurl yourself out over the abyss? Leap into the void with no designer clothes, no Pinot noirs, no make-up, no credit cards, no excuses, no lies, no history, no mythology, no trickery or deceit— knowing that you will be carried aloft, buoyed up only by, your ass saved only by, the intensity of your realness? ... [*Slaps him lightly.*] Harry? Wake up.

HARRY: The dog ran home with its tail between its legs...

NINA: [*Slaps him harder.*] Harry, Harry, can you wake up? Or are you already blind to the things that only ghosts, the innocents and madmen can see?

HARRY: My face, my dog face...

NINA: [*Strikes him very hard.*] Wake up, Harry. You're dying and the hour is late. The flesh is falling from our bodies. Moments of exquisite perfumed pleasure are slipping away into oblivion. Look, look at this face, this skin, taste my breath—fresh peaches. Harry, you, this divine animal—what an incredibly intricate piece of imagination beating inside of you. Take it out, take it out and share, dream, I give you permission... [*She pushes her back against* HARRY, *leaning the back of her neck near his face.* HARRY *rubs his face against it, inhales deeply, then begins to smother her nape in kisses.*] Bite me. Yes, go on, don't be afraid. Bite me in the back of my neck. Make me feel your eyes. Know that you still aren't asleep. [*He nibbles.*] No, no, I said really bite me... [*Harry bites her hard and holds on.*] Ahhhh ..[*She pulls free and faces him, surprised by his ardor.*] Harry... [*Laughing.*] Harry, Harry, Harry... His arm is waking up. He's getting his muscle back. And now he wants to feel... Grab at the world with his heart... Did I tell you about my vision... Why I was committed to the convent?

HARRY: "Committed"?

NINA: [*Laughing.*] I mean, "Why I ENTERED the convent"? [*Beat.*] Because of what I saw—a Man with a bleeding heart. A Man rising into the air...

HARRY: Fuck the heart, the man rising...

NINA: All in due time, all in due time—but for now we mustn't throw out the baby with the bathwater. Remember, Harry, my vision's also your dream ...

HARRY: Harry's unconscious. Harry has no eyes. Harry's orbiting some distant planet with newly grown wings ...

NINA: [*As* HARRY *falters.*] Harry? [*As he struggles, grabbing his chest.*] Harry?

HARRY: Better not to ... better not to feel ... this kind of thing ... anything. Because if you do, if you do ... Better to hide. Run home, your tail between your legs ... Be the dog ... Silent, obedient, dog-face ... Because if you, if you open up, feel, let yourself breathe, howl ....

NINA: What happens?

HARRY: Because if you do ...

NINA: What happens? Harry?

HARRY: Then, then ...

[SAM *enters dragging the* DOG, *played by* JOE. SAM *offers* HARRY *the knife.* DOG's *head is lit.* JEFF *bursts in.*]

JEFF: Julie phoned. They know. The administration goons are on their way.

HARRY [*As* SAM *looks at him accusingly.*] You betrayed me. The one time I found something. Opened up. My heart ... [SAM *slashes the* DOG's *neck.* DOG/JOE *falls to the ground. Silence.*] I told them. It was me. I told the school officials what we were planning to do. [*Beat.*] They like people like me. They do. Quiet, hard working. The model minority. We always do what we're told, we're always bowing our heads — we're not dangerous, we're not sexual, we're always wearing this silent frozen mask while inside I want to rage and scream ... [JOE *gets up, dusts himself off. He takes the knife from* SAM *and puts it in* HARRY'S *hand.*]

NINA: Don't be afraid.

JOE: We all get a second chance.

NINA: Kill the dog ...

[JOE *and* NINA *whisper into* HARRY'S *ears from both sides while embracing him, stroking him.*]

JOE: Kill the dog ...

NINA: Kill the dog ...

[*Both keep repeating "kill the dog."* HARRY *has the blade raised. The sound has been building throughout.* HARRY *screams and drives the blade into his own chest. Blackout.*]

[*Loud club music.* EXOTIC DANCERS *appear, dancing for ten seconds, erotic, insane. Blackout. Silence. Hold.*]

[*We hear a song similar to Louis Armstrong's "What a Wonderful World." A match is struck. Upstage we see and hear a comet grace the sky.*]

[HARRY *and* JOE *slowly appear, both dressed identically in sleek tailored black suits with white T-shirts on underneath. Barefoot, both wearing Homburgs.* HARRY *lights* JOE's *cigarette.* JOE *holds it between his third and fourth fingers. He inhales deeply, then blows smoke rings.*]

[HARRY *notices a growing red stain on the front of his own white T-shirt. He's bleeding from the heart. Slowly* JOE *begins to rise off the ground, nonchalantly blowing smoke rings.* NINA *appears, watching the peculiar spectacle, holding a red umbrella. She is dressed normally except for a nun's head covering. She stares in wonder for a beat, then points at her unfolding vision, delighted.*]

NINA: Look, look, Raoul!

[*We hear a dog barking happily.* NINA *laughs like a schoolgirl. She kisses* HARRY *on the cheek and softly barks at him. They both laugh.* NINA *joins* JOE *and they exit arm in arm. Blackout on all except* HARRY, *as Louis Armstrong continues underneath.*]

HARRY: I was at this wine tasting party. When I saw . . .

[LILLIAN *appears, with a man dressed in an expensive dark suit. They hold wine glasses. She waves to him.*]

LILLIAN: Harry?

HARRY: When I went up to talk to her I noticed she was with someone who looked familiar. Then I realized who it was.

SAM: Harry? It's me.

HARRY: I couldn't believe it. It was . . .

SAM: Sam . . .

HARRY: [*Overlapping.*] Sam . . . For some reason I had thought he was dead . . .

SAM: No, I'm a stockbroker.

HARRY: He appeared very conservative and . . .

SAM: Yes, I'm very rich.

HARRY: [*Staring.*] I couldn't get over it — I stared . . .

SAM: What, I look like some foolish old man now?

HARRY: We both laughed . . .

SAM: Would you like to try this Pinot? It's quite good.

HARRY: He wore a Jerry Garcia tie.

LILLIAN: I gave it to him. [HARRY *turns his attention to* LILLIAN; SAM *withdraws. She stares at* HARRY.] You seem different. Your face?

HARRY: [*Thinking about it, touching his cheek*] My face? Hmmm...

LILLIAN: I'm happy now. Are you?

[*Beat.* HARRY *watches as* LILLIAN *fades to black. Then he looks to another part of the stage.*]

[*Louis Armstrong fades as* HARRY'S MOTHER *and the* FISHERMAN *appear. They sit side by side fishing. We hear birds, the river.* MOTHER *reaches into her bag and pulls out a piece of fried chicken, wraps the bottom in a napkin and hands it to* HARRY'S *father. She then holds out a musubi (rice ball) for him to eat so he doesn't have to use his hands, which hold the imaginary pole. They laugh and she wipes the corner of his lip.*]

FISHERMAN: Would you like to go to Kauai with me? It's across the river?

[MOTHER *nods.* FISHERMAN *sweeps* MOTHER *up in his arms and takes her across the river,* MOTHER *laughing happily.*]

MOTHER: Harry? You didn't give me a story. You didn't let me really speak.

HARRY: Would you like to?

MOTHER: [*Thinking.*] No, I'm not finished yet...

[*They dim to darkness, their laughter disappearing in the distance.* HARRY *stands alone in a pool of light, the sound of wind blowing somewhere. Music rises — melancholic, mournful, beautiful sadness.* HARRY *closes his eyes — then, slowly, opens them again.*]

HARRY: I awoke from a deep sleep. I had the strangest feeling. That I had been asleep for a very long time. [*Looks around, inhales deeply.*] Fresh air has a flavor, did you know that? Peaches? And Night... [*Thinking.*] Night is... [*Surprised at his own thought.*] ... day standing on its head... [*Quietly laughs at the thought.*] I awoke with a sense of fullness. Yes, fullness. And the one thing I knew. Was that I would dance. Yes, dance. Dance any chance I could get...

[*A song similar to "Is That All There Is?" begins to play.* HARRY *sways for a beat, then moves into a brief dance. It should be fun, not take itself too seriously.* PEGGY LEE *appears and moves toward* HARRY, *handing him a red rose.*]

PEGGY LEE: Harry...

HARRY: I've been expecting you...

[*She enters his arms. They begin to slow dance. We see that it is* LILLIAN *this time beneath the blonde wig and dress. Lights tighten to a pool around them. They stare into each other's eyes. It's a warm, deep exchange. They drink deeply of each other. She slowly takes off the blonde wig. Their eyes never leave each other. He draws her closer to him. She rests her head on his shoulder. The wig hanging by her side, now falls to the ground.* HARRY'S *hand moves to stroke the nape of her neck. They continue to slow dance. Very slow fade to black. Music swells, then out.*]

END OF PLAY

Amy Hill

TOKYO BOUND

EDITOR'S NOTES

In the last ten years, solo performance has become its own genre, its best-known practitioners a diverse group ranging from Laurie Anderson to Eric Bogosian to Anna Deavere Smith to Roger Gueveneur Smith. Within the Asian American theatre community, the one-person show has become especially popular — partly, of course, because it is so economical, but principally because theatre, especially in these days when it is overshadowed by film, thrives today as it gives voice to those who have had no voices. The one-person show allows the solo performer to state his or her individual truths for which the history books have had little room.

In a moment, an entire new anthology could be compiled of distinctive and provocative work by Asian American solo performers. A highly incomplete list would certainly include pioneer Brenda Wong Aoki (*The Queen's Garden*), NPR commentator Sandra Tsing Loh (*Aliens in America*), character actor Dennis Dun (*Dragon Dream*) and Mari Sunaida (*Hybrid Vigor*). Writers in this volume such as Lane Nishikawa and Denise Uyehara have also been solo performers, while Dan Kwong, working at the Santa Monica performance venue Highways, has not only performed his own work, but has been a teacher and curator urging actors and other artists to explore the form.

Amid this proliferation of self-revelation, writer/actor Amy Hill has been at the forefront. A writer whose work has been telecast on the PBS series *The Puzzle Place*, she is best known to the public for her performances in the ABC situation comedies, *All-American Girl* and *Maybe This Time*. But much of that work arose from the success of a trilogy of monologues, of which *Tokyo Bound* is the first.

In *Tokyo Bound*, Hill invents and re-invents herself, seeking a persona that makes some kind of sense. The pun in the title reveals her conflicts: Japan as destination, Japan as inescapable restriction. Though Hill's mixed-race heritage has clearly been the catalyst for some painful experiences, Hill does not wear her pain on her sleeve, and in fact the success of her performances owes as much to her own exuberant personality as to the wit and humor of the text. But over the course of the evening we realize that the personality we see has been forged slowly, by a donning and discarding of other masks. At the end of the evening, having been a geisha, a punk, a media starlet, and a dutiful daughter, we must decide if the Amy Hill backstage is still another persona — or a constellation formed by all the stars she has shown us.

Also key to the story, obviously, is Hill's relationship with her mother, who still plays an important role in Hill's life. It could be argued that the reticence of parents has partially inspired the boom in Asian American solo performance — artist after artist testifying to the difficulty of getting their parents to speak about painful immigration or internment experiences, testifying to the challenge of piercing the mystery and commemorating a history that will die if it remains untold.

Are performance texts unique to the people who write them? Wallace Shawn's monologues have been performed without his presence, and if ever there were an idiosyncratic performer, Shawn is it. Similarly, while Hill's zeal as a performer is hard to equal, it is interesting to contemplate whether the texts written by her, by Loh and Aoki and Nishikawa and all the rest, will have life as performance texts after the performers themselves have moved on. It is partly to encourage that possibility that *Tokyo Bound* is included in this volume — stories like Hill's deserve a lasting life in the theatre.

Tokyo Bound was first produced at East West Players in Los Angeles, California, on August 8, 1991. Written and performed by Amy Hill. Directed by Anne Etue. Dramaturgy by Judith Nihei; Set Design by Chris Tashima; Lighting Design by Rae Creevey; Costume Design by Lydia Tanji; Sound Composition and Design by Scott Nagatani.

SETTING: *Empty stage with large geta — Japanese wooden shoe — placed center stage on its side so that the bottom of the shoe is facing down stage. The words "Tokyo Bound" are written on the bottom of the shoe in Japanese characters. There is a large noren — Japanese hanging curtain — upstage, against the back wall. It serves as a screen for the slides used throughout the performance to punctuate/illustrate the text. Costume pieces are placed behind the geta and offstage. There are no props or other set pieces. All location changes are indicated by action. The show opens in* BLACK *with* MUSIC *and* SLIDES *of Japan and Amy's own photos.*

VOICE OVER: When I was seven, I would tell people I lived in a mansion in Broadmoor, with servants and chandeliers. Instead, we lived off a gravel dead-end street in the Rainier Valley. My father, a Finnish-American transplant, had moved us all from Deadwood, South Dakota to make it big as a heavy equipment operator. But it rains so much in Seattle that most construction is shut down a good part of the year. My mother was a Japanese war-bride who helped ease the financial burden by first cooking part-time in a Japanese restaurant — "Nikko, serving authentic Japanese food since 1956" — and then full-time in the Group Health hospital kitchen. Growing up, I sensed that our family situation was unique, though not necessarily to be envied, so I made it my job to re-invent who I was.

By the time I got to high school everybody knew me too well, so I had to leave Seattle, start over again somewhere else. My senior year at Franklin, I was elected president of the Foreign Exchange Club. I had plans to move to Paris and become a bohemian: sit around in cafes, smoke non-filter Gauloises, converse about politics, poetry, and art, and change my name to "Josephine." Dad said he'd pay if I went to Finland. Mom said she'd pay if I went to Japan: "You make me so happy if you go!" ...

Helsinki or Hiroshima, lutefisk or sashimi ... hmmm ...

[AMY *enters room, approaching people for directions. Speaks haltingly from an imaginary phrase book. We hear the sounds of Tokyo city streets.*]

AMY: Sumimasen, ote-arai wa doko desu ka? Sumimasen, ote-arai wa doko desu ka?

[*To audience.*]

I was looking for the bathroom. It wasn't easy. I knew how to ask, but with only two years of Japanese in high school, I didn't have a clue

what the people I asked were saying back. It was all...well...
Japanese.

[*To imaginary passerby.*]

Sumimasen, ote-arai wa doko desu ka?

[*To audience.*]

The stakes got higher as my bladder got fuller!

[*To passerby.*]

Sumimasen!

[*To audience.*]

Then, I found it.

[*Standing in front of imaginary door.*]

O-TE-ARAI.

[*She opens the door, enters and immediately notices something on the floor. She turns to the audience.*]

It was a hole in the ground. A porcelain hole. Had I wandered into the men's room?

[*She steps out and glances at her surroundings.*]

No. There were women there.

[*Stepping back in and examining more carefully.*]

They've got these little footrests on either side of the hole.

[*She gingerly places a foot on each footrest and begins to squat. Interrupting herself, she determines that she might in fact be facing the wrong direction, and turns around. Deciding she was probably right in the first place, she switches positions again. With a sigh of relief, she begins searching the stall itself and realizes her final inconvenience to the audience.*]

No toilet paper.

[*The toilet flushes. She steps out of stall.*]

That's how it began. I was eighteen, first time away from home. Alone. And, everybody's Japanese: small, dark, neat...and they all looked the *same*. I mean, it's not like I've never seen them before. My mom's Japanese. But, we're talking *nothing* but Japanese faces *everywhere*. And there I was: long brown hair to my waist, streaked with "Sun-in," bell-bottom jeans with patches, "Che Guevara" T-shirt, obviously American born, bred and fed, wearing clogs.

Maybe I should have gone to France.

The first six months, I cried everyday, called home a lot and wondered if I could handle it all: new school, new language, new lifestyle
...nude body.

[*She glances down at her body and cringes slightly.*]

No one had every seen me naked before. Not even my doctor. My
first apartment in Tokyo didn't have a bath or shower, which is very
common. I would have to use the public bath house. A room full of
naked people. All women. But...naked. I must have waited at least a
week before going.

[*Walks past imaginary stores, etc. Taking her time. Looking into the distance
furtively.*]

I walked that long, lonely two blocks.

[*She sees something in a display case and smiles at the shopkeeper.*]

Stopping to pick up snacks along the way.

[*To shopkeeper.*]

Kohii gyuunyuu o ippon. Hai. Doomo.

[*Gives shopkeeper some change and starts to move. She stops again to
request another item.*]

Keiki mo...ichi...uh...hitotsu kudasai. Hai. Doomo.

[*Continues on her way until she stops in front of large imaginary building.*]

Until I found myself in front of it. A large wooden building with a giant smoke stack coming out of the center of the roof...with sliding
frosted glass doors.

[*She opens the doors and enters cautiously.*]

To my right I saw shelving with several pairs of very sad looking
shoes. People who had their own bathrooms probably had nice shoes.
I looked own at my own sorry-looking "Dr. Scholls" and thought
"nobody'd steal these either."

[*She takes her shoes off. She carefully places them on the shelves and enters
through the second set of doors.*]

To my right, a handful of women in various stages of undress. To my
left, a wooden wall, about six feet high, separating the men's side of
the bathhouse from the women's. I could hear their voices...and
wondered if they were listening, too. Following that wall to my im-

mediate left, I looked up and saw...a man. On a platform. Overlooking the whole spectacle. He reached down.

[*She cowers slightly. Recovering, she hands him some money, and moves into the darker recesses of the changing room. She continues to glance back at the man on the platform, attempting to hide herself from his view.*]

I found an empty locker and undressed. What was I supposed to do? Leave? No. I had to get used to this. No one else seemed to care.

[*Looking around her. She covers herself with her arms and scurries to the final imaginary door, pauses and opens it slowly. She is awestruck. We can hear a cacophony of bathhouse sounds: water splashing, the echo of women's and children's voices.*]

A bunch of naked women cleaning themselves very thoroughly. I mean, scrubbing real hard and getting really clean. They were all kind of moist and pink. And, for the first time, I realize that the Japanese woman comes in all shapes and sizes. I mean, they were right there, in full view, sitting on little stools. I grab one and wait to see if it belongs to anyone. No one protests.

[*Sitting on her imaginary stool. She carefully watches and then, mimics the women around her. She fills a bucket with water. Pours it over her head. Lathers herself and then rinses off. She then notices a large communal tub. She stands and starts to get in. As her toe reaches the water, she immediately pulls it out again. It is very hot but she grits her teeth and forges ahead. As she manuevers herself into the water, she grimaces and groans in pain. Finally settled, somewhat uncomfortable, yet victorious, she notices that a small group of women have taken notice of her. She waves meekly and indicates the water is...*]

Atsui.

[*Deciding that she has been in a sufficient amount of time. She emerges from the tub, waving goodbye to the others in the tub and returns to her stool. She then notices something odd next to her.*]

There's a leg next to me. Kind of hairy. An arm. Hairy.

[*She jumps to her feet after a quick double take. She covers herself with a washcloth.*]

A man! He's not naked. He's wearing a loincloth. But again, no one blinks an eye. He gathers some used razors and empty shampoo bottles and moves on, cleaning and shuffling stools and buckets as he makes his way through the bodies.

Of course, if I'd gone to Finland, I'd have been buck naked in a sauna, slapping myself with birch branches and jumping into a snow bank.

How'd I end up with a mom and dad from two cultures that think of *bathing* as some kind of *ritual.*

Maybe I should have gone to France.

[*Dropping the towel, she moves to another area of the stage.*]

My first day at Sophia International University, I noticed a group of kids sitting on the steps outside the student lounge. They were laughing and talking. As I drew nearer, I could hear them speaking in English, but I couldn't quite understand what they were saying. One of them, Kimiko Johnson, became a friend of mine.

[*Becomes* KIMIKO, *who is speaking to some other students offstage.*]

Hey! Meet you ato de okay? Yeah. Henry Africa de ii yo! No. By myself de iku no. So. Ja. Ciao baby! Oh, hey! Genki kai? Nanka happening? Minna meeting at Henry Africa yo! Iku? Ikoo zei!

[*To audience as* KIMIKO.]

Yeah, I was raised here. I was born on base, but I was raised off base. Went to Japanese school when I was real young but kids were kinda rough on me. I really don't remember much but I changed over to private school. You know, ASIJ ... American School in Japan? I like it a lot better.

My mom's Japanese. She met my dad at the PX. My dad's career military but he's great. He doesn't speak Japanese as good as us kids but he swears really good.

There are lots of kids like me at ASIJ. We hang out a lot together. My best friend's "half," too. She's a model, so we get into discos really easy. I think all our Japanese friends like us because they think we're ... "exotic."

Anyway, I'm going to college in the states. Gonna go home to Connecticut. That's where my dad's from. I went there once, when I was six. It was great. I remember thinking, "Yeah ... this is where I belong." I hated Japan after that. I'd just sit around and dream about going back.

It's funny though. Some kids go back and say they don't like it. Say they fit in better here. They're happier here. I can't believe it. In America, you can do anything and be anything you want. Here ... I can't sing, can't dance ... don't want to be a model.

[*She notices someone in the distance and runs forward.*]

Hey, chotto! Wait up!

[*Becomes* AMY.]

I wanted to be just like Kimiko. Be Japanese when I wanted to, or

American or...both. I enjoyed being around her because growing up, I never had any friends with a family like mine. I cut my hair, got a perm and went...shopping.

[*Appears to be entering a store as she puts on gloves and a hat. We hear Japanese department store sounds.*]

When you entered a department store, there was always someone to greet you at the entrance. As you moved through the store, the clerks would welcome you as you passed their counters. And, at the foot of the escalator, there was always a young woman, wearing white gloves, holding a handkerchief, continuously wiping the handrail of the escalator as she bowed and purred... "Welcome, Welcome,"

[*She becomes the* ESCALATOR GIRL.]

"Irrashaimase, goraiten itadaite, makoto ni arigatoo gozaimasu," I love my job. I know I am very good, too. I always rinse my gloves out every night...so they are very white. And I refold my handkerchief every thirty minutes so each side of the cloth is used evenly. Some girls don't care, but I do.
Sometimes I see very cute boys, but I remember to keep my eyes down, and bow at just 45 degrees, keeping the angle of the back of my head in a straight line with my back and my left hand just so.

[*Placing it in front of lap.*]

I imagine people going up the escalator, looking back at me, admiring my expertise. Someday, I know that my husband will also be very pleased with my poise. I would like to marry out of love, but I have a picture of me in kimono, being distributed to eligible young bachelors right now by my aunt. I should be married by the time I'm twenty-three, have two children, and live in the outskirts of Tokyo in a three-room apartment until we can save enough for a small prefab house. They're so cute. I've always known what I wanted. My life is so good.

[*Department store chimes.*]

"Irasshaimase." The rooftop beer garden is now open as well as the children's insect zoo. In our seventh floor gallery space, we have an exhibit of sand paintings and paper products from Fukushima prefecture. In our six floor "Bargain Parade," Kenzo and Miyake are 75 percent off, yukata and other sleepwear are 80 percent off. In the first floor basement, American beef is now on sale at the same price as Australian and New Zealand beef, sliced thin for sukiyaki and shabu

shabu. Dresses are on floors three, four and five. All clothing is marked size M, but shoes range from size 21.5 to 24.5.

[*Becomes* AMY, *removing hat and gloves.*]

I was at least an L and wore a size 25 shoe, so everything was a bit tight. But, I was soon walking like a Japanese girl—

[*As if in pain.*]

—naturally.

And, lacking any basic knowledge in the finer points of womanhood, I studied tea ceremony, calligraphy and flower arrangement. My ikebana teacher was so perfect: so soft, gracious, feminine. I liked her a lot... Koike sensei.

[AMY *becomes very feminine Japanese woman, appearing to do flower arrangement. The sound of a koto is heard playing.*]

This is "shin," representing the heavens, "hikae," the earth, and "soe" is the sun.

[*As* AMY, *to audience.*]

She had a way about her that was utterly compelling. So... cool. So I assumed her persona outside of class as well. I'd try it on new acquaintances. Japanese acquaintances. Okay. Men.

[AMY *approaches an imaginary man, shy and covering her face as she giggles.*]

How are you? I'm fine thank you. Would you like a piece of fruit? An apple? Let me peel it for you.

[*Laughing.*]

Oh, you are so funny!

[*Checking her forehead with the back of her hand.*]

Hot? Oh no, I'm not hot. I'm fine.

[*Suddenly concerned.*]

Are you hot? Let me fan you!

[*Fanning him.*]

Feel better?

[*To audience.*]

Sometimes I got carried away.

[*Returns her attention to the man.*]

You are so smart. You are so strong. Thirsty? Oh no. Don't move.

[*Beginning to tire of the charade.*]

Let me get it for you. Tired? Let me massage your shoulders. Stop!

[*Admonishing slap.*]

You are so funny, you make me laugh too much! My name? Amy. Yes, it does mean "laughing beauty" in Japanese.

[*To audience, as she kneels and bows.*]

I was every Japanese man's dream.

[*Returning to her feet.*]

TV also provided me with a kaleidoscope of images of women. Like the weather girl...

[*Becomes* WEATHER GIRL.]

Yokohama hare, tokidoki kumori. Nagano hare, tokidoki kumori. Tokyo hare, tokidoki kumori. Kyoto kumori, tokidoki hare.

[*Becomes* AMY *again.*]

Or the cooking ladies...

[*Becomes* COOKING LADY.]

First you make the dressing. Ginger sho sho. Oshoyu sho sho. Osu sho sho. Zembu mazete. Aji o mite. Mmmm.

[*Smiles.*]

Then, you hold the radish like this, and peel...around and around. Thin like paper. Then, you slice the cucumber like this and this and this...

[*Chopping and flipping knives in the air.*]

...and...Yosh!

[*Becomes* AMY, *indicating finished product.*]

And, by the time you're done, you've created a salad that looks like a sunset, with the skyline of Toronto and tomatoes that look like dancing bears.

[*Crosses to another area of the stage.*]

In the mornings there were the "shock news" shows. Take a simple murder. Make it fun. Make it simple. Sell it.

[*Becomes outlandish, brash* NEWSCASTER.]

Here we have the crime scene. A neighborhood like yours or mine. But it's not. Sadao Matsumoto was killed right here. Sadao liked to drink. He liked women. Too bad.

Michiko Fukushige was raised in Tama Prefecture. She was born bad. She ran away from home when she was fifteen and came to Shinjuku where she met Sadao. She thought her life had taken a turn for the better. She wanted marriage. He resisted. She killed him and ate him for dinner! Matsumoto "teriyaki kabob!"

[*Becomes* AMY *again.*]

And then, way before Sally Jessy and Oprah, there were the women talk show hosts.

[*She picks up wig, glasses and scarf from offstage and becomes older woman with a hacking smoker's cough. The sounds of jazz can be heard.*]

My name is Chima. I have been doing my show now for twenty years. Just me and my many guests over the years.

[*Cough.*]

It hasn't been easy. It wasn't so common or accepted for women to be in this business. I have been very lonely. [*Cough.*]
I gave up many things in life. Marriage. Family.

[*Cough.*]

Smoking.

[*Long pause.*]

My uterus. I will have to grow old alone.

[*She dons large, elegantly coiffed blue wig, glasses and scarf.*]

How do you like my hair? I hate it. I want to cut it. Dye it brown.

[*Pause.*]

I want to make pot stickers out of scratch.

I've always been a rebel. I come from a long line of rebels from Nagasaki. Christian Martyrs. Catholics. I rebelled against that. At my first communion, I didn't *swallow* the host, I *bit* it, waiting for the blood to spew out. When I was fourteen, I gave up confession so I could have sex without forgiveness. And, I told my mother, I would never become a nun like my friend Harumi who thought the inkstains on her hand were stigmata. And when the A-Bomb fell on our city, changing Nagasaki from heaven to hell, I knew that God cared as little for me as I did for him. I refused to do what was expected anymore. And, this is what I've become.

I'm blood type-A, you know. I like to work hard. I'm ambitious. Smart. But I have to do so many stupid things. Do you know, I'm never allowed to wear the same dress twice? Who cares if I wear the same dress?

[*Pause.*]

Who cares about this stupid show? About me. About anything.

[*She exits, removing wig, etc. She returns to upstage of geta with red fluffy dress covered with Japanese snack package labels and a sequined hat. Typical Japanese "pop idol" attire. We hear the melody of a very "cute" pop song.*]

Then there were the young entertainers. Packaged by "star makers," some stick around for a year or two like "Pink Lady" or some disappear as quickly as they arrive on the scene. All they have to be is 'charming,' a word used too often in Japan.

[AMY *hops up onto geta, with her back to audience and begins to do a cute dance. She stops and looks over her shoulder to the audience.*]

Hi, I'm Koko...

[*She jumps off the geta to the stage and begins to put on her outfit as she speaks.*]

That's my new hit. I was discovered in a singing contest when I was just thirteen. My manager says "Saba (that's my real name), you don't have to worry so much about singing. People can't identify with you if you sing too well. We want to sell your personality." He says I'm "charming."
See these teeth? I'm lucky they stick out. Some girls have straight teeth. Way too boring. My manager picks all my songs for me... about love and breaking up and being lonely. I've never had a boyfriend, but I use my imagination. He teaches me all my dance moves, too.

[*Does little dance.*]

This year I've done a lot of television dramas. I've never acted before, but people say I'm talented because I cry so easily. I like those scenes a lot.

[*She looks off into distance with longing, then cries out, over-acting horribly.*]

"Yurushite! Yurushite kure yo!"

[*Ending the mood just as quickly as she fell into it.*]

Good, huh?

I also do game shows. It looks like I make up my lines but I have them written for me. They have me say things I could never imagine saying. "Reality is the mind trap of duality."

But what I really look forward to is the big year-end singing contest. Kohaku Utagassen. I'll be on the red team. Red is my lucky color. I'll be wearing a dress that looks like the Eiffel Tower with an elevator going right up the middle. It's beautiful. Costs 850.000 YEN. I can't wait. I hope I win, because this is my last year. I'm twenty-five and my manager says I have to have an "image change." I'm going to get a nose and an eye job and start wearing sexy clothes. Maybe get married. He's already picked someone out for me. Another singer. I like him, but I heard he's gay. That's alright. I think I like women better anyway. Sometimes I wish I could go back to when I was thirteen, but I guess I can't.

[*She has completed putting on her outfit and strikes beginning pose for song. The pop song heard earlier plays again, this time with the lyrics. She lip-syncs to the song and does a simple, but very typically "cute" Japanese pop dance.*]

Kini no love, moratte kurenai
Doshite your love, my way ni narenai
Shinu hodo itai na no yo!
I love you oh so much!

Anata ga, zurai, na no yo
Loving you wa, itami no moto
Shinu hodo, itai nan no yo!
I love you oh so much!

I want your love na no, give me your love na no
Kiss me and hold me so tight
dekinai kara, watashi no sekai wa tottemo tsurai!
Dame na love na no yo!

Why is your love, something that I can't have
All I need is, someone to hold my hand
My poor heart is, breaking apart over you!
I love you oh so much!

Pain and heartache, is all I know right now
You're my torment, stand up and take a bow
How much longer, can I endure you alive?
I love you oh so much!

I wnat your love more than anything else
Please just kiss me and hold me so tight

Then, take this gun and shoot
My death will free me from this hell on earth I know
I'd rather die than say good-bye
Dame na love na no yo!

Thank you!

[*She takes off the hat and dress and discards offstage. We hear a Japanese radio talk show, "Konnichi wa,* AMY *desu...." as she returns to center stage.*]

Spawning salmon in Hokkaido. That's the kind of thing we used to talk about on my radio show, "Amy's Japan." Did the whole thing in Japanese. They wanted to do a travel show from an American's perspective and it was important that I spoke Japanese fluently, but badly. I could handle that. They also wanted someone under 5'7" who wouldn't frighten the country folk. The show suited me fine. But I did all sorts of things in Japan. Well, what I was allowed to do. As a foreigner, I could teach English, translate, do language tapes... host a radio show. But, as I learned to speak Japanese fluently, I would often be treated differently, not so special. Or rather, like a Japanese woman. There's a lot of baggage attached to either identity and I knew I had to start making some choices. Something my Japanese American friends had little trouble making... or so I thought.

Candy Takanaka and I were in the same class in high school. I ran into her in Tokyo. She was in Japan doing the "junior year abroad" thing. Candy stayed with relatives in Takadanobaba. One of the stops on the green "loop" line. The train that circles the center of Tokyo.

[*Draws big circle in air.*]

The train with no beginning and no end.

[*She disappears behind noren. She shouts from behind the screen.*]

I'm not Japanese!

[*She bursts forth from noren as* CANDY *with Rayban sunglasses on.*]

I got really burnt on this trip. I mean, I came here to get in touch with my roots, you know. Get down with the "people." And all they can do is get on my case! Like, I let them know right from the get that I am American. Like they can't just tell by looking at me?

[*Gesturing, in real easy English. Points at herself, as if speaking to someone.*]

"I am an American." I use my hands a lot.

[*Does "yellow power" salute.*]

"Japanese American." I make faces.

[*Grimacing oddly and carefully pronouncing.*]

"America-jin desu." I mean, isn't it obvious?!

[*Almost shouting and pronouncing with quite an obvious American accent.*]

"Nikkei desu! Wakarimasu ka?!"

[*Giving up.*]

Wakarimasu nothin'! They got pissed off! They thought I was trying to bullshit them . . . like I could speak Japanese but I was *pretending* I couldn't! Like I was trying to bump their heads!

Or they treat me like I'm this full grown person with the vocabulary of
a six year old. Okay, five. Okay, I guess I coulda studied harder in
Japanese school. I mean, my parents forced me to go every Saturday
of my life! But, be serious. Nobody learned Japanese there. We only
went to play basketball. I mean, I didn't want to have nothin' to do
with all that bowin' and scrapin' and shit. You act like some foreigner
in my neighborhood, honey, you get your butt kicked. We were
tough. We had to be. But you wanna know the truth? *This* is tough. I
feel like . . . like my own people have turned on me . . . shit!

[*She turns and takes off her glasses.* AMY *turns back to audience.*]

All this time, I thought J-A's had it made. They had assimilated into
America . . . like teriyaki hot dogs, baseball leagues, cheerleading
squads, Buddhist Church dances. They had their own thread in the
fabric of America. But I found out they felt "different," too. They'd
come to Japan hoping to fit right in, but they didn't. I always tried to
fit in by telling people, "My mom's Japanese! Just like you guys!"
But people mostly didn't know what to make of me. So, for the time
being, I could live a dual life: American at work, Japanese at play.

I lived by the train and subway schedule. All Tokyoites do. The train
has a very tight schedule.

[*Pulls out imaginary calculator.*]

If you calculate the time you leave . . .

[*Starts to walk as if leaving home, towards station.*]

. . . the time it takes to get to the station . . .

[*Punching in numbers.*]

Trains depart every 1.5 minutes. Then, you figure 2.5 minutes for
every stop it makes between the time you get on and your destination

[*Calculates.*]

And...

[*She sees a train pulling into the station and smiles.*]

You're never late.

[*She watches the train pull in, slowly moving to a halt. The doors open and she boards.*]

When I got on at Nakano Station...

[*Looking around.*]

...there weren't any seats left. And there's a guy sitting with his legs so wide, he's taking up at least three spaces.

[*She assumes his position, reading a newspaper.*]

A lady has climbed up onto the seats with her legs tucked underneath her.

[*She sits on top of geta and poses geisha-like.*]

And, there's this other lady squatting smack dab in the middle of the aisle.

[*Squats and stares ahead with an empty look in her eyes.*]

I guess there weren't any seats when she got on either.

[*She stands and searches for something to hold onto.*]

I manage to find the only hand-grip available and settle in for the duration.

[*She sees something in the distance and becomes increasingly alarmed as it appears to close in.*]

As we pull into Shinjuku Station, I can see we're in trouble. The Japanese call it "rashu." Rush hour. The doors opened and in they came.

[*She is immediately jostled.*]

Five million, bazillion people. Being packed in by these guys in white gloves. Some had to use their whole body to force people in.

[*She ends up with her body forced forward.*]

I ended up with my breasts in the face of the man sitting in front of me. I didn't think he could breathe.

[*She strains to pull herself back to a more upright position.*]

He smiles.

[*She is suddenly startled.*]

Then, I felt something odd behind me. A hand?

[*Realization strikes.*]

A chikan?! One of those guys who feel you up on the train?!

[*She vainly attempts to get out of his reach, then silently surrenders. At first she is angry, suspicious of those around her, then perhaps a bit embarrassed by the invasion, then by turns, slightly curious and hesitatingly aroused.*]

Then I remember my father: stern, hard-nosed Finnish-American, devout Lutheran.

[*The train stops.*]

We arrive at Tokyo Station.

[*She gets off and searches the crowds.*]

I manage to catch a glimpse of my chikan. He's cute. Young.

[*Long pause.*]

I wonder if he'll be on this train tomorrow?

[*She continues to walk through station, pointing out things as she proceeds.*]

You can find everything you want in a train station: magazines, gift shops, department stores and . . . restaurants.

[*She stops and appears to be parting a curtain as she enters a restaurant. She looks at her surroundings and rather noisily makes sniffing sounds, as well as other kinds of vocalizations.*]

"Saaa. Heee. Hooo." Japanese love to make noises.

[*She sits at geta as if at a counter and reaches out to accept something.*]

Especially when they eat.

[*Sets the offering down and looks at it with anticipation.*]

Take noodles for instance. They could suck up a bowl of noodles in one breath, right into their stomachs, without spilling a drop.

[*Returns her gaze to the bowl and appears to be readying herself.*]

As the steam rises into your face, a slight sweat breaks out on your forehead. You have your spoon in one hand, your chopsticks in the other, and . . .

[*She dives in, sucking and slurping noodles, until she starts to cough and choke. She stops and slowly lifts her head. She finds a stray noodle on the tip of her nose, then in her hair and on her chin, clothing etc. until she*] *takes her hands and just wipes her whole face clean. Someone sits down next to her and she shrinks in embarrassment and defeat.*]

In the midst of my humiliation, a guy sits down next to me. He asks if I'd like some tea.

[*Doing him.*]

"Ocha o nomimasenka?"

How sweet. But I already had some, so I passed on it. But he insisted. Said he loved tea.

[*Doing him, with a little more energy.*]

"Ocha o dai suki da!"

Said he'd love to have some with me.

[*Doing him, gradually building.*]

"Ocha o nomimashoo!"

He really had a hankering for tea.

[*Doing him, just a touch crazed.*]

"Ocha o nomitai!"

What he meant was... at his place. Or, if that wasn't convenient, we could pop into a local love motel for a quick sip or two. He wanted some...

[*Imitating his desperation.*]

... tea! I may have been young, but I whacked him with my chopsticks and left. I could still hear him screaming—

[*Doing him, wailing and grabbing his crotch.*]

"Ocha! Ocha!"—as I walked out the door.

[*She stands outside the restaurant.*]

Maybe I should have gone to Finland.

[*Skips across stage with glee.*]

But I was in Tokyo and not in Seattle! Soon after the noodle incident, I took a long walk around the Imperial Palace, past the National Theater and through the gardens, when I ran into a couple of young Japanese students who started a conversation with me in very good English.

[*Stops and appears to be speaking with someone.*]

"Exchange students to the University of Michigan?" "Show me around the city?"

[*She appears to be taking a tour, until she stops, pokes her head through a door and looks around.*]

"Nice apartment, Kenji."

[*To audience.*]

Several of his friends were there and we all sat around and talked. Slowly, I noticed that the size of the gathering had dwindled to just... us two.

[*She looks at him.*]

"Maybe I should go, too?"

[*To audience, as she looks through album.*]

He pulled out some pictures of his days at U.M. His girlfriend. His host family. His other girlfriend...naked on the bed. His trips around the U.S.

[*She hesitates.*]

Naked? Well...it probably wasn't meant for others to see.

[*She returns her attention to the photos.*]

Then he got up and went to his bedroom.

[*Watches him leave.*]

When he emerged again...

[*Her eyes grow large.*]

he was...

[*She can't believe what she sees.*]

....buck naked with a hard on.

Up to this point in my life, I'd never had the opportunity to see an erect penis. And I must say, it was quite a sight. And it seemed so... large. I remembered a girl in high school health class had insisted she'd seen one at least a foot long. Well, we might have laughed then but... [*She glances at him.*]

I believed her now.

[*She looks up at him again, as if she can't believe what she's just heard.*]

He asked me to dance.

[*She pauses a moment to think it over, braces herself and then stands. She *cautiously moves toward him, stealing quick glances down to his groin. She raises her arms to his shoulders, careful to keep her body well away from his and attempts to slow dance. After several awkward moments, she breaks away into a disco dance of sorts.*]

I knew this was not the reaction he was hoping for, but not having had any sexual encounters up to this point, I wasn't sure how to react.

[*Turning to him.*]

"Maybe I should leave?" He put on his clothes and took me home. We never danced again. Maybe I should have stayed in Seattle.
Soon after this I decided I had to get "it" over with or "it" was going to get in the way of progress.

[*She stands on geta, tossing her hair back in preparation for something.*]

I was standing in the basement of Takashimaya Department Store, handing out lemons, posing as —

[*Tossing hair.*]

"California Girl."

[*Passing out lemons to passing customers.*]

"Sunkist lemons, doozo. Sunkist lemons, doozo..."

[*Sees something and stops short.*]

...when I saw him. My heart stopped. He had on a black leather jacket over a button-down shirt, jeans and boots.

[*Stepping down from geta.*]

Mr. "Black Leather Jacket" had a name. Udo. And a few weeks later I saw him at school and introduced myself. Soon he was a regular with the after school crowd that met at McDonald's for hamburgers, fries and honeydew melon shakes. One day, he came home with me. Five years later, we married.
I met Udo's parents about a month after we started having sex. We never really dated. We were friends, then we had sex, then we were a couple. That was it.
His mother was beautiful. She didn't look very Japanese, though. And ...I felt immediately...*comfortable* with her. Looking through the family album, I noticed that her brother was quite dark. Almost black. Even so, Udo insisted his family lineage was pure. He *did* say he was often teased as a child. Kids thought he looked "half" because his eyes were so large. But his mother would always reassure him, so he'd just shrug the whole thing off. So did I.

[Leaning forward, secretively.]

But, sometimes...we'd be sitting in his living room, watching Sesame Street, just to hear English...and his mother would comment on what was going on. Like she understood. I knew she didn't.

[Not thoroughly convinced.]

Just before we took that final step towards marriage, his parents called a conference. His mother pulled out the family register and there it was: her name was Yoshiko Kummar and she was born in Prajapur, India.

[She quietly kneels, assuming the character of MRS. UDO. *Carefully opening an imaginary box, she appears to gently hold up a photo that she picks from the top of its contents.]*

I've been waiting for this day. This picture was taken when I was just six. Your uncle, my brother, was eight. We had just gotten a car. None of my friends' families had one so I was so excited. We were all wearing our finest outfits and I had on new earrings that my father had given me. I still have them. I loved my father. He was a doctor and always smoked a pipe. And, he loved to give me new earrings and bracelets because he said I was his "sunshine."

[Replacing the photo.]

Two years later, he died. And, we had to return to Nagasaki. And... I couldn't speak any Japanese. I know it's hard to believe. I can't speak any English now, but...sometimes...when I listen to you two speak, I understand a little. Now you know why your uncle is so fluent. He was older so he didn't forget.

But these things were our secrets. Your grandmother and I would talk of those days often. You know the curry you love so much that obachama used to make? She learned how to in India. I miss her. And, I miss the closeness of our family. Your uncle was too...dark. We couldn't risk having him be a part of our lives. I think he and his wife and children have suffered the most. I don't know how important these things are anymore, but I know why we made the choices we did. If you choose to live in America, I hope you will find things different than here.

[She stands, becoming AMY *again.]*

Here was someone who was familiar with my pain. Someone who understood what it was like to be outside society, wanting to join in, and then creating someone who could be acceptable. We never spoke of it again, but, somehow . . . I felt like we could be each other's support.

[*Seeing someone in the distance, she smiles and bows.*]

"Ah, ohayoo gozaimasu!

[*Looking towards sky.*]

"*Ii otenki desu ne! Hai. Sore ja. Doomo.*"

[*To audience.*]

They called me "okusama," which means "wife." In the neighborhood we lived in, everybody knew the family, so I was accepted into their lives. When I went shopping for groceries, I would get special service for being "Udo's wife." When my brother-in-law got married, the bride's family came to me, and requested that I, being the senior wife, take good care of her. Protocol demanded that I comply.

[*Awkwardly but earnestly to imaginary family.*]

"Okay."

[*To audience.*]

Even though I often felt awkward at times like that. With my mother-in-law's help, I soon became quite accomplished in the "rituals" of married life.

[*The phone rings. She seems dismayed as she looks around to see if anyone else will answer it. She picks up the receiver. She speaks in textbook clear, very polite Japanese, smiling as she speaks.*]

"Moshi moshi. Ha. Sayoo de gozaimasu. Donatasama deshoo ka? Sho sho omachi kudasai."

[*To audience, her smile now vanished.*]

I hated talking on the phone. I would immediately anticipate ending the call. A very delicate maneuver.

[*She returns the receiver to her ear, smiles again and continues in Japanese.*]

"Doomo, omachidoosama deshita. Hai, wakarimashita. Otsutae shimasu. De wa, shitsurei itashimasu. Hai. Sore ja. Hai.

[*Bowing and fading her voice as she slowly pulls the receiver away from her ear and hangs up, relieved.*]

"Doomo. Doomo. Sayonara. Doomo. Doomo. Hai. Doomo."

[*To audience.*]

Growing up, it was just my mother, father, brother, sister and me. Being married meant being part of an extended family.

[*Struck by a thought.*]

A nation.

[*Climbing the geta.*]

As if, when Amaterasu climbed up into the heavens to create the Japanese race...I was there!

[*Recalling a warm memory, she sits back onto the geta.*]

One summer, "Amy's Japan" went to a tiny island called Yoron, located halfway between the Japanese island of Kyushu and Okinawa. It was very small and very untouched. You had to get there by dinghy. It was like one of those places you see in *National Geographic*, where the water is warm and clear and the sky is as blue as the starfish in the ocean and the beaches are covered with "star sand," shaped that way because it was formed from white coral.

I loved it, so I decided to stay behind for a few days to just relax. I loved telling people I was from Tokyo. I had married into a Japanese family and my Japanese was pretty good by then, too. And, I made friends with the guy who rented out the boats. He and I could talk about all kinds of stuff for hours. I admired how he'd left everything behind to just kind of live off the land, enjoy life, escape.

One night we were sitting on the beach, talking. I was filling him in on my background: being born in Deadwood, South Dakota, raised in Seattle. My dad's Finnish American. My mom's Japanese. He stopped me there. He wanted to know how my parents met.

[*She's stumped.*]

Well...I'm not too sure. I know that my mom had told me that while my dad was in Japan during the Occupation, he had pursued her very heartily and finally won her over, but I didn't know the details so I said, "I don't know."

[*She looks straight at him. He continues to question her in in voice over.*]

VOICE: Why don't you know?

AMY: Well, I just never asked. I had more important things to think about like...if I was ever gonna have a boyfriend.

VOICE: Was there something your mom wanted to hide?

[AMY *is still not quite comprehending the line of questioning.*]

AMY: Hide? That's one thing my mom never did. She was always totally honest and blunt and in your face! Sometimes I wished she'd disappear when my friends were around.

VOICE: Maybe she didn't tell you because she didn't want you to know...

[AMY *begins to understand.*]

AMY: What? I started to feel my heart race. He's saying my mother was...

[*Quietly defiant.*]

...what?

VOICE: Maybe she couldn't do any better because no Japanese man would have her. Maybe she sold herself to the first American who would take her. What'd he do? Offer her nylons and candy?

[*Hardly containing her rage.*]

AMY: I wanted to kill him. Just grab him and make him stop thinking what he was thinking.

[*Jumps up.*]

I flashed to my childhood.

[*Doing* "WHITEBREAD" LADY.]

"Your mother is so cute! Does she speak English? Can she eat American food?"

[*To audience.*]

She was a freak to me. My father told me once on this long ride back from the Washington Coast that even my own relatives didn't talk to her for six months after she arrived in Deadwood. We got hate letters and rocks in our mailbox in Seattle.
We, her own children would make fun of her accent.

[*As a* CHILD.]

"Mom, say 'Phyllis Diller', come on!"

[*As* MOTHER.]

"Firis Diris."

[*To audience.*]

Because she spoke English so poorly, we questioned her intelligence. I thought it was her fault that I didn't fit in.

[*Becoming another* KID, *taunting.*]

"What are you? Indian?"

[*To audience.*]

They called me "half" and asked me which half was which. I'd say ...

[*Indicating by tracing a line down her face.*]

"This half is Japanese. This half is American." Sometimes I'd switch.

My mother tried to deal with it once by showing me an article in Life magazine about "Ainoko" — "love children"...like me...living in Japan. It painted a pretty bleak picture. I guess she wanted me to feel lucky. But, I didn't.

Yet, here I was, years later, defending this woman — realizing how much I loved her and how much she had influenced me. She made a very difficult choice in life: turned her back on everything she knew, faced extreme racism, held a marriage together through sheer force of will and through it all, maintained her dignity.

[AMY *appears to pull a letter from her pocket and sits on the edge of the geta.*]

One day, I received a letter from my mother. For the first time, she had written to me in her own language.

[*Unfolding the letter, she reads.*]

"Watakushi no aisuru Amy"

[*Translating to audience.*]

"My beloved Amy"

[*She looks back at letter and thinks.*]

All during my childhood, she had never held me or kissed me. Not that I can recall. Yet, here she was professing her "love."

[*Again, reading in Japanese.*]

"Amy no akarusa ga mo arimasen no de, kono ie wa naka naka samishii desu ne. Hayaku, Amerika ni kaette hoshii desu."

[*Translating.*]

"Without your brightness, this house seems so empty. Hurry home."

[*Reading on, describing the contents.*]

She went on, in a very literary, poetic way to describe the weather, her thoughts on life...her loneliness in my absence.

[*She folds the letter and puts it away.*]

My mother was transformed — from this goofball, illiterate who could barely read or write English — to this formidable, intelligent woman. I think this was finally an opportunity for her, in her own language, to communicate to me like she was unable to with anyone else in her new life in America, particularly those closest to her — her own family. My mother had begun to perceive me as the one who is "Japanese" in the family, that I should understand. I did. And...I do.

[AMY *stands.*]

All these years, my mother held on fiercely to who she was, hoping that one day, her children would find their strength in the strength they had seen in her. She knew who she was and was proud of it. I always wanted to be someone else from somewhere else. I thought I needed to create an acceptable "Amy." Instead, I learned that I need to find and accept "Amy" just the way she is. I knew then that I could go home. And I'm glad I went to Tokyo.

[*Blackout. Slides and music.*]

EPILOGUE VOICE OVER: Udo and I moved to San Francisco together. Our marriage did not survive the journey. He is now living in Fremont, a suburb of San Francisco with his Japanese wife and child. Udo's mother and I have not had any contact for over six years. I miss her and wonder how she's doing... and wonder if she still thinks of me. My mother is a continuing source of revelation... and frustration. I wouldn't have it any other way.

Velina Hasu Houston

AS SOMETIMES IN A DEAD MAN'S FACE

As Sometimes in a Dead Man's Face by Velina Hasu Houston
© 1994 by Velina Avisa Hasu Houston

EDITOR'S NOTES

In a play called *Outlaws: A Place of Voices*, the characters of Pilipino writer Dom Magwili praise one of their fellow writers, a hapa writer whose work shows that "the half-breed way is a full and no-shame way." Every year more and more people check "Other" on employment applications; their diverse heritage cannot be summed up in a neat category, and so their stories are never included in employment statistics. But with Velina Hasu Houston to tell their stories, that situation may change.

Part Japanese, part African American, and part Native American, Houston is easily the most-produced Asian American woman playwright in the country. But it is interesting to note that her signature play, *TEA*, is more often produced at mainstream theatres than at theatres of color. Houston belongs to no single ethnic constituency, and perhaps that has been an obstacle to wider production of her work.

The hallmarks of Houston's work are a wry sense of humor, a commitment to feminism, and a love of language for language's sake (as in this play, more than one Houston character speaks of admiration for poet John Berryman). Many associate her work, though, with its exploration of the influence of Japanese heritage on either Japanese-Americans or Japanese immigrants to America. What some take as a romanticizing of Japan in Houston's work perhaps should be viewed instead as the influence of poetry in her work rather than a comment on Japan itself. For all the reverence Houston shows to Japanese tradition in some of her plays, there is an equal amount of clear-eyed criticism. *As Sometimes in a Dead Man's Face*, for instance, paints a less than flattering portrait of Japanese feelings about adoption, and about trusting anyone who is not Japanese.

Houston's work is also quite distinctive for its appreciation of sex in all its aspects, positive and negative. The semi-incestuous relationship between adopted siblings in this play may be disturbing, but it is also unrelentingly honest. And Houston is the only playwright I can imagine writing a successful children's theatre play about a young girl's coming-of-age that uses menstruation as its main plot point. ("I was aghast," said another woman playwright — with a smile — when *The Matsuyama Mirror* was workshopped at the Kennedy Center.)

Speaking of workshops, Houston developed this play in a staged reading at East West Players, but it has already begun to evolve since then, and may be revised further before (or even after) it receives a professional premiere. One of the most diligent and prolific rewriters I have ever seen, Houston frequently revisits and revises her work. Particularly striking in this newest draft is the dream sequence in which Samantha recovers part of her body (talk about reinventing yourself!).

Houston may examine the conflicts of a Japanese woman who attempts ritual suicide in California (*Kokoro*). She may dramatize a romance between an African American man and an Asian woman as they attend protests against hate crimes (*Tokyo Valentine*). Or, in the present play, she may depict the struggle of two mixed-race children in a world that reduces everything to black and white. Regardless of the arena, Houston is dedicated to exploring a multiethnic landscape in her work — it is the same landscape in which she lives her life.

As Sometimes in a Dead Man's Face was presented as a staged reading in The Writers Gallery at East West Players (Tim Dang, Artistic Director), on November 9, 1994, with the following cast:

SAMANTHA	Tamlyn Tomita
MAN/DANIEL	Carlos Carrasco
EMIKO	Susan Haruye Ioka

Directed by Jan Lewis. Writers Gallery curator, Brian Nelson. Stage Manager, Lily Wong.

As sometimes in a dead man's face.
To those that watch it more and more,
A likeness, hardly seen before,
Comes out — to someone of his race...

— Alfred, Lord Tennyson
In Memoriam, stanza 74

CHARACTERS

SAMANTHA	early 30s
MAN/DANIEL	early 40s
EMIKO	Samantha's mother, 55

TIME AND PLACE: *1964-1994. Kansas and California.*
SETTING: *Samantha's home.*

ACT I

SCENE 1

Two tea candles shine from one side of the stage. A heartbeat thumps. A pin of light illuminates the face of SAMANTHA *standing in front of a panel of white cloth. She wears a hospital gown. She twists and turns in her sleep, as if in pain. Light widens to low intensity as she struggles to free herself. She pulls away, moving forward from the panel. Her hand reaches to her heart and the heartbeat stops. She opens her eyes, filled with a sense of sudden urgency.*

SAMANTHA: [*Rapid, intense.*] I'm baking cookies, see. Rolled cookies cut out like Santas. And snowmen. And shaped cookies. Like wreaths and candy canes. And pressed cookies like stars. And petit fours. Love petit fours. And it's like a fire alarm. One-two: knife in the side. Three-four: double-over, somersault. Five-six: "Hi. This is Samantha. Can you drive me to the hospital? I have this pain and — . Oh, yeah. Office party. Eggnog. New date. Busy, busy, busy. Life goes on. Merry Christmas." [*Dry heave.*] Seven-eight-nine-ten: BAM. Fire alarm. I deck the halls. With me. And the world goes dark. And cookies burn. Dreams scorch. " Hello? Mom? Don't panic, but. I said don't panic. Mom...? I'm on fire." Nine. One. One.
[*A red siren light flashes and* SAMANTHA *spins around in it, ending up in a blue spotlight that fades up downstage.*]

Are you okay, do you know what day it is, how do you feel, are you still real, will you make it, can you take it. And I'm going, floating fast, narcotic never-land: a shot to turn away from blindness, a piercing of the right hip then the left. Hopeless thinkers scratch their heads by my bed, but I see nothing except a tunnel with names carved on the inside. Yours is there next to mine in several equations. They don't make sense. Didn't you go before me? Is it your hand fixing the stray hair, stroking the gray cheek, adjusting the hospital gown so my bottom won't show as they bring Demerol, morphine, embarrassment, pain? It's okay, really. I've been on that fast ride at the amusement park.

I'm ready. They can have me, all my books, my computer, my education, my house; they can have it all. I'm letting go of everything, including you. It's only memory, isn't it? A bunch of junk below heaven breathing, giving shape to this tenuous thing called a life. I'm bored of sin. A broken doll, my seamstress stands perplexed. Are you on the other side, Daniel, or is it me?

[*In voiceover,* A MAN *and* A WOMAN (MAN *and* EMIKO) *chant in whispered rhythm.*]

MAN/WOMAN: . . . appendicitis/gallstones/kidney stones/bowels . . .

[*The voiceover repeats several times. It makes* SAMANTHA *nervous.*]

SAMANTHA: The tube. The tube goes in your nose. It's about the size of a number-two lead pencil. It goes in and they say swallow hard and it shoves its way down your throat, scraping, gagging — and they say don't gag, don't cough — and it pokes into your stomach and they say good girl, Samantha, good girl. And they say appendicitis, gallstones, kidney stones, bowel obstruction, fucked-up life and they take out the knives, take out the knives, and I —

[SAMANTHA *collapses and the voiceover ceases abruptly. A silhouetted figure of a* MAN *dressed in white enters and stands with his back to* SAMANTHA's *pool of light. The sound of a man's weeping is heard, blending into the sound of a male child crying. Spotlight up on* EMIKO *as crying sounds grow muted. She wears a mask of a sad-faced Japanese woman.*]

EMIKO: [*Upset, frightened, toward audience; with Japanese accent.*] Didn't you see? She had a tattoo on her arm. A streetwalker with a tattoo. We don't know what kind of diseases he has. We don't know if he'll steal from us, beat up Sammy, kill us. He's already nine; what can we give him? Papa, listen to me. It doesn't matter if he grows up in Japan or America. Bad blood means bad life wherever you go. Japanese don't want bad blood. It doesn't wash out. It won't wash out.

[*The crying ceases and the* MAN *turns to face downstage. He wears a mask of iridescent tattoos. On his chest is the tattoo of a heart with ribbons and the word "Mom" in the middle of the heart.* SAMANTHA *suddenly stands and faces downstage. She wears the mask of a little girl. The face is violet.* EMIKO *steps downstage, in the middle of the other two.*]

Daniel, I know you resent being brought here to live in America. But you're not Chicano and you're not black and you're not white, okay? Whether you like it or not, your mother was Japanese and your father was Mexican or maybe African American; I don't know. But don't take it out on us. We're just trying to be nice to you. You're mixed, just like Samantha. Is that so bad?

[*Pause.*]

Daniel, did you steal my credit card? Someone bought girls' nightgowns and French perfume on my credit card and I can't find it. Did you steal, Daniel?

[*Pause.*]

You want to find your real mother and kill her, go ahead. You keep making trouble like this and you're going to end up dead, too.

[*The* MAN *eats with his palm as his bowl, and his fingers as utensils.*]

Do you have to eat so much, Daniel? Don't eat the narazuke! Too expensive! Not for kids!

DANIEL: I'm hungry, Mom.

SAMANTHA: Danny, I'll tell her I'm hungry and then I'll give it to —

EMIKO: Sammy? You want some narazuke with rice?

SAMANTHA: Thanks, Mom. Yes. Here, Danny.

MAN: Get some more.

SAMANTHA: Okay.

EMIKO: Sammy, Danny, your report cards came today.

MAN: Congratulations, Mom.

EMIKO: Sammy, you got As in almost every subject, but you got an A- in science class. Don't you like science?

SAMANTHA: But in class, they kill mice, Mom. They kill them.

EMIKO: So what? Look in the kitchen cabinet. I kill mice, too. With hunks of big cheese; they like that.

SAMANTHA: You give them what they like and then lead them to slaughter?

EMIKO: Danny, you got mostly Cs.

MAN: So I'm average. What's so bad about being average?

EMIKO: You can't be Japanese and Black in America and just be average.

MAN: I'm not a Jap. I'm Chicano. Comprende, Comanchera?

SAMANTHA: He has a hard time concentrating in school, Mother.

EMIKO: In school? He can hardly concentrate in life. He didn't fix his bed again today — and don't you dare fix it for him, Sammy! You can't follow him around his whole life long and fix the things that he can't or won't fix.

SAMANTHA: Sometimes I have a hard time too, Mother.

EMIKO: I had B-29 bombs falling around my head from the time I was fourteen, so don't tell me about hard times when you live in a nice, quiet community and go to school a block away. They saw us. They did. They knew we were kids, but they shot at us anyway.

MAN: I've had bombs falling around my head since I was born, Comanchera.

EMIKO: What does that mean, "comanchera?"

SAMANTHA: You see, Mother. We're different. When you mix red and blue, you get violet. It's easy when you're painting on paper, but not so easy when you're painting pigment.

EMIKO: What are you talking about?

MAN: I'm violet.

SAMANTHA: Violet.

MAN: It means I get to choose what I want to be because I don't fit into what's already there.

SAMANTHA: No, it means being real, being special.

MAN: It means camouflage. It means life is make-believe.

EMIKO: Is that what your mothers at the orphanage taught you?

MAN: They are not my mothers. [Pause.] You are not my mother. Samantha's my mother.

SAMANTHA: What? What did he say?

MAN: I said you, Samantha, are my mother.

EMIKO: Samantha, come to Mommy. Let's go out for ice cream.

[Urgent.] Let's go now.

SAMANTHA: Mom, be quiet, please. I can't hear what Daniel's saying.

EMIKO: Samantha, go to your room.

SAMANTHA: Daniel, say it again.

EMIKO: Daniel, go to your room.

[*Blackout on* EMIKO; *she exits.* SAMANTHA *and* MAN *sit back to back, leaning into each other.*]

MAN: Sam? Are you awake? I can't sleep.

SAMANTHA: What's wrong?

[*They look at each other.*]

MAN: Sam, I think she's going to try to kill me.

SAMANTHA: Who?

MAN: Mom.

SAMANTHA: She couldn't kill anybody.

MAN: Did you check the kitchen cabinet? I saw him. His head under a steel bar, cheese still in his mouth.

SAMANTHA: . . . yes . . . I saw him.

[*Blackout on* MAN *and* SAMANTHA's *spotlight.* EMIKO *enters and covers her ears. Then a loud, piercing scream is heard along with the sounds of crackling fire as* EMIKO's *mouth silently shadows the scream. As the scream fades away,* EMIKO *slowly lowers her head to stare at the audience. She fights for composure.*]

EMIKO: Don't tell anyone about what happened, you hear me? I think it was just a dream you had, Sammy. Just a dream. That smell? Why, that's just Papa's cigar. Good night. [*Pause.*] Okay, Danny, everything packed? Good. I bought you nice new clothes and tennis shoes for your little vacation. You will learn a lot, make new friends. Papa can't come to say goodbye because he's in the hospital. Asthma. From stress.

[*Meaning exactly the opposite.*]

It's . . . not your fault.

[*Pause.*]

You listen to everything the counselors tell you, okay? You can't help the way you are. You were born of war and the war's still beating on you, I guess. That's what Sammy says anyway. Now don't cry. This isn't jail. It's just reform school. Reform. Papa says that means to change, to make you better. Maybe you're okay deep down inside, but, on the outside, you are war and the war has to stop, Danny.

[*Pause.*]

Sammy's at school. She didn't want to come home to say goodbye. You've been too hard on her.

[*Pause.*]

You have. Don't lie. You almost killed her when you pushed her down the hill in her baby carriage. And then ... this. This is too much. It's not my fault your mother left you. I didn't leave you. I'm not leaving you now either. I'm not the zoo, okay? I don't know how to take care of a wild animal. I didn't have anything to do with making you wild. You came that way and I tried to tame you. It's not jail. It's a reform school.

[*Pause.*]

No, Sammy. You can't come home to say goodbye to him. Why do you want to say goodbye to someone who treats you like he did? He's not really your brother. You may never see him again and you'd be lucky if that happened. Now go to school. Forget. Let go. It's not a jail.

[SAMANTHA *and* MAN, *still in masks, enter and sit downstage of* EMIKO, *one on either side of her, as she mimes cleaning the stage area around them using her hands or perhaps a handkerchief. A straitjacket falls from the sky and the* MAN *puts it on. He and* SAMANTHA *switch places continually, moving in slow, almost surreal cadence.*]

SAMANTHA: Dear Daniel. Don't call it jail. Mom says it's a school, reform school. We're going to come visit you on Memorial Day.

MAN: Dear Sam. Don't come visit me. The guys'll give me an even harder time. They fuck me; I mean, they fuck with me. I told Mom I'm scared here, but she says it's where bad boys gotta go. It's only been six months. Feels like a year.

SAMANTHA: Dear Daniel. I turned thirteen today. Now I'm a real teenager and Mom tried to talk to me about birth control pills. It was a riot: "Sammy, I need to talk to you about the egg and the sperm, how they have a meeting."

MAN: Dear Sam. It's like jail around here, but I'm learning how to fix cars and I read a lot. The library's kind of limited, but there's a lot of poetry. You taught me how to love poetry. Thank you.

[*Pause.*]

You shouldn't be having sex. You're too young.

[*Pause.*]

Are you having sex?

SAMANTHA: Dear Daniel. I fed the birth control pills to my asparagus fern and she's growing wild, breaking out of her pot. Maybe I should have taken them.

MAN: Dear Sam. Have you figured out why Papa never stopped me? Didn't he know that whipping and words were not love?

[*Pause.*]

Why didn't he ever whip you?

SAMANTHA: Dear Daniel. Papa died. They said it was heart failure, but it was worse. Much worse. Mom says we can't talk about it. Scars from his youth.

[*Pause.*]

So much we can't talk about.

MAN: Dear Sam. Do you remember when you were little and I made you sit in front of me while I was watching TV and I used your shoulders as a foot rest? Did I do that?

SAMANTHA: Daniel, you did a lot of peculiar things that I don't understand. Did you break my arm or did I accidentally fall into that hole at the park? Did you make me fix your bed or did I just do it because I wanted to?

MAN: Get the hell over here, Sam.

SAMANTHA: Danny, ever since you came back from reform school, you're meaner.

MAN: Papa was my only real parent, okay? And he fuckin' died and fuckin' Madame Butterfly didn't even spring me so I could go to the fuckin' funeral.

SAMANTHA: Stop saying the "f" word.

MAN: You'll learn to say it, too. The world'll suck out your heart and you'll be sayin' it, too; screamin' it at the top of your lungs.

SAMANTHA: You better cool it or Mom's going to send you away again.

MAN: Fuck her. I'm twenty-one. I'm a man. She can't send me away anymore. Get over here, Sam. Pop this pimple for me.

SAMANTHA: Mom says that causes brain cancer.

MAN: Give me your allowance, Sam.

SAMANTHA: But I'm saving up for a new book. Ow! What did you slap me for? It's just chewing gum!

MAN: You want guys to look at you like you're cheap or something? Don't ever let me catch you chewing that shit again. Now get some food together, lots of it, and some blankets. Pack it all up in one of Pop's duffel bags. I'm shakin' this shithole.

SAMANTHA: You mean you're leaving us? For good? But what'll I say if Mom asks me where you've gone?

MAN: Tell her I've returned to the wild, princess. She'll applaud, with that kind of half-smile Japanese always got on their lips.

SAMANTHA: It's your real mother you should hate.

MAN: Get the hell outta here, princess. Don't come back. If you do, I swear I'll run so far and fast you'll never find me.

SAMANTHA: Mom, Daniel ran away. He's sleeping in the ravine.

MAN: You had to tell. You're gonna get it now, Sam.

SAMANTHA: Daniel.

MAN: What do you want?

SAMANTHA: I know why Mom sent you away.

MAN: [*With sarcasm.*] Because she loves me.

SAMANTHA: You can't help being the way you are. You were born of war and the war's still beating on you.

MAN: Oh, go get another A+, Sam, and leave me the hell alone.

SAMANTHA: Something happened, Daniel. Mom says something happened.

MAN: How is the weather, Samantha? How is school? How are you? I'm fine, thank you.

SAMANTHA: Daniel, do you hear me?

MAN: How is the weather, Samantha? How is school? How are you? I'm fine, thank you.

SAMANTHA: Talk to me, Daniel. She said not to trust you.

MAN: Goin' on the road now, Sam. Yours truly. Daniel.

SAMANTHA: Daniel, where are you? You have to call me again because . . . Daniel, Daniel, I've . . . fallen in love . . .

[DANIEL *is taken aback by this information; it stops him cold. They finally really look at each other.*]

MAN: What?

SAMANTHA: Love.

MAN: But.

SAMANTHA: And I'm moving to Los Angeles.

MAN: New York then. Yeah, New York. Far away.

SAMANTHA: Okay. If you have to.

MAN: Sammy?

SAMANTHA: Yes?

MAN: This guy. This love.

SAMANTHA: Yes?

MAN: Sex?

SAMANTHA: Yes.

MAN: I see. Wow.

SAMANTHA: Will you write me?

MAN: About what happened, Sammy.

SAMANTHA: What are you talking about?

MAN: You know. Why Mom sent me away. Listen, Sam.

SAMANTHA: Please call me Samantha.

MAN: Oh, Sammy . . . you've changed.

SAMANTHA: Papa's dead. Mom's older and quieter. And we're grown-up, somehow. And, Daniel, don't chew gum. Nobody looks good chewing gum or smoking cigarettes, okay?

MAN: You're not my mother.

SAMANTHA: But Daniel, you're 30 years old. You can't keep wandering the country like a vagabond. Go to school, get a real job.

MAN: Camouflage.

SAMANTHA: Maybe you can come down for Christmas.

MAN: Really?

SAMANTHA: Yeah. I guess so. Christmas is for family. Mom's remarried now. She'll spend Christmas with him.

MAN: But I met this woman.

SAMANTHA: Oh.

[*Pause.*]

Love?

MAN: Maybe.

SAMANTHA: Gee. Commitment?

MAN: Sammy? You tied to this guy? I don't want you to get messed up with some pit bull.

SAMANTHA: Oh, Daniel. You'll never change.

MAN: But you will. You will if you fuck around with the wrong guy. If somebody messes over you, I'll kill him. Goddamn it, I'll kill him. What's the name of this guy you're hangin' with? Where's he live?

SAMANTHA: Never mind, Daniel. See you on Christmas Eve.

MAN: Fuck you.

[*Blackout. Immediate blue spotlight in which* SAMANTHA *lies in her earlier collapsed position, without mask. Slowly, she rises and looks around.*]

SAMANTHA: Hey, I made it. Incision from here to Venezuela, but who cares, I was never interested in bikini contests anyway. I made it.
[*The* MAN *in silhouette, masked and in straitjacket, walks across the stage, far upstage, and exits. She is very aware of him, but doesn't look.*]

I dreamed about Daniel. And, well, it's time. I guess it's time. He disappeared ten years ago Christmas and it's almost Christmas again.

[*Loud door knocks. Enter* EMIKO *dressed in black. She hovers over* SAMANTHA, *but stares out at the audience.*]

EMIKO: Tomorrow I'll come and paint your nails.

SAMANTHA: Look, Mom. I.V.

EMIKO: And make you wakame udon. Can you eat yet? Of course. You need to eat.

SAMANTHA: I.V., Mom. I.V.

EMIKO: Yes, udon. Because it's New Year's Eve and, if you don't eat long noodles on New Year's Eve, no long life.

SAMANTHA: She mashes the udon into a pulp and presses it into my mouth when the nurse isn't looking.

EMIKO: Long life.

SAMANTHA: "Walk," the nurse says. "Bitch," I whisper under my breath.

EMIKO: Why can't she walk right?

SAMANTHA: "I'll race you down the hall," the nurse says.

EMIKO: Why is she shaking?

SAMANTHA: Shaking, I get up from the starting block. Calling her bluff. Nurse shocked. Post-operative humor. That night, she brushes my teeth. Have you been eating, nurse asks. Ask my mother.

EMIKO: I don't know what that pulp is in her mouth, Nurse. Maybe it came out of the tube.

SAMANTHA: Next morning, doctor says, this is chronic, live simply, eat simply, sleep, sleep, sleep . . .

EMIKO: Maybe he's dead, Sammy, but you're alive. Act like it.

[EMIKO *disappears.* SAMANTHA *immediately leaps from her "bed" and dances, faux-Isadora-Duncan. The* MAN *appears in the darkness, remaining an unidentifiable silhouette and mask.*]

MAN: [*Reverberating voice.*] Get back in bed, Samantha.

SAMANTHA: [*Startled and then pleased.*] Are you going to leave me a number this time?

MAN: Somebody's gonna see you, squelch you, put you out.

SAMANTHA: Here. Write it down here. Area code first.

MAN: Get back in your body, Samantha. Hurry before the nurse comes.

SAMANTHA: What about an address? Do you? Have one? You're always changing addresses.

MAN: It's gonna leave you, Sam. That body's gonna float out that door and —

SAMANTHA: Just give me the math. The numbers. Numbers.

MAN: Nurse! Nurse! There's a problem with Miss Sedgwick!

[SAMANTHA *is pulled back to the "bed," in front of the panel. She struggles and stands in front of the panel.*]

SAMANTHA: One-two. Just give me the fucking Demerol. Three-four:

[*Her eyes start to close; she fights it.*]

Three-four. Give me the math. Somebody give me the math.

[*Drops to all fours, crawls toward downstage center.*]

Five-six. Think I can't see? No evil. Think I can't hear? Seven-eight. First, I find your eyes.

SAMANTHA/MAN: "Pick them up, Sammy, baby. Pick them up."

SAMANTHA: You say. And I do. Soft. Like raw sweetbreads. Like warm rubber. Blind. Okay, okay. Got the eyes.

SAMANTHA/MAN: Can you see me?

SAMANTHA: Brain. There it is. Pieces of winter. Okay. Your hands.

SAMANTHA/MAN: Yes.

SAMANTHA: The right finger. Top half.

SAMANTHA/MAN: Okay.

SAMANTHA: Is this your leg? Is this your arm?

SAMANTHA/MAN: Where's your lips?

EMIKO: [Offstage, panic/warning.] Sammy!

SAMANTHA: Damn it, I can't find you. I can't find you. Why'd they have to do this to you? Who do they think they are?

[SAMANTHA's head jerks in the direction of the voice as the MAN looks toward the audience and runs offstage quickly. EMIKO enters with two boxes and stares reprimandingly at SAMANTHA.]

EMIKO: Here. Are these the boxes you want? Look at you: home one day from the hospital and up all night like some kind of witch or something. The doctor didn't say to sing rock-and-roll songs on your porch until midnight and stare at the moon. She said to rest. You don't have the energy you used to have, Sammy. And you will never get it back if you sit out on the porch in the cold. Stay inside.

[SAMANTHA digs through clothing and things in the box.]

SAMANTHA: I never wear this anymore and this or this or this. I don't want these books either. Do you need a toaster? I have two.

EMIKO: You can't throw away this nice sweater. I'll take it. Of course you need two toasters. What if one breaks? And look at this book! You paid thirty-five dollars for it. Why must you come home from the hospital and clean your house like your life depended on it?

SAMANTHA: [To audience.] I didn't just come back from the hospital; I came back from the dead.

[To EMIKO.]

Thanks for bringing me home, Mom. Thanks for making me okayu.

[Aside to audience, dark humor.]

I eat okayu everyday. Overcooked mashed rice sludge. It's the only thing I can keep down because, well, I just don't have the guts anymore.

EMIKO: Don't make jokes about your health.

SAMANTHA: [*To audience, laughs.*] They took my guts and I just don't have the guts anymore.

EMIKO: [*Sternly.*] It's not funny.

SAMANTHA: Next time they'll trim a little more and I'll say, "Gee, I can't stomach that."
[*Pause.*]

Here, Mom, you want this scarf?

EMIKO: But you like this scarf.

SAMANTHA: Used to. Used to.

EMIKO: Wear it or save to give to someone for Christmas.

SAMANTHA: It's silk, Mother.

EMIKO: What? You can't give away silk.

SAMANTHA: You know how good it feels to give away silk, to give away something you thought you needed but you don't? It feels real good, damn good.

EMIKO: Okay. I'll take it. [*Pause; shakes her head.*] Sammy, it's like you're trying to throw your whole life away! Go through your things when you feel —

SAMANTHA: [*Toward audience.*] Scalpel on the tray. That's for you, Samantha. Just for you. Boy scout knife to slice, sever, slash. Oh goody.

EMIKO: Forget about the cutting. Forget about what you can't get back.

SAMANTHA: Cutting away things that don't work, things I don't need, things that get in the way. All this clutter. My, oh, my. Can we give it to the thrift shop?
[*To another persona.*]

Hello, I'm Samantha. I'd like to donate a battered intestine, an ovary, an appendix, and a couple of tumors. They're perfectly good tumors! They're benign!
[*A smile.*]

I'm malignant.

[*Pause.*]

May I have a receipt please?

EMIKO: The doctor says in eight weeks you'll be like a normal person, but it'll take you at least four to six months to be your irregular busy self. Do you hear me, Sammy? Six months.

SAMANTHA: Pump that stomach! Twist that colon! Urine bag! I.V.! Teeth unbrushed! Hair uncombed! I'm ready for my close-up, Mr. De Mille.

EMIKO: Sleep. That's what you have to do. You are home now and you can thank your lucky stars that you are.

SAMANTHA: But Mom. It's almost Christmas again.

EMIKO: I'm going now. I have to feed my cat.

SAMANTHA: But Christmas, Mom, Christmas.

EMIKO: You know he cannot smell. Feline leukemia.

SAMANTHA: You have to stop taking in strays, Mom.

EMIKO: Sometimes you don't have a choice. Sometimes somebody says "this is yours" and you take it and —

SAMANTHA: Don't talk about him like that.

EMIKO: And you take it and keep it warm and it goes through your cabinets and your wallet — and you — consuming everything in sight.

[Pause.]

You want to give something away? Give him away, cut that away.

SAMANTHA: I said only the things I don't really need. And anyway, this isn't about him. It's not his fault I got sick.

EMIKO: [Angry about this.] He just feels important because you wanted to save him. Me, too. And I ended up the feast. You, too.

SAMANTHA: Good night, Mother.

EMIKO: You almost died. Now let him die.

SAMANTHA: But he isn't dead.

EMIKO: I'm dead and I have seen him on the other side. This is your chance to start all over again, Samantha. To start with an empty house, nothing, no one in it but you. His kind die hard. Probably got shot by somebody he made angry. He could do that to people, you know. Call them names, be stuck up, and — boom — next thing you know, someone's put a hole in his head.

SAMANTHA: Mother!

EMIKO: Just like yakuza in Japan. Lead a life in the streets and streets choke you, just like that.

[*Pause.*]

He's dead, Samantha.

SAMANTHA: No.

EMIKO: Just say it. This is wasting too much of your life.

SAMANTHA: Don't you ever miss him or feel sorry for him?

EMIKO: Yes, but he was never nice to me. He stole meat from my freezer to give to the black kids so they'd accept him and then they just turn around and call him chink-face, then he stole television sets to give to the Mexican kids so they'd accept him and they just turn around and call him nigger, so then he stole credit cards and money to give to all the white girls and then it's just one girl after another, one child after another and Daniel still looking for mama. [*Pause.*] I am sorry, Sammy. Whatever he was, whatever he is, he's dead. Even if he's alive, he's dead.

SAMANTHA: When your brother dies, you get to know. You get to go to church and cry. And, after a while, don't you get to stop feeling so godawful about it so that you can go on with your own restless life? Don't you?

EMIKO: Straighten your spine, Samantha. Lie in bed straight or you'll never walk right again. I'll bring you groceries tomorrow.

[EMIKO *exits.*]

SAMANTHA: Thanks, Mom.

[SAMANTHA *sleeps downstage. The* MAN *enters again with a birthday cake on a stool. The cake is beautifully, ornately floral, single candle at its center. He places it downstage center and exits.* SAMANTHA *takes no notice of him. She awakens and admires the cake.*]

SAMANTHA: [*To audience, reciting.*] Red roses you gave me. The roses are red. I paint, I paint them on this cake and pray you are not dead. Roses red like blood, like wine. There's no time left, is there? No time. For roses. Red. What shall I love instead?

[*She blows out the candle. Immediately, lights up to reveal her home: representations of a porch with old-fashioned swing, a living room/dining room, a kitchen; comfortable, tasteful atmosphere. There is antique furniture.* EMIKO *has turned on the light. She holds a grocery bag. She stands on the front threshold looking across the porch at* SAMANTHA.]

EMIKO: I'm just here to check on you.

SAMANTHA: I'm the same as I was yesterday, Mom.

EMIKO: It's his birthday again, isn't it?

SAMANTHA: You oughta know.

[EMIKO *nods, puts down the bag, approaches cake and tastes frosting.*]

EMIKO: You are such a good baker. Is he 46 today?

[SAMANTHA *takes a chunk of cake in her fingers and eats it, much to* EMIKO*'s disapproval.*]

SAMANTHA: What if he isn't?

EMIKO: Why do you make such a pretty cake only to eat it with your fingers?

SAMANTHA: I mean, what if Daniel stopped being 36 or 40 or 46?

[EMIKO *picks up the cake and stool, and heads toward porch.*]

EMIKO: Come inside. The beach wind is too cold.

SAMANTHA: Daniel likes the beach.

EMIKO: And only one candle. Looks silly.

SAMANTHA: You know I don't like fire.

[EMIKO *leaves the stool on the porch and heads inside, taking off her shoes.* SAMANTHA *follows suit.* EMIKO *places cake on table and eats a chunk with her fingers.*]

EMIKO: Did you go to the doctor today? What did he say?

SAMANTHA: She. She says I'm okay. Okay?

EMIKO: I brought you calcium.

[EMIKO *starts taking bottle after bottle of calcium out of the grocery bag and lining them up on the table.*]

On sale, so I bought many.

SAMANTHA: Gee, Mom, why didn't you just bring me a dinosaur bone to gnaw on or something.

EMIKO: Are they expensive?

SAMANTHA: That's not the point, is it?

EMIKO: You need lots of calcium, but if it's on sale, good.

SAMANTHA: Thanks, Mom.

[SAMANTHA *sweeps up as many bottles as possible and puts them in a kitchen cabinet, which is full of identical bottles. As* EMIKO *enters kitchen,*

SAMANTHA *quickly closes the cabinet. Petit fours and cookies waiting to be frosted sit on the counter on racks with bowls of icing beside them.*]

EMIKO: What are you baking?

SAMANTHA: Cookies, petit fours. Before my students leave for break, I want to give them Christmas goodies.

[*The phone rings.*]

Hello? This is she. I know the adoption papers say Masao Kawada, but Daniel Sedgwick and Masao Kawada are the same people. Can't you make an exception this once? He's been missing for ten years. Emiko Sedgwick is his mother. He just never formally changed his Japanese name. Please. Okay. All right. Thanks.

[*Hangs up the phone.*]

Social Security. They won't give out his number unless we can prove you're his legal parent, but there's nothing to connect your name with the name of Daniel, only with his Japanese name.

EMIKO: I wish I could be more help to you, but you know my cat is so old now. He needs a lot of care. He is probably wondering where I am right now. This time of year is hard for my garden, too.

SAMANTHA: For years I didn't worry about him because he's such a wanderer. I was sure I'd get the Social Security number and find him by Christmas, but here it is nearly Christmas again.

EMIKO: Only reason you put so much time into this is because you put no time into getting married and having children.

SAMANTHA: I thought you didn't want grandchildren.

EMIKO: Keiko-san knows a nice Japanese American boy, an accountant. He wants to settle down.

SAMANTHA: Nice Japanese American boys like white girls.

EMIKO: Okay, then find a nice boy who likes Amerasians.

SAMANTHA: Afro Asians.

EMIKO: And have children before it is too late.

SAMANTHA: Mom? Today, the doctor? The doctor said. She said that I can't have children. Well, not that I can't, but that I shouldn't.

[EMIKO *looks at her like she's defective. The look passes.*]

EMIKO: Well, I need to go feed my cat. I will see you later.

SAMANTHA: Okay, mom.

EMIKO: He is mad at me. Last night, I did not have my glasses on to feed him and I gave him snail pellets by mistake.

SAMANTHA: Scratch behind his ears for me.

[EMIKO *nods and exits.*]

Okay. It's time.

[*Blackout crossfading to spotlight.* SAMANTHA *walks into it with resolve. She stands as if holding a collection of things in her arms. She goes to the candles and offers the collection like she's before an altar.*]

Okay, God or Goddess or whoever's up there. Listen up. Are you listening?

[*Determined.*]

Hello? Father Malcolm? This is Samantha. I'm fine. Losing my guts has given me the guts to do this, so listen because I have to do this now. To save my life. I need to bury someone. No. I haven't killed anybody and I'm not going to kill anybody, at least not like what you mean. I just need to bury someone. I need your prayers. Flight, Father Malcolm. It's all about flight. If I can do this, one day I'll be able to race you down the hall. Any hall. Do you understand?

[*Lights crossfade and* SAMANTHA *follows the light.* EMIKO *enters and places a black chiffon veil over* SAMANTHA; *it is long enough to brush against her shins.* EMIKO *exits.* SAMANTHA *kneels downstage, fidgeting with the veil.*]

Accept my prayer on behalf of Daniel and let him into whatever kind of club you have up there. No one took him into their arms and blessed him when he was a child, so could you do that for him now? Nothing formal like you see in all that portraiture when they paint you pink and make your hair blond; something from the gut, please. You took some of mine, so give it to Daniel.

[*Pause.*]

Now listen, I want you to care for him and love him, or at least teach him what those things really are because I never could get close enough to do it and if I couldn't, nobody could. Give him green pastures and restore his soul and all that stuff, but give him nice pictures to look at and good poetry. Yeats, Tennyson, Berryman, Schwartz.

[*Pause.*]

There's a question in the forty-second psalm and I hope it isn't rhetorical, because it sure seems real to me: "Why art thou so full of heaviness, O my soul? and why art thou so disquieted within me?"

[*She removes the veil and crumples it in anger. Blackout.*]

SCENE 2

[SAMANTHA, *sans mask, hums "Deck the Halls" to herself in a folk-rock fashion, slow cadence as she moves to the porch swing and sits. She swings; the swing occasionally creaks.*]

SAMANTHA: "Deck the hall with boughs of holly,
"Fa-la-la-la-la-la-la-la-la.
"'Tis the season to be jolly,
"Fa-la-la-la-la-la-la-la-la.
"Don we now our gay apparel,
"Fa-la-la-la-la-la-la-la-la … "

[*Falters, unable to remember the last line.*]

Behold the ancient Yuletide carol? Toll the ancient Yuletide carol?

[*Pause.*]

For whom the bell tolls.

[*Pause; sings the last line.*]

"Fa-la-la-la-la-la-la-la-la."

[*The song has made her unhappy. She gets up. It is a struggle. Her look of strength gives way to labored walking, as if the lower torso has no power. She stumbles. Commenting on the stumble:*]

Curses.

[*She enters the house, crossing to kitchen. There is an ikebana arrangement in the making on the table with a big watering can next to it. There is a glass of water by the faucet. She drinks it. She hears the porch swing creak and looks in that direction, but dismisses it. Again, the creak. Another look. Couldn't be anything. She finishes her water. She tears a leaf off an aloe plant, sits, lifts her dress, and massages the meat of the aloe on a long, neatly straight vertical scar that marks her from navel southward. A knock at the door. She's startled. She drops her dress and stands. The porch swing creaks. The* MAN *appears by the swing. He is well-dressed; he wears a plain mask that conceals his entire face. Everything about him seems ordinary except for his mask.*]

SAMANTHA: Who is it?

MAN: It's uh, uh . . . I'm with Citizens for a Better Environment.

SAMANTHA: I'm sorry. I'm preparing dinner for my family . . . of ten. Could you just leave some literature for me and I'll read it later?

MAN: I promise it'll only take five minutes.

SAMANTHA: I just came back from a funeral, okay? A funeral.

MAN: It wasn't your mother or anything, was it?

SAMANTHA: Just leave the literature.

MAN: You aren't interested.

SAMANTHA: I'm interested in the environment, but nobody will be around to have to worry about it anymore if we annoy each other to death first. What does it matter if my nose is breathing when my head has been cut off? Don't leave the literature.

MAN: I don't smell dinner.

SAMANTHA: You guys come at dinnertime on purpose, don't you. You know I'll be home so you come with your questionnaires, surveys, number two lead pencils, and knuckle wraps.

[*She draws close to the imaginary door. She can't see a thing. Frustrated, she opens the door. He backs away as she gasps.*]

MAN: Remember me?

SAMANTHA: What's with the mask?

MAN: A substitute for the real thing.

[*Her hand automatically goes to her abdomen. He observes this. She quickly pulls it away, but doesn't know what to do with her hands.*]

MAN: I think you remember me.

SAMANTHA: Did I give you a donation before?

MAN: Yes.

SAMANTHA: I used to do that. Buy everyone's candy or peanuts — I'm allergic to peanuts — or donate at least fifty dollars. But not anymore.

MAN: Because you're dealing with the real thing now.

SAMANTHA: What? Whatever. I can't help you. Sorry. I've given everything away.

MAN: Except your . . . ten children.

SAMANTHA: Okay, okay, no children. The doctors took the tools away. I said all right, gave them the tools. It's a family of one.

MAN: No one's at the table, huh?

SAMANTHA: I am. That's one.

[*Pause.*]

What's your name?

MAN: Daniel.

SAMANTHA: [*Disturbed.*] Daniel.

MAN: Yes.

SAMANTHA: I know — I mean, I knew — someone named Daniel before. He's dead.

MAN: Dead?

SAMANTHA: Yes. I buried him.

MAN: I'm sorry.

SAMANTHA: It was just about an hour ago.

MAN: [*Surprised.*] An hour ago? Why today?

SAMANTHA: Because he's dead.

MAN: . . . like you almost were.

SAMANTHA: What? Me? No, not me. I'm a very healthy person. Aerobics, yoga, health food.

MAN: Your neighbor told me.

SAMANTHA: My neighbor lies. She eats chocolates and lies.

[*A goodbye.*]

Well, thanks, gotta go.

MAN: No, Samantha.

[*He strides past her.*]

SAMANTHA: How do you know my name?

[*He goes to sit in the kitchen area. Flabbergasted, she follows.*]

MAN: Because I live inside you.

SAMANTHA: Cut the shit. Who are you?

MAN: Daniel. The one you gave your soul to save.

[*Pause.*]

And now I will return the favor.

SAMANTHA: Daniel couldn't save himself, much less anybody else.

MAN: You take me apart — the devil and the saint that only you saw; take me apart — the good from the bad — and eat what tastes good, eat all that you need until you feel invincible again.

SAMANTHA: Again?

MAN: Like before you began saving Daniel.

SAMANTHA: [*Spooked, uncomfortable.*] You have to go, Mister.

MAN: Like when you were five.

SAMANTHA: I didn't save Daniel.

MAN: Sure you did.

SAMANTHA: Look, he's dead. Now I'm starting the rest of my life. Here's how you can save me: go.

MAN: Samantha...help me die into life.

SAMANTHA: Perhaps the police can help you.

[*She reaches for a telephone. He cracks it into pulp. She's shocked, steps back.*]

MAN: Sam.

SAMANTHA: Don't say that. Not like that.

MAN: Sammy, listen.

SAMANTHA: Jesus. You even sound like him or maybe I can't remember because it's been so long.

MAN: I love you, my dear young woman.

SAMANTHA: I can't even stand it when a living man comes back and spouts that bullshit. But a dead man? Give me a fuckin' break. You're dead. Gone. History. I don't need some priest of ruin knocking on my door a second time in my life. I gave at the office. Now go, goddamn it or I'll make you die again.

MAN: You said "you."

SAMANTHA: What?

MAN: You said "you." Like you believe I'm Daniel.

SAMANTHA: Why do you want to upset me like this? You had to leave. I used to plant trees, fight smokers, and only flush the toilet once a day, but I gave all that away.

MAN: You think he's dead because he's been missing for ten years.

[*She tries to run out of the house; he stops her, reporting.*]

Daniel is adopted before you're born. He's the only brown Amerasian in the orphanage outside Tokyo and your father, upstanding African American soldier that he is — medal of good conduct, citations for bravery — he can't leave the little boy in Japan. And so he brings him to the United States, thinking he'll fit in just like that because, after all, he's half American. But the hard part is, he's half Japanese. Square peg. Square peg.

[*Pause.*]

You just think he's dead.

SAMANTHA: Daniel's dead, damn it.

MAN: Your mother killed me a long time before, so you buried an old corpse.

SAMANTHA: My mother loved him.

MAN: Bullshit.

SAMANTHA: Look, I waited ten years, not sleeping at night, eating poorly, suffering nightmares when missing persons and private detectives came up with zeroes. They said maybe it was amnesia or maybe Daniel had been killed in a way that his body couldn't be recognized.

MAN: Why didn't you look for me? Not private dicks or police. You. You should've gone and looked for me. If it'd been you who disappeared, I would've searched the whole goddamn planet for you. Nobody else's look would've been good enough.

[*Pause.*]

So where's he buried?

SAMANTHA: In the only place that counts.

MAN: You put flowers on your head every May? 'Cause that's where he's buried.

SAMANTHA: Look, Mister. Do you know what it feels like to have no grave to go to, no deteriorating body to pray over? There's no place to lay down your grief. No place to —

MAN: Lay it on me.

SAMANTHA: Oh yeah. Right.

MAN: You know. It's like that with soldiers missing in action, right? The family can never move from anger and grief, to grief and finally letting go. They need to dig their eyes into a dead body, see the gray flesh, weep for their sins, weep for how they didn't sew clothes for him or cook special things for him or talk to him sweetly or realize that he simply didn't speak the language and never could, never would.

[*Unsettled with a strange feeling, she stares at him and he looks away. He is embarrassed about his mask.*]

SAMANTHA: How did that happen to you?

MAN: Fire.

SAMANTHA: Fire? I'm terrified of fire.

MAN: Why?

SAMANTHA: [*Thinks hard, looks troubled.*] Well, hell, it burns. You can't ever fix that. I mean, look at you.

[*Immediately sorry, embarrassed.*]

Sorry. I dream about it, you know.

MAN: And what's burning? In your dream.

SAMANTHA: I don't know. What am I supposed to see?

MAN: It's your dream.

SAMANTHA: [*Points to mask.*] Did that recently happen to you?

MAN: Like I said. It all started years ago . . . trying to save somebody.

SAMANTHA: How many years ago?

[*The* MAN *is silent.*]

Tell me the truth. Did you know him?

MAN: Yes.

SAMANTHA: Really?

MAN: And no.

SAMANTHA: No one really knew him but me.

MAN: Don't brag.

SAMANTHA: [*Urgently.*] You see, I had to let Daniel die.

[*The* MAN *adjusts his mask as* SAMANTHA *stares.*]

Who are you?

MAN: Who are you?

SAMANTHA: Samantha.
[*Pause.*]

After all these years.

MAN: And who is she?

SAMANTHA: I don't have to answer to you.

MAN: But you have to answer to you.

SAMANTHA: ... she's a person who can live without attachments. It's like ripping bandages off tender skin when love disappears, you see. Ripping fucking bandages. No thanks. Give me your literature and go.

MAN: Tennyson?

SAMANTHA: Tennyson?

MAN: Yes. And Delmore Schwartz.

SAMANTHA: Delmore. Nice. Real nice. Good work, Sherlock. I mean your literature for being a citizen for a better environment.

MAN: I don't have any. There's none left.

SAMANTHA: [*A farewell.*] Well then.

[*She gestures toward door.*]

MAN: There's a hole in your universe, Sam. I came because you almost died ...

SAMANTHA: My neighbor doesn't know I almost died, okay? She just knows I had surgery. How do you know I almost died? How do you know?

MAN: Because I'm alive, Sammy.

[*Pause.*]

SAMANTHA: Take off your mask.

MAN: Are you certain?

[*She nods slowly. He takes off his mask to reveal a disfigured face.* SAMANTHA *gasps and faints. He holds her in his arms. Lights crossfade to a space out of time, a downstage spotlight in which* EMIKO *stands wearing an apron and her mask.* SAMANTHA *enters in her violet mask. Both present younger personas.* EMIKO *points towards audience.*]

EMIKO: You want to see something funny? Look at the table.

SAMANTHA: [*Looks.*] Yes?

EMIKO: How many people do you see?

SAMANTHA: [*Counts.*] I see you and Papa on one side.

EMIKO: Yes?

SAMANTHA: And me on the other side.

EMIKO: You see three, right?

[SAMANTHA *nods.*]

But there are four people. Really. Four. You stand over here and you can see Daniel, too. But you stand over there and Daniel disappears. Isn't that funny?

[SAMANTHA *isn't so sure.*]

Teach him not to use his chopsticks in the rice like that. It hurts my soul every time I see it. Why can't he be good like you? Why can't he use manners?

[*Lights dim and* EMIKO *falls to her knees, mimicking in action what* SAMANTHA *reflects in her direct address to audience.*]

SAMANTHA: All the way down the street, Japanese stare at her baby strapped to her chest. Curious about this mixed-race boy. Curious. The mother, a storm, holds him tightly, stops to rest on office steps. Japanese bustle by, heads bent so low to the ground that their asses face heaven. Americans walk by, heads held so high that their asses kiss hell. She slips the bundle away from her chest and lays him down on the wooden steps. He begins to cry. She nods. That's okay, baby, everything will be all right. America will save you or kill you. There's nothing in between. At the orphanage, he's the mama-sans' favorite. He sings and dances to Japanese folk songs. The soldiers clap and bring chocolate, sugar, flour, canned milk. The mama-sans say dance some more, dance you freak, their hearts the whip, dance. And he dances and dances and dances. And it will rain again. Rain. Again.

[*Lights shift again and* EMIKO *returns to looking at the unseen table. She laughs.*]

EMIKO: You stand over here and you can see Daniel, too. But you stand over here and Daniel disappears. Isn't that funny?

[*Lights crossfade to a spotlight on* MAN *in tattooed mask. It goes off and on, flashing, as* SAMANTHA *enters and stands on its periphery, struggling to see the* MAN. *Suddenly the light stops flashing and the* MAN *and* SAMANTHA *stare at one another, and then out towards the audience. It is the past.*]

MAN: She talks like all the mama-sans at the orphanage: do this, Danny; do that, Danny; dance, Danny; stand up straight, don't slouch like a yakuza, don't smile so big, don't hold your head up so high, don't eat so fast; help me with your sister, Danny; isn't it nice to have a sister; push her carriage ... down the hill.

[EMIKO *enters screaming hysterically. She is in mask.* SAMANTHA *covers her ears. As* EMIKO *enters the periphery of the light, she ceases screaming and* SAMANTHA *uncovers her ears.*]

EMIKO: Danny, no! Don't push the baby carriage down the hill! Papa, help! Help! Danny pushed Samantha's baby carriage down the hill!

SAMANTHA: Four years old.

EMIKO: [*Beams.*] Happy birthday, Sammy!

MAN: Sammy Sedgwick won't remember this.

EMIKO: I made a cake.

MAN: [*Surprised.*] Cool.

EMIKO: From a box. See?

MAN: Uh, why'd you cook it in a frying pan?

EMIKO: Frosting is too liquid, but tastes good.

SAMANTHA: Thanks, Mom.

MAN: Got any doughnuts?

SAMANTHA: Five years old.

MAN: The German lady next door teaches Mom how to make a cake.

SAMANTHA: I ride my tricycle in the park and stare at Daniel riding his bicycle.

MAN: Papa bought it for me.

SAMANTHA: And Mom said:

EMIKO: Too expensive. He's just going to let all the neighborhood boys use him. I mean, use it. The bicycle.

MAN: Sam, your little tricycle cost as much as my bike.

SAMANTHA: Cost? I don't understand cost.

MAN: Never mind. You wanna ride a big boy's bicycle?

SAMANTHA: I try to get on and I fall off the seat.

MAN: Into a hole where one of the big red clay pipes is exposed and —

EMIKO: Bang. Crack. Ohhhhhhhh.

MAN: Just like that.

EMIKO: Her arm is broken in two places, Danny! Papa, call the doctor! Call the ambulance! Hurry, hurry, hurry.

SAMANTHA: [*Overlapping.*] Hurry, hurry, hurry.

[*Beat.*]

Six years old.

MAN: You're fat and ugly and no one will ever love you. Look at you, wearing that stupid dress Mom made you. You look like a goddamn ballerina Barbie doll. Barbie isn't Polynesian. Barbie isn't brown. And she speaks English real good and her mother knows how to bake a goddamn birthday cake, okay?

EMIKO: We come home and Danny's been a good babysitter. He loves his little sister so much. Everything okay, Danny?

MAN: Fix my bed and clean up my room and don't tell Mom or Papa or I'll kill you.

EMIKO: Everything okay, Danny?

SAMANTHA: His bed is wet. Yuck. I fix it anyway. I don't tell Mom.

EMIKO: Did you fix Danny's bed for him?

SAMANTHA: I fixed my own bed.

[*To audience.*]

I never lie to my mother, but she has a way of not listening that allows you to skirt around the truth sometimes.

EMIKO: Good girl. You fix your bed so nice. Danny, your bed smells funny.

MAN: Japanese don't believe in adoption. Bad blood they say. Bad blood.

EMIKO: Papa, I don't want to adopt him. All the rules he's every going to learn about life he's learned.

SAMANTHA: What do you mean he's not my real brother?

EMIKO: Papa found him at an orphanage, a place where they keep children that nobody wants.

SAMANTHA: Then why did you want him?

EMIKO: Papa loves Daniel.

SAMANTHA: Me, too, Mama.

EMIKO: But Daniel makes you cry.

SAMANTHA: Sometimes you make me cry, too, Mama, but I love you.

EMIKO: Love, love, love. Different meaning for everyone so it's empty word.

SAMANTHA: Daniel, are you real?

MAN: She walks away, leaving me on some step in the rain, never looking back.

SAMANTHA: The opposite of real is . . .

MAN: She wants to pretend the war is a dream and that she never had a Yankee child. Not her. That only happens to bad girls.

SAMANTHA: Untrue, unreal.

MAN: Artificial.

EMIKO: Fake.

MAN: Yeah. Made in Japan.

SAMANTHA: I always thought he was my real brother.

EMIKO: Papa, don't buy a used car. Drive it a few miles and soon it'll break down on you. When you least expect it and you need it most, it'll leave you stranded.

SAMANTHA: Papa, do people find each other? Is that how families get made?

EMIKO: How many people sitting at the table, Sammy?

MAN: Real.

EMIKO: Three, Sammy. I see three.

SAMANTHA: Non-fiction.

EMIKO: You and Papa on one side. See, Sammy?

MAN: To be or not to be.

EMIKO: And me on the other.

SAMANTHA: Concrete.

MAN: May I please be excused?

EMIKO: Did you hear something, Sammy?

SAMANTHA: Genuine.

EMIKO: You stand over here and you can see Daniel, too. But you stand over there and Daniel disappears. Isn't that funny?

[*Lights crossfade to table and kitchen area, back to present day.* SAMANTHA *moves away from the man quickly. She is without mask; he wears the plain mask.*]

SAMANTHA: Who told you these things?

MAN: Daniel.

SAMANTHA: When did you see him last?

MAN: Today.

SAMANTHA: If you were Daniel, you would have called me on Easter or Christmas or my birthday. You never missed calling me on those days. You would've let me know you were all right.

[*Pause.*]

You would've been here for Christmas like you promised.

MAN: Like this?

SAMANTHA: You would've known that it wouldn't have mattered.

MAN: Wouldn't it?

SAMANTHA: No.

MAN: Then touch my face.

[*She can't.*]

See?

SAMANTHA: If you were Daniel, I'd touch it.

MAN: Then touch it.

SAMANTHA: I could have your teeth checked, match your dental records.

MAN: I have false teeth now.

[*Pause.*]

I could've had amnesia. Or be in a witness protection program.

SAMANTHA: Daniel wouldn't do anything to help a country he so despised.

MAN: Maybe in Japan.

SAMANTHA: Ditto.

MAN: Of course, there's always that possibility that Daniel's disappearance was . . . deliberate.

SAMANTHA: [*She hadn't ever thought about that.*] No.

MAN: Maybe I just didn't — don't — want to see you. Maybe I realized you were just another mama-san trying to get me to dance your way: wear a tie, Daniel; finish college, Daniel; don't sleep around so much, Daniel; you can't rely on your looks to get you through life, Daniel.

SAMANTHA: . . . men and women alike turned to look at Daniel when he walked by.

MAN: Fuck you. That's your truth and nobody else's. You want truth? You have a birthmark the shape of Ireland on your left buttock.

SAMANTHA: What? How do you know that?

MAN: Your neighbor told me.

SAMANTHA: Right.

MAN: And a long scar from north to south on your otherwise perfect belly. Let me see it.

SAMANTHA: What else did my neighbor tell you? The diameter of my cervix?

MAN: I saw your birthmark when I bathed you. When you were five and I was thirteen. Emiko always let me bathe you, until the time I broke your arm.

SAMANTHA: Did you break it or was it just an accident?

MAN: Just stop it, Sam. Stop.

SAMANTHA: What do you want from me?

MAN: For you, not from you.

SAMANTHA: What do you want for me?

MAN: A better environment.

[*Pause.*]

You're the only person who truly loved me.

SAMANTHA: I didn't love Daniel.

[*Pause.*]

I hated Daniel.

[*Pause.*]

I felt sorry for Daniel.

MAN: When I heard you were in the hospital, I couldn't understand what was wrong, couldn't understand why it was life-threatening. I thought maybe it was just a matter of time and you'd disappear.

SAMANTHA: Go Mister . . . whatever your name is. Go make the environment green. Flush my toilet on the way out. I buried Daniel, okay? And you don't get to exhume him, parade his soul around like a flying elephant, spit on his grave.

[*The* MAN *spits on her head and she reels with disgust.*]

MAN: Yeah, I spit on his grave. That's his grave.

SAMANTHA: Get out.

MAN: Let me out, Sammy. Trot me out without all your reformer trappings and just look at me for what I am: not beautiful, not tame...not dead.

[*She stares at him with fear and uncertainty.*]

Remember how you'd listen to the Beatles by the old stereo, those waffling LPs, their voices anathema to Emiko as you pretended that George Harrison was dancing in the living room.

SAMANTHA: George Harrison?

MAN: Five years old. You and George Harrison. You pretended to dance with him. And I told you to listen to Otis Redding.

SAMANTHA: And I did.

MAN: Listen to me again.

SAMANTHA: We were supposed to meet. Daniel and I. Meet and talk about things I had on my mind, things that weren't right all the way back from childhood, things I hadn't remembered before.

MAN: Yes.

SAMANTHA: [*Getting upset.*] And he was going to say I'm sorry and I was going to hate him all over again.

[*She looks at him and then slaps him.*]

You ruined my life. I had to build it back like blocks, like Legos, like Lincoln Logs, but too many pieces were lost.

MAN: Okay. That's a good start.

SAMANTHA: Wait, I'm sorry. Daniel ruined my life, not you. Daniel.

[*Confused, angry at her confusion.*]

Who are you? You don't even have a goddamn petition for me to sign.

[*He goes "outside," sits on the porch swing. It creaks. He starts to sing in the same slow, folk rock fashion as she did earlier:*]

MAN: "Deck the halls with boughs of holly,
Fa-la-la-la-la, La-la-la-la..."

[*She steps outside and stares at him. He stops singing, uses his hand to hide his face from her piercing gaze.*]

SAMANTHA: You're Daniel. If you sing that song like that, then you're Daniel. That was how we sang it.

MAN: I don't want you to let me be Daniel. I want you to take me for who I am.

SAMANTHA: That's all I can do. Daniel isn't here before me, not as I knew him or as I can ever know him again. But you're here. You can be you and, if you call yourself Daniel, then I guess you are. Daniel, Curtis, Steven, whatever. You.

MAN: I'm Daniel. Daniel Sedgwick.

SAMANTHA: [*Indicating burn.*] Does it hurt?

MAN: No.

[*Indicating her scar.*]

Did they hurt you?

SAMANTHA: It only hurts late at night. I wake up to silence, like I did in the hospital. It feels . . . alone.

MAN: Oh, Sam . . .

SAMANTHA: Wanna have dinner with me?

MAN: Yeats. Remember Yeats. He said, "And tear the heart out of her side,/ And lay the heart upon her hand/ And bear that beating heart away . . . "

SAMANTHA: "And then did all the Muses sing."

MAN: Take it, Sam. Take everything I've got. It's okay. I'm willing to die for you, not for her, but for you. Somewhere there's a better life and I'll rise to it.

[*She touches his face lightly and then leans forward and kisses him gently on the forehead. Blackout.* END OF ACT I.]

ACT II

SCENE 1

The MAN *and* SAMANTHA *sit opposite of each other at the kitchen table. He eats with chopsticks. She sifts through a box of men's clothing.*

MAN: It's been so long since I've had perfect Japanese rice. Thanks.

SAMANTHA: It's all in the washing, you know. If you've got the right kind of rice, it's all in how many times you wash it. The more, the better.

MAN: To get it as clean as possible, huh.

SAMANTHA: Yeah.

MAN: You don't really believe I'm Daniel. That's why you kissed me. You never would've kissed Daniel. But Sam, you're the only tribe I belong to.

SAMANTHA: Tribe? What are you talking about "tribe?" You mean family.

MAN: I've known you since you were born.

SAMANTHA: No. I started my life today at church. When I buried you. Official, Episcopal priest and everything.

MAN: No. First you have to go back. Then you can go forward. I'm here to help you go back.

SAMANTHA: You can't stay.

MAN: I have to stay long enough.

SAMANTHA: She's coming. She comes every day. To make sure I'm still breathing, like she did when I was an infant.

MAN: But if I'm not really Daniel, it doesn't matter. Call her and tell her not to come.

SAMANTHA: She'll know something's wrong.

MAN: Something is wrong. Something's been wrong for a very long time.

SAMANTHA: Look, I'm like you. I have no history. It's better that way.

[Pause.]

Don't be afraid of her.

MAN: You see, when I went to that school, that jail, I died then. Into stone. Stuck in stone, in what she believed I could be. Which was nothing. If you die with love, for love, you can die into life.

SAMANTHA: I wasn't at school the day you left for reform school. I was next door playing with Tamako's daughter. I tried to come say good-bye, but Mom wouldn't let me.

MAN: Does she still make the rules? Is that why you buried me alive?

SAMANTHA: Here.

[Pushes the clothes towards him.]

These are your things. I guess they're out of style now.

[The MAN puts on a shirt. It fits.]

MAN: What you said earlier.

SAMANTHA: Yes?

MAN: About hating Daniel. You mean now or for the last twenty-five years?

SAMANTHA: Stop it. I don't hate you.

MAN: But you do.

[*Pause.*]

You don't want to remember that part.

[*Pause.*]

When I got up in the night to take a piss and I stopped in your room, I watched you for a long time before you woke up. All the baby fat was falling off. You were this clean, brown, lean thing and I didn't want anybody to ever touch you or I'd kill them. And I knew Mom was going to kill me. I knew, before long, I wouldn't be there to protect you and I didn't know what to do. Walking into a trap, it was like walking into a trap.

[*He crosses to living room. She follows with the box.*]

SAMANTHA: Where are you going?

MAN: I can't make you go back.

[*He heads to the door. She throws down the box and stops him. He throws her off of him with a force that shocks her, hurts her feelings.*]

SAMANTHA: What, what, what?

MAN: You wanted to kill me, too. You wanted me deader than Emiko did. Say it.

SAMANTHA: I wished —

MAN: Yeah?

SAMANTHA: I wished you were never born.

[*He is stunned; he lets go of her. She puts her head down.*]

Okay?

MAN: Fair enough? But don't you ever wonder what really happened?

SAMANTHA: You'd better go. It's okay. When Daniel disappeared, I didn't wish he wasn't born anymore. Let's leave it at that.

MAN: She brainwashed you.

SAMANTHA: She's the best mother anybody could ever hope for.

MAN: All right, Sam. But watch out for the cheese in the trap.

[*Outside,* EMIKO *approaches the house with groceries. She enters and stares at* SAMANTHA *and then at the* MAN, *as if he's a fixture.*]

EMIKO: I bought groceries.

MAN: Mom, it's okay. She knows it's me.

EMIKO: [*Peering at him without recognition.*] You don't have to call me "ma'am," young man. You can call me Emiko. I'm Sammy's mother.

SAMANTHA: Mother, it's Daniel.

EMIKO: Daniel is dead.

MAN: Give it up, Emiko.

EMIKO: He's dead. You stupid idiot, letting a man come in and tell you anything and you believe it. Are you that desperate?

SAMANTHA: But he said —

EMIKO: He isn't. You want to believe someone, anyone is your brother, but your brother's dead. Maybe he never lived.

SAMANTHA: But he knows things. He knows.

EMIKO: [*Unnerved.*] Did he hurt you? I know he did. I know it. Answer me before I call the police. He broke in and he raped you, right? That's what we'll say. He raped you.

[EMIKO *goes for the phone. The* MAN *pushes her onto the sofa and holds onto her fisted hands with vigor.*]

MAN: Nobody's callin' the police or Papa or the dead bitch who left me in Tokyo almost forty-five years ago. It's just you and me and the princess, Emiko. Just you and me and her.

[*Blackout. Immediate spotlight on* SAMANTHA, *downstage center. The* MAN *appears behind her in his tattooed mask, stepping forward to share the spotlight. It is the past. The sound of fire crackling fades in, slowly escalating.*]

SAMANTHA: Christmas, 1984. Daniel is coming today, without Jane or Genevieve, Natasha or Barbara. He goes through them like they're a stack of paper napkins.

MAN: Samantha? I'm in Louisiana and I —

SAMANTHA: Louisiana? But you said you'd be here in L.A. for Christmas.

MAN: I need some money, Sam. Barbara was in trouble, owed some money to some jerk and I brought her down here to take care of it —

SAMANTHA: Daniel, are you in trouble?

MAN: Some guys came to the apartment and —

SAMANTHA: Is it drugs?

MAN: They were looking for Barbara and the guys had guns and —

SAMANTHA: Daniel, what is going on?

MAN: Fuck you, Sam. I just need some money.

SAMANTHA: I haven't got a lot of extra money.

MAN: Just wire me some money.

SAMANTHA: How much?

MAN: A thousand dollars.

SAMANTHA: And I don't have the right to ask why?

MAN: I'll pay you back at the end of the month.

SAMANTHA: Who is this Barbara? I thought she was a nice girl with a radio job.

MAN: Nice girls with radio jobs can get into a lot of trouble.

[*Beat.*]

Just like nice girls from Kansas who move to California and get nice little television jobs.

SAMANTHA: All right, all right. I'll send it. When will you be here?

MAN: . . . tomorrow.

SAMANTHA: Are you sure?

MAN: I'll be there, okay?

SAMANTHA: And we'll talk. Daniel, we have to talk.

MAN: I don't know what you're so worried about, but listen, Sam. Life isn't worth a fuckin' dime, okay? We want to pretend that it's precious, but it isn't. It's tenuous. Fleeting. You can't change it. Dwell on it and it'll kill you. Who cares what happened to you? You're still alive. You got a thousand dollars to spare which is more than what most people can do. You got a house. Tomorrow, you could be on a slab at the morgue.

SAMANTHA: Thank you for that enlightening forecast.

[*Pause.*]

I just need to talk about it. Before I go to the morgue. Then I'll be okay.

MAN: You'll never be okay. You want to know why? Because you were born of war and the war's still inside of you.

SAMANTHA: Not me. That's you. You.

MAN: And it's never going to stop, baby. So just let it go.

SAMANTHA: Fuck you, you heartless bastard.

MAN: See? I told you you'd learn how to say fuck you. And nobody says it as good as a good girl.

SAMANTHA: Daniel.

MAN: Yeah, baby.

SAMANTHA: Don't get hurt.

MAN: I'll be fine. See you tomorrow. Uh, Barbara and I might get married, you know, elope or some kinda shit like that.

SAMANTHA: Married? That's . . . nice.

MAN: That's a real fuckin' Midwestern thing to say. Manana, mi linda pobrecita.

SAMANTHA: Is there a number where I can reach you?

[*The* MAN *exits as the sound of crackling fire crescendos.* SAMANTHA *looks frightened.*]

The day after Christmas, 1984. Daniel isn't here.

[*Pause.*]

Christmas, 1986. Missing persons can't find him without a Social Security number.

[*Pause.*]

Christmas, 1989. Private eye says: grisly death, amnesia, deported because he refused to be naturalized as a U.S. citizen, maybe mistaken for Cuban or something.

[*Pause.*]

Christmas, 1990. My girlfriend calls. She's watching some TV show about missing persons. Afro-Asian or Polynesian male in a coma. She calls the station. But, shit, the man's only seventeen.

[*Lights widen,* EMIKO *enters in mask.*]

EMIKO: Thank God it's not Daniel.

SAMANTHA: You never loved him.

EMIKO: Think if it was Daniel. You'd spend your whole life taking care of a vegetable. You can't fix that, Sammy.

SAMANTHA: I wanted it to be Daniel.

EMIKO: Better he just dies.

SAMANTHA: Just to know for sure whether or not he's —

EMIKO: Vegetable.

SAMANTHA: I think I wanted it to be him.

EMIKO: Admit it. You're relieved it's not Daniel.

SAMANTHA: No.

EMIKO: Yes. You want it over, but you want it over easy. Like your eggs. Like anything else that makes you sick to your stomach.

SAMANTHA: I can't stomach this.

EMIKO: Are you all right, Sammy? You don't look so good, Sammy.

[*The fire sounds grow louder.*]

SAMANTHA: I'm fine.

EMIKO: I'll call the doctor. What doctor should I call?

SAMANTHA: I'm fine. What could be wrong? Good manners, Phi Beta Kappa, pretty dresses, and life is green tea ice cream. I'm fine.

EMIKO: Did you have a bowel movement today?

SAMANTHA: My bowels are twisted up in knots, Mother, and not from my diet or Daniel or Papa. Not from anything but...

EMIKO: What?

SAMANTHA: [*Stares hard at her mother.*] The death of truth. You've given me everything, Mom, told me everything, right?

[*No response.*]

Right? So where's it hiding? Where's it buried?

[*The fire sounds crescendo and fade out as lights fade on* SAMANTHA *and* EMIKO.]

SCENE 2

Lights fade up on present day. EMIKO, SAMANTHA *sit on sofa; no masks. The* MAN *in plain mask ties* EMIKO'*s hands together.*

SAMANTHA: Daniel, don't tie her up.

MAN: Shut up. She makes me nervous.

EMIKO: Whoever you are, you don't fool me. I know my own son when I
see him.

MAN: Your son? Don't make me vomit, Mrs. Sedgwick.

SAMANTHA: Mom, this is Daniel. There was a fire.

EMIKO: Fire? You remember?

SAMANTHA: He got burned.

EMIKO: Oh, that fire.

SAMANTHA: What fire? Why do you say it like that?

MAN: Yes, Emiko. Why do you say it like that?

EMIKO: What are you going to do to us?

MAN: I'm already doing it to your daughter.

EMIKO: [*Frightened, panicked.*] What did you do to her?

MAN: The one thing you as her special mother never wanted me to do.
I'm taking her back.

EMIKO: She never belonged to you.

SAMANTHA: So you do believe he's Daniel.

EMIKO: You never belonged to any man.

SAMANTHA: Or woman.

MAN: I'm taking her back to remember.

EMIKO: Remember what?

MAN: You know, Emiko. You want to tell her first?

SAMANTHA: What? What is it?

EMIKO: Lies. All lies. My Daniel is dead. How can you come into our lives
like this making a mockery of the dead?

MAN: Because you killed me. Mrs. Sedgwick, I think you owe me an apology.

EMIKO: Go to hell.

MAN: Last chance. 'Fess up — and I mean everything — so she can finally
understand that it wasn't just me.

EMIKO: I said go to hell.

MAN: Tell her the truth or I'll —

SAMANTHA: Daniel, no.

MAN: Or I'll...give you a big, fat piece of cheese and lock you in the kitchen closet where steel things go SNAP.

[EMIKO *laughs nervously.* SAMANTHA *goes to her, the* MAN *pushes her back.*]

The truth, Mrs. Sedgwick.

SAMANTHA: Please, Daniel. Mother, tell me.

EMIKO: There's nothing to tell.

MAN: You fuckin' liar. Tell her or, goddamn it, I mean it, cheddar metal.

[*He tightens the ropes on her hands. Lights crossfade to a downstage spotlight. It is the past. The* MAN *appears in the spotlight with no mask and damaged face. He waits impatiently for someone.* EMIKO *appears with no mask. He hands her a piece of paper.*]

MAN: Just write me under this name in care of this woman and let me know Sammy's all right.

EMIKO: You don't deserve to know her.

MAN: Be that as it may, I need to know she's all right.

EMIKO: I know what "comanchera" means now.

MAN: Don't tell her how to find me.

EMIKO: I will do this for you if you promise never to see her again. She's always trying to fix your life. Well, hers is broken, okay?

MAN: Did you have anything to do with breaking it?

EMIKO: I just love her the best way I know how.

MAN: Don't kiss my ass now, Emiko. Don't ruin it. I want to remember you loving your goddamn cats, Shinanoyaki teacups and Japanese soap operas more than you loved your own flesh and blood.

EMIKO: You're not my flesh and blood.

MAN: [*Hurt, hiding it.*] I mean Sam. Samantha. You fed her too much, choked her. Just like you did to me.

[*Pause.*]

You have to give her space. Then she'll fly, Mom.

EMIKO: Don't call me "Mom." I am not your Mom.

MAN: And you never wanted to be. I know.

[*Pause.*]

You look at me and you see a nigger but you look at Samantha and you see a Polynesian princess. Why is that?

EMIKO: Because you act like a nigger. And you don't have to be black to be a nigger.

MAN: I know.

[*Pause.*]

Because you're a nigger, too.

EMIKO: You go die. Die. Because she already thinks you're dead and good riddance. I won't tell you where she goes, how she's doing. I won't.

MAN: Okay, then I'll tell her myself. I'll go to her —

EMIKO: No! Don't go to her. You don't want to hurt, but you hurt.

MAN: Fuck you.

EMIKO: See?

MAN: I won't hurt her. Not after saving Barbara and . . .

[*Points to mask with anger.*]

. . . this.

EMIKO: Fire will follow you all of your life. But still there will be women. And you will grow big, sucking up their lives. And then you'll come looking for Samantha and you will not understand how little is left.

MAN: You see blood, but I tell you it was just love. You know about hard love, Emiko, you know.

EMIKO: What was there to give us a sense of hope about you except that perfect face? Nothing. Sammy will cringe when she sees you, just like I did. And there will be no love.

MAN: Liar.

EMIKO: You know it is true or you wouldn't have come to me today. You would have gone to her.

MAN: [*An admission she's right.*] Promise me you'll take care of her. Promise me you won't tell her to marry somebody just because he's rich. Promise me you won't talk circles around her 'till her head blows off, or visit her and move all the stuff around in her kitchen so she can't find things anymore.

EMIKO: What do you know? What have you ever known?

MAN: It's about saving you. Not her.

EMIKO: When Papa died, he said he only had one regret: that he forced me to adopt you.

[*Pause.*]

DANIEL: Papa never said that. He loved me.

EMIKO: Yes. But, Danny, love gets tired.

DANIEL: Goodbye, Emiko. And don't think I wouldn't have chosen the orphanage over America. I just might've. I just might've. I'd rather know I wasn't free from the git-go, rather than to think I was and learn the hard way that it was just a myth. Lots of myths in America. Your country.

EMIKO: It's not my country. I didn't ask to come here.

DANIEL: But you could've said no. It's more your country than it'll ever be mine because it looks at you, sees an immigrant and gives you a break sometimes. But it looks at me and sees an American, a nigger, a spic, a gook; it looks at me never understanding that I can't speak the language either. You see, Emiko, I can't speak the language.

EMIKO: If I could have found your mother and asked her to love you from your first breath and then every day like every child needs...

DANIEL: Just remember, Emiko. People are better than you think they are.

[*Blackout.*]

SCENE 3

[*Lights up. The present.* EMIKO *is gagged.* SAMANTHA *looks at her with shock.*]

MAN: So she never told me nothing, Sam. And I was so fucked up that I thought you really wouldn't wanna see me like this so I stayed away. And then she calls me after ten years, fuckin' hysterical, screamin' like a kamikaze, saying, "Daniel, Daniel, Sammy almost die, Sammy might die."

SAMANTHA: [*Stunned.*] Mom...you lied to me.

MAN: And to me. Sent me a fuckin' hundred dollar bill for my birthday every August with a note that said, "Sammy okay."

[*He rips the gag off* EMIKO's *mouth.*]

What the fuck you got to say for yourself?

EMIKO: I...I think you needed the money. That is why I sent it.

MAN: I'm not talkin' about the fuckin' money.

EMIKO: Your birthday. I wanted to buy you something you liked.

MAN: [*Disgusted with* EMIKO'*s lack of discernment.*] Holy myopia.

SAMANTHA: But, Mom, you told me he was dead.

EMIKO: Well . . . inside he was dead.

SAMANTHA: Ten years, Mom.

MAN: Do you know what it's like to be a fuckin' ghost for ten years?

SAMANTHA: [*Another unsettling realization.*] You really are Daniel.

DANIEL: Yes, Sammy.

SAMANTHA: Oh, God. I thought — I just thought —

EMIKO: You wanted him to be Daniel, so you thought —

SAMANTHA: [*To* EMIKO.] Are you sure he's Daniel?

EMIKO: . . . yes.

SAMANTHA: Oh my stars.

> [*Confused,* SAMANTHA *starts to leave the house, but the* MAN *holds onto her.* EMIKO *tries to stop him. He pushes her away with great force, knocking her onto the floor. She crawls to side stage.* SAMANTHA *tries to help her, but the* MAN *won't let her.*]

MAN: Now that you know it's me, Sam . . .

SAMANTHA: Yes?

MAN: You have to go all the way back.

SAMANTHA: Daniel, you're home now. You're safe. We'll all be together again. Everything is okay. I'll make some tea.

> [*A spotlight fades up downstage. The* MAN *points to it.*]

MAN: Sammy, stand over there.

SAMANTHA: Daniel.

MAN: Stand over there.

> [SAMANTHA *goes to the spotlight, stands.*]

Ask me what I was thinking that day, the moment before. Ask me what the fuck I was doing.

> [*Lights fade out on home. It is the past.* SAMANTHA *shivers in violet mask. The* MAN *in tattooed mask enters her light. He puts a chenille house robe,*

fuzzy slippers on her. They assume younger personas. EMIKO *watches from a prone position as if frozen, able only to respond visually.*]

MAN: It's time to go to bed.

SAMANTHA: But Mom and Papa said I could stay up until ten.

MAN: You're eight. That means you have to be in bed by eight o'clock. You can't stay up until ten until you're ten.

SAMANTHA: [*To audience.*] My parents went to a V.F.W. dance and Danny is in control. Mom would rather hire a babysitter, but Papa said she had to trust Daniel.

MAN: Go to bed.

[*The* MAN *fades into the darkness. Light dims on* SAMANTHA.]

SAMANTHA: I'm afraid to go to sleep in the pitch dark. He turns on the lamp. He's angry about turning on the lamp. Takes my favorite lace dress. Pulls it over the lampshade.

[*Pause.*]

I try to leave the room to go to the bathroom. Sends me back in. Slams the door. I pee in the bed, peeing not out of need, but out of fear. I look at my papier-maché Easter bunny that I made at school. Crepe paper fur starts to singe from the heat of the lamp. I go to the door again to tell Daniel that the sky is falling.

[*The* MAN *in tattooed mask reappears, hovering over her as they relive the incident.*]

MAN: I march into the room. She lies on the bed smelling like piss. Goddamn you, Sammy! You're supposed to be clean.

SAMANTHA: He smells me.

MAN: [*Simultaneous with last line.*] I smell her.

SAMANTHA: And puts his hand on my stomach. The sheet goes over my head. And I try to push him away.

MAN: [*Simultaneous with last sentence.*] And she tries to push me away.

SAMANTHA: . . . and he's crying.

MAN: [*Softly.*] Yes.

SAMANTHA: And I can see my dress on the lamp starting to burn.

MAN: Don't worry, Sammy. It's nothing.

SAMANTHA: And I say, "Daniel, we're going to burn."

MAN: "Don't push me away," I tell her.

SAMANTHA:/MAN: Don't.

SAMANTHA: And his head sinks between my legs. His smell.

MAN: [*Simultaneous with last sentence.*] Her smell.

SAMANTHA: Daniel, what are you thinking?

MAN: Don't think.

> [SAMANTHA *screams loud and long. He covers her mouth and suffocates the scream.*]

MAN: And my mother's house is no longer immaculate, but awkward and impure like me.

SAMANTHA: "Go to sleep," he says. "But fire," I whisper.

MAN: I take my sister into my body and she takes me into her and —

SAMANTHA/MAN: — we are one . . . dirty . . . and one . . .

MAN: I close the door, tie a rope from its doorknob to another doorknob, tie it tightly so she can't get out and then I go back to the television set. War movie. I like war movies.

SAMANTHA: The fire spreads to the bunny and then the wall. Room fills with smoke. "Danny, but I can't go to sleep without my bath."

MAN: And I curse children who won't sleep. That's what the mama-sans did at the orphanage. "Sleep you little half-breeds, sleep." They'd say it in English because they thought we only spoke Japanese. But I understood.

SAMANTHA: Don't you hear me, Danny?

MAN: [*Simultaneous.*] Don't you hear me, Mom? Tonight I'm cleaning up my own mess, leaving no traces. I'll go to the kitchen where I can't hear the noise, maybe there's doughnuts, maybe maki-zushi.

SAMANTHA:/MAN: Fire burns through the wall.

SAMANTHA: Dead wall.

> [EMIKO *struggles and breaks free, leaping on him, trying to choke him.* SAMANTHA *begins to cough. As they continue to struggle, her cough becomes uncontrollable, blending with the sounds of crackling fire. The* MAN *gets the best of* EMIKO *and starts choking her with an intent to kill.* SAMANTHA *flings off her mask and tries to stop him. Sounds intensify. Lights fade out. All exit. Immediate spotlight downstage into which* EMIKO, *dazed, enters in mask.*]

EMIKO: I think I'd like you to paint it peach. It's funny, isn't it? The burn's shaped like a heart, just tear off the right side and it's a heart, isn't it?

Can you get all the bad stuff out? Will the room be normal once again?

[*Pause.*]

There was a robber. Yes, I think that's what it was.

[*Pause.*]

There was a fire.

[*Slow beat, reacts to unseen presence.*]

Hi, Sammy. You want some o-senbei and o-cha? No? You want to talk? Talk about what? Nothing's wrong with the wall in your room. How can you be in the wall when you're standing right here in from of me? It's peach, Sammy. A perfectly beautiful wall. What are you talking about "fire?" Go to bed, Sammy. There's nothing to be afraid of.

SCENE 4

Lights up. The present. The MAN *and* SAMANTHA *sit in the kitchen.* SAMANTHA *is maskless; the* MAN *wears the plain mask.* EMIKO, *without mask, lies down on the sofa.*

MAN: You see, your doctors got all the bad things out, but me.

SAMANTHA: Goddamn you, Daniel. What was I looking for all those years. I really was your mother. Mother of invention. Get out. Just go.

[*He doesn't move.*]

EMIKO: [*Quiet sadness.*] Many times I told you: Daniel is not a prince or saint. Daniel was just a boy who didn't have a chance. And I didn't know how to give him one.

MAN: [*To* SAMANTHA.] You have to forgive. For you, not for me.

[*The* MAN *takes* SAMANTHA's *hand and holds onto it tightly. She tries to struggle free, but he won't let her go.*]

You're the only thing I ever loved or needed because you're the only one who ever truly loved me.

SAMANTHA: Just go. I started cleaning out my things this week and I intend to continue. Starting now.

EMIKO: Well, I'm sorry, Daniel.

MAN: I always wanted to be a piece of your china, Emiko.

[*Pause.*]

Hard love. It's all so hard.

[*Pause.*]

I'm tired now.

EMIKO: Rest here. I will cook for us.

SAMANTHA: No, Mom.

[*But* EMIKO *smiles, heads to kitchen.*]

MAN: You can have my share.

[*He prepares to leave.*]

SAMANTHA: Where will you go?

MAN: Back to my assumed identity. But I guess Daniel Sedgwick was assumed, too. I was born Masao Kawada. Did you know that?

SAMANTHA: But how will I find you, in case, you know, something happens to Mom or something?

[EMIKO *reappears from kitchen.*]

EMIKO: Sammy, Danny, would you like wakame in the miso shiru?

[*The* SIBLINGS *stare at one another. He is poised to leave.*]

How about potato?

MAN: Don't feed me. Save it for yourselves.

EMIKO: But, Danny, I said I am sorry. I said.

MAN: What exactly do you expect, Emiko?

EMIKO: [*Searches for an answer and then —*] Truth. Now there can be truth.

MAN: Isn't that funny. Truth. Whose truth? Yours? Mine? Sammy's?

SAMANTHA: How about mine? I'm the only one everybody lied to.

MAN: No whining.

SAMANTHA: Fuck you and, by the way, it wasn't George Harrison. It was John Lennon, okay? John Lennon. And he's dead, too.

MAN: [*Softly.*] But you're not anymore.

EMIKO: And neither are you, Danny.

SAMANTHA: Mom? Go home now, okay?

[*On* EMIKO's *stricken look.*]

Not forever. Just for now. For today. Next week maybe I'll cook for you.

MAN: Goodbye, Mrs. Sedgwick.

EMIKO: Didn't I tell you about Sammy's operation? I didn't lie to you in the end.

MAN: Thanks...Mom.

EMIKO: [*This is enough; she's happy.*] You are welcome, Danny. Bye-bye. Be a good boy. You try, okay?

[EMIKO *exits.*]

SAMANTHA: And you stay.

DANIEL: Then take off your mask.

SAMANTHA: I'm not wearing one.

DANIEL: Let me see your scars, Samantha.

SAMANTHA: NO. Damn it, you've seen behind my mask. You've seen the real scars. This one is nothing, just a memorial to all the others, the ones that turned my body against itself.

[*The* MAN *tears at her dress.*]

Stop it!

[*They tussle; he holds her down and touches her scar.*]

MAN: [*Sad.*] Samantha.

SAMANTHA: "...why art thou so full of heaviness..."

MAN: They cut you open.

SAMANTHA: "...and why art thou so disquieted..."

MAN: Oh Sam.

SAMANTHA: Better environment.

MAN: It — I mean — Sam...I —

SAMANTHA: My seam. My ridge. Tierra Madre.

MAN: It's okay.

SAMANTHA: Of course it's okay. No big deal, really.

MAN: It is a big deal, but it's okay.

SAMANTHA: It is not a big deal.

MAN: Okay.

[*He rubs the scar.*]

SAMANTHA: Don't.

[*Then he kisses it and she pushes him away. He comes forward again. They kiss and then separate.*]

MAN: I . . . I can't be with you.

[*She just looks at him.*]

Not anymore. Not this close.

SAMANTHA: Because of the scars.

MAN: I made them.

SAMANTHA: I mean yours, Danny.

MAN: Find a thinking, clean man and live together, okay?

SAMANTHA: You know, we can fix your face, revise the scars.

MAN: I like it just the way it is. Goodbye, beauty.

[EMIKO *appears on the porch and stands by the swing. The* MAN *leaves the house.* SAMANTHA *sits on sofa, stares into space contemplatively. The* MAN *looks at* EMIKO. *She walks up to him with great hesitation and then hugs him, his hands up in the air not knowing what to do with this hug. Finally, he embraces her. Lights fade out on the* MAN, EMIKO, SAMANTHA, *crossfading to downstage spotlight which* SAMANTHA *enters.*]

SAMANTHA: Dear Father, I confess that I have sinned against you in thought, word and deed, for what I have done and for what I have left undone. And that's that. If you forgive me, I'll forgive you for all the cruel jokes you've played on us. This time, you take care of Daniel. You hear me? Take care of him, teach him.

[*About to walk away, she stops and covers her ears for a moment.*]

Uh-uh. No way. Don't talk to me about right and wrong or what might be true or what might not be true. The newspapers lie, the poets lie, mothers lie, you lie. We all lie down in our beds of truth and spit at the angels. Well, thanks for nothing. Do me a favor, okay? Don't be so black and white. So goddamn black and white.

[*Lights crossfade to a space out of time, a spotlight in which* SAMANTHA *and* EMIKO *stand side by side as* SAMANTHA *motions towards an unseen table.* EMIKO *trembles.*]

SAMANTHA: Mother, how many people do you see sitting at the table?

[*Pause.*]

EMIKO: . . . f-four.

SAMANTHA: Say it again, Mother. Speak clearly.

EMIKO: Four.

[*Blackout.*]

END OF PLAY

David Henry Hwang

BONDAGE

EDITOR'S NOTES

I did a double-take when first reading *Bondage*, when his characters describe their setting as "a bondage parlor on the outskirts of Encino." You see, I *live* on the outskirts of Encino.

Let me hasten to add that I do *not* live in a bondage parlor. And yet, not to get too facile about it, Hwang is suggesting here that we all do. Anonymous communications on the internet have recently demonstrated the degree to which many people are eager to escape the labels of race, gender, and age, and to interact with someone free of the baggage that comes with such labels. To be able to put on a mask and be accepted for yourself, knowing that your race was neither an incentive nor a disincentive. . . how rare, how provocative.

A practical consideration for producing *Bondage* is the extent to which the actors' racial identities can be concealed until they are unmasked. While a clever costume design may hide the ethnicity of Mark, for example, anyone attending the premiere would know that actor B.D. Wong was Asian, even if they weren't familiar with his star-making performance in *M. Butterfly*. Addressing this production challenge, short of happening on actors with nondescript names or handing out programs at intermission, will take some ingenuity.

It will take more than ingenuity to overcome the struggle faced by characters like Mark to be taken seriously as romantic leads. Asian men have it rough in current fiction and film. Projects which deftly break stereotypes about Asian women, such as *The Joy Luck Club* or *Double Happiness*, present Asian fathers and boyfriends who are insensitive, invisible or gay. Perhaps the next generation of leading actors (Russell Wong, Jason Scott Lee) will change that.

Yet Hwang is writing about far more than the plight of Asian men; he addresses stereotypes about African Americans, Latinos, Italians, men and women alike. A change is gonna come, as the song may say, but it's a long time coming. With the same year that *Bondage* premiered at Louisville, Hwang went to New York with a large farce about racial issues, *Face Value*. The latter play closed quickly, and though it may be reworked in the future, its initial failure suggests that Americans are not yet ready to laugh about some kinds of racial politics. But the success of *Bondage* also shows that the topic won't go away, either.

Masks figure prominently in the preceding plays by Philip Kan Gotanda and the subsequent play by Velina Hasu Houston. The recurrence of the image suggests that for many, race is a mask that affords protection and yet traps its wearers. *S.A.M I Am*, later in this volume, also features a character whose strength is anonymous interaction, even creating a fictional identity for himself. All this points to a yearning to move beyond the minefield of race, even while acknowledging that few ideas add as much to the richness of one's social identity as one's race. "Only connect" is the goal for these authors' characters — and awareness of race can either help or hinder that simple human connection.

Bondage was first produced by the Actors Theatre of Louisville (Jon Jory, Producing Director) at the 16th annual Humana Festival of New American Plays, on March 1, 1992, on a double bill entitled "2 Acts of Love," with the following cast:

MARK   B.D. Wong

TERRI   Kathryn Layng

Directed by Oskar Eustis. Scenery by Paul Owen; Lighting by Mary Louise Geiger; Costumes by Laura A. Patterson; Stage Manager, Debra Acquavella. *Bondage* was commissioned by the Actors Theatre of Louisville.

CHARACTERS

TERRI   late-twenties, female

MARK   early-thirties, male

PLACE: *An S & M parlor on the outskirts of Los Angeles.*

TIME: *Present.*

A room in a fantasy bondage parlor. TERRI, *a dominatrix, paces with her whip in hand before* MARK, *who is chained to the wall. Both their faces are covered by full face masks and hoods to disguise their identities.*

MARK: What am I today?

TERRI: Today — you're a man. A Chinese man. But don't bother with that accent crap. I find it demeaning.

MARK: A Chinese man. All right. And who are you?

TERRI: Me? I'm — I'm a blonde woman. Can you remember that?

MARK: I feel . . . very vulnerable.

TERRI: You should. I pick these roles for a reason, you know.

[*Unchains him.*]

We'll call you Wong. Mark Wong. And me — I'm Tiffany Walker. [*Pause.*]

I've seen you looking at me. From behind the windows of your — engineering laboratory. Behind your — horn-rimmed glasses. Why don't you come right out and try to pick me up? Whisper something offensive into my ear. Or aren't you man enough?

MARK: I've been trying to approach you. In my own fashion.

TERRI: How do you expect to get anywhere at that rate? Don't you see the jocks, the football stars, the cowboys who come 'round every day with their tongues hanging out? This is America, you know. If you don't assert yourself, you'll end up at sixty-five worshipping a Polaroid you happened to snap of me at a high school picnic.

MARK: But — you're a blonde. I'm — Chinese. It's not so easy to know whether it's OK for me to love you.

TERRI: C'mon, this is the 1990s! I'm no figment of the past. For a Chinese man to love a white woman — what could be wrong about that?

MARK: That's . . . great! You really feel that way? Then, let me just declare it to your face. I —

TERRI: Of course —

MARK: — love —

TERRI: It's not real likely I'm gonna love you.

[*Pause.*]

MARK: But . . . you said —

TERRI: I said I'm not a figment of the past. But I'm also not some crusading figure from the future. It's only 1992, you know. I'm a normal girl. With regular ideas. Regular for a blonde, of course.

MARK: What's that supposed to mean?

TERRI: It means I'm not prejudiced — in principle. Of course I don't notice the color of a man's skin. Except — I can't help but notice. I've got eyes, don't I?

[*Pause.*]

I'm sure you're a very nice person . . . Mark. And I really appreciate your helping me study for the . . . physics midterm. But I'm just not — what can I say? I'm just not attracted to you.

MARK: Because I'm Chinese.

TERRI: Oh no, oh heavens, no. I would never be prejudiced against an Oriental. They have such . . . strong family structures . . . hard working . . . they hit the books with real gusto . . . makes my mother green with envy. But, I guess . . . how excited can I get about a boy who fulfills my mother's fantasies? The reason most mothers admire boys like you is 'cause they didn't bother to marry someone like that themselves. No, I'm looking for a man more like my father — someone I can regret in later life.

MARK: So you're not attracted to me because I'm Chinese. Like I said before.

TERRI: Why are you Orientals so relentlessly logical?

[*She backs him up around the room.*]

MARK: Well, for your information . . . it doesn't — it doesn't hurt that you're not in love with me.

TERRI: Why not?

MARK: Because I never said that I loved you, either!

[*They stop in their tracks.*]

TERRI: You didn't?

MARK: Nope, nope, nope.

TERRI: That's bullshit. I was here, you know. I heard you open yourself up to ridicule and humiliation. I have a very good ear for that sort of thing. [*Cracks her whip.*] So goddamn it—admit it—you said you love me!

MARK: I did not! If I don't tell the truth, you'll be angry with me.

TERRI: I'm already angry with you for lying! Is this some nasty scheme to maneuver yourself into a no-win situation? God, you masochists make life confusing.

MARK: I came close. I said "I love—," but then you cut me off.

TERRI: That's my prerogative. I'm the dominatrix.

MARK: I never finished the sentence. Maybe I was going to say, "I love . . . the smell of fresh-baked apple pie in the afternoon."

TERRI: That's a goddamn lie!

MARK: Can you prove it? You cut me off. In mid-sentence.

TERRI: It does . . . sound like something I would do. Damn. I'm always too eager to assert my superiority. It's one of the occupational hazards of my profession.

[*Pause.*]

So I fucked up. I turned total victory into personal embarrassment. God, I'm having a rotten day.

MARK: Terri—

TERRI: Mistress Terri!

MARK: Mistress Terri, I—I didn't mean to upset you. It's OK. I wasn't really going to say I loved apple pie. Now—you can whip me for lying to you. How's that?

TERRI: I'm not about to start taking charity from my submissives, thank you. That's one good way to get laughed out of the profession.

[*Pause.*]

Sorry, I just—need a moment. Wouldn't it be nice if they put coffeemakers in here?

MARK: Look—do what you want. I'm a Mexican man, and you're an Indonesian—whatever.

TERRI: What went wrong—was I just going through the motions?

[MARK *kneels behind her, places his hands gently on her shoulders.*]

MARK: You feeling OK today?

TERRI: Of course I am! It just . . . hurts a girl's confidence to stumble like that when I was in my strongest position, with you at your weakest.

MARK: Why were you in such a strong position?

TERRI: Well, I was — a blonde!

MARK: And why was I in such a weak one?

TERRI: Oh, c'mon — you were . . . an Oriental man. Easy target. It's the kind of role I choose when I feel like phoning in the performance. Shit! Now, look — I'm giving away trade secrets.

MARK: Asian. An Asian man.

TERRI: Sorry. I didn't know political correctness had suddenly arrived at S & M parlors.

MARK: It never hurts to practice good manners. You're saying I wasn't sexy?

TERRI: Well . . . I mean . . . a girl likes a little excitement sometimes.

MARK: OK, OK . . . look, let's just pretend . . . pretend that I did say "I love you." You know, to get us over this hump.

TERRI: Now, we're pretending something happened in a fantasy when it actually didn't? I think this is getting a little esoteric.

MARK: Terri, look at us! Everything we do is pretend! That's exactly the point! We play out these roles until one of us gets the upper hand!

TERRI: You mean, until I get the upper hand.

MARK: Well, in practice, that's how it's always —

TERRI: I like power.

MARK: So do I.

TERRI: You'll never win.

MARK: There's a first time for everything.

TERRI: You're the exception that proves the rule.

MARK: So prove it. C'mon! And — oh — try not to break down in the middle of the fantasy.

TERRI: Fuck you!

MARK: It sort of — you know — breaks the mood?

TERRI: I'm sorry! I had a very bad morning. I've been working long hours —

MARK: Don't! Don't start talking about your life on my time!

TERRI: OK, you don't need to keep —

MARK: Sometimes, I really wonder why I have to be the one reminding you of the house rules at this late date.

TERRI: I didn't mean to, all right? These aren't the easiest relationships in the world, you know!

MARK: A man comes in, he plops down good money . . .

TERRI: I'm not in the mood to hear about your financial problems.

MARK: Nor I your personal ones! This is a fantasy palace, so goddamn it, start fantasizing!

TERRI: I have a good mind to take off my mask and show you who I really am.

MARK: You do that, and you know I'll never come here again.

TERRI: Ooooh — scary! What — do you imagine I might actually have some real feelings for you?

MARK: I don't imagine anything but what I pay you to make me imagine! Now, pick up that whip, start barking orders, and let's get back to investigating the burning social issues of our day!

TERRI [*Practically in tears.*] You little maggot! You said you loved me . . . Mark Wong!

MARK: Maybe. Why aren't I sexy enough for you?

TERRI: I told you — a girl likes a little excitement.

MARK: Maybe I'm — someone completely different from who you imagine. Someone . . . with a touch of evil. Who doesn't study for exams.

TERRI: Oh — like you get "A"s regardless? 'Cuz you're such a brain?

MARK: I have a terrible average in school. D-minus.

TERRI: I thought all you people were genetically programmed to score in the high-90s. What are you — a mutant?

MARK: I hang out with a very dangerous element. We smoke in spite of the surgeon general's warning. I own a cheap little motorcycle that I keep tuned in perfect condition. Why don't I take you up to the lake at midnight and show you some tricks with a switchblade?

[*He plays with the handle of her whip.*]

Don't you find this all . . . a lot more interesting?

TERRI: I . . . I'm not sure.

MARK: I'm used to getting what I want.

TERRI: I mean . . . I wasn't planning on getting involved with someone this greasy.

MARK: I'm not greasy. I'm dangerous! And right now, I've got my eye set on you.

TERRI: You sound like some old movie from the 50s.

MARK: I'm classic. What's so bad about — ?

TERRI: Oh, wait! I almost forgot! You're Chinese, aren't you?

MARK: Well, my name is Mark Wong, but —

TERRI: Oh, well . . . I'm certainly not going to go out with a member of the Chinese mafia!

MARK: The Chinese — what? Wait!

TERRI: Of course! Those pathetic imitations of B-movie delinquents, that cheap Hong Kong swagger.

MARK: Did I say anything about the Chinese mafia?

TERRI: You don't have to — you're Chinese, aren't you? What are you going to do now? Rape me? With your friends? 'Cuz I've seen movies, and you Chinatown pipsqueaks never seem to be able to get a white woman of her own free will. And even when you take her by force, it still requires more than one of you to get the job done. Personally, I think it's all just an excuse to feel up your buddies.

MARK: Wait! Stop! Cut! I said I was vaguely bad —

TERRI: Yeah, corrupting the moral fiber of this nation with evil foreign influences —

MARK: Vaguely bad does not make me a hitman for the tong!

TERRI: Then what are you? A Viet Cong? Mmmm — big improvement. I'm really gonna wanna sleep with you now!

MARK: No — that's even more evil!

TERRI: Imprison our hometown boys neck-high in leech-filled waters —

MARK: No, no! Less evil! Less —

TERRI: Will you make up your goddamn mind? Indecision in a sadomasochist is a sign of poor mental health.

MARK: I'm not a Chinese gangster, not a Viet Cong . . .

TERRI: Then you're a nerd. Like I said —

MARK: No! I'm —

TERRI: . . . we're waiting . . .

MARK: I'm . . . I'm neither!

[*Pause.*]

TERRI: You know, buddy, I can't create a fantasy session solely out of negative imagines.

MARK: Isn't there something in between? Just delinquent enough to be sexy without also being responsible for the deaths of a few hundred thousand U.S. servicemen?

[TERRI *paces about, dragging her whip behind her.*]

TERRI: Look, this is a nice American fantasy parlor. We deal in basic, mainstream images. You want something kinky, maybe you should try one of those specialty houses catering to wealthy European degenerates.

MARK: How about Bruce Lee? Would you find me sexy if I was Bruce Lee?

TERRI: You mean, like, "Hiiii-ya! I wuv you."

[*Pause.*]

Any other ideas? Or do you admit no woman could love you, Mark Wong?

[MARK *assumes a doggy-position.*]

MARK: I'm defeated. I'm humiliated. I'm whipped to the bone.

TERRI: Well, don't complain you didn't get your money's worth. Perhaps now I'll mount you — little pony — you'd like that, wouldn't you?

MARK: Wait! You haven't humiliated me completely.

TERRI: I'll be happy to finish the job — just open that zipper.

MARK: I still never said that I loved you, remember?

[*Pause.*]

TERRI: I think that's an incredibly technical objection this late in the game.

MARK: All's fair in love and bondage! I did you a favor — I ignored your mistake — well, now I'm taking back the loan.

TERRI: You are really asking for it, buddy . . .

MARK: After all, I'm not a masochist — no matter how this looks. Sure, I let you beat me, treat me as less than a man —

TERRI: When you're lucky . . .

MARK: But I do not say "I love you!" Not without a fight! To say "I love you" is the ultimate humiliation. A woman like you looks on a declaration of love as an invitation to loot and pillage.

TERRI: I always pry those words from your lips sooner or later and you know it.

MARK: Not today—you won't today!

TERRI: Oh, look—he's putting up his widdle fight. Sometimes I've asked myself, "Why is it so easy to get Mark to say he loves me? Could it be . . . because deep inside—he actually does?"

MARK: Love you? That's—slanderous!

TERRI: Just trying to make sense of your behavior.

MARK: Well, stop it! I refuse to be made sense of—by you or anyone else! Maybe . . . maybe you *wish* I was really in love with you, could that be it?

TERRI: Oh, eat me!

MARK: 'Cuz the idea certainly never entered *my* head.

TERRI: Oh—even when you scream out your love for me?

MARK: That's what we call—a fantasy . . . Mistress.

TERRI: Yeah—*your* fantasy.

MARK: The point is, you haven't beaten me down. Not yet. You may even be surprised sometime to see that I've humiliated you. I'll reject *you* for loving me. And maybe, then, I'll mount *you*—pony.

TERRI [*Bursts out laughing.*] You can't dominate me. I'm a trained professional.

MARK: So? I've been your client more than a year now. Maybe I've picked up a trick or two.

TERRI: I'm at this six hours a day, six days a week. Your time is probably squandered in some less rewarding profession.

MARK: Maybe I've been practicing in my spare time.

TERRI: With your employees at some pathetic office? Tsst! They're paid to humiliate themselves before you. But me, I'm paid to humiliate you. And I still believe in the American work ethic.

[*Cracks her whip.*]

So—enough talking everything to death! I may love power, but I haven't yet stooped to practicing psychiatry, thank you. OK, you're a — a white man and me — I'm a Black woman!

MARK: African-American.

TERRI: Excuse me — are you telling me what I should call myself? Is this another of our rights you're dying to take away?

MARK: Not me. The Rev. Jesse Jackson — He thinks African-American is the proper —

TERRI: Who?

MARK: Jesse — I'm sorry, is this a joke?

TERRI: You're not laughing, so I guess it's not. Tell me — the way you talk . . . could you be . . . a liberal?

MARK: Uh, yes, if you speak in categories, but —

TERRI: Um. Well, then that explains it.

MARK: Explains what?

TERRI: Why I notice you eyeing me up every time I wander towards the bar.

MARK: Let me be frank. I . . . saw you standing here, and thought to myself, "That looks like a very intelligent woman." [*She laughs.*] Sorry. Did I — say something?

TERRI: What do they do? Issue you boys a handbook?

MARK: What?

TERRI: You know, for all you white liberals who do your hunting a little off the beaten track?

MARK: Now, look here —

TERRI: 'Cuz you've all got the same line. You always start talking about our "minds," then give us this look like we're supposed to be grateful — "Aren't you surprised?" "Ain't I sensitive?" "Wouldn't you like to oil up your body and dance naked to James Brown?"

MARK: I can't believe . . . you're accusing *me* of —

TERRI: Then again, what else should I have expected at a PLO fundraiser? So many white liberals, a girl can't leave the room without one or two sticking to her backside.

MARK: Listen — all I said was that I find you attractive. If you can't deal with that, then maybe . . . maybe *you're* the one who's prejudiced.

TERRI: White people — whenever they don't get what they want, they always start screaming "reverse racism."

MARK: Would you be so . . . derisive if I was a Black man?

TERRI: You mean, an African-American?

MARK: Your African-American brothers aren't afraid to date white women, are they? No, in fact I hear they treat them better than they do their own sisters, doesn't that bother you even a bit?

TERRI: And what makes you such an expert on Black men? Read a book by some other whitey?

MARK: Hey — I saw *Jungle Fever*.

TERRI: For your urban anthropology class?

MARK: Don't get off the subject. Of you and me. And the dilemma I know you're facing. Your own men, they take you for granted, don't they? I think you should be a little more open-minded, unless you wanna end up like the 40% of Black women over 30 who're never even gonna get married in their lifetimes.

[*Silence.*]

TERRI: Who the fuck do you think you are? Trying to intimidate me into holding your pasty-white hand? Trying to drive a wedge through our community?

MARK: No, I'm just saying, look at the plain, basic —

TERRI: You say you're attracted to my intelligence? I saw you checking out a lot more than my eyes.

MARK: Well, you do seem . . . sensuous.

TERRI: Ah. Sensuous. I can respect a man who tells the truth.

MARK: That's a . . . very tight outfit you've got on.

TERRI: Slinky, perhaps?

MARK: And when you talk to me, your lips . . .

TERRI: They're full and round — without the aid of collagen.

MARK: And — the way you walked across the room . . .

TERRI: Like a panther? Sleek and sassy. Prowling —

MARK: Through the wild.

TERRI: Don't you mean, the jungle?

MARK: Yes, the . . . Wait, no! I see where you're going!

TERRI: Big deal, I was sniffing your tracks ten miles back. I'm so wild, right? The hot sun blazing. Drums beating in the distance. Pounding, pounding . . .

MARK: That's not fair — !

TERRI: Pounding that Zulu beat.

MARK: You're putting words into my mouth . . .

TERRI: No, I'm just pulling them out, liberal.

[*She cracks the whip, driving him back.*]

What good is that handbook now? Did you forget? Forget you're only supposed to talk about my mind? Forget that a liberal must never ever reveal what's really on his?

MARK: I'm sorry. I'm sorry . . . Mistress!

TERRI: On your knees, Liberal!

[*She runs the heel of her boot over the length of his body.*]

You wanted to have a little fun, didn't you? With a wild dark woman whose passions drown out all her inhibitions. [*She pushes him onto his back, puts the heel to his lips.*] I'll give you passion. Here's your passion.

MARK: I didn't mean to offend you.

TERRI: No, you just couldn't help it. C'mon — suck it. Like the lily-white baby boy you are.

[*He fellates her heel.*]

TERRI: [*Cont'd.*] That statistic about Black women never getting married? What'd you do — study up for today's session? You thought you could get the best of me — admit it, naughty man, or I'll have to spank your little butt purple.

MARK: I didn't study — honest!

TERRI: You hold to that story? Then Mama has no choice but to give you what you want — roll over!

[*He rolls onto his stomach.*]

You actually thought you could get ahead of me on current events!

[*She whips his rear over the next sequence.*]

MARK: No, I mean — that statistic — it was just —

TERRI: Just what?

MARK: Just street knowledge!

TERRI: Street knowledge? Where do you hang out — the Census Bureau? Liar! [*She pokes at his body with the butt of her whip.*] Don't you know you'll never defeat me? This is your game — to play all the races — but me — I've already become all races. You came to the wrong place, sucker. Inside this costume live the intimate experiences of ethnic groups that haven't even been born.

[*Pause.*]

Get up. I'm left sickened by that little attempt to assert your will. We'll have to come up with something really good for such an infraction.

MARK: Can I — can I become Chinese again?

TERRI: What is your problem? It's not our practice to take requests from the customers.

MARK: I — don't want you to make things easy on me. I want to go back to what you call a position of weakness. I want you to pull the ropes tight!

TERRI [*Laughs.*] It's a terrible problem with masochists, really. You don't know whether being cruel is actually the ultimate kindness. You wanna be the lowest of the low? Then beg for it.

[*He remains in a supplicant position for this ritual, as she casually attends to her chores.*]

MARK: I desire to be the lowest of men.

TERRI: Why?

MARK: Because my existence is an embarrassment to all women.

TERRI: And why is that?

MARK: Because my mind is dirty, filled with hateful thoughts against them. Threats my weakling body can never make good on — but I give away my intentions at every turn — my lustful gaze can't help but give offense.

TERRI: Is that why you desire punishment?

MARK: Yes. I desire punishment.

TERRI: But you'll never dominate your mistress, will you?

[*Pause.*]

Will you?!

[*She cracks her whip.*]

All right. Have it your way. I think there's an idea brewing in that tiny brain of yours. You saw me stumble earlier tonight — then, you felt a thrill of exhilaration — however short-lived — with your 40% statistic. All of a sudden, your hopes are raised, aren't they? God, it pisses me off more than anything to see hope in a man's eyes. It's always the final step before rape.

[*Pause.*]

It's time to nip hope in the bud. You'll be your Chinese man, and me — I'll be an Asian woman, too.

[*Pause.*]

Have you been staring at me across the office — Mark Wong?

MARK: Who? Me?

TERRI: I don't see anyone else in the room.

MARK: I have to admit —

TERRI: What?

MARK: You are . . . very attractive.

TERRI: It's good to admit these things. Don't you feel a lot better already? You've been staring at me, haven't you?

MARK: Maybe . . .

TERRI: No, you don't mean "maybe."

MARK: My eyes can't help but notice . . .

TERRI: You mean, "Yes, sir, that's my baby." The only other Asian American in this office.

MARK: It does seem like we might have something in common.

TERRI: Like what?

MARK: Like — where'd your parents come from?

TERRI: Mom's from Chicago, Dad's from Stockton.

MARK: Oh.

TERRI: You didn't expect me to say "Hong Kong" or "Hiroshima," did you?

MARK: No, I mean —

TERRI: Because that would be a stereotype. Why — are you a foreigner?

MARK: No!

TERRI: I didn't necessarily think so —

MARK: I was born right here in Los Angeles!

TERRI: But when you ask a question like that, I'm not sure.

MARK: Queen of Angels Hospital!

TERRI: Mmmm. What else do you imagine we might have in common?

MARK: Well, do you ever . . . feel like people are pigeonholing you? Like they assume things?

TERRI: What kinds of things?

MARK: Like you're probably a whiz at math and science? Or else a Viet Cong?

TERRI: No! I was editor of the paper in high school, and the literary journal in college.

MARK: Look, maybe we're getting off on the wrong foot, here.

TERRI: Actually, there *is* one group of people that does categorize me, now that you mention it.

MARK: So you *do* understand.

TERRI: Asian men.

[*Pause.*]

Asian men who just assume because we shared space in a genetic pond millions of years ago that I'm suddenly their property when I walk into a room. Or an office.

[*Pause.*]

Now get this straight. I'm not interested in you, OK? In fact, I'm generally not attracted to Asian men. I don't have anything against them personally, I just don't date them as a species.

MARK: Don't you think that's a little prejudiced? That you're not interested in me because of my race? And it's even your own? I met this Black girl a few minutes ago — she seemed to support her brothers.

TERRI: Well, her brothers are probably a lot cuter than mine. Look, it's a free country. Why don't you do the same? Date a Caucasian woman.

MARK: I tried that too . . . a couple of women back.

TERRI: I'll tell you why you don't. Because you Asian men are all alike — you're looking for someone who reminds you of your mothers. Who'll smile at the lousiest jokes and spoon rice into your bowl while you just sit and grunt. Well, I'm not about to date any man who reminds me even slightly of my father.

MARK: But a blonde rejected me because I *didn't* remind her of her father.

TERRI: Of course you didn't! You're Asian!

MARK: And now, you won't date me because I *do* remind you of yours?

TERRI: Of course you do! You're Asian!

[*Pause.*]

MARK: How — how can I win here?

TERRI: It's simple. You can't. Have you ever heard of historical karma? That's the notion that cultures have pasts that eventually catch up with them. For instance, white Americans were evil enough to bring Africans here in chains — now, they should pay for that legacy. Similarly, Asian men have oppressed their women for centuries. Now, they're paying for their crime by being passed over for dates in favor of white men. It's a beautiful way to look at history, when you think about it.

MARK: Why should my love life suffer for crimes I didn't even commit? I'm an American!

TERRI: C'mon — you don't expect me to buck the wheel of destiny, do you? This is the 1990s — every successful Asian woman walks in on the arm of a white man.

MARK: But — but what about Italian men? Or Latinos? Do you like them?

TERRI: I find them attractive enough, yes.

MARK: Well, what about their cultures? Aren't they sexist?

TERRI: Why do you stereotype people like that? If pressed, I would characterize them as macho.

MARK: Macho? And Asian men aren't?

TERRI: No — you're just sexist.

MARK: What's the difference?

TERRI: The — I dunno. Macho is . . . sexier, that's all. You've never been known as the most assertive of men.

MARK: How can we be not assertive enough and too oppressive all at the same time?

TERRI: It's one of the miracles of your psychology. Is it any wonder no one wants to date you?

MARK: Aaargh! You can't reject me on such faulty reasoning!

TERRI: I can reject you for any reason I want. That's one of the things which makes courtship so exciting.

[*Pause.*]

It seems obvious now, the way you feel about me, doesn't it?

MARK: It does not!

TERRI: C'mon — whether Black, Blonde, or Asian — I think the answer is the same. You . . . what?

MARK: I . . . find you attractive . . .

TERRI: Give it up! You feel something — something that's been driving you crazy.

MARK: All right! You win! I love you!

TERRI: Really? You do? Why, young man — I had no idea!

[*Pause.*]

I'm sorry . . . but I could never return your affections, you being so very unlovable and all. In fact, your feelings offend me. And so I have no choice but to punish you.

MARK: I understand. You win again.

[*He heads for the shackles.*]

TERRI: Say it again. Like you mean it.

MARK: You win! I admit it!

TERRI: Not that — the other part!

MARK: You mean, I love you? Mistress Terri, I love you.

TERRI: No! More believable! The last thing anyone wants is an apathetic slave!

MARK: But I *do* love you! More than any woman —

TERRI: Or man?

MARK: Or anything — any creature — any impulse . . . in my own body — more than any part of my body . . . that's how much I love you.

[*Pause.*]

TERRI: You're still not doing it right, damn it!

MARK: I'm screaming it like I always do — I was almost getting poetic, there . . .

TERRI: Shut up! It's just not good enough. *You're* not good enough. I won't be left unsatisfied. Come here.

MARK: But —

TERRI: You wanna know a secret? It doesn't matter what you say — there's one thing that always makes your words ring false — one thing that lets me know you're itching to oppress me.

MARK: Wha — what do you mean?

TERRI: I don't think you want to hear it. But maybe . . . maybe I want to tell you anyway.

MARK: Tell me! I can take the punishment.

TERRI: What sickens me most . . . is that you feel compelled to play these kinds of parlor games with me.

MARK: What — what the hell are you — ?!

TERRI: I mean, how can you even talk about love? When you can't approach me like a normal human being? When you have to hide behind masks and take on these ridiculous roles?

MARK: You're patronizing me! Don't! Get these ropes on me!

TERRI: Patronizing? No, I've *been* patronizing you. Today, I can't even keep up the charade! I mean, your entire approach here — it lets me know —

MARK: I don't have to stand for this!

TERRI: That you're afraid of any woman unless you're sure you've got her under control!

MARK: This is totally against all the rules of the house!

TERRI: Rules, schmules! The rules say I'm supposed to grind you under my heel! They leave the details to me — sadism is an art, not a science. So — beg for more! Beg me to tell you about yourself!

[*Panicked,* MARK *heads for the wall, tries to insert his own wrists into the shackles.*]

MARK: No! If I'm — If I'm defeated, I must accept my punishment fair and square.

TERRI: You're square all right. Get your arms out of there! Stand like a man! Beg me to tell you who you are.

MARK: If I obey, will you reward me by denying my request?

TERRI: Who knows? Out of generosity, I might suddenly decide to grant it.

MARK: If you're determined to tell me either way, why should I bother to beg?

TERRI: For your own enjoyment.

MARK: I refuse! You've never done something like this before!

TERRI: That's why I'm so good at my job. I don't allow cruelty to drift into routine. Now, beg!

MARK: Please, Mistress Terri . . . will you . . . will you tell me who I really am?

TERRI: You want to know — you wanna know bad, don't you?

MARK: No!

TERRI: In the language of sadomasochism, "no" almost always means "yes."

MARK: No, no, no!

TERRI: You are an eager one, aren't you?

MARK: I just don't like you making assumptions about me! Do you think I'm some kind of emotional weakling, coming in here because I can't face the real world of women?

TERRI: That would be a fairly good description of all our clients.

MARK: Maybe I'm a lot more clever than you think! Do you ever go out there? Do you know the opportunities for pain and humiliation that lurk outside these walls?

TERRI: Well, I . . . I *do* buy groceries, you know.

MARK: The rules out there are set up so we're all bound to lose.

TERRI: And the rules in here are so much better?

MARK: The rules here . . . protect me from harm. Out there — I walk around with my face exposed. In here, when I'm rejected, beaten down, humiliated — it's not me. I have no identifying features, and so . . . I'm no longer human.

[*Pause.*]

And that's why I'm not pathetic to come here. Because someday, I'm going to beat you. And on that day, my skin will have become so thick, I'll be impenetrable to harm. I won't need a mask to keep my face hidden. I'll have lost myself in the armor.

[*He places his wrists in the wall shackles.*]

OK—I bent to your will. You defeated me again. So strap me up. Punish me.

TERRI: But why . . . why all these fantasies about race?

MARK: Please, enough!

TERRI: I mean, what race *are* you, anyway?

MARK: You know, maybe we should just talk about *your* real life, how would you like that?

[*Pause.*]

TERRI: Is that what you want?

MARK: No . . .

TERRI: Is that a "no" no, or a "yes" no?

MARK: Yes. No. Goddamn it, I paid for my punishment, just give it to me!

[*She tosses away her whip, begins to strap him up.*]

What are you doing?

TERRI: Punishment is, by definition, something the victim does not appreciate. The fact that you express such a strong preference for the whip practically compels me not to use it.

[*Pause.*]

I think I'd prefer . . . to kill you with kindness.

[*She begins kissing the length of his body.*]

MARK: Please! This isn't . . . what I want!

TERRI: Are you certain? Maybe . . . I feel something for you. After all, you've made me so very angry. Maybe . . . you're a white man, I'm a white woman—there's nothing mysterious—no racial considerations whatsoever.

MARK: That's . . . too easy! There's no reason you wouldn't love me under those conditions.

TERRI: Are you crazy? I can think of a couple dozen off the top of my head. You don't have to be an ethnic minority to have a sucky love life.

MARK: But there's no . . . natural barrier between us!

TERRI: Baby, you haven't dated many white women as a white man lately. I think it's time to change all that.
[*Pause;* TERRI *steps away.*]

So — Mark . . . Walker. Mark Walker — how long has it been? Since anyone's given you a rubdown like that?

MARK: [*After a pause.*] I usually . . . avoid these kinds of situations . . .

TERRI: Why are you so afraid?

MARK: My fright is reasonable. Given the conditions out there.

TERRI: What conditions? Do you have, for instance, problems with . . . interracial love?

MARK: Whatever gave you that idea?

TERRI: Well, you . . . remind me of a man I see sometimes . . . who belongs to all races . . . and none at all. I've never met anyone like him before.

MARK: I'm a white man! Why wouldn't I have problems? The world is changing so fast around me — you can't even tell whose country it is anymore. I can't hardly open my mouth without wondering if I'm offending, if I'm secretly revealing to everyone but myself . . . some hatred, some hidden desire to strike back . . . breeding within my body. [*Pause.*]

If only there were some certainty — whatever it might be — OK, let the feminists rule the place! We'll call it the United States of Amazonia! Or the Japanese! Or the gays! If I could only figure out who's in charge, then I'd know where I stand. But this constant flux — who can endure it? I'd rather crawl into a protected room where I know what to expect — painful though that place may be. [*Pause.*]

I mean . . . we're heading towards the millennium. Last time, people ran fearing the end of the world. They hid their bodies from the storms that would inevitably follow. Casual gestures were taken as signs of betrayal and accusation. Most sensed but no one knew on which side of such a division they themselves might fall.

[*Silence.*]

TERRI: You want to hear about yourself. You've been begging for it so long — in so many ways.

MARK: How do you know I just said anything truthful? What makes you so sure I'm really a white man?

TERRI: Oh, I'm not. After all these months, I wouldn't even care to guess. When you say you're Egyptian, Italian, Spanish, Mayan — you seem to be the real thing. So what if we just say . . .

[*Pause; she releases him.*]

You're a man, and you're frightened, and you've been ill-used in love. You've come to doubt any trace of your own judgment. You cling to the hope that power over a woman will blunt her ability to harm you, while all the time you're tormented by the growing fear that your hunger will never be satisfied with the milk of cruelty.

[*Pause.*]

I know. I've been in your place.

MARK: You . . . you've been a man? What are you saying?

TERRI: You tell me. Fight back. Tell me about me. And make me love every second of it.

MARK: All right. Yes.

TERRI: Yes . . . WHO?

MARK: Yes, Mistress Terri!

TERRI: Yes — who?

MARK: Yes . . . whoever you are . . . a woman who's tried hard to hate men for what they've done to her but who . . . can't quite convince herself.

TERRI [*Pushes him to the ground.*] Is that what you think?

[*Beat.*]

TERRI: [*Cont'd.*] Tell me more . . .

MARK: You went out — into the world . . . I dunno, after college maybe — I think you went to college . . .

TERRI: Doesn't matter.

MARK: But the world — it didn't turn out the way you planned . . . rejection hung in the air all around you — in the workplace, in movies, in the casual joking of the population. The painful struggle . . . to be accepted as a spirit among others . . . only to find yourself constantly weighed and measured by those outward bits of yourself so easily grasped, too easily understood. Maybe you were harassed at work — maybe even raped — I don't know.

TERRI: It doesn't matter. The specifics never matter.

MARK: So you found your way here — somehow — back of the Hollywood Star — something — roomfuls of men begging to be punished for the way they act out there — wanting you to even the score — and you decided — that this was a world you could call your own.

TERRI: And so, I learned what it feels like to be a man. To labor breathlessly accumulating power while all the time it's dawning how tiring, what a burden, how utterly numbing — it is actually to possess. The touch of power is cold like metal. It chafes the skin, but you know nothing better to hold to your breast. So you travel down this blind road of hunger — constantly victimizing yourself in the person of others — until you despair of ever again feeling warm or safe — until you forget such possibilities exist. Until they become sentimental relics of a weaker man's delusions. And driven by your need, you slowly destroy yourself.

[*She starts to remove her gloves.*]

Unless, one day, you choose to try something completely different.

MARK: What are you doing? Wait!

TERRI: It's a new game, Mark. A new ethnic game. The kind you like.

MARK: We can't play — without costumes.

TERRI: Oh, but it's the wildest interracial fantasy of all. It's called. . . two hearts meeting in a bondage parlor on the outskirts of Encino. With skins — more alike than not. [*She tosses her gloves away.*] Haven't we met before? I'm certain we have. You were the one who came into my chamber wanting to play all the races.

MARK: Why are you doing this to me? I'm the customer here!

TERRI: No, your time is up. Or haven't you kept your eyes on the clock? At least I know I'm not leaving you bored.

MARK: Then. . .shouldn't I be going?

TERRI: If you like. But I'm certain we've met before. I found it so interesting, so different your fantasy. And I've always been a good student, a diligent employee. My Daddy raised me to take pride in all of America's service professions. So I started to. . .try and understand all the races I never thought of as my own. Then, what happened?

MARK: You're asking me?

TERRI: C'mon — let me start you off. I have a box in my closet —

[*She runs her bare hands up and down his body as he speaks.*]

MARK: In which you keep all the research you've done. . .for me. Every clipping, magazine article, ethnic journals, transcripts from Phil Donahue. Blacks against Jews in Crown Heights — your eyes went straight to the headlines. The rise of neo-Nazism in Marseilles and Orange County. And then, further — the mass-murderer in Canada who said, "The feminists made me do it." You became a collector of all the rejection and rage in this world.

[*Pause.*]

Am I on the right track?

TERRI: Is that what you've been doing?

MARK: And that box — that box is overflowing now. Books are piled high to the hems of your dresses, clippings slide out from beneath the door. And you . . . you looked at it . . . maybe this morning . . . and you realized your box was . . . full. And so you began to stumble. You started to feel there was nothing more here for you.

TERRI: If you say it, it must be true.

MARK: Is it?

[*She starts to unlace her thigh-high boots.*]

TERRI: I'm prepared to turn in my uniform and start again from here.

MARK: You're quitting your job?

TERRI: The masks don't work. The leather is pointless. I'm giving notice as we speak.

MARK: But — what if I'm wrong?

TERRI: I'm afraid I'll have to take that chance.

MARK: No, you can't just — what about your hatred of men? Are you really going to just throw it all away when it's served you so well?

TERRI: I've been a man. I've been a woman. I've been colorful and colorless. And now, I'm tired of hating myself.

[*Pause.*]

MARK: And what about me?

TERRI: That's something you'll have to decide.

MARK: I'm not sure I can leave you. Not after all this time.

TERRI: Then stay. And strip. As lovers often do.

[*As* TERRI *removes her costume,* MARK *turns and looks away.*]

MARK: I worry when I think about the coming millennium. Because it feels like all labels have to be rewritten, all assumptions re-examined, all associations redefined. The rules that governed behavior in the last era are crumbling, but those of the time to come have yet to be written. And there is a struggle brewing over the shape of these changing words, a struggle that begins here now, in our hearts, in our shuttered rooms, in the lightning decisions that appear from nowhere.

[TERRI *has stripped off everything but her hood. Beneath her costume she wears a simple bra and panties.* MARK *turns to look at her.*]

I think you're very beautiful.

TERRI: Even without the metal and leather?

MARK: You look . . . soft and warm and gentle to the touch.

TERRI: I'm about to remove my hood. I'm giving you fair warning.

MARK: There's . . . only one thing I never managed to achieve here. I never managed to defeat you.

TERRI: You understand me. Shouldn't I be a lot more frightened? But — the customer is always right. So come over here. This is my final command to you.

MARK: Yes, Mistress Terri.

TERRI: Take off my hood. You want to — admit it.

MARK: Yes. I want to.

TERRI: The moment you remove this hood, I'll be completely exposed, while you remain fully covered. And you'll have your victory by the rules of our engagement, while I — I'll fly off over the combat zone.

[TERRI *places* MARK'S *left hand on her hood.*]

So congratulations. And goodbye.

[*With his right hand,* MARK *undoes his own hood instead. It comes off. He is an Asian man.*]

You disobeyed me.

MARK: I love you.

[*She removes her own hood. She's a Caucasian woman.*]

TERRI: I think you're very beautiful, too.

[MARK *starts to remove the rest of his costume.*]

At a moment like this, I can't help but wonder, was it all so terribly necessary? Did we have to wander so far afield to reach a point which comes, when it does at last, so naturally?

MARK: I was afraid. I was an Asian man.

TERRI: And I was a woman, of any description.

MARK: Why are we talking as if those facts were behind us?

TERRI: Well, we have determined to move beyond the world of fantasy . . . haven't we?

[MARK'S *costume is off. He stands in simple boxer shorts. They cross the stage towards one another.*]

MARK: But tell the truth — would you have dated me? If I'd come to you first like this?

TERRI: Who knows? Anything's possible. This is the 1990s.

[MARK *touches her hair. They gaze at each other's faces, as lights* FADE TO BLACK.]

CURTAIN

Lane Nishikawa and Victor Talmadge

THE GATE OF HEAVEN

EDITOR'S NOTES

Lane Nishikawa has been one of the seminal forces in keeping Asian American theatre alive, in an era when any theatre at all struggles to survive. Whether as co-director of the Asian American Theatre Company in San Francisco, as an actor in such plays as *Sansei* at the Mark Taper Forum or *The Ballad of Yachiyo* at Berkeley Repertory Theatre/South Coast Repertory, or as a performance artist in solo shows such as *I'm on a Mission From Buddha*, Nishikawa stays in vibrant motion.

His collaboration with Victor Talmadge on *The Gate of Heaven* makes for an unusual play in many respects. First, the sheer telling of a story of friendship between men of such divergent backgrounds is original enough. Most interethnic stories are tales of conflict; while Sam and Leon have their disagreements, the bond between people born a world apart forms the heart of this evening. Second, the play recognizes the importance of ritual to a culture—and by presenting it as a play, itself a form of ritual, the authors offer a new ceremony to honor both the similarities and the differences between Jewish and Japanese.

And in many ways, the play is a documentary, inspired as it is by the lives of the authors' fathers. *The Gate of Heaven* provides a wealth of information that may well be new to the average theatregoer, from the presence of Japanese American soldiers at Dachau to the tensions between Jews in the United States and Argentina. Yet the amount of factual and cultural information in the play should not distract from its richness as a text for actors.

For all the data the play provides, some of its most intriguing moments occur in what is not said. Sam's dialogue during the poker game becomes more and more succinct as the game goes badly for him. Leon never explains why it takes him so long to find a romance, but tellingly, the only woman he ever speaks of is Sam's own wife—and when he finally does fall in love, he still describes the woman by comparing her to Sam's wife. Sam's own frustration with Leon's misguided attempt to compliment him ("You're so Japanese!") is never spelled out—Sam just presses the intensity of their judo match harder and harder.

Los Angeles Times theatre critic Laurie Winer, in her review of the play, noted the special billing given to dramaturg David Henry Hwang. Since few people know what dramaturgs actually do, the notice was appreciated at least by this writer. The dramaturg serves sometimes as an editor, sometimes as an advocate for the producing theatre to the playwright or for the playwright to the producing theatre. He or she may provide background research, a sounding board, or therapy. In one troubled production, my dramaturg title made me a go-between; the director and the playwright were just tired of talking to each other.

In *The Gate of Heaven*, Hwang's input as dramaturg has served the writers well, for the play has deepened and sharpened between the pre-production draft I first read, and the current version (which is labeled Draft 12 — calling to mind the old adage that no work of art is ever finished, only abandoned for a time). The participation of Hwang and director Benny Sato Ambush saw the use of the kurokos in the script expanded, so that they sometimes play characters in the story instead of merely moving scenery and props. As the creative parties continued to develop the script for production, a gun and the obstacle of the door were added to Scene 6, the stories retold in Scene 7 became more personal and less general, and so on. And further productions may see still more refinements of the text. Though it may stymie academics and historians, there is rarely a final version of any theatrical text — only a multiplicity of texts that continue to evolve through time (a multiplicity we are starting to see in film, with the proliferation of "director's cut" and "producer's cut" releases).

Given the extent to which tales of the Holocaust as well as the Japanese internment camps in this country have been previously documented and dramatized, it is a marvel that this story has taken so many years to reach the theatre. Perhaps various cultures have fought too long in isolation. Using kurokos and stage managers, shakuhachi music and klezmer music, productions of *The Gate of Heaven* can inspire a different way of recognizing our disparate pasts.

The Gate of Heaven was first produced at the Old Globe Theatre (Jack O'Brien, Artistic Director) in San Diego, California, in association with Laura Rafaty and Benjamin Mordecai and Philadelphia Festival Theatre for New Plays at Annenberg Center, on March 5, 1996, with the following cast:

SAM	Lane Nishikawa
LEON	Victor Talmadge
KUROKOS	Eric Almquist, James O'Neil, Erika Rolfsrud

Directed by Benny Sato Ambush. Original story concept by Lane Nishikawa. Dramaturg, David Henry Hwang. Scene Design by Ralph Funicello; Light Design by Kevin Rigdon; Composer, Michael Roth; Sound Design, Jeff Ladman.

This play is dedicated to our fathers, James T. Nishikawa and Max Talmadge; to the survivors of the 442 and to the victims and survivors of the Holocaust.

CHARACTERS

LEON EHRLICH   A Polish-Jewish concentration camp survivor of Dachau. He ages from 20 to 70 during the play. He has a strong dialect at the beginning of the play which becomes more Americanized over time.

KIYOSHI "SAM" YAMAMOTO   A Japanese American Nisei (second generation) from Hawai'i. He ages from 20 to 70 during the play. He has a Hawai'ian pidgin dialect which he loses over time.

KUROKOS   The Japanese "shadow" people who move furniture and props and, at times, become characters in the play.

ACT ONE

SCENE 1

It is April 29, 1945. A single slide fades up to reveal a Japanese American soldier carrying a survivor of Dachau. We are at Dachau, Germany. Sound fades in with large cannon fire in the background. It slowly blends into taiko drums. Lights fade up to reveal SAM *the soldier and* LEON *the prisoner in the same position as in the photo. The slide fades out.*

SAM *slowly puts* LEON *down.* SAM *takes out his canteen and splashes water on* LEON'S *face.* LEON *slowly opens his eyes but they have a ghostly look.* LEON *looks at* SAM *and reacts with fear.*

SAM: Don't worry. American. [SAM *points to himself and holds his dog tags out.*] See, U.S. Army. I'm not Japanese. I'm an American.

[SAM *takes out an Army blanket and wraps it around* LEON, *who is shivering.* SAM *puts a hand on* LEON'S *shoulder and brings the canteen up to* LEON *and motions for him to drink.*]

SAM: [*Cont'd.*] You want some water?

LEON: Va-ser.

[LEON *opens his mouth, but he is too weak to drink himself.* SAM *lifts the canteen to* LEON'S *lips and holds it for him.* LEON *gags on the water.*]

SAM: Slow down.

[SAM *slowly pours water as* LEON *drinks.*

SAM: [*Cont'd.*] Go slow. Vaser.

[SAM *reaches into the duffel bag and pulls out a piece of chocolate.*]

SAM: [*Cont'd.*] You want something to eat? Maybe just a little sugar. Here, chocolate. Cho–co–late.

[LEON *opens his mouth and* SAM *slowly breaks off a piece. He holds it in front of* LEON. LEON *is too weak to chew. He cannot fit the piece into his mouth.* SAM *shows the piece of chocolate to* LEON *for a second, then puts it into his mouth and chews it.* SAM *takes his dog tags, brings them up to his mouth, and spits out the chewed chocolate. He spoonfeeds* LEON. *He watches as* LEON *is barely able to swallow.* LEON *doubles over, holding his stomach.*]

SAM: [*Cont'd.*] I'm going to get you a medic.

[SAM *starts to get up but is stopped by* LEON *who holds onto his hand.* LEON *begins to kiss* SAM's *hand.* SAM *indicates that he'll be right back.*]

SAM: [*Cont'd.*] I'll be right back. I'm just going to get the medic. Don't worry, don't worry. I'll be right back.

[LEON *holds onto* SAM *and keeps him from leaving.* SAM *yells in the direction of the medic.*]

SAM: [*Cont'd.*] Medic! Medic! You gotta help this guy out. He's dying. [SAM *waits for a response.*] You'll get to him? [*Calling out to Medic.*] Help us! Somebody help us! [*To himself.*] Somebody help us.

[*Lights fade to black.*]

[*A month later. Lights fade up on* SAM *at Regiment Headquarters. In halflight, a* KUROKO *enters with military bearing. He stands before* SAM, *produces a box. He opens the box, produces a Silver Star and pins the medal on* SAM's *chest. He steps back and remains.*]

SAM: Thank you sir. I just want to say that I am honored to receive this. Yes sir, that was some battle back there in France. I was just doing my duty, sir. Oh, I'm from Hawai'i, sir. Yeah, a lot of us are from the Islands. Yes sir, the weather is much warmer there. I miss the sun, and the beaches, too, sir. [SAM *takes out a "sen nin bari," a 1000 stitch belly band, from his pocket.*] Can I ask a favor, sir? I was wondering if you could send this back to Shigamoto's family. It's a "sen nin bari," a 1000-stitch belly band. The women back home made it. They each put their own stitch in it and then pass it around to relatives and friends until there's a thousand stitches. You wear it into battle around your stomach. It's so the spirit of a thousand loved ones can be here with us. I wanted to make sure it got sent back with Shig's stuff to his family in Rohwer, Arkansas. They're in the internment camp. My family was lucky since we're from Hawai'i but I got relatives at Tule Lake. Sir, how can they lock us up, we're all citizens. They're in the middle of nowhere, surrounded by barbed wire. [*Pause.*] You know, sir, that German camp we passed through. I couldn't believe that anyone could treat fellow humans like that. Yes, sir, it is a tragedy.

[*Pause.*]

SAM: [*Cont'd.*] After the war? Well, I'm hoping to be an officer. Just like you, sir.

[SAM *smiles and taps his belly.*]

SAM: [*Cont'd.*] Oh, yes I do, sir. I'm wearing mine.

[*Lights fade to black.* KUROKO *exits.*]

A few months later. Lights shift. SAM *removes jacket and scarf, boots and pants, hands them to* KUROKO. *He wears only T-shirt, dogtags, civilian pants.* KUROKO *begin to exit, but* SAM *stops the one with his field jacket, who turns back.* SAM *removes Silver Star from jacket.* KUROKO *exits. We hear a* VOICE *under the scene.*]

OFFICER: This Summary Court Martial Hearing finds you, Sgt. Yamamoto, guilty of conduct unbecoming a Non-Commissioned Officer.

[*Slide of Truman decorating the 442.* SAM *looks between slide and the medal. He takes out his own "sen nin bari" and wraps it around the Silver Star. Lights fade to black.*]

SCENE 2

The year is 1955. We are at an interrogation room at the Presidio U.S. Army base in San Francisco. Lights fade up to reveal LEON *in his late twenties, now a medical Army officer, with a box and an official folder with him. There is a blanket on a table and two chairs.*

[LEON *checks to make sure everything is set correctly.* SAM *enters, dressed in a suit.*]

SAM: Excuse me, sir, this letter says I'm supposed to report here today at 1700 hours . . .

LEON: Sit down.

[SAM *looks curiously at* LEON, *then slowly sits in the chair across from him.* LEON *stares at* SAM *but gets no response.*]

LEON: [*Cont'd.*] Your name is Kai . . . yashai . . . Ya-me . . . mato. You were a sergeant. Your serial number was N2084942.

SAM: Yes. But it's pronounced Ki-yo-shi Ya-ma-mo-to.

LEON: Ki-yo-shi Yama-mo-to. Ya.

SAM: But people call me Sam.

LEON: Ya. You were born in Hawai'i?

SAM: Yes. In Wahiawa.

LEON: Va-hi-e-va. Ya. Va-hi-a-va.

SAM: No. Wahiawa.

LEON: You are an American?

SAM: [*Slightly irritated.*] Of course.

LEON: You're not Japanese, you're an American citizen?

SAM: No, I am Japanese, and yes, I am an American citizen.

LEON: I see. Do you need some water?

SAM: No.

[LEON *takes out a chocolate bar and places it on the blanket.*]

LEON: Cho-co-late, bar?

SAM: What?

LEON: Now you live here in San Francisco?

SAM: Yes.

LEON: You work for the Chevron Oil Company?

SAM: Yes. In the accounting department.

LEON: Are you married?

SAM: Yes.

LEON: [*Smiles to himself.*] Is she pretty?

SAM: What?!

LEON: Alright. You were one of the men who fought in the European campaign during the war.

SAM: That's right.

LEON: You were with the 442nd?

SAM: Actually, the 522nd Artillery of the 442.

LEON: You were assigned to Battery B of the artillery unit?

SAM: Yes.

LEON: Now, Samuel . . .

SAM: The name's Sam.

LEON: Sorry. Let's get this information straight. You're from Hawai'i, but you live here now.

SAM: Yes.

LEON: You're married.

SAM: Yes.

LEON: Children?

SAM: Two. A boy and a girl.

LEON: Two children? [*Laughing to himself, then covering.*] Are they citizens?

SAM: Yeah . . . [*More irritated.*] Hey listen . . .

LEON: Mr. Yamamoto, I suggest you try and answer the questions without comment.

SAM: Fine. Are you with the O.S.S.?

LEON: I must remind you, I am asking the questions today. You'll get a chance to ask your questions later. [LEON *pushes the blanket toward* SAM.] Now, do you remember April of 1945?

SAM: No.

LEON: NO?!?

SAM: That was a long time ago.

LEON: Think. It was snowing. I'm referring to a particular concentration camp in Germany.

SAM: Ah yes, yes, I remember.

LEON: There was a tremendous battle fought to reach this camp.

SAM: I remember. How could I forget that?

LEON: It was near the end of the war.

SAM: Are you with N.A.T.O.?

LEON: Please, Mr. Yamamoto . . . if you must know, I am an officer with the U.S. Army.

SAM: But I've been out of the service for nearly ten years.

LEON: What can you tell me about April 29, 1945?

SAM: Is that what this is all about? What am I being accused of?

LEON: What are you afraid of, Mr. Yamamoto?

SAM: Nothing.

LEON: Then what can you tell me about the instructions you were given regarding April 29, 1945?

SAM: Nothing. I don't want to talk about it.

LEON: You can talk about it with me.

SAM: What do you want from me?

LEON: Your memory. [LEON *sits on the table and touches the blanket.*] I want your memory, Samuel.

SAM: The name's Sam. [*Pause.*] Let me see your orders.

LEON: I thought I was dead. All I can remember is how incredibly cold it was. How bright everything was. There was snow everywhere. I could see things but I couldn't feel. I had no sensations at all.

[SAM's *eyes drift from* LEON *to the blanket; he unfolds the old Army blanket.*]

LEON: [*Cont'd.*] Then all of a sudden I'm floating onto the snow. The next thing I remember is being outside and breathing in the fresh air.

[*We see* SAM'S *name crudely written on the blanket.* SAM *realizes who* LEON *is.*]

LEON: [*Cont'd.*] I'm an American now, too!

SAM: You made it!

LEON: I found you! I finally found you!

[LEON *grabs* SAM, *hugs him and kisses him.* SAM *seems a bit awkward, not used to this outward display of affection between men.* LEON *touches* SAM'S *face. Lights crossfade.*]

SCENE 3

Later that night. Sound fades in with cafe noise and a beat poet reciting a poem. Lights fade up on SAM *and* LEON, *who are drinking in a North Beach cafe.*

LEON: . . . for two years I was a refugee in a Displaced Persons Camp in Europe. Through the Jewish Agency I was placed on the ship Arlosolov headed for Palestine. The British who controlled didn't want us there and sent the ships to the Island of Cypress. Suddenly the Irgun, the Jewish underground, hijacks our boat and I am enlisted in the fight for statehood. The Nazis, the British and the Arabs. It was a long struggle.

SAM: From freedom fighter to shrink. I can't believe it. Imagine. A doctor. And on top of that, a military doctor.

LEON: [*Raises his glass.*] To the United States Army, it saved me twice!

SAM: I'll drink to that.

LEON: L'chaim.

SAM: L'chaim.

[*They drink.*]

LEON This is my favorite hangout. People get up and perform for you. It's great.

SAM: So what happens in two years when you're out? Are you going to start your own practice?

LEON: Yes. Here in San Francisco.

SAM: Why a psychiatrist?

LEON: [*Laughs.*] Let me tell you a story. In a little Southern town where the Klan was riding, a Jewish tailor had the chutzpah to open his little shop in the middle of Main Street. To drive him out of town, the head of the Klan sent a gang of hoodlums to annoy him. Day after day they at the entrance of his shop yelling, "Jew! Go home Jew! Get out of here, Jew!" Finally, out of desperation, the tailor cooked up a plan. The following day, when the boys came to jeer at him, the tailor came out and said, "From today on, any boy who calls me a Jew will get a dime from me." Then he gave each of the boys a dime.

SAM: He gave them a dime?

LEON: Delighted, the boys came back the following day and yelled even louder, "Jew! Jew! Get out of here, Jew! Who needs you!" The tailor came out with a big smile on his face. Then he gave each of the boys a nickel and said, "A dime is too much. I can afford only a nickel today." The boys went away satisfied because after all a nickel was money too. However the next day, when the boys came back, the tailor gave them only a penny each. "Why do we get only a today?" "That's all I can afford today." "But two days ago you gave us a dime and yesterday we got a nickel. It's not fair, mister!" "Take it or leave it. That's all you're going to get." The boys huddled together, turned around and yelled back, "You don't think we're going to call you a Jew for one lousy penny?"

SAM: [*Raises his glass.*] To the shrink! Kampai.

LEON: Kam-pa-e? Kam-pai.

[*They drink.*]

LEON: [*Cont'd.*] Samuel, that's a Biblical name. In Hebrew, it is pronounced "Schmuel."

SAM: My real name is Kiyoshi.

LEON: It means, "His name is God."

SAM: Actually, I'm called Sam because nobody wants to pronounce Yamamoto. It's too long. So they shortened it to Yam. Then people started to call me Sam. You know, Yam. Sam. See. So it kind of stuck.

LEON: Samuel, there is a Talmudic expression. A man has three names.

SAM: Talmudic?

LEON: Right, Talmudic. Writings about the Bible. A man has three names. One he is born with. One others give him. And one he must earn himself.

[LEON *thinks for a moment, then raises his glass.*]

LEON: [*Cont'd.*] To Schmookie! Samuel. Schmuel. Schmookie.

SAM: Schmookie?

LEON: Your third name. You earned it.

SAM: L'chaim.

LEON: Kampai.

[*They drink.*]

LEON: [*Cont'd.*] I owe you my life, Schmookie.

SAM: No you don't.

LEON: Yes I do. I saw you, a strange Oriental soldier peering down at me.

I thought I was hallucinating. I thought Japan had won the war and I was about to be killed. And then I heard your voice. You were speaking English. An angel with a Japanese face. I owe you my life.

SAM: You want to see an angel? [SAM *takes out his wallet and shows* LEON *a picture.*] We met at a USO dance back in 1946. I spotted her in group of giggling girls. She smiled at me and I was hooked.

LEON: Ahzisi punim. [LEON *kisses his fingers like a French chef.*] A sweet face.

SAM: Her name is Ruby. I love this woman. What a gal. [SAM *points to another picture.*] And this is my daughter, Emerald.

LEON: And this is your son, Onyx? [*They both laugh.*]

SAM: [*Looks at the pictures.*] They are my jewels, Leon. [*Points.*] That's my boy, Steven.

LEON: You are blessed with a beautiful family, Sam.

SAM: And . . . that's my car.

LEON: So, CPAs are now driving Oldsmobiles?

SAM: What do shrinks drive?

LEON: We drive people crazy. [*They both laugh.*]

SAM: You have any pictures?

LEON: No.

[*There is an awkward moment.*]

SAM: So, how did you find me? I mean, there's gotta be a couple hundred thousand Buddhaheads in the States.

LEON: It wasn't easy. I started with the name on the blanket. But every S. Yamamoto that I could find, was not you. I went through the Army files and found all the Yamamotos who served with the 442. There were 68 Yamamotos. I wanted to narrow it down to those who liberated Dachau but the Army gave me no cooperation. So on my own I found out more about the 442. On a hunch I started looking for Yamamotos who have been given medals for their bravery. I didn't have to look far. Under the Silver Star Medal of Gallantry were two Yamamotos. One had died in action, and the other was from Hawai'i. I called and was told that Kiyoshi had moved to San Francisco. [*Pause.*] It took six more months to develop my little "dibbuky" scheme. To get clearance for that office, two bottles of the colonel's favorite single malt scotch. A former member of the Red Bull Division helped me secure your back records. [LEON *smiles.*] You should have seen the look on your face when you walked through the door. I thought I was nervous. Admit it, you were frightened. I felt like Broderick Crawford stalking my prey.

SAM: I haven't heard from the Army in ten years, I just thought . . .

LEON: What?

SAM: We got a lot of medals.

LEON: But the Silver Star . . .

SAM: The war's over. It's not something . . . I like to talk about.

LEON: Why?

SAM: Take Dachau. Nobody wanted to believe that we had helped to liberate a concentration camp in Germany while our families were being held in camps back home. Some guys were ordered not to talk about it. Some guys were afraid to because we had no orders to open the gates. Some guys were afraid to because we had no orders to give out food. The rations were for U.S. G.I.s. We were also part of a big push moving the Germans out. Other U.S. battalions opened up other compounds at Dachau. Nobody wanted to believe that the 522nd had done the same.

LEON: "Der grester vaytog iz der vos men can im far andereh nicht arroysogn." [*Translating.*] "The greatest pain is the one you can't tell others about." [*Pulls out a small wrapped box, hands it to* SAM.] Samuel, I believe when someone does you a favor, you have to return it.

[SAM *looks at the present and then pushes the box back to* LEON.]

SAM: Yeah, but where I come from, when someone gives you a gift you have to give them something back. I got nothing for you.

[LEON *pushes the box back to* SAM.]

LEON: You've already given me enough.

[SAM *opens the box. He holds up a silver medallion on a chain.*]

LEON: [*Cont'd.*] This is a mezuzah.

SAM: Mezuzah?

LEON: Ya, mezuzah. It contains . . . ah . . . the "Shma" — the heart and soul of the teachings of Moses and what he brought to my people.

SAM: Fits in here? [*They laugh.*]

LEON: And now I will perform for you.

SAM: What?

[LEON *stands on a chair and begins to chant to the crowd.*]

LEON: "Va-y-mair ado-shem el moshe..."

SAM: Leon, what are you doing?!

[LEON *continues to chant and daven for* SAM; SAM *looks around the cafe and is getting embarrassed.*]

SAM: [*Cont'd.*] Leon! People are staring at us!

[*Lights fade to black.*]

SCENE 4

The year is 1959. We are at SAM's *house. Lights fade up on* SAM *and* LEON *facing off in Sumo wrestling positions.* LEON *charges at* SAM *head first;* SAM *sidesteps and deflects* LEON's *energy, throwing him out of the imaginary ring. They both laugh.*

LEON: Wonderful. Samu?

SAM: No, Sumo. Okay, what's this all about?

LEON: I was standing on the street and this parade was coming at me. In the center of the parade there was this beautiful woman. I thought it was Ruby. She looked exactly like her. She was on this float and, and, and she just floated by.

SAM: Hey, how come you haven't called any of the women Ruby lined up for you.

LEON: I've... been too busy.

SAM: They won't wait forever, you know.

LEON: I wanted to be up there on that float with her and before I knew it I was following. The parade stopped in the middle of the street where there were all these booths and exhibits.

SAM: Cherry Blossom Festival.

LEON: The air was filled with this sweet syrupy smell... and...

SAM: Teriyaki chicken.

LEON: ... and as I walked along thousands of different flowers...

SAM: Ikebana.

LEON: ... it smelled like the perfume counter at Macy's. It was spectacular, Sam; I was surrounded by all these families. I followed these two little kids to this one game where they played basketball. The prize was a little Japanese wooden doll.

SAM: Kokeshi doll.

LEON: An American game with a Japanese prize. It's wonderful. These precious children, so excited about who they are. It was at this point that I went into the church and saw the Sumo match. [LEON *gets up and motions* SAM *to stand.*] Show me another move. It was so incredible because it was so simple.

SAM: I can't show you simple.

LEON: Yes, you can. Come on.

SAM: Sumo is a tradition. It is a lifelong commitment. If you really want to learn something, I can teach you judo.

LEON: Judo? Great! Teach me.

SAM: Well, it takes a lot of time and practice.

LEON: I understand that, Sam. Everything takes time but you have to start somewhere. Show me a move. Teach me a move.

[SAM *grabs* LEON *and throws him to the floor.*]

LEON: [*Cont'd.*] What's that? That's not Sumo. Where's the facing off? The distance? The positioning? The focusing? The ritual?

SAM: Judo has lots of ritual.

LEON: Not like Sumo.

SAM: What are you, an expert now? Look, I know they're different but what I'm saying is that judo might be easier for you to learn than Sumo. It's like baseball or football.

LEON: What do you mean?

SAM: Judo, karate, kendo, back in Hawai'i, it's part of the normal school day. They're sports.

LEON: You hit a ball with a stick, that's one thing. You throw somebody around, that's another thing. But being put in a 12 foot circle, using your strength, your intellect to force your opponent out, I'm sorry, there is no comparison.

SAM: Look, you don't know what you're talking about.

LEON: The concentration it takes. The anticipation. These two men, there was nothing else on their minds. It was so . . . pure! Does judo or karate have that?

SAM: Sure they do. All martial arts have a spiritual side.

LEON: It's the gestalt! The ritual of everything. Come on, show me another move.

SAM: Alright.

[LEON *assumes a Sumo position.*]

SAM: [*Cont'd.*] No. No Sumo. We're going to try something else. Just stand normally. [SAM *assumes a karate stance.*] Now, I want you to concentrate on my face. You have to focus. I want you to clear your mind and think only of my face. When you feel the time is right and you are truly ready, hit me.

[LEON *begins to take a swing at* SAM, *then stops.*]

LEON: I can't . . .

[LEON *laughs nervously.* SAM *doesn't move.* LEON *positions himself again, then swings.* SAM *deflects it and immediately returns to his stance.*]

LEON: Amazing.

[LEON *throws a punch.* SAM *deflects and throws a series of blows to* LEON'S *body and face but never touches him.*]

LEON: This is wonderful! [*Steadies himself, focuses, remains very still, trying to mirror* SAM.] You are a spiritual man, Samuel.

SAM: Judo, karate, kendo, aikido, are spiritual.

[*They both move, circling each other.*]

SAM: [*Cont'd.*] They represent a way of life.

LEON: That's it! Life is a ritual to you. Yes, I understand.

SAM: Each form has a discipline to it.

LEON: Discipline, yes.

[LEON *throws a punch and* SAM *blocks and parries, hitting* LEON *in the chest.*]

LEON: [*Cont'd.*] Ow!

SAM: Are you okay, Leon?

LEON: Your eyes, where were you looking?

[SAM *touches the point below his chest and above his abdomen.*]

SAM: At your ki. Your center of energy.

LEON: That's easy to remember. Ki, just like your name, Kiyoshi.

[*They continue circling.*]

LEON: [*Cont'd.*] You can't learn this in school.

[SAM *circles in silence.*]

LEON: [*Cont'd.*] You have totally embraced the ways of your people in your everyday life. It's beautiful. I love it. It is like Judaism. Look all around you. Your home. It's so . . . neat. Everything has its . . . perfect place.

SAM: That's because of Ruby.

LEON: No, it's not. It's you. When I had dinner here the other night, you lit incense in front of those pictures. Then you put out some food and rang a little gong. It was for relatives that passed away, yes?

SAM: You like that, huh? Hit me.

LEON: You are so . . . Japanese.

SAM: No I'm not, hit me.

LEON: Okay, ki. The energy. I'm feeling connected, I'm feeling very connected. I want you to teach me everything. I want to feel what you feel.

SAM: You want to know how I feel? Hit me!

LEON: To truly know a man, you must first understand his culture.

SAM: Will you just stop talking and hit me?

[LEON *hesitates, then throws a punch at* SAM. SAM *grabs* LEON *by the wrist and forces him to his knees.* LEON *is getting a little upset and frustrated.*]

LEON: Yes. That's very good, I . . . alright . . . alright!

[SAM *releases* LEON.]

SAM: End of lesson.

[LEON *suddenly attacks* SAM. SAM *quickly counters, pinning* LEON *to the ground by the throat. He violently raises his fist and is about to strike* LEON *but stops himself.* LEON *curls up in a fetal position, responding to war memories more than* SAM's *actions.*]

LEON: Nein . . . das is nicht mein . . . du nem es . . . bitte. ("No . . . this is not mine . . . you take it . . . please.")

SAM: You alright, Leon? I'm sorry. I just reacted. Leon?

[LEON *sits up.*]

LEON: We had a Cherry Blossom Festival, Sam. In my village father would lead us in a hora, a circle dance under the new moon. Everyone would stand, hold hands and dance; laughter and singing, always laughter and singing. Because she was so tiny, my sister Rivki hung between David my brother and me and would sweetly swing like a little porcelain bell. We were connected, together as one. I could feel the heat of our hands as we danced, the energy of our connection. We danced and danced. Father would blow the Shofar, the ram's horn, welcoming in our New Year. Mame would tuck us into bed and tell us stories about the family. She would lean over and whisper in my ear, "The oldest child has the responsibility to pass these stories on, promise me." She would blow out the candles and sing to us our favorite song, the Alef-Base. We lay in bed, eyes wide open, unable to sleep, waiting for the morning's celebration. It was ours, Sam, that night, year after year, just ours. It's as if they are all here, tonight, still alive... [Points to his center of energy.]... right here.

[SAM gets up and crosses to LEON. SAM holds out his hands and helps LEON up. SAM resumes the karate stance.]

SAM: One more time. Only now, I'm going to hit you...and you block.

LEON: Okay.

SAM: You have to go through Hell to get to Heaven, Leon.

[LEON eagerly assumes the karate stance.]

SAM: [Cont'd.] Only no more talking. Clouds the mind.

[They circle each other with smiles on their faces.]

LEON: [Whispering.] What you are doing, Samuel, is binding me to your community. Cultures create rituals in order to keep the community together...

[SAM puts his finger to his lips.]

SAM: Ssssh.

SCENE 5

The year is 1963. It's late in the evening. We are at LEON'S house. Sound fades in with the swearing in of Lyndon Baines Johnson as President of the United States, other events surrounding the assassination, and the country's reaction. This plays under and throughout the scene. Lights fade up on LEON'S living room. LEON cleans a pistol as he watches the news of the funeral. SAM enters the scene but remains outside LEON'S door.

SAM: Leon? Leon, let me in.

LEON: My chest is about to explode!

SAM: Open the door!

LEON: My heart is breaking!

SAM: Are you sick, Leon? You need a doctor?

LEON: They killed Kennedy, Sam. They let him die.

SAM: Other presidents have been killed. It was just some nut case.

LEON: So was Hitler.

SAM: Open the door.

LEON: [*Ignores* SAM.] He was a Catholic, Sam.

SAM: What are you talking about?

LEON: Don't you see? He was different. And look what they did to him.

SAM: C'mon, this doesn't have a thing to do with his religion.

LEON: Congratulate me, Sam. I have it all figured out, the way to make it in America. It's a beautiful plan. You come to this country; they take you in. You don't speak their language; they teach it to you. You don't know the rules; they bend them for you. You believe in a different God; they build you a church. You work hard for them; they take care of you. You make it to the top; and then they kill you. Whenever you're different, they kill you.

SAM: You're taking this way too far. One man killed him, not the entire country.

LEON: Someone had to pull the trigger. Whenever you are different, they will kill you. The most dangerous evil is the one that convinces us it does not exist. I hate being stupid! Thirty years ago, they lulled us to sleep, Sam. We shut our eyes and refused to see. I didn't think it could happen again. You can be walking down the street and all of a sudden . . . boom. Don't you see, the lunatics are running the asylum! Nero is fiddling! Wake up, it's over!

SAM: Leon, it's cold out here.

LEON: Go away! [*Pause.*] When I first got to Israel. I was so desperate to find someone. Her name was Chia, she was beautiful, shining black eyes. A soldier, every Monday morning she would leave our kibbutz to patrol the Golan. One Wednesday night she never came back. Go away! As soon as I get close to you, you'll die. [*Pause.*] It's a disease. The world is diseased. Texas is diseased. [*Pause.*]

SAM: Texas isn't so bad, Leon. I actually passed through there on my way to basic training in Mississippi. You know they made us keep the shades down on the trains because they didn't want anyone peeking in and seeing the Jap cargo. It was the first time I had ever witnessed prejudice. The further south we went the more clearcut the lines were. They had "white" and "colored" drinking fountains and toilets. We didn't know where to sit on the bus, up front with the Caucasian guys or in the back with the colored guys. We decided to sit in the back. They got pissed at us, told us to go sit in the front. Whenever we went into town, we got into beefs with the locals or other G.I.s. They hated us. Used to call us monkeys, or Tojo's boys. The meanest G.I.s were the Texans. You just had to "ganbare." Suck in your gut and show no fear. You know what I mean, Leon?

LEON: Yes.

SAM: So, one day after we got shipped overseas, we got orders to rescue this Lost Battalion. They were trapped on a hill behind enemy lines two miles east of Biffontaine. They were considered "doomed." Days had gone by and nobody could get them out. So, they gave the mission to the 442. It was six days and nights of the worst fighting I had ever been in. When we reached the hill, Colonel Pursall said, "Our orders are to fix bayonets." It was suicide. The Germans threw everything at us. Guys were dropping on both sides of me. We lost so many men . . . but we finally reached the top. The guys we rescued were starving, ammo was so low, they felt they wouldn't have lasted another day. They were scared. When they saw it was American G.I.s and not Germans coming over the hill, they rushed up and started hugging us. Tears were coming out of their eyes. The Lost Battalion we saved . . . was from Texas. "Shikata ganai," live for the future, you can't change the past. Did you know that to this day, every year, the Texas battalion invites the whole 442nd . . . whoever is still alive . . . they invite us all to Texas for a big barbecue and to celebrate that day. So, you see, Leon, ganbare. Texas isn't so bad, shikata ganai.

LEON: I don't understand what's going on, Sam.

SAM: Nobody does.

[SAM *holds out his hand.* LEON *gives* SAM *the gun. Lights fade to black.*]

SCENE 6

The year is 1967. We are at SAM'S *house. Sound fades in with a children's party and laughter. Lights fade up on* LEON. SAM *enters with a sake bottle and cups.*

SAM: What are you doing out here? The party's inside. You want some more cake?

LEON: I've already had two pieces.

SAM: How about some more sake? You can never have enough sake. Ruby just heated it up.

LEON: Ahzisi punim.

SAM: I love that woman. [SAM *kisses his fingers like a French chef. He pours them a drink, they toast, then drink.*] What a gal!

[LEON *smiles weakly.*]

SAM: [*Cont'd.*] So, how'd you like my son's bar mitzvah?

LEON: Schmooks, it was a lovely . . . ceremony.

SAM: This was a great idea of yours, Leon. Did you see the look on Steven's face when he opened up the box and took out the BB gun?

LEON: I really think the BB gun was a little too much.

SAM: Or when I put the beanie on his head? I know it didn't fit quite right, but I didn't know what size to get.

LEON: Schmookie, size doesn't matter.

SAM: I know, he didn't read any passages in Jewish.

LEON: It's Hebrew.

SAM: But the haiku poem. That should count for something, right?

LEON: I didn't understand it.

SAM: Okay, I know it wasn't a real Jewish bar mitzvah, but . . .

LEON: Schmookie, it was a wonderful ceremony.

SAM: . . . but when you first told me about this way of . . . I just thought . . . that Steven might . . . what I mean is . . . I don't know . . . here, we don't have anything like it. In Japan, you're welcomed into the community. In America, because we're Japanese, we're not embraced as men. My father, he was a real tiger. He'd bite my head off if I rubbed him the wrong way. [*Pours himself some sake.*] He was picked up as an undesirable eleven days after Japan bombed Hawai'i and taken to this prison in Corpus Christi because he was a kendo master. They questioned him for nearly two years but he refused to answer. Didn't matter, he couldn't speak English. [*Downs his glass of sake.*] His spirit was tempered steel. But over the years, he could never talk to me about what they did to him. I had to learn on my own to be a man in America. You got to fight harder, work harder. I don't want Steven to go through what I did. I want to be there for him. You know what I mean?

LEON: I understand.

SAM: Hey, wasn't that cute when he said, "Thank you for the savings bond, Uncle Leon."

[LEON *doesn't respond.*]

Come on, let's go inside.

LEON: I've got to say goodbye, Sam.

SAM: What?

LEON: We're at war.

SAM: Vietnam?

LEON: Israel was invaded yesterday.

SAM: Oh, no.

LEON: They have planes leaving tonight. You know, Sam, it's been seventeen years since I looked up at the mountain city of Safat, the home of the Kabbalah.

SAM: The Kabbalah?

LEON: The Jewish mystics. Every Friday I would stand in the middle of town. The narrow streets. The sandstone buildings. Sam, the smell of challah, the Sabbath bread, the wines. I'd peek into windows as they took out their best silverware. I was back in the ghetto, but here there were no boundaries. People came and went as they pleased. A young man in a long black coat stopped and stared at me. He smiled and said, "You are one." I didn't understand. As he walked away, Sam, I could feel his peace, his faith. I was surrounded by the sense of possibility. Israel is our homeland. It must be protected.

SAM: You're an American now. This is your home.

LEON: I'm also a Jew.

SAM: [*Pause.*] You're going as a doctor, right?

LEON: Yes, but . . .

SAM: What is it, Leon? What's the matter?

LEON: Sam, I . . . I can't face the bloodshed. [*Pause.*]

SAM: You know what today stands for? You told me, bar mitzvah means, "son of a good deed." You told me, the deed of becoming a man is accepting responsibility to his community.

LEON: [*Smiles.*] This was a wonderful ceremony, Sam.

[SAM *turns to leave, obviously disappointed.* LEON *stops him.*]

The beanie doesn't matter. The music, the gifts, it all doesn't matter. All the bar mitzvahs that I have attended had no father who loved his son as much as I have seen in this home. It was a proud moment, yes?

SAM: [*Smiles.*] Yes, it was.

LEON: I love you, Schmooks. [LEON *hugs* SAM.]

SAM: I...I...

[SAM *can't get out the words.* LEON *smiles, gives* SAM *the sake cup, and salutes.*]

LEON: Goodbye.

[SAM *watches* LEON *exit.*]

SAM: Hurry back home, OK, soldier.

[*Lights fade to black.*]

SCENE 7

The year is 1973. We are at LEON'S *house. Lights fade up on* LEON *who is addressing a dinner table full of guests going through the celebration of Passover.*

LEON: Shalom, my friends. Shalom. I welcome you all, particularly Sam Yamamoto and his wife, Ruby. In all of our years of friendship this is the first Passover seder Sam has attended. It is a very special night. [*Pause.*] Tonight is a time to relax, drink some wine, and share each other's company. [*Imitates Yul Brynner in "The Ten Commandments."*] "Moses, Moses, Moses."

SAM: That's Yul Brynner. [*They laugh.*]

LEON: My father, Mortechai, was the first to teach me about Moses. He was a Chazan...a cantor. He would chant the services in synagogue and sing them in his heart. He taught me the basic principle of Judaism, the "Shma." "Shma Yisroel Adonai Elohainu Adonai Echad," "Here O Israel The Lord Our God, The Lord Is One." Oneness, the oneness of life, of all life.

[*Lights crossfade to* SAM *as he turns out from his seat, his mind drifts from* LEON'S *speech.*]

SAM: April, 1945. Germans on the retreat. SS already pulled out.

Tremendous push, taking towns, villages. What's this? Some kind of camp. Barbed wire. Guard towers. Dachau. Shoot off the lock. Open the gates. Bodies on the ground, moving. Hundreds of them. Secure the perimeter. Ay, he get one pulse. Got to get him to dry ground. Remember, prisoners choking to death. Need to feed him and give him some water. He's so helpless looking up, waiting to be fed. I never felt so scared. That feeling came over me one other time, the very first moment I held my newborn son.

[*Lights crossfade to* LEON *continuing his Passover speech.*]

LEON: Pesach is on the first full moon of Spring, the renewal and rebirth of the Earth. It is the story of Moses and our exodus from Egypt. We were slaves in Egypt, the first group of slaves in history to wage a successful struggle for freedom. We are not the last. People are struggling for freedom everywhere, Cambodia, South Africa, Ireland, even here in our own backyards. Egypt in Hebrew is Mitzrayim from the word Tzar. It means narrow and inhibited.

[*Lights crossfade to* SAM *as his memory continues.*]

SAM: Listen, they are not the enemy. We just gotta keep our heads. We been through worse than this. We just got to stick together and walk out of here. We're a unit. We're one. Remember, show no fear.

[*Lights crossfade to* LEON.]

LEON: What have we learned since then? What have we learned since the last war? I have learned that Arabs and Jews are cousins. We both call Abraham our father. Yet only last summer in Munich we witnessed the senseless killing of the Israeli athletes by terrorists. To see death feeding off of life. Our family is being destroyed.

[*Lights crossfade to* SAM.]

SAM: Steven was three years old. At two o'clock in the morning I found him sitting in the hallway, sobbing. He looked up at me: "What's going to happen to us when we die? What's going to happen to you and Mom and Emerald?" "No worry, we going meet up in a better place. Go say one prayer, special one for the family." Imagine, three years old, carrying all that weight.

[*Lights crossfade to* LEON.]

LEON: I cannot wait for the next war. Oneness, the oneness of life. This story of redemption, the story of Moses, Moses the great, my guiding teaching, my philosophical anchor, is an example, no, it is proof that the world can be changed.

[*Lights crossfade to* SAM.]

SAM: Remember how we used to take trips back to Hawai'i during the summer. It's good Steven and Emerald got to know who their grandparents were. That old Japanese "furo" downstairs in the back was a great bathtub. You could sit in it up to your neck. The room was dark and steamy but the water was nice and hot. Steven hated to go down there because of the cockroaches, toads and lizards. The fear in his eyes would search the floor for a refuge. I would pick him up and hold him in my arms under the shower and then take him into the furo with me. Once he got in, his fears would subside, and he would play with his boats.

[*Lights crossfade to* LEON *and* SAM.]

LEON: When the Pharaoh refused to free the Jews from bondage, God sent ten plagues to Egypt. The harshest punishment he levied on the Egyptians was in retaliation to their killing the firstborn sons of the Jews.

SAM: Steven came up to me and showed me the letter from the draft board.

LEON: God sent the Angel of Death on the first full moon of spring into the houses of all Egyptians to kill their firstborn sons.

SAM: He had that same look of fear.

LEON: God instructed Moses to paint lamb's blood above the doors of all Jewish homes.

SAM: He asked me what he should do.

LEON: The Angel of Death would "pass over" these homes sparing the lives of their firstborn sons.

SAM: I told him, "Thirty years ago, I volunteered to fight against Germany, Italy and Japan. Whoever was an enemy of our country."

LEON: Tonight as we recite the ten plagues, we dip the end of a finger into our wine cups and cast a drop of wine onto our plates for each plague.

SAM: "There is a part of the bushido in all of us that we must observe."

LEON: In doing so, we diminish our own pleasure and remember to have compassion even for our enemies.

SAM: "It is our code of honor."

LEON: Dam, blood . . .

SAM: Why is it that we never learn? Huh, Leon?

LEON: Tsfardeya, frogs . . .

SAM: I taught him everything I could to make sure that he would survive in this world.

LEON: Kinim, vermin . . .

SAM: Ruby won't talk to me.

LEON: Arov, beasts . . .

SAM: She says I shouldn't have let him go.

LEON: Dever, cattle disease . . .

SAM: She says I should have stopped him, maybe sent him away.

LEON: Sh'khlin, boils . . .

SAM: His sister, Emerald, just walks into his room, lays down on his bed and cries.

LEON: Barad, hail . . .

SAM: His body comes back from Saigon tomorrow.

LEON: Arbeh, locusts . . .

SAM: They're going to give me a check and the American flag.

LEON: Khoshekh, darkness . . .

SAM: I don't think I can go down there myself.

LEON: Makat b'khorot, slaying of the firstborn . . .

SAM: Will you go with me, Leon? Pray for him.

[*Lights crossfade as* SAM *and* LEON *move downstage. They stand over Steven's coffin. We hear a Buddhist gong. Incense is lit.* SAM, *holding a "juzu," silently prays. Then* LEON, *wrapped in a talis, begins reciting a special Jewish prayer for the dead, The Mourner's Kaddish.*]

LEON: "Yisgadal ve-yiskadash sh'mey rabbo, be'ol'mo deevrochirooset, ve'yamlich malchoosey be'chayeychown u'vyownmeychown u'vchayey de'chol baiss yisroale, ba'agolo uvisman koreev ve'imroo omaine."

[*Lights fade to black.*]

ACT II

SCENE 1

The year is 1974. It's late in the evening. We are at SAM'S *house. Sound fades in with big band music in the background. Lights fade up on* SAM, *dressed in a robe sitting in his living room.* SAM *is having a dream.*

SAM: That's a pretty dress you have on. But not as pretty as . . . you. Ay, where you going? Come on, no make like that, huh. I been watching you all night. I can't take my eyes off of you. You like dance? [SAM *begins to dance with an imaginary Ruby.*] Your name is . . . Ruby. That's my favorite color. Just joking, eh. [*Pause.*] I knew I could make you laugh. [SAM *laughs. He holds Ruby closer as they dance. He pulls his right arm back and looks at it. He sees it is covered with blood. He screams and looks at Ruby, who has turned into a bloody body.*] What's this? Blood!

[*We hear taiko drums, then cannon fire.* SAM *is handcuffed from behind and pulled up. We hear police sirens.*]

SAM: [*Cont'd.*] Get these handcuffs off of me! Look, I'm a sergeant! What do you think? Of course this is my uniform! Goddamn it, let me go!

[SAM *is tossed to the ground before a* KUROKO.]

SAM: [*Cont'd.*] Captain, sir . . . it wasn't our fault.

[KUROKO *turns to exit.*]

SAM: [*Cont'd.*] But, sir, they . . .

[KUROKO *transforms into* SAM'S *father, kneels.* SAM *kneels before him.*]

SAM: [*Cont'd.*] Oto-san. Father. Yamenakatta.

[KUROKO *slaps,* SAM *reacts.* KUROKO *exits.*]

SAM: [*Cont'd.*] I didn't quit.

[*We hear desert winds as lights shift. His dream takes him to the internment camp in Tule Lake, California.*]

SAM: [*Cont'd.*] Auntie Yuki, are you packed? Let's go. They got a train waiting to take you home. You can leave here. Tule Lake is just a bad dream. [SAM *looks at the gates.*] Who's that by the fence? He's too close. The guards are going to shoot him. [*We hear* LEON *from offstage.*]

LEON: Schmooks.

SAM: Leon? Oh my God, it's Leon! They're going to shoot Leon! I've got to save him.

[SAM *rushes up and uses his body to shield* LEON. SAM *turns to face the guards.*]

SAM: [*Cont'd.*] Don't shoot! American, don't shoot!

[*We hear a loud gunshot. Gates open and* KUROKOS *spill out as dead bodies.* SAM *is now in a battlefield.*]

My God, look at all the bodies. [*Pause.*] Check 'em, see who's alive. This one's gone. The back of his head's blown off. I'll check his tags. [*Pause.*] This guy's name is . . . Steven . . . Yamamoto. It can't be! Ruby! Ruby, where are you? It's Steven! Come and take him home.

LEON: [*Entering.*] Schmooks.

SAM: Don't worry. They're going to fix you up. Medic! Medic! Hurry, he's not breathing! Oh God, look at all the blood. Gotta stop the bleeding. [SAM *frantically attempts to mop up blood with his jacket.*] Gotta stop the bleeding. Don't worry, Steven, we're going to get help.

[LEON *begins to wake* SAM *from his dream.*]

LEON: Schmooks.

SAM: What are you standing around for? He's dying.

LEON: He's dead, Sam.

SAM: No! You're a doctor, help him!

LEON: Sam . . . [LEON *shakes* SAM.] Sam!

[SAM *slowly comes back to reality.*]

SAM: Leon? Where's Ruby?

LEON: She and Emerald are waiting in the bedroom. Ruby called and said this was your worst one yet.

SAM: Why didn't you help Steven? You loved him, didn't you?

LEON: Deeply, like my own son.

SAM: I couldn't save him. He was right there in my arms. Ruby was with me. [*Pause.*] I gave away my son, Leon.

[LEON *takes* SAM'S *pulse, then gently puts his arm down.*]

SAM: [*Cont'd.*] I buried all my friends from the 422. That's why I moved here to the mainland. I couldn't stay there with their ghosts. They came to see me every night, and I wanted to go with them.

LEON: It's not your time, Sam.

SAM: When I first came over, I went to visit my relatives in Stockton.

Ruby and I didn't know anybody else. I couldn't look them in the eye. Everything was taken from them during the war. Everything.

LEON: Sam, many people suffered and lost.

SAM: I couldn't save my buddies. I couldn't help my family. What else do I have to give? I have nothing left.

LEON: You have Ruby and Emerald.

SAM: They hate me.

LEON: [*Gently.*] One day an SS officer said to me, "If you ever survive, no one will believe you. No one will want to believe what has happened here in Dachau." He laughed and continued, "So we have already won." We are survivors, Sam. We're alive to make sure the ghosts don't die a silent death. They need our voice.

SAM: I miss him, Leon.

LEON: Let's get you to bed.

[*Lights fade to black.*]

SCENE 2

It is July 4, 1976. We are at a downtown street corner. Sound fades in with fireworks and street noise in the background. Lights fade up on SAM *and* LEON.

LEON: No, I don't want to eat there.

SAM: Why not?

LEON: It's too . . . American.

SAM: It's a great restaurant.

LEON: I want to eat . . . sushi.

SAM: What? Did you say sushi?

LEON: Yeah. Isn't that how you pronounce it?

SAM: You want to eat sushi on July 4, 1976, the bicentennial of our country?

LEON: Yes. Let's pick up Ruby and Emerald and go to a sushi place.

SAM: Sushi bar.

LEON: Great. I need a drink. All this backslapping has given me a headache.

SAM: Ruby wants prime rib. And Emerald doesn't eat sushi. She doesn't like it.

LEON: She doesn't like fish?

SAM: Do you even know what sushi is?

LEON: Yeah, it's fish, and . . . and . . . rice . . . and it's Japanese.

SAM: It's raw. It's uncooked. It's every kind of sea creature you can think of.

LEON: Sounds great. Let's go.

SAM: I was counting on . . . some leg of lamb tonight. Tell you what, my treat. You can have some fried chicken, something American. Tonight's a celebration.

LEON: Let's be more exotic. Since we're . . . celebrating.

SAM: Yes, but it's an American celebration.

LEON: Yes, but America is made up of different exotic kinds of people.

SAM: Yes, but this exotic person wants leg of lamb.

LEON: I know, let's go to a Cuban restaurant. I know a great place. You can get lamb at a Cuban restaurant.

SAM: Cuban? On the fourth of July? I want some good old American home-cooked food.

LEON: Home-cooked food. Did you ever cook sushi in your home?

SAM: You don't cook sushi. I told you, it's raw. You prepare it.

LEON: Well, did you ever prepare sushi in your home?

SAM: Sure, lots of times.

LEON: So for you, sushi could be home-cooked food, right? For a Cuban American, Cuban food could be home-cooked food, right? So you tell me what is good old American home-cooked food?

SAM: I don't know. What I do know is that Ruby wants prime rib. The car is this way. [SAM *starts to cross stage left.*]

LEON: Tell you what. Italian.

[SAM *turns and looks back at* LEON.]

They discovered America, right?

SAM: What do you know about America?

LEON: What's there to know?

SAM: Are you an American?

LEON: Last time I checked my papers.

SAM: Aha. See, you need papers. I was born here.

LEON: Does that mean we have to eat lamb legs?

SAM: Don't you see that this goes deeper than food.

LEON: Nothing is deeper than food.

SAM: Listen to me. I'm trying to be serious. People judge me by what I do . . . who I am . . . how I look . . .

LEON: But that's normal.

SAM: No, it's not normal.

LEON: We can't help the way we look or sound or where we were born.

SAM: Look at the two of us. Because you're white, you're treated like you were born here. I'm the one who was born here, but I'm treated like a foreigner.

LEON: I agree with you, Sam, that's wrong. But the answer is not to play the game like everyone else.

SAM: But I don't have that choice. I can't help being different. You can. Those two people today from Ohio who asked you for directions, you, not me, because you're white, they thought you were an American. And then after you opened your mouth, they thought you were German.

LEON: Can you believe that? Of all countries, Germany.

SAM: They were afraid to talk to me, afraid I wouldn't understand them. That's what I mean, Leon.

LEON: I know what you mean, Sam, but I'm not white.

SAM: Is this one of your Talmudic riddles?

LEON: Seriously. I get treated differently all the time. This is a Christian country. Take any holiday. . . Christmas. If you don't celebrate Christmas, you might as well be from another planet.

SAM: Christmas isn't really religious anymore. It's more about shopping and Santa Claus.

LEON: Exactly. St. Nicholas. How many Chanukah carols do you know?

SAM: What about Easter? OK, never mind, that's about Jesus.

LEON: Hmm . . . all the best Christmas carols were written by Jews.

SAM: I got one . . . Halloween.

LEON: All Hallows Eve. It originated as the night of revelry before All Saints' Day.

SAM: Forget it. You're nuts.

LEON: No, I'm a Jew. So I know.

SAM: You don't know. You think you know everything but you don't.

LEON: Let's go find Ruby and Emerald.

SAM: If you know so much, why the hell did you tell Steven he could dodge the draft?

LEON: What?

SAM: You thought I didn't know?

LEON: No, I just . . . frankly, it never occurred to me, we just . . .

SAM: Never occurred . . . ? How could you even think that he should be part of a protest march! Don't you see how much harder that would have made life for him? You didn't even think before telling my son he shouldn't join the Army! Didn't you see he would be not only be taking a stand against his country, but doing it with this Japanese face?

LEON: Sam, have you been sitting on this for all these years? I don't think there's any point to . . .

SAM: That's easy to say now.

LEON: He asked for my opinion.

SAM: He was scared. Like any man would be. Did you help him be brave? No, you shot off your mouth with your crazy ideas!

LEON: It was an unjust war. We had no respect for who they were.

SAM: Respect? What about when they brought his coffin off the plane?

LEON: That was horrible, I agree, I . . .

SAM: Those protesters were spitting on it!

LEON: Don't forget, I was a soldier too, Sam. I was ashamed. Sam, did you know how Steven felt about the war?

SAM: Of course I did. We sat down, had a good long talk.

LEON: He felt the same way I did.

SAM: That's insane.

LEON: Sam, it's true.

SAM: You can say that now, since he's not here to . . .

LEON: But in the end, he respected you more. That's why he went into the Army. He went for you.

SAM: He went because I raised him to do his duty to his country!

LEON: All right. That's enough.

SAM: What? You don't think this is his country?

LEON: Sam, you're twisting my words. I'm the last person in the world you should accuse of . . . of . . .

SAM: Of prejudice? Why? Because you know what it's like to be me?

LEON: Yes. I know what it's like to be hated.

SAM: I suppose you think you understand what it's like to be a black man, too?

LEON: Suffering is suffering, oppression is oppression.

SAM: That kind of attitude is . . . arrogant!

LEON: Sam, you are looking for a scapegoat. Which is the one thing I will not be, even for you!

SAM: I wish, just once, when we were together, you didn't treat me like your exotic friend!

LEON: I don't treat you like that!

SAM: Would you think it was so strange that I want to eat a steak on the Fourth of July if I were white?

LEON: When you look at me, my face, after all these years, am I your enemy? Sam, that is the very definition of racism!

SAM: This isn't about what happened to you in the war. This is about life in America. You're white and I'm not. And you can't understand. Look at this face! Steven and I are different than you! You don't know what it's like!

LEON: I don't know what it's like to be different? My family, my whole world was destroyed because I'm different!

[LEON *storms off.* SAM *watches* LEON *leave, then turns and walks off in the opposite direction. Lights fade to black.*]

SCENE 3

The year is 1980. We are at the Japantown Center. Lights fade up on

LEON, *who is in a conference room rehearsing his speech to the Japanese American Redress Committee.*

LEON: Thank you for inviting me here today. Since 1967, I have been lecturing to many different groups . . . no, too stiff. I have been speaking at various Jewish Centers around the country. Hatred and fear are . . . no.

[SAM *enters, then sees* LEON *and exits.* LEON *does not notice* SAM.]

LEON: [*Cont'd.*] It is a great honor to be able to speak to you, the Japanese American Redress Committee. No. I am honored that you have invited me here today. No.

[SAM *enters and stands behind* LEON.]

LEON: [*Cont'd.*] Thank you. There is a story of Heaven and Hell in the Talmud. Two great big rooms with identical banquet tables filled with mountains of food are surrounded by people with their hands tied to the arms of their chairs. In one room, the people are starving to death, unable to feed themselves. They are in Hell. In the other room there is laughter and rejoicing. The people are feeding each other. Let us work together to create a Heaven here on Earth.

SAM: It's Chinese . . . [LEON *turns and sees* SAM.]

LEON: How long have you been here?

SAM: Ruby brought me. She showed me your name in the Japanese paper. Pretty impressive. [*Pause.*] She wanted to come. She's sitting out in the auditorium. Her family was interned.

LEON: I didn't know.

SAM: The story you were telling. It's a Chinese tale. I heard it when we were kids.

LEON: You've heard this story?

SAM: Yeah, except I heard they were tied to their chairs and had chopsticks that were too long to feed themselves. So, you had to feed the person across the table from you. [*Pause.*] It's a beautiful story.

LEON: We all have stories, Sam.

SAM: Yeah, but nobody can tell them like you, huh?

LEON: How's Emerald?

SAM: She's good. She's grown up into a real lady. We go visit her when we can. How's your practice?

LEON: Fine.

SAM: That's good.

LEON: Sam, why don't you talk to the committee? It's great they asked the Jewish Federation for support but I believe they need to hear from their own, too.

SAM: I'm no talker.

LEON: Think of it like Passover. You'll be bearing witness by telling your story. And besides, it's easy if you imagine all those people in the audience wearing funny hats.

SAM: I can't.

LEON: Okay.

SAM: [*Looks at his watch.*] Leon . . .

LEON: [*Overlapping.*] Well, I'm on.

SAM: Good luck.

LEON: Chinese, huh?

SAM: Yeah. [*Pause.*] Leon?

LEON: Yes.

SAM: You mind if I watch from the side?

LEON: Be my guest.

SAM: Ruby already has a seat and I don't want to disturb anyone by walking in now.

LEON: Sure, Sam.

[*Lights crossfade to* LEON *as he takes his place in front of the Redress Committee.* SAM *peeks in from the shadows.*]

LEON: Thank you. I am honored that you have invited me here today. My name is Leon Ehrlich. I am a survivor of Dachau. There is a story of . . . of . . . Heaven and Hell . . . No. [*Pause.*] You have to go through Hell to get to Heaven. [*Turns to* SAM, *then back to the audience.*] The Germans had led us to an open field. We knew it was our last march. We were so weak we could not stand. I lay there for hours. I could only see white. I was buried under all this snow. The next thing I knew was that I was being rescued by an American soldier. A Japanese American soldier. He saved me. It was a basic act of human kindness. He has taught me what American prejudice is. He showed me that even when you risk your life for your country and lose your son for your country and have your family imprisoned by your country, there is no gratitude, no acceptance. Prejudice still remains. My teacher, my friend is here tonight. I want to introduce him to you. His name is Kiyoshi Yamamoto. It's been four years since I've seen him. His friends call him Sam.

[LEON *motions for* SAM *to step forward.* SAM *sheepishly joins* LEON *on the stage at the microphone.*]

SAM: Ah . . . ah . . .

LEON: [*Whispering.*] Sam . . .

[LEON *gestures to the top of his head: "funny hats."* SAM *turns back out to the audience.*]

SAM: I think what you're . . . I think what we're doing here is really important. Thank you. [SAM *quickly exits.*]

LEON: Um . . . thank you, Sam. I would like to read an excerpt from a diary written by a young boy in the camps during the war. [*Takes out a piece of paper and reads.*] "I wish I was home. I have none here. It gets so cold at night. The buildings we live in are just made of wood. The wind blows in through the windows and doors and it goes everywhere. I'm always cold. When I look out at the mountains all I really see are the barbed wire fences. I want to look past them, through them, but the guards point their rifles at me and keep me from getting too close. The wind blows right through the fence. It is the only thing that can escape. Will I have escape? Will I ever go home? I wish I was wind." George Masao Matsumoto. Manzanar, California. [*Puts away the letter.*] In my life I have heard the Holocaust never existed. I have heard that most people don't believe that America had internment camps. I believe that there are two types of anger. There is the anger which causes us to say things we do not mean, which comes from the darkest place in our own hearts.

[LEON *looks over at his friend,* SAM, *now back offstage, nods, then returns his attention to the audience.*]

And then, there is righteous anger, which battles the darkness to bring light to the world. In righteous anger, you and I are one. My humanity is bound up with your humanity. I am because you are. Thank you for inviting me. Domo arigato. Shalom.

[*Lights fade to black.*]

SCENE 4

The year is 1983. We are at LEON *office. Lights fade up on* LEON *giving* SAM *a physical evaluation for a job application.*

LEON: How's your health?

SAM: I'm fine.

LEON: How's your blood pressure?

SAM: It's fine. I'm in good shape.

LEON: What do you want me to put down?

SAM: Put down that I'm fine.

LEON: I'm going to have to ask you some questions.

SAM: That's what I'm here for. What question do you want to start with?

LEON: Okay. How have you been sleeping?

SAM: Fine, I get my eight hours. I go to bed early. I sleep pretty soundly. Ruby complains about my snoring.

LEON: What about your nightmares?

SAM: I don't get them as often as I used to. What's that got to do with my work?

LEON: You've had no nightmares since you were laid off?

SAM: No.

LEON: How do you feel about your employer?

SAM: I feel fine.

LEON: Schmooks, do you feel anything except "fine" about things? Every time I ask you a question, you say you feel fine.

SAM: Okay, how do I feel about my employer? Is that the question?

LEON: Your former employer, yes.

SAM: I still don't understand what that has got to do with anything. I'm applying for a new job with a different company with a new employer. All I need is a physical, for job clearance. Just help me fill out the form. Stop acting like a meshugenah.

LEON: Schmooks, why are you so defen . . . what's bothering you?

SAM: I know what defensive means, and you're making me feel that way by turning this into a chance to shrink my head.

LEON: Sorry. You're in my office. Force of habit, I guess.

SAM: Nothing personal, but I couldn't imagine going to a shrink.

LEON: You mean, professionally, I hope.

SAM: All that talk about how I feel. Who cares? Like on TV when the news reporter goes to interview the relatives of some poor victim, they always ask, "How do you feel?" What are they going to say, "I feel great"?

LEON: And you. . .you got laid off. So excuse me if I'm surprised when you say you feel fine.

SAM: That's a sneaky one, Leon.

LEON: That's why we get to charge by the hour. Just tell me this. . .how many people were laid off?

SAM: A few guys.

LEON: Were they as high up as you?

SAM: No.

LEON: [*Scans the medical form.*] How do you feel about working for another big corporation?

SAM: I have no problem with it.

LEON: They may have to lay off people, too.

SAM: I don't have any control over that. Besides, I think the economy is going to change. Are we finished?

LEON: Do you want us to be finished?

SAM: Yeah. I think I've had enough.

LEON: Good. Now you sit here.

SAM: Huh?

LEON: [*Gets up and motions to his chair.*] Sit here.

SAM: What are you doing? [SAM *goes to the chair,* LEON *lays down on the couch.*]

LEON: Now we talk about me.

SAM: Okay, how have you been sleeping?

[LEON *lets out a laugh.*]

SAM: [*Cont'd.*] What's so funny?

LEON: Last night, I slept not very well.

SAM: Are your lungs hurting?

[LEON *lets out another laugh.*]

SAM: [*Cont'd.*] What is it?

LEON: "Mah nishtarah ha lilah ha zeh . . ."

SAM: What are you doing?

LEON: Why is this night different from all other nights?

SAM: Which night?

LEON: How do you make empanadas?

SAM: Empanadas?

LEON: Isn't that an Argentinean dish?

SAM: I don't know.

LEON: I want to learn to make an Argentinean dish. I want to play Argentinean music. I want to learn Argentinean dances.

[LEON *gets up and begins to dance and hum an Argentinean song.*]

SAM: You're the one who needs a doctor.

LEON: It's time for me.

SAM: For what?

LEON: For her.

SAM: What, you found a woman? Is she a shiksa?

LEON: It's a mechiah. A gift from God.

SAM: You're in love with a mechiah from Argentina?

LEON: [*Shows* SAM *a photo.*] I found my mate. My Ruby. Her name is Eva. What a gal.

SAM: This is serious stuff.

LEON: When Eva is around, the world is never the same. Things become possible.

SAM: When do I get to meet her?

LEON: After I meet her parents.

SAM: Wait a minute. How old is Eva?

LEON: [*Laughing.*] Old enough.

SAM: Well, I hope so. What does this woman do for a living? Is she a citizen? Does she have a green card? She's an immigrant, right?

LEON: Schmooks, I'm an immigrant.

SAM: Oh yeah.

[*They laugh.*]

LEON: She's Jewish.

SAM: Great. When's the wedding?

LEON: The wedding?

SAM: Yeah.

LEON: I don't know.

SAM: Oh, you haven't asked her yet.

LEON: Her family hates me.

SAM: What?

LEON: For some reason and we're talking about a Jewish family, Sam, for some reason, I'm too American for them. You see, they hate Americans. And me, Leon Ehrlich, concentration camp survivor, all they see is my American passport. It's not enough that I speak Hebrew, it's not enough that I love their daughter. They don't know me, yet they hate me.

SAM: There's Jews in Argentina?

LEON: Of course, there are Jews everywhere. There, I'm "Yankee Doodle Dandy," here, I'm "Fiddler on the Roof." Jews hate Jews for not being the right kind of Jew. Can you believe it, Sam?

SAM: [*Aside.*] There's Jews in Argentina?

LEON: If you went down to Argentina to meet Eva's parents, didn't open your mouth or tell them who you were, I wager they would embrace you more than they embrace me.

SAM: What do you mean?

LEON: Look in the mirror.

SAM: What?

LEON: You're Japanese.

SAM: So, you want me to go down there?

LEON: What do I do? They won't let us get married.

SAM: You could . . . shack up with her.

LEON: She's old-fashioned. It's one of the things I love about her.

SAM: Okay. They won't approve the marriage. How did they end up in Argentina?

LEON: They've been there since before the war, from Russia, in the twenties.

SAM: Why do they hate Americans?

LEON: Because we've gone in there and tried to tell them what to do.

SAM: I'll tell you what you have to do. You just gotta go down there and meet them. As soon as they see you, they'll know you're as Jewish as they are. Just do one of your chants.

LEON: Eva's gone down there to speak with them. If she comes back, then we'll get married.

SAM: People are so goddamn stupid! This shit always happens. Why can't they just accept you for who you are?!

LEON: They fired you, right, Schmooks?

SAM: Huh?

LEON: Your work. They fired you.

SAM: No. [*Pause.*] I resigned.

LEON: Resigned? Why?

SAM: I felt that . . .

LEON: What?

SAM: I felt that they were not giving me my due.

LEON: What do you mean?

SAM: I've been with that company for almost fourteen years. I know what goes on in the payroll department. I see the figures. I saw the bonuses. They were pushing another controller up.

LEON: Surely, you talked to them.

SAM: I talked to them. I presented a pretty damn good case.

LEON: And?

SAM: They told me they were well aware of everything. They said they were pleased with my work. But they had other priorities. So I left.

LEON: It's because you're Japanese.

SAM: That's . . . that's not it.

LEON: You are a gifted CPA. There is no rational reason for them to treat you this way.

SAM: This country rewards people for how hard they work! That's the way it's supposed to run.

LEON: But you are the hardest working man I know.

SAM: He's got an M.B.A.

LEON: You've got years of experience. You should report this company!

SAM: No!

LEON: But they are racists! Can't you see that?

SAM: No!

[LEON *looks at the job application. He signs it and gives it to* SAM.]

LEON: I wish you more luck there at Mat-su-ha-ra Electronics.

[SAM *begins to leave again;* LEON *stops him.*]

Sam. If Eva . . . when Eva comes back, I want you to be my best man.

SAM: Oh . . . I'd be honored to be your best man.

[*They shake hands.* SAM *begins to leave again, then stops and turns back to* LEON.]

Do you think that everything I fought for . . . meant nothing?

LEON: No. What is it, Sam?

SAM: When I came home from Europe, I stopped off in New York City. It was my first time in the Big Apple. We had just left this kind of a "thank you" event given by the Japanese community. I had on my dress uniform with my medals on my chest. I was so proud because none of the old men and women had ever seen a Silver Star before. It was hanging right next to my Purple Hearts. [*Pause.*] I guess I was kind of a celebrity. [SAM *crosses downstage. Lights crossfade to a spot on* SAM, *now at the Redress hearings in Washington, D.C.*] My neck was sore from looking up at the skyscrapers. My buddies from the 422 and I got off the subway at midtown around 47th Street and Broadway, and walked into the best restaurant we could find. We hadn't had an American meal for nearly two years. We asked for a booth and were seated. I could just taste the big T-bone steak I was about to order. The waiter came over to our table with the restaurant manager. They told us we had to leave. They didn't serve Japs at their establishment. I couldn't believe what I was hearing. I couldn't even breathe. I looked around the restaurant at the other customers and you know what . . . they were laughing at us. My buddies looked at me wondering what to do. I had the highest rank at the table. A couple of people started throwing food from their plates yelling, "Remember Pearl Harbor!" I stood up and nodded to my men and we marched toward the door. Everyone we passed threw their drinks at us. Then a bunch of guys charged at us screaming, "Japs go home!" [*Clears his throat.*] The Police Department turned us over to the MPs. They charged us with being drunk and disorderly and instigating a public disturbance. We had put two guys in the hospital. They held us responsible for the property damage. It was the word of everyone in that restaurant against the six of us. The Army said we were a disgrace to the uniform. I told them since I was the ranking soldier I would take full responsibility. My commanding officer called me into his office. He was a man I knew and trusted. He told me the court wanted to set an example and was considering taking away my rank; they were talking full court martial proceedings; they were talking dishonorable discharge; but. . . if I resigned, all of the charges would be dropped. My record would be kept intact. [*Pause.*] The Army gave us a chance to prove ourselves when America was pointing the finger at our patriotism. The Army allowed us to be men. The Army was going to be my life. [*Recites from memory.*] "By direction of the President of the United States, for Gallantry, in connection with military operations against a hostile force, Sergeant Kiyoshi Yamamoto distinguished himself by heroic action." What they couldn't take were my medals. We weren't drunk. We just wanted a meal. We were so glad finally to be home. Senators, I love this country. I'm an American. You have to pass this reparations bill. You can't let this happen again. Thank you.

[*Lights fade to black.*]

SCENE 5

The year is 1985. We are at SAM's *house. Lights fade up on* SAM *and* LEON *seated at a table with two chairs.* LEON *places a box on the table.*

LEON: Open it.

SAM: Not another gift, Leon.

[SAM *shoves the box toward* LEON.]

LEON: It's a special occasion.

[LEON *gently slides the box back.*]

SAM: Every gift is a special occasion. I don't have anything for you. [SAM *shoves the box toward* LEON.]

LEON: Open it. [*Once again,* LEON *gently slides the box back.*]

SAM: If you keep this up, I'm going to go broke.

LEON: Just open the damn thing.

SAM: [*Opening the box.*] It's a mah jong set. [*Puzzled.*] Do you play?

LEON: All the time. And it's one of the many things that you and I have in common.

SAM: Leon, mah jong is a Chinese game.

LEON: Well . . . but you said you played it, right?

SAM: I never said that.

LEON: Fine, it's a gift. Let me tell you why I got it for you.

SAM: It's like when you thought all Oriental women had their feet bound.

LEON: It's Asian women, Sam.

SAM: Right, right. But you just assumed it was all Oriental women.

LEON: What are you saying?

SAM: I'm saying I don't know where every good Thai restaurant is. I'm saying I don't know a damn thing about that Filipino family that moved in down the block from here. I'm saying that you assume me to know everything instead of asking to be sure!

LEON: So, you don't play mah jong?

SAM: No, I do play mah jong, but you see, you assumed I did because you thought it was a Japanese game.

LEON: What are you getting so meshugah about?

SAM: Go is a Japanese game.

LEON: What game are we playing now?

SAM: What if I assumed that you celebrated New Year's Day on January 1st? What if I assumed that every doctor was Jewish? Wouldn't that upset you? What if I assumed that you cooked kibbutzes like a malasada?

LEON: Sam, you don't eat kibbutzes, it's knishes.

SAM: Oh. [*They both laugh.*]

LEON: Enough already, let's play.

SAM: No, not until you tell me why you bought this for me?

LEON: So now you're interested all of a sudden?

SAM: Tell me.

LEON: I forget.

SAM: Please, I want to know. [*Pause.*] Let's play.

LEON: Okay.

[SAM *dumps out the tiles onto the table. They begin washing the tiles and setting up the walls.*]

SAM: So, you going to tell me why you bought this?

LEON: What's a malasada?

SAM: A Hawai'ian knish.

LEON: Roll the dice.

SAM: No, you go ahead, you roll first.

LEON: No, you roll.

SAM: You're in my house, you roll first.

LEON: Fine. [LEON *rolls; they begin to play, taking their turns at rolling the dice and picking up tiles.*]

SAM: So? Come on, Leon, tell me why?

[LEON *takes out a letter and shows it to* SAM. *He points out the name.*]

LEON: Chee-ne Suge-haha.

SAM: What?

LEON: Chu-nu Sugi-huhu.

SAM: [*Reading.*] Chi-u-ne Su-gi-ha-ra.

LEON: He was the Consul General from Japan assigned to Kovno, Lithuania before the war.

SAM: And? What?

LEON: I have a cousin.

SAM: Alive?

LEON: She's in New York. She wrote to me. It took her a while to find me but she did. I just spoke to her on the phone last night. I'm going to visit her in a month.

SAM: I don't understand. You told me you thought all your relatives had died.

LEON: All, except Sarah Tomach. This Sugihara gave out exit visas to war refugees from Lithuania to Japan. He gave out thousands of them, and Sarah was one of the thousands. Do you believe it? From Lithuania, Sarah ended up in Japan in 1941. She was on the last boat that left Japan for America. The war broke out when she was halfway across the Pacific.

SAM: Pearl Harbor?

LEON: December 7, the captain of the ship decided to push on instead of turning back. Sam, I have a cousin! At last, Leon is not alone in this world.

SAM: I wanted it to work out with Eva, too.

LEON: I know.

[SAM *folds the letter and hands it back to* LEON.]

SAM: Hey, you want to play my favorite Japanese American game?

LEON: Sure.

[SAM *gets a deck of cards, shuffles, puts them down.*]

SAM: Cut.

LEON: [*Cutting the deck.*] What are we playing?

SAM: [*Dealing the cards.*] Five Card Draw. Guts to open. Nothing wild.

LEON: What do we use for chips?

SAM: Let's use the tiles. They're a nickel each. Ante up.

[*They look at their hands.*]

SAM: [*Cont'd.*]We should have a party in honor of Sarah. You going to bet?

LEON: A nickel.

SAM: A nickel? I call.

LEON: Two cards.

SAM: Two cards, huh? Is she married? Does she have kids?

LEON: Yes, she's married.

SAM: Dealer takes four.

LEON: I should have bet a dime. I raise you a nickel.

SAM: A nickel?

LEON: Are you in, Mr. Rockefeller?

SAM: Are you going to stay at her house?

LEON: I'll be getting a hotel.

SAM: I call. Two eights.

LEON: You stayed in with two eights?

SAM: What do you got?

LEON: Two tens.

SAM: Deal.

[LEON *shuffles*, SAM *cuts*, LEON *deals, they ante up.*]

LEON: It's beautiful.

SAM: Got a good hand.

LEON: No, I mean to think that both Sarah and I were saved by Japanese.

SAM: It took a lot of courage to do what he did.

LEON: This Sugihara was a true tzadik. A righteous man.

SAM: It gives you a warm feeling inside to know there were people like him out there, huh? He deserves a dime bet.

LEON: I call without looking. And I raise a nickel in your honor. You're my Sugihara. How many cards you want?

SAM: I see your nickel. I'll take four.

LEON: Four? I should have bet a dime. Dealer takes one.

SAM: A nickel. So, you going to be leaving me and moving to New York?

LEON: New York? I see your nickel and raise a dime.

SAM: You know, to be closer to Sarah and her family.

LEON: We'll see. You in or out.

SAM: I raise a dime.

LEON: Sam, can I ask you a question?

SAM: Sure.

LEON: As long as I've known you, you've never asked me about the camps. Why is that?

SAM: I wondered, but it wasn't my place to ask. If you wanted to tell me, you would have.

LEON: I'm a healer. That is what I do. I have dedicated my life to that one cause. But Sam, I am still trying to heal.

SAM: You're a mensch.

LEON: I call. Two pair, sevens and fours.

SAM: Three deuces. I pulled two.

LEON: You pulled them?

SAM: Just dumb luck.

LEON: There's an angel watching over you.

SAM: [*Gathers the cards and begins to shuffle.*] I love playing poker.

[*Lights fade to black.*]

SCENE 6

One month later. We are in New York. Lights fade up on LEON *in a hotel room, upset.*

LEON: I saw Sarah today, Sam. I drove for two hours before I had the courage to meet her. I circled her house eighteen times, for good luck. [*Pause.*] When she opened the door, I stared at her face. It was my mame's face, same high cheekbones, full round lips. . .all the women in our family. I couldn't stop smiling and laughing and kissing, kissing everything in sight. Sarah's hands, her eyes. I started singing the Alef-Base. I took her in my arms and danced. She looked like she was suffocating. She began to cry. She ran into her bedroom and shut the door. "I can't do this. My memories hurt too much. You're too Jewish." [*Pause.*] What's too Jewish, Sam? I got to go. When you get this message, you don't have to call me back. [LEON *hangs up the phone. He takes a worn letter from his pocket.*] She ran away from me in horror. Eva ran away, too. "Mayer and Deborah Abramowitz request the honor of your presence at the marriage of their daughter Eva Ruth to Dr. Jorge Levine, son of Walter and Goldie Levine, on May, 1, 1983, in Buenos Aires, Argentina." She was to be my bride, mame. Eva and I vowed to each other that we would have a family. A family to tell our stories to. . .remember my promise, mame? [*Pause.*] They would not accept me. [*Pause.*] Oh God, haven't the Ehrlichs suffered enough? Don't we deserve a future? [*Begins to cry.*] Forgive me, mame. . . [*Starts singing the Alef-Base song.*] "Oy-fen pripochic, brent a fireull. Une shtubis haste. Un der Rebeleh urn in kleine kinderlach dehm Alef-Base."

[*Lights fade to black.*]

SCENE 7

The year is 1996. We are in a hospital. Lights fade up to reveal LEON *gazing out a window. There is a bed and chair in the room. The light shines in through the blinds on* LEON. LEON *painfully gets up and begins to do Tai Chi.* SAM *enters, holding a paper bag. He watches* LEON *in silence.* LEON *finishes the Tai Chi exercise.*

LEON: I heard your footsteps as you were coming down the hall.

SAM: Have you had breakfast yet?

LEON: If you can call it that.

SAM: You want me to get you some take-out?

[LEON *laughs and coughs, walks toward* SAM, *extends his hand. They shake and* LEON *pulls* SAM *to him for a little hug.*]

LEON: Missed you the last few days.

SAM: We went to visit Emerald and her new baby. Boy, he's growing fast. Ruby made you some macadamia nut cookies. [SAM *puts the bag down next to the bed.*]

LEON: Give her my love.

[LEON *coughs uncontrollably.* SAM *watches with concern.*]

So, what's the latest news?

SAM: Well, I've been thinking about . . . ki.

LEON: Energy flow.

SAM: Yes. The spirit of the body. Conducting energy in and around you to influence your environment and health. Mastering the physical world and all of its pain, taking your body intact and rising all at once.

LEON: Mind over matter.

SAM: Ascension. It is what Buddha was said to have done.

LEON: And Moses.

SAM: And Jesus.

LEON: You should be treating me. I should be at home. [*Coughs.*] I had a thought about you the other day.

SAM: Oh yeah.

LEON: I wondered what was the need that drove Sam to bond with Leon?

SAM: Need?

LEON: I wondered if during the war, you were driven by a special need to help me because you couldn't help your own people.

SAM: It was just a reaction. Any human would help anyone.

LEON: History and experience tell us — not every human helps every other. You could not possibly save all of your people, Sam. And yet you chose to save me.

SAM: Just because a man can't save his own doesn't mean he'll decide to save someone else.

LEON: This is also true.

SAM: I don't think there's an answer to your question. Must be a mystery.

LEON: Sam, you have always been wiser than you know. [coughs.] My father and I were separated from the rest of the family as soon as we entered the camp. In the middle of the parade ground stood Dr. Sigmund Rasher holding a ceremonial sword. The sword moved effortlessly from right to left to right. Suddenly my father and I were in front of the doctor. "Is this your son?" "Yes, yes, I am." I was holding my father's hand so tightly because I did not want to lose him. The sword moved to the right and we were taken to the hospital. We were given numbers, and told to undress and run quickly in front of the doctors. They called it a "selection." There was Rasher with the same hard unfeeling eyes injecting serum into fathers and sons. For "volunteering," our "reward" was two pieces of bread and more salt than the other prisoners. We were given daily injections and examinations. One morning I awoke to my father's screams. He was delirious with fever. His bedsheets were soaked, and he was shaking. I kissed his forehead. For the briefest moment he recognized me and said, "Leon, icht schtarb. Nem mein broit. Du vest es darfin. I am dying. Take my bread. You will need it." I refused, but when he lost consciousness, I took his gift. I am the strong one, I thought. I need them for myself. To this day I am shamed by this. The fools withdrew some of my blood and injected him with it. They separated us and sent me to the barracks. Every day I begged to see my father. Then for some reason they took me to him. He is naked and lying in his own excrement. His eyes are open but cannot follow or focus. He is blind. He is deaf and paralyzed. I take his hand and place it on my face. His fingers reach my mouth, "Tate." He tries to speak but his lips are cracked and dry. I ask the guards for water, they laugh and hand me a small metal cup. When I return, his bed is empty. They have removed him while he is still alive. I lay down in his bed staring at the ceiling until they beat me and make me leave. It was the last time I saw a member of my family alive . . . until now. [LEON *coughs, holding his chest, then crosses to the chair.*] I am because you are.

SAM: Leon, as long as I live, as long as my children and grandchildren have a breath in their bodies, they will know about your life and the life you gave me.

[SAM *looks at* LEON, *who does not move.* SAM *crosses and checks* LEON'S *pulse.* LEON *has passed away.* SAM *looks up to the heavens, then down.*]

SAM: [*Cont'd.*] I brought you a gift today, Leon. [*Fights back tears as he takes a small box from his coat.*] I thought about this and told Ruby what I was going to do and she agreed it was a good idea. So, don't you enryo. You know what that means, Leon, don't you hold back. I guess you're the last one I should think would hold back, huh? [*Holds up his*

Silver Star medal.] It's my Silver Star. [*Pause.*] It saved me, many a time. Whenever I felt like the world was coming in at me, I just took it out and held it. It gave me a lot of strength. I just thought you might need some of its warmth too. [SAM *pins the medal on* LEON'S *chest. He gently lifts* LEON *up from the chair and slowly carries him to the bed.*] Leon Ehrlich . . . "has distinguished himself by heroic action." [*For a moment, it mirrors the image at the beginning, at liberation.* SAM *puts* LEON *down and gently rocks him. Then* SAM *takes out the mezuzah from underneath his shirt.*] And I'll always have this . . . to think of you.

[*A color slide fades up. It is a moment back in 1945 when* LEON *has regained his senses and is reaching out to* SAM. SAM *begins the Mourner's Kaddish.*]

SAM: [*Cont'd.*] "Yisgadal ve'yiskadash sm'mey rabbo, be'ol'mo deevro chiroosey, ve'yamlich malchoosey be'chayeychown u'vyownmeychown u'vchayey de'chol baiss yisroale, ba'agolo uvisman koreev ve'imroo omaine."

[*Lights and the slide slowly fade to black.*]

END OF PLAY

Dwight Okita

THE RAINY SEASON

EDITOR'S NOTES

For a writer dealing with gay issues, Dwight Okita is strikingly free of bitterness and alienation. Homosexual characters rarely surface in Asian American drama, but when they do (as in the remarkable plays of Han Ong or Chay Yew), they lead tortured existences. Ong's characters wander an urban netherworld that brutalizes them at every turn; Yew's protagonist in *Porcelain* is driven by love to commit murder, while his hero in *Half Lives* is scorned and rejected by his mother for his sexual orientation. The traumas these characters endure are mirrored backstage: at least one board member of an Asian American theatre company has resigned rather than watch the theatre produce gay work. In this context, it is utterly novel that Harry, in *The Rainy Season*, has a mother who thinks her son's life would be easier if he liked women, but that's about the limit of her censure. Her principal concern is that she just wants her son's company.

The striking, even refreshing lack of anger and alienation in Okita's portrait of gay romance is part of what makes *The Rainy Season* unique. Another part of its uniqueness is in the partner Okita has chosen for Harry: the tale-spinning Brazilian, Antonio. The intersection between Asian and Latino cultures — both of which hold homosexuality in taboo — is almost never depicted in theatre or film. The only other play addressing it that comes to this writer's mind is Eugenie Chan's *Emil: A Chinese Play*. Perhaps this "gap in the literature" (as academicians would put it) will be explored soon.

In the meanwhile, it is interesting to note that while Asian characters are often exoticized in romantic stories, here it is Okita's young lover, Harry, who is doing the romanticizing — while Antonio, redolent with the mystery of the rainforests, is the exotic Other. And yet, as with many other characters who project exotic stereotypes onto their foreign lovers, Harry ends up paying a price for his susceptibility to Antonio's mystique. In fact, it is arguably Antonio's perception of what Harry really wants that precipitates the conflict between them. Regardless, at the end of the day, Harry is a champion of neither Asian American nor gay politics — he is simply Asian American and gay. The lack of a political axe to grind may simply be a part of Okita's nature — but it may also reflect the genesis of the play in Chicago. Most critics in search of Asian American theatre seek the stages mentioned in Dorinne Kondo's introduction to this volume — companies on the East or West Coasts, many of which arose during the political tensions of the 1960s and 1970s. But the 1990s have seen a slowly growing Asian American theatre movement in the midwest. Chicago's Angel Island Theatre Company (which has commissioned further work from Okita) is one such example, as are a number of groups in Minneapolis: the Hmong Theatre Project, Rick Shiomi's Theatre Mu, and The Playwrights' Center (which has hosted a series of development workshops specifically addressing Asian American work). It is worth speculating that these midwest groups, born well after the political broilings of years past, will write new and unexpected chapters in the history of Asian American theatre.

The Rainy Season is not the sort of play, frankly, that becomes the darling of the Theatre Communications Group; it wears its heart on its sleeve, and its poetry is the simple language of everyday life. Yet it is precisely the kind of play that a theatregoer, entering a small alternative stage and watching actors driven by as much commitment as charisma, will remember long after more abstruse plays have seen their day. It bears the earnest quality, in some scenes, of being a first play — but Okita's career, which has since generated a volume of poetry, a Joseph Jefferson citation for work with Bailiwick Repertory on The Hiroshima Project, and new work for the HBO Writers Project (My Last Week on Earth), is clearly just beginning.

The Rainy Season was first produced by Zebra Crossing Theatre and North Avenue Productions at Chicago Dramatists Workshop, Chicago, Illinois, on February 20, 1993, with the following cast:

HARRY	Raymond J. Mark
ANTONIO	Edward F. Torres
MOM	Cheryl Hamada
TIWANA	Ronda Bedgood
JOSH	George Seegebrecht
DAD	Marc Rita

Directed by Marlene Zuccaro. Developed in part at Chicago Dramatists Workshop. Special thanks to Russ Tutterow, Marlene Zuccaro, Cheryl Hamada, Eddie Torres, Patsy Okita, Dick Dotterer, Greg Nishimura and the many Latino boyfriends who (for better or for worse) inspired this play.

CHARACTERS

HARRY   30, Japanese American, gay, son of MOM and DAD. A hopeful romantic atttracted to Latino men. An aspiring artist, he works an office day job.

MOM   58, Japanese American. Very young-looking and acting, tries to be hip. Charming and girlish. Retired.

DAD   late 50s, Japanese American. He passed away four years ago. Was an elementary school science teacher. The thinker in the family, with Mom the perpetual student.

ANTONIO   26, Latino male, heavy Portuguese accent. An irresistible storyteller, cute.

TIWANA   34, African American, straight. She alternates between being urbane and down-to-earth.

JOSH   32, European American, Jewish, straight. A little clueless, but well-intentioned.

PROLOGUE:

Lights go down. In the dark, we hear rainfall, music. Slowly light comes up behind the picture window of MOM'S *living room.* MOM *and* HARRY *are silhouetted standing at window, watching it rain. Hold on this image for a moment and fade to black. In the half-light,* HARRY *moves to press button on his answering machine to play messages. He then moves into dark as messages play. We can just barely make out* HARRY'S *actions in the dark — opening his mail, taking off his tie.*

MOM: [*On machine.*] Uh, Harry — this is your Ma. Watch Public Television tonight at 8. There's a show called "The Japanese: Who They Are and How They Got That Way." It should be very inspirational. I saw the previews and it looked pretty good.

[BEEP.]

MOM: [*Cont'd.*] Harry? What do *you* think we should do about Dad's ashes? Jojo wants to . . . well . . . scatter them from a plane — over Mount Fuji. But Dad's not from Japan and he was afraid of heights. Do you think that's right? We should call a family conference. I need input.

[BEEP.]

MOM: [*Cont'd.*] This is just your Ma again. Where *are* you? I just came back from grocery shopping and the fridge is packed to the gills. We got rotisseried chicken and soda pop — do you want to come over to eat? It's about 5:30 right now and —

[HARRY *shuts off machine mid-message and speaks directly to the audience.*]

HARRY: My mother's a pretty funny lady. But I think she abuses my machine. [*Beat.*] I suppose if I called her more often, she wouldn't have to leave so many messages. Ever since my Dad died a few years ago, I've been pretty conscious of that sort of thing.

Once I recorded the sound of my parents laughing. It was an ordinary moment. They were sitting in the living room sending out Christmas cards and they came to this lady down the block who'd been *divorced* so many times — they couldn't remember what *name* to send it to. It struck them as *very* funny. They just burst out laughing and couldn't stop. It was such a wonderful sound — I said to myself, "I must always remember this sound." So I run to my room and get my tape recorder and stand in the hallway recording them.

My strongest memory of growing up is standing at the window with my Mom watching it rain. We'd stand there for hours . . . mesmerized. What were we looking at anyway? I dunno. Everyone needs a hobby, I guess. But it was like we were waiting for something . . . or someone . . . to come out of the rain and — I don't know — save us, I suppose. Take us into the light. That's what I was thinking about anyway. I have no idea what she was thinking about.

SCENE 1

Next day, Friday night, MOM'S *place. Lights come up on* MOM *and* HARRY *at* MOM'S *condominium. She's reading a newspaper on the sofa.* HARRY *is eating dinner at the table. He casts increasingly hostile glances at* MOM *till finally he speaks.*

HARRY: [*Annoyed.*] Well?

MOM: [*Still reading newspaper.*] What?

HARRY: I'm here.

MOM: Uh-huh.

HARRY: I don't believe you! You leave *twenty* messages blinking on my answering machine telling me you went shopping and everything that's in your refrigerator, you beg and plead for my company and finally I come over and you know what you do?

MOM: What?

HARRY: You read the paper!

MOM: Well, what do you want me to do? Sing and dance for you?

HARRY: Just be with me. Sit at the table with me like we're part of a family. Like the old days.

MOM: This is what we *did* in the old days. Dad and Jojo and I would watch TV and you'd eat at the table. That's 'cause you were always late. I think you were just anti-social.

HARRY: I was shy, Mom. I was maturing. I was finding myself.

MOM: Why couldn't you find yourself at the table . . . like the rest of us? Anti-social.

HARRY: You said you wanted to have a family conference.

MOM: Oh yeah. What should we do about Dad's ashes? Jojo wants to scatter them from a plane —

HARRY: [*Overlapping.*] — scatter them from a plane over Mount Fuji. I know, I heard. So where's Jojo?

MOM: He went to the movies.

HARRY: [*After a beat.*] Isn't it kind of hard to have a "family conference" with one-third of the family missing? Is he avoiding me?

MOM: No, he's practicing not being here. He says he wants to move to Seattle.

HARRY: That's great! Don't you think?

MOM: Sure.

HARRY: So what do *you* want to do about the urn?

MOM: Well, I don't see why we have to scatter him at all. He only died four years ago. It's kinda nice to have him around the house.

HARRY: You should really get out more. [*Beat.*] You know, that urn weighs a ton. I think we should move it off that shelf before it crashes through.

MOM: Okay, then that's what we'll do. Can you move it, Harry?

[*He moves urn to lower shelf.*]

MOM: [*Cont'd.*] Well, *that's* settled. Want some sody pop?

HARRY: Sure.

[MOM *gets Pop from fridge and serves them both.*]

HARRY: [*Cont'd.*] Do you ever think about Dad?

MOM: No. Well, sometimes when I'm dusting.

HARRY: Sometimes I feel him watching me.

MOM: You mean like he's watching over you?

HARRY: No. Like he sees what I'm doing. What I'm going through. Only he seems . . . different somehow.

MOM: How?

HARRY: Well, he's more talkative for one thing —

MOM: He talks to you?

HARRY: — more carefree.

MOM: Well, he would be, I suppose.

[*Pause.*]

HARRY: I have fires burning inside me.

MOM: What kind of fires? Romantic?

HARRY: No, not that kind! Fires made of everything I want to do. Everything I want to be. I have this friend — he's a filmmaker from Poland. He was giving this party and he says: [*In Polish accent.*] "Harry, I know how *hungry* you are to meet interesting people. You must come to my party." I *love* that! And he's right. And that's a fire.

MOM: I don't think I have any fires inside *me*.

HARRY: I bet you do. Think about it. When you go to bed at night and you lie there in the dark — what keeps you awake?

MOM: I don't think when I'm in bed — I sleep! I'm too tired to think. Well . . . I'd like to travel, I guess.

HARRY: So that's a fire. Where to?

MOM: Japan, Europe, anywhere.

HARRY: Okay, what else?

MOM: I think maybe . . . one day . . . I'd like to have my own dress shop. A cute one with lacy curtains. I'd do alterations too.

HARRY: Have you ever wanted to write down your life story? About you and Dad? Me and Jojo?

MOM: Do you think it'd get published?

HARRY: You never know. But I mean, just as a way to tell yourself what you did in this lifetime. To tell your kids.

MOM: Oh, that's a good idea! Shall I? Do I have an interesting story to tell?!

HARRY: Don't go fishing for compliments.

MOM: Am I fishing?

HARRY: Yes.

MOM: Well, how else will I know if you don't tell me!

[*She starts rummaging through bookcase.*]

MOM: [*Cont'd.*] I didn't know my life would make an interesting story that someone would want to publish! I didn't know that! I must have a spiral notebook in here somewhere. [*She finds it.*] Here we go!

HARRY: You're just a woman on fire.

MOM: How 'bout you? What's your fires?

HARRY: I want to be famous. I want to say things that everyone will hear —no matter how far away they are . . . [*Pause, relishing the thought.*] I want someone to talk to in the dark when the whole world is sleeping.

MOM: You could always sleep over here anytime you like.

HARRY: That's not what I mean.

MOM: It's so nice when you're here. It's like old times.

HARRY: No it's not. It's totally different. It's like . . . "new times." [*Sarcastically.*] The universe is expanding and so am I. Continents drift while we sleep. It's an exciting time we live in, these new times: AIDS, co-dependence, drive-by shootings, crystals . . . you really should get out more.

MOM: How would you know how much I get out? You're not home enough to know!

HARRY: This is not my home, Mother. It's my home away from home.

MOM: Harry, are you happy? You don't sound happy.

HARRY: Don't start.

MOM: Do you get lonely . . . living by yourself? People aren't meant to live alone. It's not natural.

HARRY: I know. I considered a roommate.

MOM: You've got too many papers in your house. Throw them out! Open up the curtains. If your house is messy, you feel messy inside.

HARRY: I've got to go.

MOM: You said you wanted to have a real conversation. How 'bout now?

HARRY: I've really got to go. [HARRY *moves to the door and stops. Reconsidered, pausing in doorway.*] I was looking through my closet last night. I found my journal from ten years ago. Know what my birthday wish was on my twentieth birthday? To have a lover.

MOM: That's one of your fires.

HARRY: Some fire. That's what I wished for last week — on my *thirtieth* birthday!

SCENE 2

The next day, Saturday morning, at a bus stop. HARRY *and* ANTONIO *notice each other as they wait for bus. There is a strong attraction between them, flirting.* ANTONIO'S *Portuguese accent is rich, charming.*

ANTONIO: Nice country you have here.

HARRY: I'm sorry?

ANTONIO: I said, nice country you have here.

HARRY: Oh, it isn't mine.

ANTONIO: Were you born here?

HARRY: Yeah.

ANTONIO: Then it's yours.

HARRY: Well, I mean, I don't own it. It's not like it's *all* mine. This land is your land, this land is my land — ya know what I mean?

[*Beat. No response from* ANTONIO.]

HARRY: [*Cont'd.*] That's a song.

ANTONIO: That's a song?!

HARRY: Yes.

ANTONIO: Sounds like a silly song.

HARRY: Maybe.

ANTONIO: I'm from Brazil. Do you know Brazil?

HARRY: [*Singing to the tune of "Brazil."*] Brazil . . . ya dah dah dah dah dee . . . Ya dah dah dah dah dah dee . . .

ANTONIO: Yes. Now that's a song.

HARRY: It's okay. A little . . . overplayed.

ANTONIO: Whose fault is that? I can't help it if Americans love Brazilian music. And Americans can't help it if they love what they love. Why do you think people love our music? Because it's the sound of someone reaching for their happiness and finding it in the palm of their hand.

HARRY: Do you find happiness "in the palm of your hand?"

ANTONIO: When I listen to Brazilian music.

HARRY: And when you don't?

ANTONIO: Then I'm on my own.

HARRY: So who do you know in town?

ANTONIO: No one. I've been here for seven months and I have no friends. It's tragic. Where are you going today?

HARRY: I was headed for a coffee house. It's always pretty lively on a Saturday.

ANTONIO: Maybe I could join you. You could show me around a little. Be my . . . ambassador of good will.

HARRY: [*Avoiding the question.*] I *love* Brazilian music. To me it represents everything that's alive and free, joyful and aware, primitive yet profound . . .

ANTONIO: Was that a yes or was that a no?

HARRY: That's an I don't know.

ANTONIO: What don't you know?

HARRY: I don't know *you*, for one thing. And my mother told me not to talk to strangers.

ANTONIO: Do you do everything your mother tells you?

HARRY: Everything. She also told me . . . if I sleep with boys . . . they'll like me better.

ANTONIO: Do you want to sleep with me?

HARRY: Yes and no. Yes, I want to sleep with you. No, I'm not going to.

[*Pause.* ANTONIO *looks at* HARRY *flirtatiously.*]

HARRY: [*Cont'd.*] We shouldn't do everything we want to do, should we? I mean, I don't want you to think I just walk up to people at bus stops and . . . go to bed with them. [*Pause.*] I wish you wouldn't look at me like that . . . with those big . . . dreamy . . . Brazilian eyes of yours.

ANTONIO: You're very American. You want to do one thing, but you do the other. In my country — if a man wants a man, and the feeling is mutual . . .

HARRY: Is the feeling mutual?

ANTONIO: Maybe.

HARRY: That's no answer!

ANTONIO: "Yes and no" is a *better* answer??

HARRY: At least I have strong feelings both ways.

ANTONIO: I wish I could be more clear. It's a long story.

HARRY: I have time.

> [*At this point,* DAD *appears as if from out of nowhere. A snippet of signature music underscores each time* DAD *appears, mystically.* DAD *wears a bathrobe, carries a bowl of popcorn in one hand and a soda in the other. He stands in the background, watching.* HARRY *and* ANTONIO *don't notice.*]

ANTONIO: It has nothing to do with you, really. I'm just kind of strange that way. I'll tell you about it someday.

HARRY: I don't know if I'll know you that long.

ANTONIO: I hope so. I'd like that.

HARRY: What?

ANTONIO: To know you.

HARRY: Really?

ANTONIO: Really. So will you take me to your coffee house where the life is?

> [HARRY *hesitates, then turns wordlessly and begins to walk away.* ANTONIO *watches him go. Then* HARRY *turns back and calls to* ANTONIO.]

HARRY: Are you coming or what?

ANTONIO: Was that a yes? I couldn't tell. You know, the American language comes very easy to me. If only you Americans would learn to use it properly.

HARRY: Oh, shut up and walk, will ya?

ANTONIO: Seriously. Are you sure you want to spend some time with me? You'll miss your bus.

HARRY: That's okay. [*Big smile.*] I wasn't waiting for one.

> [*Lights come to half.* HARRY *and* ANTONIO *freeze in tableau. Spotlight on* DAD. HARRY *reacts to* DAD's *appearance though* ANTONIO *remains frozen in tableau.*]

DAD: [*To* HARRY.] You always were good at making friends. Well, I take that back—you were very quiet for a few years. During college. You called it your "Dark Ages." It was a time of great soul searching and revelation.

When you were little, you used to ask lots of questions. Your mother used to say: "Keep asking questions, Harry. That's how you get smart." And you did. You wanted to know everything and everyone.

One day you sat me down on the living room sofa. You looked real serious. "Dad, do you think I worry too much?" you said. "Do I seem unhappy to you?" I don't even remember what I said, but whatever it was — I know it wasn't enough. So go ahead, Harry. Ask me a question. For old times' sake. Ask me a hard one. I'm all ears.

SCENE 3

Monday morning, at the office. Lights rise on HARRY *with co-workers* JOSH *and* TIWANA, *office temporaries.* HARRY *is studying his desk calendar.* JOSH *and* TIWANA *staple industriously.*

HARRY: Oh, Josh. The days are just flipping past us. See!

[HARRY *flips pages of calendar, grabs the pages of days to come.*]

HARRY: [*Cont'd.*] We only have *this* many days left in the year.

[*He grabs the pages of days past.*]

HARRY: [*Cont'd.*] What the hell did we do with *these* days?

[HARRY *and* JOSH *laugh.*]

JOSH: They're behind us. They're history. We looked a gift horse in the mouth.

HARRY: That is one phrase I've never understood. What does that mean, "We looked a gift horse in the mouth?"

JOSH: It has something to do with not trusting what's been given to you for free.

HARRY: Oh, like Greeks bearing gifts, the Trojan horse with the soldiers inside.

JOSH: Right. So my point is that maybe time flies — not because we're having fun — but because we're just not paying attention. And because our days are handed to us on a silver platter. Maybe if we had to do hard labor on Alcatraz for each day of life we were given, *maybe then we'd remember what we did last weekend!* [*Catches himself getting car-*

ried away.] Sorry. I always get philosophical when I collate. Oh, speaking of gifts — I was talking to Lucy and she says to me, "Josh — I didn't know you were Jewish. You know *Linda's* Jewish." Wink, wink. As if she'd be interested in me.

HARRY: How do you know she wouldn't be interested?

JOSH: That's right. How do I know?

HARRY: [*As if reading headlines.*] "Rising Woman Executive Runs Off With Office Boy." "She had him as a temporary, but she wanted him permanently!"

JOSH: Temp Stud. He took more than dictation.

HARRY: Her memos said no, but her eyes said yes.

TIWANA: You guys are so crazy! Don't be talking that talk during office hours, okay? You know how I get. Honey please!

JOSH: I don't think I want to hear this. Maybe I should leave you two breeders alone.

TIWANA: Leave you two *whats* alone?

HARRY: Breeders. It's gay slang for, you know . . . [*Whispers, mock-secretively.*] Heterosexuals.

TIWANA: That's terrible! That makes us sound like rabbits. Like all we do is procreate the human species. I'm *all for* meaningless sex!

JOSH: Hallelujah! Amen, sister!

TIWANA: Who you calling sister, white boy?

HARRY: *Tiwana*, Josh's just trying to be multicultural.

JOSH: Well, Alvin Toffler predicts that multiculturalism is gonna be the big trend for the 90s. All one people, you know?

HARRY: Take me. I'm Japanese American, but I love Latins, I dance black, and I grew up in a Jewish neighborhood. And some of my best friends are white heterosexuals.

TIWANA: There goes the neighborhood!

JOSH: We better keep it down or our bosses are gonna give us some real work to do.

HARRY: I'm enjoying this. You guys are like a family to me.

JOSH: Harry's starting to feel all warm and fuzzy inside.

HARRY: No, really. Don't you guys feel that way?

TIWANA: Like a family. Uh-huh.

JOSH: It's just a job to me. A couple years down the road when I'm rich and famous — you'll be lucky if I recognize you on the street.

HARRY: [*To* JOSH.] So, are you seeing anyone these days?

JOSH: No.

HARRY: Who was the last person you saw?

JOSH: Joanne Fletcher.

HARRY: And?

JOSH: We had nothing in common. Except that she liked to fall asleep on my shoulder while we watched TV. She'd put her head on my shoulder, or sometimes on my lap —

HARRY: She was at her best in a death-like position.

JOSH: At the end of the evening, she'd wake up —

HARRY: — and then ruin everything.

JOSH: No, at the end of the evening, she'd say in this really nasal voice — [*Imitates her.*] "Well, I had a really nice time." My friend George said I should get her in bed. So I pictured going to bed with her, but I kept seeing her afterwards turning to me and saying: [*In nasal voice.*] "Well, I had a really nice time." I just couldn't go through with it. Anyway, I asked myself, "Do I really want this?" and I said, "No, I like myself better than that."

[TIWANA *rips sheet of paper out of her typewriter and storms offstage.*]

TIWANA: [*Cont'd.*] Was it something I said?

HARRY: She's probably jealous. You know she's crazy about you, don't you?

JOSH: Yeah, right. It's amazing how she conceals her feelings for me.

HARRY: That's how I know she likes you. Have you ever dated a black woman before?

JOSH [*Thinks for a beat.*] No, not actually.

HARRY: Have you ever dated a woman who wasn't white?

JOSH: Well, let's see. [*Thinks for a second.*] No.

HARRY: Have you ever dated a woman who wasn't Jewish?

JOSH: Of course! Once or twice! I'm not close-minded.

HARRY: See, I've dated men of every race, creed and color. I guess that's one of the benefits of being gay. I figure: I'm already out of the mainstream — so what's the difference if I go out a little further. Besides, it opens up the dating pool.

JOSH: I don't know, Harry. Relationships are hard enough for me to handle when they're regular. It's not like I go out of my way to *avoid* women who aren't white. I just don't go out of my way to pursue them. Some black women I think are very attractive.

[JOSH *gestures toward* TIWANA'S *desk. Just then* TIWANA *walks back.* HARRY *and* JOSH *just stare at her for a moment.* TIWANA *gives them a funny look.*]

HARRY: How 'bout you, Tiwana? Are you involved with someone these days?

TIWANA: I'm in a relationship with myself these days. I'm getting to know me . . . getting to know all about me.

HARRY: Sounds cozy.

TIWANA: Can't beat the company.

HARRY: But don't you want someone to take up your time? Give you backrubs, put the cream in your coffee?

TIWANA: Honey please! I didn't have that when I was in a relationship!

HARRY: Josh, could you do me a big favor? Could you ask Nancy if she's got any White-Out in the stockroom? I'm running low.

JOSH: You can borrow mine.

HARRY: I'd really like a fresh bottle.

JOSH: I don't know, Har. I've got some serious collating to do.

HARRY: I'll buy you lunch today.

JOSH: I'll be right back. You're my witness, Tiwana.

TIWANA: Okey dokey.

[HARRY *waits for* JOSH *to leave.*]

HARRY: What do you think of Josh?

TIWANA: What do you mean, "What do I think of him?"

HARRY: He's a handsome man.

TIWANA: He's not bad.

HARRY: I think he likes you.

[TIWANA *looks at him skeptically.*]

HARRY: [*Cont'd.*] I mean he hasn't said it outright, but he's definitely implied it on several occasions.

TIWANA: Are you trying to matchmake?

HARRY: No. I just want my friends to be happy. I truly believe we're here to share our lives with someone. If a tree falls in the forest and there's no one there to hear it — I'm convinced: it does not make a sound. A life must have a witness, you know.

TIWANA: Well, I put love on the back burner a few years ago. And that's where it's stayed.

HARRY: You probably left it on the stove, forgot all about it — and now it's all burned up.

TIWANA: It just isn't important to me right now. But it's on the list. I'm just not gonna worry about it.

[JOSH *comes back, gives* HARRY *white-out.*]

HARRY: [*To* JOSH.] Thanks.

JOSH: What's on your list, Tiwana.

TIWANA: Nothing.

HARRY: I met this guy over the weekend. I'm walking down Clark Street and I see this classically handsome Latin man waiting at the bus stop, right? And he looks . . . so lost, so sweet.

JOSH: And all of a sudden — you had this burning desire to ride the bus.

HARRY: Exactly. So I'm waiting there, pretending to be looking down the street and we're kind of noticing each other and he says totally out of the blue, "Nice country you have here," in this great Portuguese accent. We're getting together this Saturday for lunch.

JOSH: Stuff like that never happens to me.

HARRY: I'm a terrible flirt. Even on my darkest days, in my most depressed moods — I've been able to flirt.

TIWANA: Sounds like the beginning of a meaningful relationship to me!

HARRY: Gimme a break, Tiwana. We're just getting to know each other.

TIWANA: Correction: you picked him up at a bus stop. Now aside from the fact that he's Hispanic and cute, what exactly do you think you have in common?

HARRY: I refuse to discuss this with a jaded romantic.

TIWANA: Seriously, Harry. What do you think love is?

HARRY: I know it when I see it.

TIWANA: Do you?

[*Beat.*]

TIWANA: [*Cont'd.*]Think about it. Just think about it. We'll talk about it later.

SCENE 4

Coffeehouse on Chicago's Northside. HARRY *and* ANTONIO *deep in conversation, having muffins and coffee.*

HARRY: And then what?

ANTONIO: Then I came here.

HARRY: Why?

ANTONIO: I have an uncle who's a diplomat at the United Nations.

HARRY: But the United Nations is in New York.

ANTONIO: I know that. I decided to come here to study foreign relations at the University of Chicago. You know, how to build bridges of trust between countries, how to have what you Americans call a "power lunch." What a concept.

HARRY: And you don't have a lover?

ANTONIO: No.

HARRY: Why not?

ANTONIO: [*Joking.*] No one likes me.

HARRY: I find that hard to believe.

[*Beat.*]

ANTONIO: Do you like games?

HARRY: What kind?

ANTONIO: Antonio will teach you a game. I call it "The Magic Wand Game." I play it whenever I meet someone new.

HARRY: Did you learn this game in Brazil? Is this a game you learned under the coconut trees as a boy?

ANTONIO: No. You learn this game in life. You learn this game if you are lucky. This is a game you can learn from Antonio.

HARRY: I'm ready. I think.

ANTONIO: I have a magic wand that *really* works, okay? You can make three wishes, but you must be careful, 'cause you may get what you wish for. After you tell me your three wishes, I will tell you if you get these wishes or not. Okay?

HARRY: Okay.

ANTONIO: What do you wish for if you could have any three things in the whole wide world?

HARRY: Hmm. Number one. I want to do something great. Number two . . . I want to make a living doing what I love. And number three . . . I want to share my life with someone.

ANTONIO: I see. Hmm.

[*Beat.*]

MOM: [*Cont'd.*] You won't get any of these.

HARRY: Why not?

ANTONIO: Too general. You must learn to dream in detail. You say you want to share your life with someone, but you don't say who.

HARRY: What if I don't know who?

ANTONIO: Oh well.

HARRY: What are your three wishes?

ANTONIO: I want a good job translating Portuguese for Americans making twenty thousand a year to start. I want my mother to visit me in America so she can stop worrying about me. I wish for peace in El Salvador by 1999. And I want to find a cute apartment on the north side.

HARRY: That's *four.*

ANTONIO: Okay, forget about El Salvador.

[*They both laugh.*]

HARRY: That's pretty good. Okay. Ask me again.

ANTONIO: I have a magic wand that really works. What do you wish for?

HARRY: I'd like to spend this summer in Brazil where I can live in the rainforest . . . and meet many interesting people.

ANTONIO: Excellent! Much more precise. Harry, I have an idea!

HARRY: Oh, no.

ANTONIO: Why do you say, "Oh, no"?

HARRY: What's your idea?

ANTONIO: Come to Brazil with me.

HARRY: I knew it!

ANTONIO: You love it.

HARRY: Says who? Antonio, how long have we known each other?

ANTONIO: A week.

HARRY: You see, I make it a point never to leave the country with anyone I haven't known for at least . . . a month.

ANTONIO: That's why you need to go. To broaden your sunrises.

HARRY: You mean horizons. Anyway, I don't have the money.

ANTONIO: I know.

HARRY: I don't have the time.

ANTONIO: I know. But do you have the wish?

HARRY: What?

ANTONIO: Where there's a wish — there's a way.

HARRY: This reminds me of the movie *Splash*. It's an American movie.

ANTONIO: Allow me.

[ANTONIO *takes* HARRY'S *muffin and butters it for him during* HARRY'S *speech.* ANTONIO *butters the muffin without being self-conscious, in a sensual, labored, erotic manner.* ANTONIO'S *tongue could be hanging out.* HARRY *is distracted.*]

HARRY: Tom Hanks plays this guy — all his life he wants to meet that special person — but no luck, right? So he finally decided to give up looking and live alone. He winds up meeting this woman who's the woman of his dreams! But he finds out she's a mermaid, see?

[ANTONIO *hands* HARRY *his buttered muffin;* HARRY *takes a bite out of it.*]

HARRY: [*Cont'd.*] That means she's like this little fish who lives in the sea. So at the end of the movie, she asks him to come live with her in the sea and leave his world behind forever.

ANTONIO: What does he do?

HARRY: [*Thinks for a while.*] I can't remember. But you see, it's like you're the mermaid and you're asking me to leave everything I know behind.

ANTONIO: No, Harry. I asked you to spend summer in Brazil with me. Nothing more, nothing less. At the end of summer, you are free. To go. To stay. You choose. It's simple, yes?

HARRY: You make it sound simple. Tell you what. Come to my place next Saturday night and we'll talk. I'll even cook dinner for you.

ANTONIO: I'll be happy to come.

HARRY: Seven o'clock sharp, okay?

ANTONIO: Seven o'clock.

HARRY: [*Writing in his calendar book.*] "Antonio, dinner at seven." See, I'm writing you in.

[ANTONIO *stares at* HARRY'S *calendar, then grabs it from* HARRY.]

ANTONIO: Oh my gosh! That hurts my eyes. How do you *read* that thing!!

[ANTONIO *studies the book.*]

ANTONIO: [*Cont'd.*] You should have it framed and hung on a wall in a museum somewhere. Harry, I think you need a bigger calendar book.

HARRY: Or a smaller life. So it's a date then?

ANTONIO: Absolutely. You'll see. Life is much simpler than you think.

HARRY: It's so crazy — to just get up and go to South America!

ANTONIO: Look, you can't plan everything in your little calendar book.

HARRY: Why not?

ANTONIO: Because life is too big — it won't fit. 'Cause you must let yourself be a little scared sometimes. In my country, we talk a lot about the mysterious nature of our lives from moment to moment. Bow down to it. Be happy you don't know everything. That sometimes you can be surprised by the gifts of life. Don't question them . . . just smile . . . and hold out your hands.

[*Beat.*]

ANTONIO: [*Cont'd.*] And by the way, he goes to the sea.

HARRY: What?

ANTONIO: At the end of the movie, he goes with the fishwoman to live in the sea.

HARRY: You saw it?

ANTONIO: No.

HARRY: How do you know?

ANTONIO: I know.

HARRY: How?

ANTONIO: It's simple. He met someone who cares for him — which never before happens in all his days, yes?

HARRY: Yeah.

ANTONIO: What else could he do?

[*Pause.*]

So where's your boyfriend?

HARRY: Oh . . . I don't know.

ANTONIO: You don't know where your boyfriend is?

HARRY: He's probably . . . doing some shopping . . . [*Confessing.*] I don't have one.

ANTONIO: Why not? You should have someone.

[*Beat.*]

ANTONIO: [*Cont'd.*] Maybe he's out there.

HARRY: Who?

ANTONIO: Your lover.

HARRY: Oh, yeah.

ANTONIO: Maybe he's walking toward you right now.

HARRY: I hope so.

ANTONIO: Maybe he's closer than you think.

HARRY: That'd be nice.

[*Pause.*]

ANTONIO: I like the way you took care of me today. I liked waiting at the bus stop close to you. I liked buttering your muffin. [*Seductively.*] I want to butter your muffin again. Dream with me tonight. In the jungle.

[*Hot, tropical music plays underneath. Lights rise on "rain curtains" on the set, which are set into motion by fans.*]

HARRY: Wow! Are Brazilians all naturally romantic, or do you work at it?

ANTONIO: We are very romantic. In my country, we have a time of year — in your time, it would be somewhere between spring and summer. We call it the rainy season. At first we have drizzles, then monsoons. The rains are so heavy . . . cities flood, cars float like toys in the street. Or there is a mudslide and a house vanishes overnight. It's a dangerous time — anything can happen. A study has shown more people fall in love during the rainy season than any other time of year. I think, because it is the one time of year we realize how alone we are, how alone we have always been. And so, we turn to each other. We give in. We surrender to all that we know. In the rainy season.

[*Music fades out, as do the lights on the rain curtains.*]

HARRY: [*Abruptly, as if snapping out of trance.*] I have to go, Antonio. There's a movie that's on tonight I want to tape. Call me, okay?

ANTONIO: Sure. I'll call you. Good night, Japanese.

SCENE 5

A few days later, Tuesday at MOM'S.

HARRY: I met someone last week. Did I tell you?

MOM: You're always meeting people. What are you — the Welcome Wagon?

HARRY: I have a gift for starting relationships. Keeping them going is where I get confused.

MOM: Maybe this is a sign you should date a girl. Maybe you'll never find happiness with a man.

HARRY: Maybe you're right, but I'll die trying. I *love* men. Men are cool. Women are great too. But men . . .

MOM: So what's his name? This person.

HARRY: His name is Antonio. He's from Brazil and he has this great third world accent.

MOM: Brazil. That's where the nuts come from. You sure go for those international types.

HARRY: Yeah. People at home anywhere in the world. "Global citizens," I call 'em.

MOM: Global citizens. That's nice! To be at home anywhere in the world.

HARRY: You know, I've lived my whole life in Chicago and it's been great. But after a while, you get curious about the rest of the world. Don't you? Just like you wanting to go to Europe or Japan. [*Beat.*] If someone asked me to go away for a few months to live in . . . let's say . . . another country . . . what would you think about that?

MOM: Why do you ask?

HARRY: A hypothetical question.

MOM: Well, if your brother stayed with me, it'd be okay.

HARRY: Let's say he can't.

MOM: Oh, I think maybe I'd miss you.

HARRY: But would you mind if I went?

MOM: I don't know. Is this true?

HARRY: Would you tell me I couldn't go?

MOM: [*Getting uptight.*] I don't know! Why are you asking me if it's not true?! You want to go to Brazil?

HARRY: Antonio asked me. I didn't say yes, I didn't say no.

MOM: That's so far! How do you know he's not a terrorist?

HARRY: I just wanted to run the idea past you. It's just for the summer. But if you tell me not to go — I won't go.

MOM: [*Short pause.*] Don't go.

HARRY: Mom!

MOM: Don't go! You said if I told you not to go —

HARRY: That's not what you're supposed to say. You're supposed to say: "Go, son. Be happy! See the world!"

MOM: You watch too many movies.

HARRY: You don't watch enough movies.

MOM: Oh, is that so, Mr. Sassy Pants?

HARRY: I want you to meet him.

MOM: No.

HARRY: What?

MOM: No.

HARRY: No what?

MOM: Why do I have to meet him? He's your friend, not mine.

HARRY: He's more than my friend.

MOM: [*Startled.*] Oh.

HARRY: What does that mean? "Oh." If it was a woman, you'd be dying to meet her.

MOM: But he's not. [*Pause.*] I know I said I was ready for this but . . . first Dad dies. Then Jojo says he's moving to Seattle. Now you want me to meet your future husband? It's too much!

HARRY: Great! We've only talked about this for the past *ten years*. Don't ever tell me that I didn't try to include you in my life. And remember, this was the day we knew each other a little less.

MOM: Oh, will you stop that! You're being so nasty.

HARRY: [*Calmer, with affection.*] Mom, there were these two guys I knew who were lovers. They were both from Louisville, Kentucky and they were both named David—which was kinda confusing. Anyway, they'd been together for seven years. *Seven years!* I never had a relationship last seven *months!* Anyway, I missed my train one night and they let me stay at their place, right? I remember, it was raining and I slept on the sofa in the living room. But I couldn't sleep. I found myself looking around the room—I don't know what I was looking for, and I didn't want to...you know...be nosy. But I wanted to know ...*what holds people together.* Do you know what I mean?

So I'm looking around in the half-dark and I come to this bookcase *filled* with books. I looked at that bookcase and I saw seven years of companionship. I saw everything I never had. And I hated them for having it, for having each other all those years.

See, Mom—I'm a great morning person. I love to wake up—I could wake up all day. But if I never wake up with someone—who's gonna know?

MOM: [*After a beat.*] Wow. What a good public speaker you are. You get that from your father.

HARRY: Did you hear what I said?

MOM: Yes. I don't know what holds people together, Harry. I don't even know how people *get* together. You know, when I met your father, I was almost thirty years old myself. I thought I was gonna be an old maid. I accepted that as a real possibility. I didn't mind. If it wasn't in the cards, it wasn't in the cards. [*Beat.*] And that's when I met your father! Isn't that funny? It was only after I stopped trying to find a fella that I found one. It was at a picnic. Your Dad was so smart. He knew about anthropology and existentialism. [*Laughs.*] I couldn't even spell those words! I remember we were standing around under a willow tree. I was wearing my yellow dress—and he spilled Hawaiian Punch on it! He was so embarrassed. We were trying to clean it up together and finally he said: "You know, I think pink is your color." We burst out laughing and couldn't stop. We just clicked.

HARRY: That is a great story. Did you think to yourself...this is the guy?

MOM: No, I didn't think about marrying him—I just thought I had found a good friend. Friendship is more solid than love 'cause love...people fall out of love. [*Beat.*] I don't know about meeting your friend. Let me think about it, okay?

HARRY: Okay.

[*Lights go down partially on* HARRY *and* MOM. *They freeze in a tableau in half-light.* DAD's *musical snippet is heard.* HARRY *looks to the audience as if he hears something.* MOM *remains frozen in tableau. Spotlight up on* DAD.]

DAD: I think your mother exaggerates a little when she says I was a great public speaker. I was a "good" public speaker. As a "private" speaker —I was less impressive. Except when I was with your Ma. We had a chemistry going.

Hey, remember the time you took me to a Polish art film? But then, I love the movies. Give me some popcorn and I'll follow you anywhere. But this film was particularly bad—no camera movement and too many subtitles. But that wasn't the point. It was the first time you and I spent time together socially. . .like friends. And you set it all up. I think you were pleased we went at all.

I always thought one day you and I would have this great conversation. . .about life and love and the movies.

It never happened, you know.
So go ahead, Harry. Ask me something. Ask me a question you'd ask of the dead. But make it count. We simply *have* to stop meeting like this.

SCENE 6

A few days later. ANTONIO'S *place.*

HARRY: [*Upset.*] HAVE YOU EVER HEARD OF THE PHONE?

ANTONIO: I didn't think I needed to call —

HARRY: What did you think I was going to do? Did you picture this? What did you think was gonna happen at seven o'clock?

ANTONIO: What are you getting so upset about? I wasn't there —I'm here now. You need to learn to relax.

HARRY: Do you know what I did yesterday? This is pretty funny. I woke up at four a.m. and started cleaning. I threw away papers by the truckload — my neighbors thought I was moving. I vacuumed, I mopped. I bought a new tablecloth. Then at noon, I started to do something I've never done before: I started to cook for someone. I didn't know what I was doing. I surrounded myself with ingredients.

By afternoon, the smell of butter filled my apartment. So at seven o'clock . . . my place looked like a hotel. And I waited for you to ring my buzzer. At 7:15 I called your house and got your machine. At 7:30 I wondered if you were lost. By 8:00 . . . by 8:00, I said, "Fuck it," and I went for a walk.

ANTONIO: Harry, I didn't know it was that important to you! You should've *told* me.

HARRY: Antonio, I don't do *anything* that's not important to me! If it's not important — why do it at all? Yesterday, I thought you were important. I don't know what I feel today.

ANTONIO: I'm sorry. What else can I say?

HARRY: Is this what life is like in Brazil? Unimportant. Carefree? Easy come, easy go? Maybe yes — maybe no? IT WAS YOUR IDEA TO GO TO BRAZIL! Where were YOU last night?

ANTONIO: Take it easy! It's a little thing. What are you getting so upset about?

HARRY: Because I happen to like you. And it's a very important thing. I know it seems small — one dinner, one night. But you put all these things together and you've got a big thing. You've got trust — or you've got nothing. You want to be a diplomat? Try showing up for dinner next time. You want to build bridges. Build one to me.

ANTONIO: Maybe there won't be a next time.

HARRY: Don't threaten me.

ANTONIO: I think you should go.

HARRY: Do you want me to?

ANTONIO: I don't want to stand here and be insulted. You insult my country and my honor.

HARRY: [*Calmer.*] Why didn't you come to my house last night? I was really looking forward to it.

ANTONIO: I forgot.

HARRY: Tell the truth.

ANTONIO: I told you before. I couldn't make it!

HARRY: Why?

ANTONIO: Why. Why. Too many questions.

HARRY: Talk to me.

[*Pause.*]

ANTONIO: I wasn't ready.

HARRY: For what?

ANTONIO: If I came to your house for dinner—this would mean something, yes?

HARRY: It would probably mean you're hungry.

ANTONIO: In my country, it means you're hungry for more than food. It means you're hungry for a lover.

HARRY: I don't get it. I ask you to come to my house for dinner and it means I want to marry you. You ask me to come halfway around the world with you—and it's "just a trip: nothing more, nothing less."

ANTONIO: Harry, I have invited many people to come to my country. No one has ever come. Even when they say yes, they probably will never come. So I am . . . safe. And I like it this way. But dinner is more dangerous. You have a certain time, a place. There is an understanding. There are pictures. Each person has pictures of who he thinks the other person is—beautiful pictures. But how can we ever live up to them?

HARRY: You know, my mother thinks you're a terrorist.

ANTONIO: Maybe I am.

HARRY: You wouldn't scare anyone. Except maybe yourself.

ANTONIO: I started to come last night.

HARRY: And?

ANTONIO: And I'm sorry I didn't.

HARRY: It's all right. I have leftovers. You can't escape my cooking that easily. I'm not sure if you can reheat chicken Kiev, but we'll find out.

ANTONIO: Harry, what can I do to make it up to you?

HARRY: Well, there is one thing . . .

ANTONIO: Name it.

HARRY: I feel stupid even asking . . .

ANTONIO: Whatever you wish.

HARRY: Teach me the samba.

ANTONIO: What?

HARRY: I want to learn the samba. Now can you teach me or not?

ANTONIO: Why the samba?

HARRY: You don't think I'm gonna go halfway around the world with you to South America and not know how to do the stupid samba, do you?

ANTONIO: You are coming?!

HARRY: I wouldn't miss it for all the nuts in Brazil. Of which there are many, I'm sure. [*Beat.*] I want to see the rainforests. What are they like?

ANTONIO: They're beautiful. And the trees are huge. Five or six men holding hands cannot circle one. I'd like to show them to someone before... before anything happens to them. Maybe we can save them, Japanese. Do you think?

HARRY: I don't know. Anything's possible.

ANTONIO: I'd like to try. I feel I *owe* them something. Does that sound so funny?

HARRY: No.

ANTONIO: So tell me, Harry. How can you be so free to come to Brazil? What about your job, and your time, and...

HARRY: I look at it this way. I don't know if anything's ever gonna happen between us. I don't even know if I'm gonna like Brazil—

[ANTONIO *cuts him off, puts his finger to* HARRY'S *lips.*]

ANTONIO: Shh — no more talk, Japanese. Time to dance.

[*They take a long look at each other. Then they go into a dance position. But* ANTONIO, *instead of moving into the dance hold, embraces* HARRY. *Surprised,* HARRY'S *arms are still frozen in a dance frame. The song* "Brazil" *plays underneath.* HARRY *hugs* ANTONIO *back. Then* ANTONIO *begins the dance lesson, but instead of samba, he's teaching swing.*]

HARRY: Antonio, this isn't the samba.

ANTONIO: Shhh!

[*They continue dancing, laughing.* ANTONIO *stops dancing and kisses* HARRY. *He leads* HARRY *offstage. Intermission.*]

SCENE 7

It's after work, Friday. JOSH *and* HARRY *are sitting at bar.*

JOSH: This has been one helluva week. A week that will live in infamy.

HARRY: Why's that?

JOSH: Well, you won't believe this, Harry, but —

[TIWANA *comes back to the bar after powdering her nose. She sits next to* JOSH.]

HARRY: What won't I believe?

JOSH: Oh, nothing. Just the workload this week — it was unbelievable. How was your week?

HARRY: It was the best of weeks. It was the worst of weeks. What does it mean when someone stands you up?

JOSH: This is gonna be good.

HARRY: [*To* TIWANA.] What I mean is — is there ever a situation where someone stands you up and it's forgivable?

JOSH: I think it's case by case.

TIWANA: Cut to the chase. Who stood you up?

HARRY: Antonio. We had a dinner date. That's the "worst of weeks" part. The "best of weeks" part is — well, we finally slept together. I was thinking about your question, Tiwana — what do you think love is.

TIWANA: What'd you come up with?

HARRY: I think love is a kind of miracle. Like Halley's Comet — something that comes maybe once in a lifetime. If you're not careful, you could be in the bathroom when it comes.

JOSH: That's a terrifying thought. [*To* TIWANA.] Can I get you something? [*To himself.*] In the bathroom.

TIWANA: The usual. No really. What do you think love is?

HARRY: What can I say? It's all been said before.

TIWANA: Say it one more time. Define it. Know it. You can't just sit around and groove on the ambiguity.

HARRY: Love is . . . love is a foreign country I've never been to. I've seen postcards of it. I've had friends who've gone and come back. I think some people are born there and never leave — and others spend their whole lives trying to get in, and are turned away at the border. All I know is I feel like a tourist and that's a lonely way to feel.

I think Sam and I were in love. He made me a steak dinner one night when I was working late. No one's ever done that for me before.

TIWANA: What happened?

HARRY: He moved back to Ecuador. Why would anyone want to live in the hottest country on earth? He'd rather live in Ecuador than be with me. So who cares if I'm alone. I was a bachelor at 20, and I'm a bachelor at 30.

[JOSH *and* HARRY *toast.*]

HARRY/JOSH: Bachelors.

TIWANA: You know what your problem is? You think love is a goal. Something you either have or haven't got. But love is a process. Just because you're single now doesn't mean you haven't made progress. Think about it. Your first boyfriend was suicidal and slept with razor blades under his pillow. Your second guy was handsome and utterly lacking in ambition — but harmless. Your last guy was an architect for heaven's sake. Cute, full of life, but a little green in the love department. But light years ahead of your first. Do you see my point? Each one was a little closer to the right one.

JOSH: Yeah, yeah! It's like — what's his name — Darwin's theory of evolution.

HARRY: Huh?

JOSH: Sure. The cool thing about evolution is — each time the animals evolved they got smarter and stronger. Don't you get it, Harry? It's not just that our boyfriends and girlfriends are getting better — it's really about us evolving! The funny thing is . . . no one knows where they are on the evolutionary scale. But you just have to have faith that you're moving forward.

HARRY: Damn! You guys are deep! You gave me goosebumps. [*Beat.*] I was standing in the xerox room yesterday looking into the courtyard in the middle of our building — and every time I look into the middle of office buildings, I think two things. One. This would be a great location for a Hitchcock movie and Two. What am I DOING here?

TIWANA: You're making rent money, for one thing.

HARRY: But am I evolving? We're temporary office workers. Modern day gypsies. Closet artists. If this was the 70s, we'd be waiters by now. I'm gonna miss you guys.

TIWANA: Where you going?

HARRY: South America.

JOSH: You're kidding. He's kidding, right?

HARRY: It's just for the summer.

JOSH: But Harry, you know they're just gonna replace you with another temp.

HARRY: We're all replaceable. Life itself is just a temporary assignment.

JOSH: Who am I gonna hassle in the morning? Tiwana always comes in on time.

HARRY: You'll find someone.

JOSH: Can I have your White-Out? After you leave, I mean?

HARRY: It's yours. Well, I gotta go pick up some plane tickets. See you guys on Monday.

[HARRY *starts to exit.*]

TIWANA: You know what this means, Josh, don't you? It means . . . we're gonna have to . . . get to know each other.

JOSH: I can think of worse ways to spend a summer. 'Scuse me for a second.

[*He catches up to* HARRY.]

JOSH: [*Cont'd.*] Harry, I just wanted to thank you. You were right. Tiwana's crazy about me. And now with you leaving, she and I can really get to know each other. Last night, we went to a concert — Paul Simon and Ladysmith Black Mambazo. It was awesome.

HARRY: Looks like it's been a helluva week for all of us. Sometime, the four of us — we'll have to go on a double date.

JOSH: Sure. Well, I better see how Tiwana's doing. We're getting to know each other. Getting to know all about each other. Oh, I almost forgot. Last night at the concert, she told me to give you this really weird message. She said she checked the back burner and it wasn't all burned up. It was just getting warm. She said you'd know what it meant.

HARRY: [*Smiles.*] You guys have fun.

SCENE 8

One and a half weeks later. Sunday night at HARRY'S. *Lights rise on* HARRY *holding a paperback book, speaking to audience.*

HARRY: I can't swim.

[*He thinks for a second, then looks into the book.*]

HARRY: [*Cont'd.*] NOWNG SAY NADAHR!

[*Then from memory.*]

HARRY: [*Cont'd.*] I can't swim. NOWNG SAY NADAHR.

[*Flirtatiously.*]

HARRY: [*Cont'd.*] He swims like a fish.
EHL NAHDA KOHM OONG PAYSH.
He swims like a fish.

[*The door buzzer rings.* HARRY *answers the intercom.*]

HARRY: [*Cont'd.*] Hello?

[*A voice mutters on the speaker.*]

HARRY: [*Cont'd.*] Oh, come on up.

[HARRY *hides the books under his bed, fixes his hair. Then* ANTONIO *enters.*]

HARRY: [*Cont'd.*] BOAH TARD, ANTONIO, KOHM SHTAH?

ANTONIO: Fine thanks.

[*Beat.*]

ANTONIO: [*Cont'd.*] What did you just say?

HARRY: I said "Good afternoon, Antonio, how are you?"

ANTONIO: When did you learn to speak Portuguese?

HARRY: I bought this handbook: *Portugues Can Be Painless.* Impressed?

ANTONIO: Harry, you're gonna love Brazil. We'll walk through the rainforests. We'll dance with my friends till the sun goes down.

HARRY: Do you think Brazilian happiness is different from American happiness?

ANTONIO: Absolutley. In America, happiness doesn't come naturally. You have to work really hard at it. Here, a person is forever making plans, running to get to places — running for their lives. In Brazil, happiness comes to you, it finds you. Even the rain falls differently here. In my country, the rain falls in solid sheets of water. . .like someone in heaven is pouring water from a pan. But here, the rain falls like it's afraid it might hurt the earth. Like it's got worries of its own.

HARRY: Do you have to work hard to feel happy here?

ANTONIO: Of course. I'm becoming very Americanized.

HARRY: I love to listen to you. And it's not just 'cause of your accent.

ANTONIO: I feel really comfortable with you, Harry. It's strange—

HARRY: If I tell you something, promise you won't laugh? I have this fantasy about you.

ANTONIO: Really? Tell me!

HARRY: Sometimes I picture you . . . in a kitchen somewhere.

ANTONIO: [*Lustfully.*] A kitchen, huh? I LOVE it. Go on.

HARRY: You're standing there . . . your hands deep in hot water, your arms covered in soap suds . . .

[ANTONIO *begins to strip, kicking off shoes and socks.*]

ANTONIO: Oh, Harry—you're exciting me! What next, baby?

HARRY: Then you pull a dirty dish out of the water and you scrub it with your brush—

[ANTONIO *pulls off his shirt.*]

ANTONIO: Scrub it with my BRUSH! I follow you! I like to play rough!

HARRY: And then you turn and hand the dish to me, right?

[ANTONIO *climbs onto bed, stands over* HARRY.]

ANTONIO: The dish—that dirty dish . . .

HARRY: No, it's CLEAN now. You just washed it!

ANTONIO: Whatever. Get to the good part!

HARRY: [*Standing on bed.*] And then . . .

[*The big finish.*]

HARRY: [*Cont'd.*] I DRY IT!

[*Pause.* ANTONIO *waits expectantly.*]

ANTONIO: And then you dry it.

[*Beat.*]

ANTONIO: [*Cont'd.*] That's it? I don't get it. That's your hot fantasy?

HARRY: I didn't say it was hot. I said it was my fantasy. Oh, and I forgot to mention, we're both about ten years older.

ANTONIO: Harry, not only is that not hot—that's depressing.

[ANTONIO *gently mock-slaps* HARRY *on cheek.*]

HARRY: No, it isn't. It's beautiful. Two men doing dishes together, growing old together. That's my fantasy: husbands.

ANTONIO: You're a weird guy.

HARRY: We've never done it before. We've known each other now for, what, four weeks — and I still don't know what it's like to wash dishes with you. Why is that?

ANTONIO: We have to leave *something* to the imagination, don't we? Some mystery?

HARRY: You're a walking mystery.

ANTONIO: You say that like it's a bad thing.

HARRY: It's a terrible thing. I want to to the imagination, don't we? Some mystery?

HARRY: You're a walking mystery.

ANTONIO: You say that like it's a bad thing.

HARRY: It's a terrible thing. I want to *know* you. I want to *learn* you. I'm tired of, well . . . "grooving on the ambiguity."

ANTONIO: Grooving on the who? Listen, Harry — in my country, the less people know about you, the more they wonder. They more they wonder, the more they *respect* you!

HARRY: [*Mock angry.*] Well, you're not in Brazil now, are you? You're in America, goddammit! And in America, WE WANT ANSWERS — AND WE WANT THEM NOW. WE WANT THE WHOLE TRUTH AND NOTHING BUT THE TRUTH. And when we do dishes in America, by golly, we do them like this!

[HARRY *has now gotten out a washcloth and a dinner plate.*]

ANTONIO: I don't believe you're doing this.

HARRY: Okay, Antonio — you wash, I'll dry.

ANTONIO: Harry, I don't want to do dishes. You can't make me.

HARRY: Just to see how it feels.

ANTONIO: I *know* how it feels. It's not that exciting, believe me.

HARRY: What did we do last night for fun?

ANTONIO: Rented scary movies.

HARRY: Which was *your* idea. Tonight it's my turn to choose. Now shut up, dear, and wash.

[HARRY *slaps the dinner plate against* ANTONIO'S *bare chest.*]

ANTONIO: Jesus!

[ANTONIO *washes a plate, but without enthusiasm. He barely tickles the plate with his fingers.*]

ANTONIO: [*Cont'd.*] Okay, I'm washing a plate.

[HARRY *gives him a disapproving look. Then* ANTONIO *puts on a big grin and scrubs the plate in exaggerated circles with big arm movement.* HARRY *smiles, ceremonially takes the plate in his hands and dries it with a towel in careful, circular motions.*]

HARRY: Wow! This is incredible! Try a coffee mug.

[*He hands* ANTONIO *a mug.*]

HARRY: [*Cont'd.*] But this time, imagine we've been together for ten years. We've just had our tenth anniversary cake — chocolate cake with banana ice cream, followed by a pot of coffee. Now, wash the mug . . . with all that in mind.

[ANTONIO *mimes washing the mug, his face beaming with domestic bliss. He sensually caresses the inside of the mug as he cleans it.*]

HARRY: [*Cont'd.*] Perfect! Just perfect! Hold that pose!

[*With* HARRY'S *free hand, he grabs a camera and snaps a picture of the two of them washing dishes together. The flash goes off.*]

HARRY: [*Cont'd.*] I have to sit down.

ANTONIO: Yes, you need to rest, Harry. I think you've been breathing too much kitchen cleanser.

HARRY: Thank you, Antonio.

ANTONIO: For what?

[*Beat.*]

HARRY: Oh! I got you something.

[HARRY *presents* ANTONIO *with a large box, nicely wrapped.*]

ANTONIO: A present? I love presents!

HARRY: We've been together for exactly one month today. So it's kind of our anniversary. Open it.

ANTONIO: Will I like it?

HARRY: That's up to you.

[ANTONIO *puts box down.*]

ANTONIO: I'm gonna wait.

HARRY: For what?

ANTONIO: I want to savor the moment.

[*He waits a beat or two.*]

ANTONIO: [*Cont'd.*] Okay, I'm done.

[*He grabs the box and impatiently unwraps it.*]

ANTONIO: [*Cont'd.*] What can it be, what can it be?

[*He pulls a pillow from the box.*]

ANTONIO: [*Cont'd.*] Oh, Harry — it's, it's . . . a pillow.

HARRY: Do you like it?

ANTONIO: I don't know what to say.

HARRY: I figured since you've been staying over, you might want a pillow of your own.

[ANTONIO *is not quite reacting.*]

HARRY: [*Cont'd.*] If you don't like it . . . you can return it for something else.

ANTONIO: And here all along I thought I was the romantic one. And then you go and — do this.

[ANTONIO *kisses* HARRY.]

ANTONIO: [*Cont'd.*] I love my pillow. Want to help me . . . break it in?

HARRY: I thought you'd never ask.

[*They quickly jump into bed, lights dim.* ANTONIO *places pillow on bed. They carefully lie down on it, enjoying it for a few moments.*]

HARRY: [*Cont'd.*] Antonio?

ANTONIO: Huh?

HARRY: This is my favorite part.

ANTONIO: What?

HARRY: This. Talking in the dark. Good night.

[*After a few moments, a flash from the camera goes off.* ANTONIO sits up *in bed, giving* HARRY *an annoyed look.*]

SCENE 9

A few days later, Wednesday early evening at MOM'S. HARRY *faces the audience.* MOM *is at the table, pouring tea.*

HARRY: Looks like rain. Antonio says it rains a lot in Brazil. "Like someone in heaven is pouring water from a pan."

MOM: That's nice.

HARRY: I want you to be strong and survive on your own.

MOM: I'm tougher than I look. I signed up for a creative writing class yesterday at City College. And they don't even grade on a curve.

[*Beat.*]

MOM: [*Cont'd.*] Everyone I love goes away.

HARRY: I have the same problem. Must run in the family.

MOM: It runs in the world. Your Dad was the first guy I felt comfortable with. In fact, conversation — I just didn't know how to do it. But you get the right two people together . . . and the conversation makes sense.

HARRY: Of course all my friends find you absolutely charming.

MOM: Am I charming? What IS it about me that people find charming?

HARRY: Don't go fishing.

MOM: [*Laughs.*] Am I fishing?

HARRY: Yes.

MOM: Things'll sure be different without Jojo around, huh?

HARRY: It'll be good for both of you.

MOM: You don't want to move in, do you?

HARRY: I've got an apartment.

MOM: I know. But I'll have plenty of room. And think of the fun we could have. We could go shopping together, see a movie, you'd have someone to talk to at the end of the day . . .

HARRY: Mom, I love you. But I can't be Dad for you.

MOM: Boy, are YOU sassy! Who ASKED you to be Dad for me? That's okay. Forget it. I'll just put an ad in the paper for a roommate.

HARRY: What do you want me to say?

MOM: You can be so selfish sometimes. When you were a baby, I coulda said, "Let Harry be raised by the neighbors, I'm too busy having FUN!"

HARRY: Mother, you live in the third largest city in the United States. You live in walking distance of no less than fifty restaurants, theatres and shops . . . there's so much to do and still you live like you're in the suburbs.

MOM: I don't need things to do! I need someone to do them with! [*Pause.*] When your Dad was alive—he used to take me places. Or sometimes, we'd just drive—we weren't going anywhere. We were just driving . . . out into the world. Our little adventure. I never trusted myself behind a wheel. I know I should learn, but I have no desire.

HARRY: There are the drivers of the world . . . and there are the driven.

MOM: Harry, do you know in all my life I've never owned a driver's license. Isn't that funny? You'd think I woulda grown up by now.

HARRY: You're pretty grown up.

MOM: I'm scared to be alone.

HARRY: Please don't ask me to move in . . .

MOM: It gets so quiet . . .

HARRY: We'd get on each other's nerves.

MOM: What if a burglar snuck into my house in the middle of the night and I was all alone?

HARRY: You think you'd be in any *less* trouble if I was here?

MOM: What if I disappear one day?

HARRY: We all disappear . . . we all return. That's no big deal.

MOM: Well, go then. Abandon your mother. Do what you want—you're gonna do it anyway.

HARRY: Mom, you're asking for my life and I can't give that to you. You've had thirty-three years with a man who loved you and knew you . . . who bought you cheap flowers at the A&P and gave you two sons. I've had a couple months with lovers who were strangers to me.

MOM: It's not my fault you sleep with strangers! I never taught you that!

HARRY: What?!

MOM: Your father and I dated for months before we even kissed. We had things in COMMON!

HARRY: You don't think that's important to me?

MOM: I don't know WHAT's important to you anymore.

HARRY: No. You don't. You have no idea.

MOM: Which is why you should move in.

HARRY: Wrong. Let's back up a minute. First of all, it's none of your business who I do or do not sleep with! Secondly, and more importantly, WHO do you think I pattern myself after? What couple do I compare all my relationships to? You and Dad. People ask me what my parents were like together, you know what I tell them? "They were the perfect couple, they were best friends, they had things in common!" What do I want? I want what you had.

[*Beat.*]

MOM: He went to the Jewel.

HARRY: What?

MOM: When Dad bought me flowers—he went to the Jewel. Not the A&P. We've never lived near an A&P. Not in Hyde Park, not on 99th Street, not in Blue Island, and not now.

HARRY: Jewel. Right.

MOM: And they weren't "cheap flowers." They were inexpensive yet beautiful flowers. Carnations usually . . . white ones.

HARRY: [*Angry.*] What the hell difference does it make WHAT they were or WHERE he got them? The point is: you GOT flowers! I would've KILLED to get flowers from someone! No one's ever loved me that much.

[*The sound of thunder crackles in the distance. A rainstorm is brewing. We hear it raining under the rest of this scene.*]

MOM: What do you mean no one's ever loved you? Lots of people have loved you.

[*Beat.*]

MOM: [*Cont'd.*] I have.

HARRY: I mean someone who loved me because they were *in* love with me.

MOM: Louie liked you.

HARRY: [*Laughing.*] Yeah. Just when I thought our relationship was finally going somewhere—I bought a pillow. He always complained when he stayed over I only had one pillow. So I went to the store and bought this nice goose feather pillow. He never slept on it.

MOM: Why not?

HARRY: He took one look at the pillow and ran.

MOM: He was scared.

HARRY: I wasn't trying to force him into anything. I was just buying him a pillow.

MOM: Some people aren't ready to settle down.

HARRY: But when I bought Antonio a pillow — he didn't run. He slept on it. With me!

[*Pause, and then with some pain.*]

HARRY: [*Cont'd.*] Do you know what it's like to feel like a freak? Like no one's ever gonna love you back? To walk down Clark Street on a Sunday afternoon and see lovers windowshopping and wonder, "What's wrong with me? What do they know that I don't know?" You keep thinking this trip is a *trip away* from you. It isn't a trip away from anything — it's a trip *toward* something.

MOM: Did I ever tell you the time Dad and I saw balloons floating over a wheat field in Iowa?

HARRY: Yes.

MOM: Dad and I had been driving all night and in the morning we saw —

HARRY: I don't want to hear it.

MOM: Harry —

HARRY: All your stories are better than mine! They're more vivid, they're sweeter. You don't have to prove to me how full your life has been — PROVE TO ME THAT YOU WANT ME TO HAVE A FULL LIFE TOO!

MOM: All I've ever wanted was for my children to be happy.

HARRY: Prove it. Let go. Just open your hands and let go. It's easy.

MOM: Let me finish my story.

HARRY: It's too late for stories. Live in the past and you get stuck there.

MOM: I'm trying to tell you something too. See, in the morning we were in Iowa City and we saw these two balloons flying over the crops —

HARRY: I'm gonna say this so you can understand it, and I don't even care if you listen.

MOM: See —

HARRY: Mom, Antonio *likes* me. He asked me to go to Brazil for the summer — and I'm going with him.

MOM: See, one balloon was red — and it was coming downward —

HARRY: We leave in three days.

MOM: — and it looked *beautiful.*

HARRY: I love you . . .

MOM: A man in a dark shirt waved hello to me.

HARRY: . . . and I will always love you.

MOM: [*Laughing.*] Dad and I laughed so hard . . .

HARRY: Wherever I am . . . I send my love in your direction.

MOM: . . . the other balloon was navy blue. It was flying off into the distance. That was exciting and fun to see.

HARRY: [*Overlapping.*] Are you delirious? Can you hear me?!

MOM: [*Overlapping.*] See, Harry, it was flying off into the distance, and I was excited too!

HARRY: I forwarded my phone to your house. Please pick up my mail once a week.

MOM: [*Overlapping.*] What I'm trying to tell you is: those balloons weren't just balloons — THEY WERE A SIGN.

HARRY: I'll write.

MOM: I was the red balloon floating downward and you were the blue one floating off into the distance.

HARRY: Take care of yourself.

[HARRY *exits.* MOM *follows* HARRY *to doorway, calling after him.*]

MOM: The point is, Harry, I wasn't sad — I was excited, see? I'VE CHANGED MY MIND! I'M HAPPY THAT YOU'RE GOING TO BRAZIL. I'M HAPPY THAT YOU FOUND SOMEONE YOU LIKE. I'M HAPPY FOR YOU, HARRY!

[*Then softer, sadly, to herself.*]

MOM: [*Cont'd.*] Can't you see . . . how happy I am?

[*The steady hush of continuous rain still can be heard in the distance. Lights fade to black.*]

SCENE 10

About the same time of evening as previous scene. JOSH *is sitting at coffee-house table alone.* ANTONIO *walks in.*

JOSH: Antonio?

ANTONIO: Yes, you must be Josh.

[*They shake hands.*]

JOSH: Yes, thanks for coming. I hope it didn't seem . . .

ANTONIO: I'm happy to come. How did you get my phone number?

JOSH: Harry gave it to me a while back. He wanted me to have it, I guess.

ANTONIO: Of course. You know, Harry has always hoped that you and I would become friends. I'm sure he would be pleased. I'll tell him we talked.

JOSH: Oh, that really isn't necessary. [*Beat.*] Harry really likes you. You know that, of course. And you like Harry, right?

ANTONIO: He's wonderful. The best.

JOSH: Well, Harry's my buddy. I'm just looking out for him.

ANTONIO: Sure. I understand.

JOSH: What — what do you understand?

ANTONIO: You want to check up on me.

JOSH: Right. I guess you could say that. I mean . . . you care about Harry, right?

[*Beat.*]

ANTONIO: What is this all about, Josh? You have something on your mind. Tell me. Maybe I can help.

JOSH: Do you love him?

ANTONIO: I don't know what that means. I like him. I'm concerned about him.

JOSH: Harry thinks you want to take him to South America and show him the rainforests, so that you can propose to him there. Ask him to be your lover.

ANTONIO: I never said that! That's Harry and his wild imagination.

JOSH: Why ARE you going to Brazil with him?

ANTONIO: When I came here to the States . . . I was alone. Harry took me under his wing, introduced me to new people, took me to new places. He showed me his world. I wanted to return the favor.

JOSH: But it's more than that to Harry.

ANTONIO: Look, Josh. I appreciate what you're trying to do but — don't take this the wrong way, but I really don't think this is any of your business.

JOSH: You're right. I know. But Harry's my friend and you're Harry's friend. So it BECOMES my business. Know what I mean? All I'm saying is . . . be a mensch.

ANTONIO: A what?

JOSH: It's a Yiddish term. It means — be a man. Be human. Be kind. [*Beat.*] I hope you guys have a great trip. By all means, show him your world, Antonio. Return the favor. But be a mensch.

ANTONIO: What makes you think I'm not one — a mensch, as you call it? You think because you tell someone to be a man that he becomes one? If I say, "Josh, be more like Harry. Or Josh, be less Jewish. Be less white" — does that makes it so? I don't think so.

JOSH: I know. I'm sorry. I don't even know you. I'm sure you're a very nice person. Hey, please don't tell Harry we talked, okay?

[ANTONIO *starts to exit coffeehouse. Then he stops.*]

ANTONIO: You know, Harry's really lucky to have both of us for friends. Don't you think?

[ANTONIO *waits for a response.* JOSH *just forces a smile.* ANTONIO *leaves.*]

SCENE 11

This scene takes place in the middle of the night, maybe five hours after the previous scene. The steady sound of rainstorm continues. HARRY *enters* MOM'S *place. It's dark with only a small light on.* MOM *has gone to bed.* HARRY'S *umbrella and jacket are wet. He walks around, looking at things — sentimental objects. It should almost be reminiscent of the way* HARRY *describes staying over at the house of the two Davids, wondering what holds people together. Finally* HARRY *stares at a family portrait.* DAD *comes onstage, carrying a bowl of popcorn and a Coke, wearing bathrobe and slippers. He goes to sit in his regular chair.* HARRY *stands still, unsure what to do.*

HARRY: Dad?

DAD: [*Calmly.*] What?

HARRY: Is that you?

DAD: Uh-huh.

HARRY: What are you doing here?

DAD: I live here.

HARRY: Well . . . yeah. You used to live here.

DAD: Yes I did. I wanted to see the old place again. See how the paint job was holding up. Looks pretty good, don't you think? But enough shop talk. How are you?

HARRY: I'm fine. How are you? I mean —

DAD: Don't worry about it. I'm fine.

HARRY: You're dead, aren't you?

DAD: Absolutely.

HARRY: You know what, Dad? I thought I saw you parked in the parking lot at Walgreen's last spring!

DAD: [*Laughing.*] That wasn't me.

HARRY: Is this a dream? Am I dreaming you?

DAD: Does it matter?

HARRY: No. It's good to see you.

DAD: It's good to be seen. Again. So did you figure out what you wanted to ask me? Ask now or forever hold your peace.

HARRY: Well, okay . . . I keep thinking people love me — and they don't. I mean they do, but not the way I want them to. No one ever loves you the way you want them to, do they?

DAD: They do their best.

HARRY: See, I find love really confusing. It comes so easily to some people. Am I ever gonna find someone to talk to in the dark when the whole world is sleeping?

DAD: Harry, this is all I know. It's all I learned. The people in your life that make you happy are there because you earned them. And the people who make you suffer are there to teach you something.

HARRY: Can a person make you happy and make you suffer at the same time?

DAD: Of course. When that happens, that's called: Being In Love.

HARRY: That's how I feel about Antonio.

DAD: The important thing is to learn what he's there to teach you. If you choose to learn — you can move forward. If you choose not to learn — you go in circles.

HARRY: What happens if you don't choose?

DAD: You don't learn.

HARRY: What if I'm not smart enough?

DAD: For what?

HARRY: To learn the lesson.

DAD: [*Looking at his watch.*] Will you look at the time! I gotta run.

[DAD *starts gathering his things, moves toward the door.*]

HARRY: Wait, Dad! Can't you tell me something a little more encouraging?

DAD: That IS encouraging. It means you have a choice. All the good you do comes back to you. All the bad you do comes back to you. So the good news is: the universe is fair. All the love you give today — might seem like it's wasted. But one day, that love will be returned to you. It might come back from a different direction, but it comes back. Well, I gotta run.

HARRY: Where are you going?

DAD: [*Smiling.*] I don't know. I love you, Harry. Know that. Oh, and tell your Ma I said hi.

[DAD *exits.* HARRY *doesn't notice, lost in trying to write down notes.* MOM *enters.*]

HARRY: Wow, I've got to write this stuff down so I don't forget it. "All the love you give today might seem like it's wasted. But one day, that love will be returned to you." That is so cool. How'd you get so smart, Dad?

[*No answer.*]

HARRY: [*Cont'd.*] Dad? Are you still with me?

MOM: Harry? Are you still here? You want to stay over — we've got extra blankets. Why don't you?

HARRY: Sure. I'll stay. Mom! I saw Dad again. He said to say hi to you.

MOM: Oh! Hi back AT him. You want some pajamas? There's chicken in the fridge if you're hungry.

HARRY: Chicken sounds good. Mom!

MOM: What?

HARRY: I'm thirty.

MOM: So. That's not so bad. You know how old your Ma is?

HARRY: How old?

MOM: Old enough.

HARRY: What's it like? To be "old enough"?

MOM: Oh, Harry . . . it went really fast.

HARRY: I love you.

MOM: I love you too. Turn off the lights when you're through, okay? Don't waste electricity.

HARRY: Okay.

MOM: Oh, I finished some notes on those memoirs you wanted me to write. It's just a start. You can look at them in the morning. Night.

[HARRY *lies down on sofa with comforter. He turns off the light and looks at* MOM'S *memoir. He smiles as lights fade to black.*]

SCENE 12

A few days later, Friday afternoon at HARRY'S. *It's the day before* HARRY *and* ANTONIO *are to leave for Brazil.* MOM *is helping to pack some things in a suitcase on the bed. There's a knock at the door.* ANTONIO *enters carrying a bag.*

ANTONIO: Hi, is Harry around?

MOM: Oh, he went to the store. He should be here soon.

ANTONIO: Could you tell him I came by? My name is Antonio.

MOM: Oh!

[*Pause.*]

MOM: [*Cont'd.*] I've heard a lot about you.

ANTONIO: I can imagine. Harry told me to come by at 2:00. He said there was something he wanted to show me.

MOM: That's funny. He told me he was expecting a delivery at 2:00 and not to leave the house till it came. I think this is a set-up!

ANTONIO: What do you mean?

MOM: Well, Harry wanted me to meet you for the longest time . . . and so . . . I guess I'm meeting you now.

ANTONIO: That was pretty sneaky. Well, it's nice to meet you.

[ANTONIO *shakes her hand gallantly. There's an awkward moment.*]

MOM: [*With great relief.*] Well, that's settled.

ANTONIO: I didn't realize Harry had a sister. Let alone such a charming one.

MOM: [*Very flattered.*] I'm not his sister. I'm his mother!

ANTONIO: Impossible.

MOM: It's true.

[*Beat. She approaches him with a secretive air.*]

MOM: [*Cont'd.*] Can I ask you a question?

ANTONIO: Sure.

MOM: What is it about me that *you* find charming?

ANTONIO: That's easy. You have the voice of a young girl — it's almost like a song. You find joy in small things. Harry's told me a lot of stories about you. You're very Brazilian in your way, I think.

MOM: I think I see what Harry sees in you. [*Beat.*] You're a poet.

ANTONIO: No, I'm not.

MOM: You coulda fooled me.

ANTONIO: I fool a lot of people.

MOM: Well, you can wait here if you want. He should be here any minute.

ANTONIO: Oh, I really can't stay. Actually, there was some stuff I wanted to talk to Harry about. Maybe I could just leave a message with you.

MOM: Sure.

ANTONIO: Could you tell him . . . something's come up. I can't go on the trip tomorrow.

[*Beat.*]

MOM: You're not going to Brazil?

ANTONIO: It's a long story. He can call me if he has any questions.

MOM: [*Getting a bit frantic.*] But you have to go! He bought his ticket! He made arrangements. He's got it all planned out.

ANTONIO: I really can't talk about it now. Could you just give him the message?

MOM: I said I was his mother—not his secretary. You know what your problem is? You're too charming! You can say no in about a million different ways, and it all sounds like yes. And the problem with Harry is...he only hears the yes. 'Cause that's all he wants to hear. Look— what you guys do is your business. But if you have any feelings at all for Harry, just tell him what you want. 'Cause I think he's falling in love with you.

ANTONIO: He is?

[HARRY *walks in with groceries.*]

HARRY: I couldn't find any dried plums, but I got some dates and raisins. They're kind of in the same family...Antonio!

MOM: I think you two have something to talk about. I'm going for a long walk around the world, Harry. Don't wait up for me.

[MOM *exits.* HARRY *kisses* ANTONIO.]

HARRY: Are you all packed? I'm almost done, but I always overpack. I can't believe you finally met my mother. She's something, isn't she?

ANTONIO: Yes. Just like her son. You know...I'll always picture us... eating muffins in your northside coffee house where the life is.

HARRY: You don't have to picture it. We can go back there any time.

ANTONIO: I'll always remember the way...you took care of me.

HARRY: What are you talking about?

ANTONIO: Harry—

HARRY: What?

ANTONIO: I'm not going.

HARRY: What do you mean?

ANTONIO: I like you very much.

HARRY: Uh-huh.

ANTONIO: I don't feel about you the way you feel about me.

HARRY: How do I feel about you?

ANTONIO: [*With difficulty.*] You look at me and see us sailing off into a South American sunset. This isn't just a trip to you—it's a honey- moon. I like you—but I don't want to marry you.

HARRY: I don't want to marry you either! It's just two friends going on a trip. Remember? Nothing more, nothing less.

ANTONIO: I've never loved anyone before. I wouldn't know where to begin.

HARRY: Who said anything about love?!

ANTONIO: I know you think I'll feel different later, once we get there. But I never feel different later. I just feel stupid.

HARRY: What was all that talk about Brazil—how the rains come and people fall in love, how they surrender to all that they know in the rainy season?

ANTONIO: That was a story I made up.

HARRY: WHAT?!

ANTONIO: People love to hear stories. Even if they aren't true.

HARRY: [*Getting angry.*] You lied to me! I believed you and you lied to me.

ANTONIO: I wanted you to like me.

HARRY: Now I'm really confused.

ANTONIO: Remember when I met you, I told you I was kind of strange, and that I'd tell you about it someday?

HARRY: I think it's time.

[*Pause, then with some difficulty.*]

ANTONIO: When I was a little kid in Brazil, the other kids used to make fun of me because I didn't know what I wanted to be when I grew up. They called me Antonio Sin Suenos—that means Antonio, the Dreamless One. See, Harry, in Brazil, a person is known by their dreams. Carlos wanted to be a great soccer star. Isabella wanted to *rule South America!* Little Evita we called her. Of me, they'd just say, Poor Antonio. He lacks imagination. So I made up my mind to prove them wrong.

[*Pause, with great difficulty.*]

ANTONIO: [*Cont'd.*] I STARTED MAKING THINGS UP!

[HARRY *is listening now.*]

ANTONIO: [*Cont'd.*] — where I lived, who my family was, what I wanted to be. I WANTED TO HAVE AN INTERESTING LIFE, BUT I DON'T KNOW HOW. And if I couldn't have one—at least I wanted people to think I did.

[*Faces* HARRY *directly.*]

ANTONIO: [*Cont'd.*] Harry, I don't study foreign relations at the University of Chicago. I drive a cab all night and I live off my tips.

[HARRY *tries to turn away, but* ANTONIO *restrains him.*]

ANTONIO: [*Cont'd.*] My sister didn't die in a mudslide like I told you. She lives in a suburb of Brazil. She watches too much television. My Brazil is not your Brazil. It's a poor country. A few people can afford to live in luxury, but most of us are poor. On the streets, they steal your wallet when you're not looking. And time . . .

[*Takes* HARRY'S *hand.*]

ANTONIO: [*Cont'd.*] . . . time steals the rest. We were born under different stars, Harry. And there's nothing we can do . . . to change that.

[*Long pause. Then* HARRY *speaks, abruptly.*]

HARRY: I'd love to stay and talk . . . but I've got a plane to catch.

ANTONIO: You're going?

HARRY: Of course. I've got the time off, I've got the ticket, and most important — I have the wish. You taught me that.

ANTONIO: But you don't know anyone there.

HARRY: Sometimes I don't think I know anyone *here*.

[*Pause.*]

HARRY: [*Cont'd.*] Antonio, tell me one thing that's true. Does it rain in Brazil?

ANTONIO: Like there's no tomorrow. Like tomorrow would have to be postponed because of so much rain. When it rains in Brazil — man, it pours!

HARRY: Good!

ANTONIO: I have something for you.

[ANTONIO *offers* HARRY *a bouquet of white carnations that he has been hiding in a bag. But* HARRY *doesn't take them right away.*]

HARRY: What's this?

ANTONIO: White carnations, I think.

HARRY: What are they for?

ANTONIO: For you.

HARRY: I don't get it.

ANTONIO: There's nothing to get. They're flowers, you put them in water.

HARRY: How'd you pick white carnations?

ANTONIO: They were on sale at the Jewel.

HARRY: They're really nice. But you know, in America we give flowers at the *beginning* of the relationship.

ANTONIO: In Brazil, we give them at the end . . . to say thank you.

HARRY: Is that true? Don't answer that.

> [ANTONIO *hands* HARRY *the bouquet gallantly.* HARRY *takes it, studies the flowers a moment, then throws them into the air like confetti.*]

ANTONIO: What the hell are you doing! Are you crazy?

HARRY: I can't take these!

ANTONIO: [*Picking up flowers.*] Why not?

HARRY: Because they don't mean anything.

ANTONIO: You said you always wanted flowers!

HARRY: No. I never wanted flowers. I wanted what flowers could mean! And these don't mean anything.

> [*Beat.*]

HARRY: [*Cont'd.*] And they're late.

> [*Thunder cracks. A storm is beginning. Rain sounds.*]

ANTONIO: What?

HARRY: These flowers are late!

ANTONIO: I told you, in my country we give flowers at the end —

HARRY: — Bullshit! No one gives flowers at the end of a relationship! YOU'RE LYING . . . YOU'RE LATE . . . AND YOU'RE IN AMERICA!

ANTONIO: You know why you're alone?

HARRY: Tell me.

ANTONIO: Because you think the world revolves around you!

HARRY: You think it doesn't? Prove it. I got you to come here today, didn't I?

ANTONIO: I came here because I wanted to!

HARRY: No. You came here because I wanted you to. You're under my spell. You were my last wish.

ANTONIO: What are you talking about?

HARRY: It's the old Magic Wand game. You were my last wish. I wished for your happiness—and that your happiness included me. But that if you weren't good for me, that I'd know it. And it worked. You know why I'm alone, Antonio? Because I'm a romantic in an unromantic age . . . and I have lousy taste in men.

[HARRY *is struck by a thought.*]

HARRY: [*Cont'd.*] That's it, isn't it? That's what you were here to teach me.

ANTONIO: I have no idea what you're talking about. You're acting really weird, Harry.

HARRY: Thank you, Antonio. And goodbye.

ANTONIO: Japanese, I think if you tried to—

HARRY: [*Cutting him off.*] I said goodbye. Don't make me say it again.

[ANTONIO *starts to say something, but gives up. He puts the flowers on* HARRY'S *bed, exits. Steady sound of rain. Lights fade to a spot on* HARRY *as he moves forward to address audience. He puts on sportcoat, has his suitcase in hand.*]

HARRY: My strongest memory of growing up is standing at the window with my Mom watching it rain. She wrote a story about it in her creative writing class and her teacher thinks it could get published!

[*Partial light rises and then fades up on* MOM *as seen behind rain curtain scrim.*]

HARRY: [*Cont'd.*] Anyway, we used to stand there forever . . . mesmerized. [*Laughs.*] It was like we were waiting for something to come out of the rain and save us. But I'll tell you a secret. We spent an awful lotta time . . . at an awful lotta windows . . . and nothing ever came out of the rain, but more rain.

[*The song "Brazil" comes in under, a version sung in Portuguese by a male singer. The music gets louder and fuller.*]

HARRY: [*Cont'd.*] Lately I think what I've got to do is stop hanging around windowsills and get out of the damn house. Go out into the rain. Get a little wet. And see for myself . . . what's there.

[HARRY *takes a last look at this place. He picks up one white carnation from the floor, smells it, smiles, exits. The song comes up full. Lights fade to black.*]

END OF PLAY

Garrett H. Omata

S.A.M. I AM

EDITOR'S NOTES

As both a divinity student and a comic book writer, Garrett Omata brought a unique perspective to the stage. In his first produced play, *S.A.M. I Am*, Omata tied together the world of personal ads, conflicts over interracial dating, and the curious literary success of certain angry white males with nothing much to say—and made of these discrete elements a romantic comedy with both a heart and a mind.

The play, which has been produced thus far at Los Angeles' East West Players Asian American Thare Company in San Francisc, Theatre Mu in Minneapolis, and at Stockton's Asian American Repertory Theatre, succeeds most strongly with young audiences who are used to seeing stories about their parents on stage—the struggles of the Issei and the Nisei, the history of the internment camps, the tragedies of racial hatred—but rarely see themselves on stage. John, Lohman, Betty and Jackie are all as recognizable as they are funny.

The growth of the play is both a testament to and a caveat against the development process so predominant among LORT theatres today. Omata started writing as a student in the David Henry Hwang Writers Institute, a program instituted by Hwang and East West Players, with various corporations providing grant support specifically to develop interethnic writing for the theatre. After an intriguing experimental drama about beauty and voyeurism in modern photography, Omata turned to comedic scenes that became one of the Institute's success stories. The first reading of *S.A.M. I Am*, at the Powerhouse Theatre in Santa Monica, was one of the funniest staged readings I've seen, and the audience response prompted further development of the play.

Yet as the play wended through further readings, the play seemed to lose some of its comedic edge. The cause of this puzzled everyone, until finally Omata and his colleagues agreed that the play had been diluted by one too many scenes that perfectly explained everything. A prologue scene, for example, in which John dreams of romancing Jackie while Jackie dreams of Sam Shepard, seemed to sum up the play perfectly—so perfectly that the following scenes, which had previously seemed so light and quick-witted, now seemed to dwell on the obvious. By cutting some of the "developed" scenes, Omata delayed revealing just where the play was headed, and kept us involved in the journey.

The ending was similarly debated. Various endings were tried nearly every night of previews—one in which the two couples fight their way through the mob, another in which they were left wrapped in each other's respective embraces. Simplicity finally won out. After John makes his statement to the public, a brief scene in which John and Jackie glance affectionately at each other across the space between their apartments ends the play. They may become romantically involved, or they may not, but they have each grown and carved out a space for themselves and their work. Few couples achieve that much, either on or offstage. We are left realizing that Omata's death in early 1997 robbed the Asian American theatre of one of its freshest new voices.

S.A.M. I Am was first produced at East West Players (Tim Dang, Artistic Director), in Los Angeles, California, on January 19, 1995, with the following cast:

JOHN	Doug Yasuda
LOHMAN	Eddie Mui
JACKIE	Joanne Takahashi
BETTY	Cindy Cheung
NORMAN	Jeff Dente
GERALDINE	Shay Phillips
LEONARD	Daniel Getzoff

Directed by Heidi Helen Davis. Set Design by Jim Barbaley; Light Design by Frank McKown; Costume Design by Marcelle Marie McKay; Sound Design by Taiho Yamada. The play was developed in a workshop with the David Henry Hwang Writers' Institute.

CHARACTERS

JOHN HAMABATA	27, Japanese-American
LOHMAN CHIN	26, Chinese-American
JACKIE SHIBATA	24, Japanese-American
BETTY HAMABATA	24, Japanese-American, John's cousin
NORMAN	40, Caucasian
GERALDINE	23, Caucasian
LEONARD GJAFFRY	21, Caucasian
VOICES:	DATELINE VOICE — FEMALE
	LARRY
	ANNOUNCER

ACT I: SIR, YOU'RE NO SAM SHEPARD

SCENE 1

The kitchen of an Italian restaurant. JOHN, *a twenty-seven-year-old Japanese-American man, is dressed in an apron, white shirt, black slacks and ugly tie.* LOHMAN, *a good-looking twenty-six-year-old Chinese man, wears a white shirt and red apron.*

JOHN: Look, one more time. The dipper.

LOHMAN: Yeah, the dipper.

JOHN: The dipper sterilizes the flatware.

LOHMAN: The what?

JOHN: Flatware! The spoons, the forks, the knives.

LOHMAN: Yeah, yeah, the flatware. Right.

JOHN: You dip the flatware rack into the dipper and the boiling water sterilizes the flatware.

LOHMAN: Kills the germs.

JOHN: Right.

LOHMAN: Before the dipper, germs. After the dipper, no germs.

JOHN: You got it. Now, before you dip the flatware rack into the dipper, the flatware is not clean.

LOHMAN: The spoons and forks and knives.

JOHN: And even if they look clean, you are not supposed to set them out on the tables for our customers to put in their mouths.

[*Pause.*]

LOHMAN: Ohhhhh! You mean they've been putting it —

JOHN: In their mouths.

LOHMAN: I fucked up, John. I fucked up.

JOHN: It's okay, Lohman.

LOHMAN: I'm not gonna get fired, am I?

JOHN: Just don't do it again, all right?

LOHMAN: Scout's honor, man. Before dipper, germs. After dipper, no germs. Scout's honor.

JOHN: Thanks, Lohman. [*Pause;* LOHMAN *stares at* JOHN.] What!

LOHMAN: Wow, you're really it! The assistant manager!

JOHN: What. So what.

LOHMAN: It's just — you really did it. Remember, right after the day you dropped out of college — you were washing dishes, you said you'd be a waiter one day. So you got to be a waiter. Then you said, nah, I wanna be a cook instead. And when you were a cook, you said, "Hey, a monkey can manage a restaurant!" Remember? Remember what you said?

JOHN: "Just hang the key around his neck."

LOHMAN: And look at you! The assistant monkey!

JOHN: Shhhhh! [*Aside.*] It's all in the lips.

[JOHN *makes kissy sound and bends over like he's kissing butt.* NORMAN *enters out of* JOHN'S *view.* NORMAN *is a fortyish man who looks like he played college sports but now mainly drinks beer.*]

LOHMAN: Uh, hey, Norman.

JOHN: Hi, Norman.

NORMAN: Hey, boys. John, a minute?

JOHN: Right, Norman.

[LOHMAN *moves away, practicing to dip the flatware rack.*]

NORMAN: Three syllables, John?

JOHN: Discipline.

NORMAN: Discipline. Easy to remember, don't you think?

JOHN: Yes, Norman.

NORMAN: Kind of rolls off the tongue. Dis-ci-pline.

JOHN: Sure does, Norman.

NORMAN: Between you and me, I don't mind a good joke. Hell, you know me...

JOHN: You're a funny guy, Norman.

NORMAN: I love a good one, man. And you know I'm not above laughing at my own foibles. It's a known truth. But, around the help...

JOHN: You're absolutely right. We are management.

NORMAN: We are management. Good. I don't want to be repetitive. I hate that. I hate repetivity. I hate —

[LOHMAN *enters carrying a copy of a weekly newspaper, the L.A. Independent.*]

LOHMAN: Excuse me, Norman, but I need — I require the aid of the esteemable assistant manager for a very important reconnaissance.

[NORMAN *exits.*]

JOHN: Please don't say you've lost your retainer in the pizza dough again.

LOHMAN: I just need to leave an hour early. I got a date coming by.

JOHN: And you're meeting her here?

LOHMAN: I want her to see me in a tie.

JOHN: A new girl? I thought you were seeing that blonde.

LOHMAN: She is, there's just a different face underneath.

JOHN: Okay, I'll cover you. I think the VCR can wait for me an hour longer.

LOHMAN: I told you, John, any time you wanted — I can get you the woman of your dreams.

JOHN: No, you can get me the woman of your dreams. You don't like the women of my dreams. [*Phone rings.*] I'll get it. [LOHMAN *exits as* JOHN *answers the phone.*] Pinoni's Pizza Palace!

BETTY'S VOICE: [*Disguised.*] Is this John Hamabata?

JOHN: Yes, can I help you?

BETTY: I hope so. This is Jackie.

JOHN: Jackie Shibata?

BETTY: You know, I heard you wanted to see me.

JOHN: Oh yeah. I love — I mean I'd love to see you.

BETTY: When?

JOHN: Anytime. It can be anytime.

BETTY: How about now.

JOHN: Now? Right now?

BETTY: I haven't had lunch yet...

JOHN: We could have lunch.

BETTY: But you know, I don't feel like lunch in Los Angeles.

JOHN: We could go someplace else.

BETTY: I've always wanted to have lunch in Hawai'i.

JOHN: Hawai'i...?

BETTY: Would you do that for me, John? Would you take me to Hawai'i for lunch?

JOHN: [*Short pause.*] Sure, Jackie. I'll take you to Hawai'i.

[*Lights come up in* JACKIE *and* BETTY'S *apartment.* BETTY *is holding the telephone receiver.*]

BETTY: [*In her own voice.*] Sucker!

JOHN: Betty!?

BETTY: Hey, cuz. When do we take off?

JOHN: I don't believe you. I hate you!

BETTY: This is really for your own good. Now what do you have to say?

JOHN: Did you ask her yet?

BETTY: The correct answer is, "Betty, I've given up on my insane need to nail your roommate."

JOHN: I can't give up, Betty! I'm already past my sexual peak!

BETTY: Really?

JOHN: Yeah, it happened on a Saturday last summer after an episode of "Three's Company."

BETTY: John, I'm going to make a healthy human being out of you if it takes two Ph.D.s in psychotherapy.

JOHN: Well, don't hold your breath.

BETTY: Are you going to pick me up, or what?

JOHN: I'll slow down as I drive by so you can jump on the bumper.

[JOHN *hangs up.* LOHMAN *walks in with* GERALDINE *on his arm.*]

LOHMAN: Yes, it's a lot of responsibility I carry here. Allow me to show you the dipper.

SCENE 2

JACKIE *and* BETTY's *apartment. A movie poster for* Country *hangs on a wall.* JACKIE *sits on a couch against a wall. On the wall, several Polaroid photos are pinned up.* JACKIE *is tall, twenty-four years old, with pretty Eurasian features. At a desk with a computer is* BETTY, *a Japanese-American woman of twenty-four, less flamboyant than* JACKIE. *A telephone sits nearby.* JACKIE *goes to her poster of Sam Shepard and uses a bronze candle lighter to light the two candles before it, as if it were a shrine.*

BETTY: Hey, you want to go to a wedding?

JACKIE: Whose?

BETTY: Lydia Yamamoto.

JACKIE: No thanks. Weddings give me zits. [*Pause.*] If I were a man, would you marry me?

BETTY: I can't marry you.

JACKIE: If I were a man.

BETTY: You mean, now?

JACKIE: If I just all of a sudden grew a penis and chest hair, then would I be the kind of person you'd want to marry?

BETTY: How big a penis?

JACKIE: I don't know!

BETTY: No really—are you going to be some kind of weird hermaphrodite? Would you still have boobs?

JACKIE: No boobs.

BETTY: Okay, that's okay.

JACKIE: Not that there's much to get rid of.

BETTY: Oh, I think your boobs are pretty big.

JACKIE: Really? You mean it? No, you don't.

BETTY: Really! If I were a guy, I'd notice them.

JACKIE: Men notice mosquito bites if they stick out.

BETTY: No, I'd think you have plenty. A handful.

JACKIE: So you'd go for me then?

BETTY: Okay, sure ... wait.

JACKIE: What?

BETTY: Who's the guy now? Am I the guy or are you the guy?

JACKIE: You're the guy, I'm the hermaphrodite.

BETTY: Sick!

JACKIE: What!

BETTY: Forget it, I can't marry you!

JACKIE: You just said!

BETTY: That's before you got kinky.

JACKIE: Okay, if you were a man and I were a man and we were both gay, then would you go for me?

BETTY: [*Pause.*] Only if you were a cross-dresser.

JACKIE: Hey, don't answer the phone if it rings. It'll probably be the TV station calling me to rewrite my leads.

BETTY: But isn't that your job?

JACKIE: I don't feel like talking to anyone, okay? Unless it's a guy ... and the answering machine will pick it up.

BETTY: What if it's my cousin John? He's giving me a ride to school.

JACKIE: Oh, he's not a guy. He's Japanese.

[*Doorbell rings.* BETTY *answers it;* JOHN *is in the doorway.*]

JOHN: Hi, ready? Umm, hi, Jackie ... !

[JACKIE *isn't paying attention. The phone rings.*]

JACKIE: Don't answer it!

BETTY: [*To* JACKIE.] Did you turn the machine on?

JACKIE: Of course I — Oh! I left the fax machine on.

[JACKIE *picks up the phone. Suddenly we are bombarded with the screeching sound of a fax signal which apparently is coming out of the answering machine.*]

MALE VOICE: Hello? Hello?

[JACKIE *picks up the receiver, but the cord has come loose.*]

JACKIE: Hello!? Brad?

[JACKIE *tries to plug the cord back in.*]

MALE VOICE: Shit. She must've given me a bogus number.

[*The line goes dead.*]

JACKIE: Brad! Brad! I'm here, Brad! [*She puts the phone down and drags herself, slump-shouldered, out of the room, mumbling to herself.*] Oh, Brad.

BETTY: John, did you ever meet my friend Alicia? She's in Depression and Suicide.

JOHN: What?

BETTY: My class.

JOHN: I don't want to.

BETTY: She's really cute, John.

JOHN: I want Jackie.

BETTY: Look, here's her resume: Alicia in formal wear — an airy autumn look; at the beach in a yellow tank suit that shows a bright summer spirit with a suggestion of sunset romance; and my favorite: an ensemble that's casual yet sexy, giving her that coquettish aura at the same time saying, "Hey world, look at me!"

JOHN: I don't want Alicia, I want Jackie! I want Jackie!

BETTY: John, you're acting like a child.

JOHN: I'm not acting. I'm very earnest. Look, if I just wanted any warm body, I'd call up a girl in one of these ads!

[*He gives her the paper. She looks at the ads.*]

BETTY: Euuww. I'm glad you have your standards. Hey, I need to go to the library. Let's go.

JOHN: Should we? She looks so despondent. She might need . . . she might need comforting!

BETTY: Who, Jackie?

JOHN: She just had a very traumatic experience!

BETTY: When the ice cream falls out of your cone, do you worry about it the next day? Do you even remember what flavor it is?

JOHN: No . . . [*Brightening.*] But, I would go back and get some more ice cream!

BETTY: John, I love Jackie, but really — what's so great about her that isn't better in someone else?

JOHN: Ever since you two moved in together, I've been — ! I get so — ! I . . . I just don't have any words for what I feel!

BETTY: So why do you want to go out with her?

JOHN: I don't know! Well, she's smart. She looks cool.

BETTY: Like how?

JOHN: Well, you know, her hair . . . her posture, I guess. Clear skin.

BETTY: Oh yeah, clear skin is very important.

JOHN: Okay, so why won't she go out with me?

BETTY: She wants something else.

JOHN: Like what?

BETTY: [*Still flipping through the personals.*] An S.W.M.

JOHN: She wants to swim? I can swim.

BETTY: No, John. See here? You're an S.A.M.

JOHN: I'm a Sam?

BETTY: Single Asian Male. [*Points to the page.*] She wants a Single White Male.

JOHN: Okay, I can't swim. What else?

BETTY: Well, for one thing, a car.

JOHN: I've got a —

BETTY: You've got a Toyota. Get a Porsche.

JOHN: Okay. Do you have a pen? [BETTY *gives him a pen;* JOHN *starts writing things down.*] Number one: Porsche. Is that it?

BETTY: Armani suits. Lunches on Rodeo Drive. And . . . oh yeah. Plastic surgery.

JOHN: Surgery?

BETTY: You have to look like Sam Shepard. He's six-four. Can you do anything about your height?

JOHN: Sam Shepard? He's the guy in the bank commercials with the stagecoach, right?

BETTY: Jackie likes Sam Shepard a lot.

JOHN: But he's so —

BETTY: Sexy...masculine...

JOHN: Old! Who'd ever go out with him?

BETTY: He's a playwright, too. He won a Pulitzer Prize, or something. Jackie likes creative men.

JOHN: [*Writes it down.*] Okay, I can do that. I can do creative.

BETTY: What about the car?

JOHN: Hey, I'll worry about the car. I can get the car.

BETTY: John...

JOHN: I can get the car!

BETTY: John...!

JOHN: What else, Betty? Tell me what else I need to do! Anything else!?

BETTY: John! Listen to me!

JOHN: I'm listening! Give me more! Tell me what I have to do!!

BETTY: What's wrong with you? You don't even know her!

JOHN: I'm not asking her to marry me. I'm just looking for a date.

BETTY: A date? Just a date!? I've got Alicia on twenty-four-hour standby!

JOHN: But Betty...! Alicia is white.

BETTY: So what?

JOHN: I like Japanese women.

BETTY: Why?

JOHN: Because...they look nice. They smell nice. They don't ask stupid questions about sushi. And when I get married, I want to be able to give my children a history. Lineage, that sort of thing.

BETTY: Jackie's only half Japanese.

JOHN: Then I'll only date half of her. The other part can go out with whatisname...Sam Stoppard.

BETTY: Sam Shepard.

JOHN: Whoever he is.

BETTY: John, besides the looks, what's really the difference between just dating a nice Japanese and a nice Caucasian?

JOHN: [*Pause.*] You know, Betty, I look at myself sometimes, and I see the same face I see every morning in the mirror. And that's okay. Then I look at the sky, and it's really blue, and I think, the sky is the same for me as it is for everybody else. And I feel like I belong here, no problem. [*Pause.*] But sometimes when I look around me, you know, at eye level with other American people—white American people—on the street, I notice all the differences between them and me, and I don't feel like me anymore. Do you know what I mean? And all of a sudden I start to think that this sky isn't mine either. It's been theirs all along. [*Pause.*] When I'm with a Japanese woman, I guess it makes me feel more American.

BETTY: [*Pause.*] I'll get her to come out here. The rest is up to you.

JOHN: Okay, fine! Fine.

> [BETTY *exits.* JACKIE *enters. She sits on the couch by* JOHN, *oblivious of him. She picks up a* Cosmopolitan.]

JOHN: Uh, tough break.

JACKIE: Huh?

JOHN: About the phone call.

JACKIE: Oh. Oh yeah.

JOHN: You must have really liked him.

JACKIE: Hmm. "Quiz: Is Your Boyfriend A Sinophile?"

JOHN: Uh, Sinophile? What's that?

JACKIE: [*Rolls her eyes.*] It's a person with a fetish for Asian things. Especially Asian women.

JOHN: Oh. [*Pause.*] So have you seen any good movies lately?

JACKIE: Some. Most of them were awful.

JOHN: Oh. Oh, yeah.

JACKIE: I mean, you would think that they'd get the idea that the audience has already seen the same dull romances and action movies. It'd be nice if they tried to make a move that had a point, you know?

JOHN: You're right, there's no point at all.

JACKIE: *Far North*, that was a movie. It was Sam Shepard's directing debut.

JOHN: Sam Shepard! Oh, he's very . . . creative.

JACKIE: But he wrote others. Remember *Paris, Texas*?

JOHN: Oh, *Paris, Texas*!

JACKIE: Could you believe it?

JOHN: I couldn't believe it.

JACKIE: It just made me cry every five minutes.

JOHN: Sad, so sad.

JACKIE: But the ending...

JOHN: So sad...

JACKIE: You think so? I thought it was actually very optimistic.

JOHN: You have a point there.

JACKIE: [*Short pause.*] You haven't really —

JOHN: No, I haven't. [*Beat.*] Would you tell Betty that I'll meet her downstairs?

[JOHN *exits; hearing the door,* BETTY *returns.*]

BETTY: Where's John?

JACKIE: He tried to ask me out.

BETTY: Why not give him a chance? He's really a nice guy.

JACKIE: That's what I'm afraid of.

BETTY: You could at least pretend to have a heart.

JACKIE: Honesty is less confusing.

BETTY: You're right. A compassionate Jackie is an oxymoron.

JACKIE: I have always stuck to my beliefs.

BETTY: Like "modern classic."

JACKIE: Sure, I've had setbacks, I've been disappointed. But I've paid my dues.

BETTY: Or "pure evil."

JACKIE: I have been true to him.

BETTY: Him? Who's him?

JACKIE: Sam. He's going to help me find my soulmate.

BETTY: [*Pushes the newspaper at* JACKIE.] I'm going to school.

JACKIE: [*Pushes the paper back at* BETTY.] You're just ignoring me because you're an atheist.

BETTY: [*Pushes the newspaper at* JACKIE.] What does religion have to do with anything?

JACKIE: [*Pushes the paper back.*] You have no faith! You don't believe I'm going to find my soulmate, do you?

BETTY: Oh, I do! Your soulmate must be, after all, desperately searching for you, too! Out of all the men in the world, I'm sure he'll conveniently show up on our little doorstep with a ring and a Mercedes! In fact, I'm sure he's been advertising for you in the newspaper all this time, under Men Seeking Soulmates!

[BETTY *throws the* Independent *at* JACKIE *and exits.*]

JACKIE: Betty, you're just so — you're so —

[JACKIE *looks through the newspaper. On the rear wall a projection of the newspaper page of "Personals" appears, with "Men Seeking Women" very evident.*]

JACKIE: Hey!

SCENE 3

LOHMAN *and* JOHN'S *apartment.* LOHMAN *is sitting on the floor with an acoustic guitar.* GERALDINE, *a pretty young Caucasian woman, is facing him on a chair.* LOHMAN *serenades her with a melodramatic rendition of The Doors' "Light My Fire."*

LOHMAN: So, whaddaya think.

GERALDINE: I think I want to make love now.

LOHMAN: Okay. Just as long as we get to have sex, too.

[*They exit into the bedroom.* LOHMAN *puts a sign on the door that says, "Stay the Hell Out!"* JOHN *enters, sees the sign, and sits on a chair, reading a magazine. He starts to hear giggling, sighing and other bumping from the bedroom.*]

JOHN: Hey, Lohman!

LOHMAN: What!

JOHN: You gonna be in there long?

LOHMAN: Hold on! [*Pause.*] Yeah!

[JOHN *turns on the TV. We hear music usually associated with nature documentaries.*]

ANNOUNCER: As the hummingbird hovers in the air above the silky petals, we can see how it aids the reproductive cycle of life. The bird directs its long beak between the petals, penetrating the moist center of the flower and drawing from it the dewy, sweet fluid which carries —

[JOHN *changes the channel.*]

NEW ANNOUNCER: And now, we return to *The Right Stuff*, starring Sam Shepard!

[*As we hear the movie,* JOHN *becomes immersed in the persona that Sam projects. He doesn't see* GERALDINE *enter from the bedroom, wearing a bathrobe and going into the kitchen. She enters again with a jar of peanut butter.*]

GERALDINE: Hi John.

JOHN: Oh! Hi! Geraldine!

GERALDINE: Sam Shepard is just too sexy, don't you think?

JOHN: I hadn't noticed. Say, I brought home some tiramisu from the restaurant. I know how much you like it.

GERALDINE: You sweetie! They just don't make guys like you anymore, John. Nice, I mean.

JOHN: Well you know, we're all being left out of the gene pool.

[GERALDINE *exits into the bedroom.* JOHN *picks up the phone and dials.* BETTY *enters, dressed in a nightgown and wearing a mudpack.*]

BETTY: Hello?

JOHN: Did you get her to change her mind? [BETTY *hangs up.*] Betty? Betty? Betty? Betty?

LOHMAN: [*Enters as* JOHN *is talking.*] I thought I said creamy-style. Chunky-style irritates my skin. Hey John, what was that all about?

JOHN: It was about having less credibility than twenty words or less at one dollar and fifty cents a word.

LOHMAN: [*Pauses to digest this, but fails.*] John, what was that all about?

JOHN: Jackie.

LOHMAN: Jackie again!? I told you, get out of this sinophile shit, man. It's unhealthy.

JOHN: What did you say?

LOHMAN: It's unhealthy.

JOHN: No. "Sinophile."

LOHMAN: It means someone who has a fetish for Oriental stuff.

JOHN: Where did you ever learn a word like sinophile?

LOHMAN: The May Cosmo. What I'm saying, man, is that —

JOHN: You read Cosmopolitan?

LOHMAN: Just for the pictures.

JOHN: Yeah, sure!

LOHMAN: What I'm saying is that it's unhealthy to be stuck on Oriental chicks.

JOHN: Why?

LOHMAN: It's their mothers, John.

JOHN: I'm not interested in their mothers.

LOHMAN: Asian girls seem OK now, but once they start sharing your closet? Bam! Polyester pants, hairnets and Top ramen! They become your mother and you become your father.

JOHN: What do you know about it? You only go out with blondes.

LOHMAN: I know. God bless America.

[JOHN *picks up the telephone, ready to make a call. Then he stops, realizing that there's no one he feels he can talk with.*]

SCENE 4

JACKIE *and* BETTY'S *apartment.* JACKIE *is on the phone, calling the personals.* BETTY *is trying to listen in.*

VOICE: Hello, this is Dateline, Los Angeles. Dateline is an innovative and technologically efficient way to help language-using people meet each other. It is also safe: not one violent homicide has been legally associated with Dateline for at least nine months. If you are a touch-tone phone user, then press 1. If you do not have a touch-tone phone, then you are probably too old or too poor for this service, and you should hang up.

[JACKIE *presses a button.*]

Thank you. At the beep, please punch in the five digit code of your potential friend. Following the client's outgoing message, you may leave your own message, taking as much time as you like. If you have found that you are not desperate enough to use this service, then hang up now.

[JACKIE *begins to hang up the phone, hesitates, then puts it to her ear again.*]

Good for you! You will now be charged two dollars a minute.

JACKIE: Two dollars!

BETTY: Per call?

JACKIE: Minute!

BETTY: Two dollars a minute?!

VOICE: Beep!

JACKIE: Code! Shoot, shoot, what is it? Wait, here it is.

VOICE: Thank you.

JACKIE: [*Checks her watch.*] Come on, come on.

BETTY: Which one are you calling?

[JACKIE *throws her the paper.*]

LARRY'S VOICE: Hi, I'm Larry. [*Long pause.*] I'm a Capricorn.

JACKIE: Hurry up, Larry.

BETTY: "SWM, Capricorn."

LARRY AND BETTY: "I'm a good-looking, successful lawyer and I'm looking for an attractive Oriental woman for intelligent conversation and romantic dinners."

BETTY: Sounds like a weirdo.

JACKIE: Shhh!

LARRY: And I have a Porsche. Leave a message where I can reach you. Thanks.

JACKIE: [*To* BETTY.] Do I just start talking? Uh, hi, Larry. My name is, uh, Jackie. I'm, umm, I'm Asian. My mother is Caucasian, and my dad is Japanese. That sounds kind of weird to most people, but —

VOICE: You may start your message . . . now.

JACKIE: Shit! Oh, sorry, Larry. I didn't mean you. I meant . . . I mean, I'm Jacqueline. [*Starts to speak in a sensual voice.*] And I'm a Scorpio. I like skiing, softball and soft music. I guess you can say I'm a Renaissance woman. I'd like to get to know you better, so why don't you call me at —

BETTY: Don't give him our number!

JACKIE: [*Ignores her.*] 999-9999. I'll be waiting for you.

BETTY: [*As* JACKIE *hangs up.*] I don't believe you gave him our number. Some lunatic is going to be calling our home.

JACKIE: He's a lawyer.

BETTY: Anybody can go to law school. Dan Quayle went to law school.

JACKIE: He's got a Porsche.

BETTY: That's okay, then! Sports car drivers are real paragons of stability and sanity.

JACKIE: And it takes real brains to buy a Toyota, right?

BETTY: Well, now that you bring him up, have I shown you John's resume? Look, here's John's SATs, his Myers-Briggs personality test, high school prom pictures... Euww, never mind.

JACKIE: Betty, he's Japanese! I don't go out with Asian guys.

BETTY: Oh, Jackie! [*Hugs her.*] I'm so proud of you! I've been waiting for this moment for so long! Admitting it is the first step to recovery!

JACKIE: It's their mothers.

BETTY: I've got the numbers of a terrific selection of 12-step groups...

JACKIE: Asian mothers ruin it for all other women!

BETTY: Here's one that offers aerobics and annual cruises to Alaska.

JACKIE: Asian guys grow up with the idea of women as their personal servants! All their lives their mothers wash their clothes and wipe their noses and make them Top ramen!

BETTY: A lot of men have mother fixa(tions) —

JACKIE: And so they don't know how to have a normal conversation with a woman.

BETTY: But all men are like —

JACKIE: And they're all insecure in bed.

BETTY: — Really?

JACKIE: It's their potty-training.

BETTY: Potty-training?

JACKIE: Mommy praises them when they go wee-wee on their own. "What a good little man!" From then on, they always have to be complimented on their performance.

BETTY: Jackie, when have you ever gone out with an Asian guy?

JACKIE: Well... I've been told on very good authority by women who swear that they know someone who really has dated a Japanese guy. [*Beat.*] Once.

BETTY: Well, there you go.

JACKIE: Don't do that.

BETTY: What am I doing?

JACKIE: When it comes to dating, you always give me this attitude! This "holier than thou" attitude! And that's completely unfair! You don't even go out!

BETTY: Yeah, so what? Should I be like you and ignore my work so I can worry about the kind of car some guy drives?

JACKIE: When was the last time you've hugged something that wasn't published by the American Psychological Association? When was the last time you dressed up to go out on a Saturday night?

BETTY: I have classes every day of the week, my master's thesis is due in just another —

JACKIE: I'm talking about a life, Betty! It's all about having a life!

BETTY: I know where my life is going, do you?

[*Phone rings.*]

JACKIE: It's the Porsche!

BETTY: Don't tell him where we live!

JACKIE: [*Picking up.*] Hi, this is Jackie.

LARRY'S VOICE: Hi, I'm Larry. I'm a Capricorn. How about you?

JACKIE: I'm a Scorpio, Larry. Just like I said on the message.

LARRY: Right, right. You're Oriental, right? I put that in my ad, "Oriental woman ... "

JACKIE: I'm Eurasian. My mom is Caucasian, my dad is Japanese. Most people think that's kind of —

LARRY: Only part? Well, I guess that's all right. You look Japanese, don't you?

JACKIE: Uh, sure. Sure. [*Beat.*] So, you're a lawyer, right?

LARRY: Yeah, sure. I'm not a trial lawyer, though. I'm not stupid.

JACKIE: You're not?

LARRY: Hell, no. No money in that. You like massages? I love a good massage. You can do that, can't you? I really love that.

JACKIE: I—I guess. If we get along, I don't see why not ...

LARRY: How about kimonos?

JACKIE: What about them?

LARRY: Would you do it in a kimono? I think that's particularly sexy. It makes me feel like I'm back in the Orient. Really, I'm not lying, Like back when I was stationed in Bangkok. I've got this incense, and when I burn it I'm just swept away. I'm in a foreign country. It all comes back to me at night, I have visions — visions all red and black and Bangkok is burning burning down around me, and my heart is pounding like the rapid fire of an M-16! [*Beat.*] The Orient is very important to me. I'm not lying.

JACKIE: I believe you.

LARRY: So?

JACKIE: So what?

LARRY: When do you want me to meet you? I always let the woman decide these things. I'm really a feminist.

JACKIE: I — I don't know.

LARRY: What's your address? I can come by and —

JACKIE: No! I'm — I'm moving soon, and it'll all be changed. Everything. In fact, they're shutting off this phone number any minute now. So I'd better say —

[*She hangs up the receiver.*]

BETTY: What's wrong?

JACKIE: He's not my type.

BETTY: What's wrong with him?

JACKIE: He's not a trial lawyer. [*Beat.*] We have to change our phone number.

SCENE 5

The restaurant. NORMAN *and* JOHN *are arguing over a boiling pot of water.*

NORMAN: Five minutes.

JOHN: At least six.

NORMAN: Five total.

JOHN: Six minutes. I'm positive.

NORMAN: Six minutes, you get cookie dough.

JOHN: Five minutes, and you have to suck on the linguini before it's soft enough to swallow.

NORMAN: I've been boiling pasta for ten years, John. I know pasta.

JOHN: My people have been making noodles for two thousand years, Norman.

NORMAN: Your people?

JOHN: We invented pasta.

NORMAN: I thought you were Japanese, John. Not Chinese.

JOHN: Okay, you got me there. Go ahead, boil the pasta for five minutes.

NORMAN: Maybe five and a half.

JOHN: [*Pause.*] Norman?

NORMAN: Yes, John?

JOHN: Do you ever leave?

NORMAN: Where should I leave, John?

JOHN: I never see you leave the restaurant. Either you're just arriving, or you're already here, chopping garlic. I've never noticed you going anywhere else.

NORMAN: Interesting. Go figure that.

JOHN: I guess I never asked, but do you have a life?

NORMAN: [*Pulls out his wallet.*] That's Nathan and that's Myung Soo, our youngest.

JOHN: Your youngest what?

NORMAN: Child, John. These are my children.

JOHN: Oh come on! Norman, this kid is black and the other one is Korean! You got these with the wallet, didn't you?

NORMAN: Maria and I adopt.

JOHN: That's your wife? Hey, not bad. She's Filipino?

NORMAN: We met at a Betty Crocker Bake-off, 1987. I got third place for my liver pate, and Maria took honorable mention for an apple strudel. Let me tell you, she was robbed. She does an apple strudel to die for. To die for.

JOHN: I never realized, Norman. I mean, I never asked.

NORMAN: John, you know how I feel about emotions.

JOHN: "The kitchen is for the men. No room for sentimentality in the kitchen."

NORMAN: None at all. But I'm going to break my rule just this once.

JOHN: Oh yeah?

NORMAN: John, you're a good man. But even so, you are flawed. Because we aren't meant to be alone, John. We are meant to unite with another, a soulmate if you will. And until we find that other, we will always be striving after phantom goals. Do you understand? Because I hate to repeat myself. I hate saying things over and over —

JOHN: Norman, I got it. Thanks for making an exception.

NORMAN: We never had this talk, John. I'm going to check the grills.

[NORMAN *exits.* JOHN *picks up the phone and calls* BETTY.]

BETTY: Hello?

JOHN: Betty, it's me.

BETTY: Forget it, John. I've gone out of business. Handle your own sex life.

JOHN: I have been handling it, that's my problem. Listen, I've been working on a plan that'll let me buy a Porsche. First, I sell my hair to a wigmaker...

BETTY: You can't afford a Porsche, John!

JOHN: I can, too! The blood bank will give me twenty bucks a visit, so one visit a week means that —

BETTY: You're an assistant manager in a restaurant, okay? And the sooner you accept that, the happier you'll be!

[*In her apartment,* JACKIE *bursts in from the front door.*]

JACKIE: Betty, look at all these responses!

BETTY: Responses from what?

JOHN: Hey, is that Jackie?

JACKIE: My personals ad! Didn't you see it in last week's *Independent*?

BETTY: John, hold on.

JOHN: Last week's *Independent*?

BETTY: You couldn't stop with our phone number. Now you had to tell them all where we live!

JACKIE: They mail their responses to a post office box. Guess which is mine.

[*She gives* BETTY *the paper. In his apartment,* JOHN *opens up his own copy.* JOHN *and* BETTY *speak in a rhythm.*]

JOHN: "Men Seeking Women."

BETTY: "Women Seeking Men."

JOHN: "Men Seeking Men."

BETTY: "Women Seeking Women."

JOHN: "White Women Seeking Latino Men..."

BETTY: "Latino Women Seeking Black Women..."

JOHN: "Asian Women Seeking White Men..."

BETTY: "Black Men Seeking Asian Father-Figures..."

JOHN AND BETTY: "Asian Women Seeking White Men With Expensive Cars!"

JACKIE: Find it yet?

BETTY: "Cigar-smoking Oriental beauty into hard rock, hard alcohol and hard bodies seeking professional S.W.M. — Single White Male — for hard times."

JACKIE: I don't smoke.

JOHN: "S.A.F. — Single Asian Female — seeking long-haired blond Swedish men over six feet, under two hundred and thirty pounds, with a boyish smile and freckles, blue-green eyes and size nine shoes. Must love me for who I am."

BETTY: "Me: Exotic Vampirella. You: Wicked Van Helsing. Tie me up but don't tie me down! Wild nights that leave us exhausted, raw and begging for more. Born again Christians, please."

JOHN: "Eurasian beauty, twenty-four, into romance and rock and roll, seeking S.A.M. — !"

BETTY: [Synchronizes with JOHN.] "Eurasian beauty, twenty-four, into romance and rock and roll, seeking Sam... Shepard type. Must be creative, thoughtful and open to new experiences. Please send photo or writing sample."

JOHN AND BETTY: Writing sample?

JACKIE: It'll weed out the F.O.B.s.

[Lights go down in JACKIE'S apartment. In the kitchen, JOHN hangs up the phone. GERALDINE enters.]

GERALDINE: Hi, John! How are you doing?

JOHN: Oh, everything's just... well, shitty, actually.

GERALDINE: Oh. [Beat.] I really don't know how to respond to that. You're supposed to say "Fine, and you?" or "Peachy, thanks."

JOHN: Sorry.

GERALDINE: No, I'm sorry. I just don't know what to say, sometimes. My pastor says I'm "sympathetically challenged."

JOHN: Pastor? I didn't know you went to church.

GERALDINE: It was kind of an accident. Like a train crash.

JOHN: So you believe in God and Heaven and that stuff, huh?

GERALDINE: Well, I have faith. I've got faith that everything that happens happens to make us better and happier. Have you seen Lohman? I'm breaking up with him today.

JOHN: He's in back, behind the grills.

GERALDINE: Is, uh, there anything I can, you know, do for you?

JOHN: Careful, don't hurt yourself. I'll figure it out. I mean . . . well, sometimes, don't you feel like you've done just about everything you can do by just being yourself? Like, everything — the air itself — just wants to force you to become something completely different and new. A new person!

GERALDINE: Well, what's stopping you? Do it!

JOHN: Do it?

GERALDINE: [*Sighs.*] While you're here wasting time, sitting on your fat butt, you could be going out and doing something about it! What are you, some kind of pansy!?

JOHN: No!

GERALDINE: Well, stop acting like it!

JOHN: Right! Okay!

GERALDINE: What do you want to be? Quick!

JOHN: Sensitive!

GERALDINE: And?

JOHN: Creative!

GERALDINE: What else? Speak up!

JOHN: Rich, white and attractive!

GERALDINE: All right! Now, get to work and I don't want to see you until you've got a million dollars and — and — Oh. Was I coming off a little too strong?

JOHN: No, that was real good.

GERALDINE: Okay, then. Well, I've got to go break Lohman's heart now.

JOHN: [*As* GERALDINE *exits.*] Jackie wants Sam? Fine, I'm going to give her Sam. [JOHN *gets a piece of paper and starts writing.*] He-man? Just watch! Sensitive? With my eyes shut! "Chapter One. I woke up this morning, and I was sad. Because... because I had a dream about my childhood dog, whose name was Gregg. And Gregg was sick. No... Gregg was dead. And his guts were splattered all over the pavement. And I started to cry." [*Beat.*] "And then I wanted to kill something really intensely."

LOHMAN: [*Enters.*] John, you're not going to believe what just happened!

JOHN: The broad dumped you.

LOHMAN: How'd you know?

JOHN: That's the way it is with broads. You turn your back for a second and you'll find a knife sticking out of it.

LOHMAN: Geez, what am I gonna do now?

JOHN: Do? You forget about it! You're a man, aren't you?

LOHMAN: Yeah, sure I am.

JOHN: Well, act like one!

LOHMAN: Okay! Yeah!

JOHN: The world is your plum! It takes a real man to pick it and suck all the life from it that you can! And only then can you be truly alive!

LOHMAN: Yeah! Let's go see a movie!

JOHN: I'm not talking about a movie!

LOHMAN: A Jackie Chan movie! [*Strikes a pose.*] *Super-Cop! Crime Story!* Come on, real kung fu action!

JOHN: Lohman, look at me! I'm busy, trying to go after something that means a lot to me. When are you ever going to really make an effort to take what you want? What do you really want?

LOHMAN: I want to see this movie! What do you want?

JOHN: I want to stop making excuses. I want to get out of this dead-end job and this dead-end life! I'm sick to death of always longing for things out of my reach! I'm going to make them within my reach! Well?

LOHMAN: On Wednesday the movie admission is half-price.

[LOHMAN *exits.* JOHN *continues writing.*]

JOHN: "Vanessa was with me last night when I felt her lips press against mine, when I traced the geography of her uneven teeth with my tongue. Sometime between that moment and this morning I let something precious slip past my notice and escape."

[JACKIE'S *apartment.* JACKIE *is reading the story* JOHN *is writing, and her voice overlaps with his as she takes over the reading.*]

JACKIE: "Doubt grips me, Nick thought. How long have I imagined her sleeping beside me? Could I actually have been alone the entire night? My fingers have memorized her face, but now in retrospect it seems like such a ghostly, transparent face. Was I really feeling the warmth of the blood in her body or was I only hearing the sound of my own heartbeat, wildly excited, one river sounding so much like two." [JACKIE *sighs dreamily.*] Oh, Nick.

SCENE 6

In JACKIE *and* BETTY'S *apartment.* BETTY *is alone. She is typing at her word processor. She stops, adding one good tap on her keyboard.*

BETTY: Oh my god. I think I'm done. My master's thesis is done. I'm done. [*Screaming.*] I'm done! I'm done! I'm done! [*Pause.*] Now what? Footnotes? I'm done. Bibliography? I'm done. Appendix? Done. Organize my desk? Done. Phone bill? Done. Grocery shopping! Done. Christmas shopping. Done. [*Points to objects in the room.*] Done, done, done, done. [*Beat.*] Oh my God. I don't have a life!

[*She picks up the phone and dials a number. In his apartment,* LOHMAN *answers the phone.*]

LOHMAN: I've gotta pee, so make it quick!

BETTY: Is John home?

LOHMAN: Nuh uh. He's working extra hours tonight.

BETTY: Would you tell him Betty called? Oh never mind. He's coming over later.

LOHMAN: Betty?

BETTY: My name is Betty.

LOHMAN: I'm Lohman. Like, "low man on the pole."

BETTY: Hi, Lohman.

LOHMAN: John's never talked about a Betty. Are you a new flame in my roommate's loins?

BETTY: No, John and I are definitely not seeing each other.

LOHMAN: Cool! Does that mean you'll have sex with me?

BETTY: I only go to bed on the second phone call.

LOHMAN: Okay. [LOHMAN *hangs up the phone.* BETTY *calls back.*] Betty! So nice to hear from you!

BETTY: I suppose I have to sleep with you now.

LOHMAN: Huh? Well, gosh. If you want to. I was gonna say we go see a kung fu movie, but hey...

BETTY: Well, we can have sex after the movie.

LOHMAN: Huh?

BETTY: Maybe you should just tell John I called.

LOHMAN: Oh. Okay.

BETTY: Were...were you serious?

LOHMAN: Were you?

BETTY: I think so. That is, about the movie.

LOHMAN: Well if you were, then I am. I guess.

BETTY: Well, OK! Umm, when?

LOHMAN: I guess we could go—Saturday?

BETTY: Uh, sure! Meet you at the Downtown Theatre?

LOHMAN: Wow! You know the Downtown Theatre?

BETTY: I saw my first Jackie Chan movie there.

LOHMAN: Wow! You like Jackie Chan?

BETTY: I've seen all his movies twice, at least!

LOHMAN: Wow! Me too!

BETTY: See you at seven?

LOHMAN: Yeah!

[*They both hang up the phone. They have a look of horror on their faces.*]

BETTY AND LOHMAN: I don't even know what s/he looks like!

[JACKIE *enters and sits on the couch, reading* JOHN'S *letters.*]

JACKIE: Oh Betty! Listen to this!

BETTY: [*Sighs.*] I don't want to!

JACKIE: This is my favorite part!

BETTY: Every part is your favorite part!

JACKIE: But he's just so—great! Nick is such an intense, passionate writer! And every day—every day he sends me a new chapter of his novel.

BETTY: And you haven't met him yet?

JACKIE: Well, no. Not really.

BETTY: "Not really?"

JACKIE: Not in the objective, physical sense. But on the level of ideas— we are as one being! Listen: " ... with the pen, he scribbled down two words. He didn't think about it; it was as if they were just lying on the edge of his brain until this very moment."

BETTY: Do you think I should go out with John's roommate? It was such a weird conversation. I didn't think it was me telling him I'd go out with him. I was some deranged, other-dimensional mirror image of Betty! A Dark Betty!

JACKIE: "A thin, knife-like thought crossed his brain, leaving an open scar in his consciousness."

BETTY: What do you think, Jackie?

JACKIE: Incredible.

BETTY: You think so? You don't think he'll be a creep?

JACKIE: No way! He can't be. I think he's just shy.

BETTY: Shy? That isn't the first word that comes to my mind.

JACKIE: Sure he is. There can't be any other explanation.

BETTY: Well, that would explain how strange he behaves. [Beat.] Should I try to call him before we go out?

JACKIE: Hey, get your own date!

BETTY: What?

JACKIE: What?

BETTY: [Carefully.] Should I call Lohman?

JACKIE: Who's Lohman? Just keep your hands off Nick.

BETTY: Oh, right. "Nick."

JACKIE: And you know how I know he's just shy? Look, he put an ad in the personals, too—just for me!

BETTY: "Wildly handsome and creative writer seeking young, beautiful and intelligent and passionate Connie Chung-like Asian girl but with less mascara. P.S. I'm white and I've got an expensive car."

JACKIE: I'm going to call and tell him to meet me Saturday night.

BETTY: Listen, John's going to be here any minute. Don't tell him anything about it.

JOHN: [*Enters from front door.*] About what?

JACKIE: Betty's got a date with someone named Lohman.

[JOHN'S *eyes glaze over. Lights fade as* BETTY *speaks.*]

BETTY: John? John? John?

SCENE 7

JACKIE *and* BETTY'S *apartment.* JACKIE *enters, with* LEONARD GJAFFRY *right behind her.* LEONARD *is twenty-one, but looks almost sixteen. He is dressed in a very trendy suit with plenty of jewelry.*

JACKIE: Go home. Go. Go home.

LEONARD: Hey, don't I even get to come in for a drink?

JACKIE: We're all out of Kool-Aid.

LEONARD: Ho ho! Jackie, you are a knife! No, a sword — a katana blade! Razor-sharp and deadly, yes, you are!

JACKIE: I wouldn't want to accidentally stab you in the heart, or cut off any other major organ, so . . . !

LEONARD: Hey, you can't just run off! After all you said in your personals message?

JACKIE: I told you: I made a mistake. A horrible, horrible mistake.

LEONARD: It might be a little easier to think of it as destiny.

JACKIE: I mistook your ad for somebody else's.

LEONARD: Gedoudda here! You described me to a tee! Intelligent, shy, a particularly talented writer! Who's this other guy?

JACKIE: Another particularly talented author.

LEONARD: Whoa! As if! It's not everybody that gets to be a contributing editor at an important magazine like *Rolling Stone*! What's this bozo written?

JACKIE: Nick is unpublished.

LEONARD: Another unpublished genius.

JACKIE: Nick sends me pages of his novel.

LEONARD: Yeah? Let me see. Believe you me, I know schlock when I see it. I read *Catcher in the Rye* when I was ten, and saw right through it. I can smell hacks like cheap perfume.

JACKIE: Okay, just one page.

LEONARD: I can't even guess why you'd defend some guy who's never shown you a good time. [*Starts to read.*] Hmm. Huh.

JACKIE: Nick is different. I can talk to Nick.

LEONARD: "A knife-like thought crossed his brain . . ." Heh heh. That's a good one. 'Sides, you said you never met him.

JACKIE: Well, okay . . . not face-to-face. But what we say to each other . . . umm, what he says to me is very special.

LEONARD: Right. Lemme see one more . . .

JACKIE: It's special!

LEONARD: Okay, special! Now gimme!

JACKIE: [*Hands him another page.*] But sometimes, you know . . . I think it's me.

LEONARD: Oh, wow. [*Starts to laugh.*] Yeah! Right on!

JACKIE: I guess you have a point. I've never met him. But I wanted to believe so much that he's the man I've been looking for that maybe, maybe I've helped to invent him. But what am I talking about?

LEONARD: I think I'm ready to go steady with this guy! Where's the next chapter?

JACKIE: I don't think I should —

LEONARD: Oh, come now! I'm a professional.

JACKIE: Go home, Leonard.

LEONARD: Babe, you're giving me literary blue balls!

JACKIE: Get lost!

LEONARD: Oh, come on! This stuff is really good!

JACKIE: I told you!

LEONARD: No, you don't understand! It's weird, but all of a sudden, I see that my whole life has been a pitiful search for self-gratification and social acceptance, and that has brought me to a depraved cliff of my own creation! God, I've got to get rid of these ridiculous clothes!

JACKIE: Are you going to leave yet?

LEONARD: Wait, what's his name? Nick Strathmore?

JACKIE: Nick Strathbourne. He answered my ad in the *Independent*.

LEONARD: Your ad? Wait, don't tell me! "Lotus Blossom of Long Beach wants to share the exotic east with generous older man."

JACKIE: Go away, Leonard.

LEONARD: This is a guy after my own heart! Are you sure he's not published? He's got to be! I can't be this lucky! When you catch him, give him my card. Tell him he can't go anywhere else! Tell him that the *Stone* will buy exclusive first publishing rights for... what's it called?

JACKIE: *Blue Skies Over Burbank.*

LEONARD: It sings! *Blue Skies!* The blue skies generation! I love it!

[LEONARD *exits.* JACKIE *pines for a moment, until a knock comes at the door. It's* JOHN.]

JACKIE: John?

JOHN: Is, uh, Betty home?

JACKIE: She's not back yet.

JOHN: Aaahh! It's almost midnight! Has she called? Did she leave a number? The movie let out three hours ago!

JACKIE: You're really worried about her, aren't you?

JOHN: Oh god. Oh god. My auntie's gonna kill me. Don't let those little Japanese women fool you. I've seen my auntie grab a pig by its hind legs and rip its throat out with her bare teeth.

JACKIE: Do you, umm, want to come in and wait for her?

JOHN: Oh. Sure, I guess.

JACKIE: Do you want something to drink?

JOHN: Huh? Oh, no thanks. [*He enters, surprised and a little suspicious of* JACKIE'S *politeness.*] Am I interrupting anything? You're all dressed up.

JACKIE: Oh, it wasn't anything special.

JOHN: Oh. [*Beat.*] Good time?

JACKIE: What?

JOHN: Going out —! I mean... you look nice...

JACKIE: Thanks. [*Beat.*] It's nice that you're worried about your cousin.

JOHN: Yeah. We're both the only children in our families, so naturally —

JACKIE: You grew close like siblings.

JOHN: We beat each other up. Until we grew up —

JACKIE: Then you became close.

JOHN: — and then Betty learned kung fu and I left her alone. [*Wandering around the room, he looks at her bookshelf.*] Elizabeth Barrett Browning! I read some of this in college.

JACKIE: You went to college?

JOHN: You have to be more than a monkey to run a restaurant.

JACKIE: Oh, sorry, I didn't mean —

JOHN: Some of her stuff really rocked my boat.

JACKIE: Uh huh. I'm sure. Like how you saw all those Sam Shepard movies.

JOHN: [*Closes the book.*] "If thou must love me, let it be for naught,"

JACKIE: "Except for love's sake only."

JOHN: "Do not say, 'I love her for her smile — her looks — her way'"

JACKIE: "of speaking gently — for a trick of thought"

JOHN: "That falls in well with me, and certes brought/A sense of pleasant ease on such a day"

JACKIE: "For these things, in themselves, Beloved, may Be changed,"

JOHN: "or change for thee — and love, so wrought"

JACKIE: "May be unwrought so."

JOHN: After poetry I got into heavy metal, and that was really cool.

JACKIE: [*Beat.*] Would you like some wine?

JOHN: Uh, sure.

JACKIE: I know you've put up with a lot from me.

JOHN: Oh no, not so much.

JACKIE: No, really. I know that . . . sometimes I can be pretty tactless and, you know . . .

JOHN: Cruel and sadistic?

JACKIE: Abrupt. I can be abrupt. Does that make me such a bad person?

JOHN: Jackie, you're fine! You have many great qualities.

JACKIE: Really? Like what?

JOHN: Well...your posture, you have clear skin... [*Sound of giggling outside the front door.*] What was that?

[JOHN *opens the front door.* BETTY *and* LOHMAN *are standing there, locked in a hot, passionate embrace.* BETTY *opens her eyes, sees* JOHN, *and shakes hands with* LOHMAN.]

LOHMAN: Thank you for accompanying me to the theatre.

BETTY: You're quite welcome. Have a pleasant life.

[BETTY *enters.* JOHN *stares her down, so she strikes a kung fu attack position and* JOHN *cringes.* BETTY *exits into bedroom.*]

JOHN: I guess I better get going now.

JACKIE: It was really nice talking to you, John.

JOHN: I had a good time.

JACKIE: I feel so comfortable and relaxed when I'm with you.

JOHN: I feel exactly the same way!

JACKIE: You know, I wish I had a brother like you.

SCENE 8

JOHN'S *apartment. He writes.*

JOHN: "Nick put his pen aside, looked at Vanessa, and—and—" [*Pause.*] "Made farting sounds with his armpit." [*Pause.*] "Nick looked at Vanessa. He was so overwhelmed that his tongue froze in his mouth and his limbs were rooted to the ground upon which he stood. Here, he thought, was the only woman who could change his life. And this confused him. Her personality was a hodgepodge of elements that were fresh and exciting, but also hateful and rude. But Nick knew that the sum of her parts was not the whole picture. It was a picture that radiated from her like light on a spectrum of quiet. It was her strength he saw, her enormous potential to love and create. Nick Strathbourne wanted to be worthy of who she would be." [*Pause.*] "Nick looked at Vanessa, and...made large farting sounds with his armpit." [*Pause.*] This is crazy. What do I think I'm doing? [*Knock at the door.*] Who is it?

LEONARD: Hello? Mr. Strathbourne?

JOHN: Who?!?

LEONARD: Am I speaking to Nick Strathbourne?

JOHN: Who wants to know?

LEONARD: My name's Leonard Gjaffry, Mr. Strathbourne, and I'm an editor at *Rolling Stone*. A friend of mine recently showed me a copy of some of your writing, and frankly, I think it's incredible! Nobody before has captured the angst, the sheer existential pain that the White Anglo-Saxon Protestant goes through coping with modern America! Your characters are so real, so gripping. It was personally very inspirational! [*Beat.*] You know, it was no picnic finding you! I had to bribe a lot of people just to get the phone numbers billed to my friend's Dateline voice mail. But then your name didn't match any of the numbers, so I've had to drive around all day to every caller on the list! Mr. Strathbourne, I want to serialize your work in our magazine.

JOHN: Oh, shit.

LEONARD: I'm going to make you the voice for every frustrated Caucasian man in America!

[JOHN *opens the door.*]

Oh, shit.

[*Blackout.*]

ACT II: THE BLUE SKY GENERATION

SCENE 1

JACKIE *and* BETTY'S *apartment.* LOHMAN *gets up from where he and* BETTY *are lying behind the couch.*

BETTY: Get up, we have to clean up before Jackie gets home.

LOHMAN: How come?

BETTY: I don't want her to know we did it out here!

LOHMAN: Come on, nobody's gonna know.

BETTY: They always know. [*Beat.*] You know, John described you much differently than you actually are.

LOHMAN: What did he say?

BETTY: He said you only go out with blondes. [LOHMAN *tries to laugh.*] Lohman, do you ever think about why I like you?

LOHMAN: No.

BETTY: You don't?

LOHMAN: Hey, I figure, why spoil a good thing? [*Beat.*] So . . . you like me, huh?

BETTY: Yes, I like you. You're really very . . . Apollonian.

LOHMAN: [*Beat.*] Is that something guys usually are?

BETTY: It means you're beautiful. It means you make me feel so . . . so . . . [*Short pause.*] Like I don't have to be me.

LOHMAN: Whaddaya mean?

BETTY: It's hard to describe. All my life, everybody I know, they always think they know me right away. It's as if I emit this aura of . . . "betty-ness," and when people get inside it, they just automatically think they have me figured out.

LOHMAN: Kind of like a car alarm.

BETTY: Exactly! It says, "She's nice!" And so people just assume things —that I want to hear their problems and help them with their homework and pick them up at the airport!

LOHMAN: Wow, you're lucky.

BETTY: What?

LOHMAN: Nobody ever trusts me like that. They just assume I'm gonna flake. My own mother won't let me drive her car unless somebody is with me! Even my little brother—and he's six! If anyone asked me to help them with their homework, I'd bust a blood vessel and drop dead!

BETTY: You can help me with my homework anytime.

LOHMAN: Betty, I gotta be honest with you.

BETTY: You do?

LOHMAN: I may have kind of led you on.

BETTY: You have?

LOHMAN: You know when I first asked you out? Over the telephone?

BETTY: Yeah . . .

LOHMAN: Well, I wasn't being totally up front with you.

BETTY: You weren't?

LOHMAN: No. See, I wasn't going to—that is, I didn't intend to really go out on a date with you. I really just wanted to see a Jackie Chan movie. Jackie Chan! Man, he's just the best! Man, if I could do what he does — I'd be . . . I'd be Jackie Chan! He does all his own stunts, you know? Not like American actors like Bruce Willis or Clint Eastwood. I just think of it — that every movie he makes, he's risking his life to help people have a little more fun in their lives. That's just so great. That's such a great way to spend your life. That's how I should live. See, nobody else would go with me and you liked Jackie Chan movies too and it was so weird because you're a girl and I never met no girl who likes Jackie Chan.

BETTY: What — what does that mean?

LOHMAN: I'm saying it's different now. I don't like you for your mind. [BETTY *is just about to respond when the doorbell rings.*] You expecting anybody?

[*He answers the door.* JOHN *rushes in. He's wearing a suit and sunglasses.*]

JOHN: Betty! Betty, I need help. Jackie's not here, is she?

BETTY: John, what are you doing here?

JOHN: Where's Jackie?!

BETTY: She's at the TV station.

JOHN: I can't do this, Betty. You have to help me with it. Listen to this sentence — [*He hesitates a second, looks around.*] Hey!

LOHMAN: What?

JOHN: [*Slightly disgusted.*] You two just had sex, didn't you!

BETTY: [*To* LOHMAN.] I told you!

LOHMAN: [*Exiting.*] I'll get the Lysol.

JOHN: Betty, listen to this: "I spoke to Vanessa in hushed tones. 'How much do you love me?' I asked. She said, 'I love you a whole bunch.'" Does that sound right?

BETTY: What is this? Don't tell me you're trying to write like Nick Strathbourne now.

JOHN: Not "like" Nick. It is Nick's writing.

BETTY: This — this is the last straw! All I have heard for four months is Nick Strathbourne! "Betty, isn't Nick a great writer?" "Betty, why hasn't Nick written to me lately?" "Look, Betty! Nick is being published in *Rolling Stone*!" "Betty, I hope that ungrateful bastard

Nick chokes on his own vomit!" You're not impressing anybody by imitating this nut!

JOHN: I'm not a nut!

BETTY: How about "reality-challenged."

JOHN: You're not listening. I've done it!

BETTY: Done what?

JOHN: I'm an S.W.M.! I'm Nick Strathbourne. Look at my suit.

BETTY: Nice!

JOHN: It's an Armani. Look out there.

[JOHN *goes to the window and points.* LOHMAN *enters and looks out with* BETTY.]

BETTY: That's a Porsche! Where did you get that?

LOHMAN: Wow! Who cares!

JOHN: John Hamabata could never afford that, but Nick Strathbourne can pay cash!

LOHMAN: Does it have a ten-CD disc changer?

BETTY: You're serious!

JOHN: [*To* LOHMAN.] Fifteen!

LOHMAN: Oh, John!

BETTY: It's true. All these months ... all those letters! It's been you!

JOHN: Yes!

BETTY: You're a celebrity! You were in *People* Magazine!

LOHMAN: I read that! Is it true about you and Princess Di?

BETTY: But where the hell have you been? Nick hasn't written to Jackie in over two months!

JOHN: You don't know how hard writing is when you think people are actually going to read it! But now I'm ready; now I have money.

BETTY: John, you can't do this!

JOHN: What? You're the one who told me to do it!

BETTY: I didn't tell you to do anything!

JOHN: You gave me the list! "Get some creativity! Get a Porsche! Rodeo Drive lunches! Plastic surgery!"

BETTY: ... plastic surgery ... ? [*Beat.*] John, take off your glasses.

[*With his back to the audience,* JOHN *takes them off.* LOHMAN *gets close to* JOHN'S *face.*]

LOHMAN: Wow, it's just like Captain Kirk when he disguised himself as a Romulan!

[BETTY *goes to the phone.*]

JOHN: What're you doing?

BETTY: I'm calling my mom. There's no way we can be blood relations.

JOHN: What, you don't like them?

BETTY: Oh come on! You're wearing blue contact lenses! What about the surgery?

JOHN: No way! I saw what they did to Roseanne! Now are you going to help me?

[GERALDINE *walks in the open door.*]

GERALDINE: Lohman, we have to talk.

LOHMAN: Geraldine!

BETTY: Geraldine?

GERALDINE: Lohman . . . ?

BETTY: Lohman . . . !

JOHN: Betty . . . !

BETTY: Lohman, who is she?

LOHMAN: Well, uh — well, uh — well, uh —

JOHN: Lohman was seeing Geraldine until she broke up with him and then he started seeing you and now she wants to get back together with him. Now will you look at this chapter?

GERALDINE: I can't believe you did this to me.

LOHMAN: Me? What'd I do?

GERALDINE: You know what you did. You — [*Looks around the living room.*] You just made love in this room!!

BETTY: How did she know he was here?

JOHN: Okay, I gave her a ride.

LOHMAN: Thanks a load, John.

JOHN: She was threatening to scratch my paint job. Now look! I need to know if this paragraph flows.

GERALDINE: Lohman, I love you!

BETTY: [*To* GERALDINE.] What?

LOHMAN: What?

JOHN: What? Betty, can we get back to something important now?

GERALDINE: You weren't supposed to start seeing other people!

LOHMAN: I wasn't? But you broke up with me.

GERALDINE: You weren't supposed to take it seriously!

LOHMAN: I wasn't?

GERALDINE: No! You weren't supposed to take anything seriously. That's why I love you!

JOHN: Betty, are you going to help me or not?

BETTY: No! I'm not!

JOHN: [*Beat.*] You're not?

BETTY: Look, John. I don't have time. I have a problem. My very own problem. Not one of yours, and not one of Jackie's. It's my very own problem in my very own life. Do you mind?

JOHN: It's okay; I'll wait.

BETTY: [*To* GERALDINE.] Listen, I think you should leave.

GERALDINE: I'm not leaving until Lohman tells me to.

BETTY: This isn't Lohman's house!

JOHN: [*To himself.*] I'm writing and writing, but where are the real words? Where are the real emotions?

GERALDINE: Emotions? I have real emotions! I can tell you how I feel!

JOHN: [*Gets out his notepad.*] Really? Okay, go ahead!

GERALDINE: Lohman . . .

JOHN: Uh huh . . .

GERALDINE: Lohman, I love you —

JOHN: Yeah, yeah!

GERALDINE: I love you — a whole bunch!

JOHN: I can't use that!

LOHMAN: Geraldine, I'm sorry.

GERALDINE: Oh, don't be sorry. Please don't be sorry.

BETTY: He's very sorry.

LOHMAN: I love Betty.

BETTY: You do?

GERALDINE: Not the way you loved me!

BETTY: Yes!

GERALDINE: You can't!

LOHMAN: It's true. [*Grabs* BETTY *around the waist.*] I love her for her body!

BETTY: Oh, Lohman!

> [*They kiss.* BETTY *picks* LOHMAN *up and drags him into the bedroom.* GERALDINE *and* JOHN *stand in silence.*]

JOHN: Want a ride home?

GERALDINE: That's okay.

JOHN: I'm sorry, I shouldn't have brought you.

GERALDINE: No, I'm sorry I was going to key your car. I guess I look pretty stupid.

JOHN: Huh? Hell, no. I was just thinking —

GERALDINE: What?

JOHN: Well, I was just thinking . . . that it was pretty brave of you to come here.

GERALDINE: Was it? It seemed kind of economical to me.

JOHN: What do you mean?

GERALDINE: See, I'm a cash-only person. I don't like being in debt — especially karmic debt, you know? So like, if I didn't come and confront Lohman, I might be wondering for years how my life might have been. I'm free and clear now, John. I don't have any regrets.

JOHN: So now you don't have any regrets?

GERALDINE: [*Beat.*] Well, you know what Nick Strathbourne says.

JOHN: What does Nick Strathbourne say?

GERALDINE: "Sometimes you've got to eat your love."

> [GERALDINE *kisses* JOHN *on the cheek and leaves the room.* JOHN *sits down to write on his notes, elated.*]

JOHN: "You know what Nick Strathbourne says!" Yeah, I know exactly what Nick Strathbourne says!

[JOHN *puts his sunglasses on, sits down and starts to write furiously.*
JACKIE *enters, slamming the door. She's agitated and upset.*]

JACKIE: John?

JOHN: [*Nonchalantly.*] Hi, Jackie. [*Beat.*] Jackie!!

[*He slams down the paper he's writing on.*]

JACKIE: Where's Betty?

JOHN: In the bedroom having sex with Lohman.

JACKIE: Oh. [*Beat.*] Can I ask you something, John?

JOHN: Sure, of course!

JACKIE: And you'd tell me the truth, right?

JOHN: Oh . . . sure!

JACKIE: You'd never hide anything from me, would you?

JOHN: Who, me?

JACKIE: Good. I don't like being deceived, John.

JOHN: Umm.

JACKIE: When someone misrepresents himself, and then tries to take to take advantage of it, do you know how that makes me feel?

JOHN: Slightly annoyed?

JACKIE: Vindictive. I don't hide it at all. I feel like seeking vengeance.

JOHN: You mean, like — ?

JACKIE: Biblical Old Testament kind of stuff.

JOHN: I, um, favor the Christian Gospels, personally.

JACKIE: Eye for an eye . . .

JOHN: Forgive and forget.

JACKIE: Ear for an ear . . .

JOHN: Turn the other cheek.

JACKIE: Limb for limb!

JOHN: Give us this day our daily bread . . .

JACKIE: I hate them, John!

JOHN: Who?!

JACKIE: The producers. The network news producers.

JOHN: [*Exhales in relief.*] Oh! I mean — what did they do to you?

JACKIE: They promised that they would give me a chance in broadcast reporting.

JOHN: Anchoring the news?

JACKIE: These past few months I've been working so hard, writing, researching, working on my complexion —

JOHN: And it's paid off!

JACKIE: I proved to them that I was capable. But today, they turned around and told me...

JOHN: What?

JACKIE: They said I'd never make it in professional broadcasting. They said I didn't...!

JOHN: What?

JACKIE: I didn't look right.

JOHN: They said what? Are they blind??

JACKIE: Guess what they said! Guess what they said was wrong with me!

JOHN: How can I? There's nothing wrong with you.

JACKIE: I'm serious, John. Guess what they said.

JOHN: Well...umm...[*Pause.*] Maybe it was —

JACKIE: What? What?

JOHN: No, never mind.

JACKIE: What? Tell me!

JOHN: Maybe...[*Beat.*] Your chin?

JACKIE: My chin?

JOHN: It wasn't your chin?

JACKIE: What's wrong with my chin?

JOHN: Nothing! It's swell! I love your chin!

JACKIE: But...!

JOHN: Well...nothing a little make-up can't cover.

JACKIE: It was my "look," John! They wanted an "Asian reporter," and I wasn't Asian-looking enough!

JOHN: What! But you're plenty Asian!

JACKIE: They said I'm too ambiguous to be on the nightly news and I don't have the appeal to capture the right demographic cross-section.

[*Hands* JOHN *a flow chart graph sheet.*] They showed me the numbers and everything!

JOHN: See? It wasn't your chin.

JACKIE: I'm qualified, John. I've got what it takes, I know it! But they can't even look past the most superficial part of me! Oh, how could you know what it's like?

JOHN: It feels awful.

JACKIE: Yes!

JOHN: Like somebody stole something you thought was yours.

JACKIE: Your heart! All the things you thought were real about yourself—

JOHN: That you're worth something, that you're good enough. It's all cut out of you. And you can't hide it. It leaves scars.

JACKIE: [*Short pause.*] I didn't do that to you, John, did I? Is that how I made you feel?

JOHN: [*Pause.*] Oh, hey! No! Where did that idea come from?

JACKIE: I just thought —

JOHN: Hey, nothing's wrong with me! If I have a problem, I go do something about it!

JACKIE: I'm really glad about that. After the last time we talked, I was afraid that—Well, I did a lot of thinking, and now I think I might have, well, wrong values, and you were — [*She sniffs him.*] Say, what's that cologne you're wearing?

JOHN: Armani.

JACKIE: Oh, I love Armani.

JOHN: It came with the suit. Jackie, I didn't (know) —

JACKIE: [*Overlapping.*] This coat is Armani? I love Armani coats.

JOHN: What a coincidence!

[JACKIE *closes her eyes and puts her hand on* JOHN'S *coat and strokes it. She inhales the cologne on* JOHN'S *neck deeply, and when she exhales, she rests her head on his shoulder.*]

JACKIE: And the smell of Armani cologne on an Armani jacket just makes me feel so —

JOHN: Hungry?

JACKIE: Huh?

JOHN: Are you hungry? I was just thinking about lunch.

JACKIE: You want to take me out to lunch?

JOHN: I know a great cafe. [*Beat.*] In Beverly Hills.

JACKIE: Beverly Hills? I love Beverly Hills!

JOHN: My car is outside.

JACKIE: But I didn't see your car when I came in.

JOHN: Oh, I sold the Toyota. It was just a transitional car, anyway.

JACKIE: But the only car I saw on the street was — !

[*She gasps.*]

JOHN: [*Nonchalantly.*] Oh, you saw it?

JACKIE: John, you seem so different than you were before. Did you always have those contact lenses?

JOHN: They're for . . . my astigmatism. But that's not important. What's important is that I want to take you for a ride in my car with the top down. I want to take you to lunch in a nice restaurant. I want to treat you the way you deserve to be treated.

JACKIE: John, I would say yes in a second —

JOHN: You would!

JACKIE: If you had asked me a few months ago.

JOHN: Excuse me?

JACKIE: John, this is hard to explain, but so much has happened to me in such a short time!

JOHN: Wonderful! Why don't you tell me about it over a margarita?

JACKIE: John, do you know who Nick Strathbourne is?

JOHN: No! [*Beat.*] I mean, the name is familiar, I think.

JACKIE: Of course! You can't turn on the television without hearing about the "Blue Skies" Generation. You probably won't believe me, but if it wasn't for me, there would be no Nick Strathbourne.

JOHN: That's for sure.

JACKIE: What?

JOHN: I believe you.

JACKIE: It was his writing that made me crazy about him. And even when Nick turned out to be a complete no-show loser, his writing continued to challenge me! It's caused me to really look at what is important in life. Like your jacket —

JOHN: My Armani jacket.

JACKIE: At the same time I want to run my hands up and down the fabric and bury my face in your chest, I'm utterly revolted at the materialism and class status that it represents.

JOHN: If you don't like it, I'll buy something else!

JACKIE: This just isn't easy, do you see? I mean, I used to think there were only two kinds of men: winners and losers. I didn't consider that there might be men like you.

JOHN: Me? What kind am I?

JACKIE: You're very special; you're nice.

JOHN: With a Porsche.

JACKIE: Right. Do you see why I can't rush into anything new? I mean, for all I know I'd only be going out with you because of your car.

JOHN: That's fine with me!

JACKIE: Or it might turn out to be a purely physical attraction.

JOHN: I'm willing to try if you are!

JACKIE: John, when we eventually go out, I promise you it will have absolutely nothing to do with any of your merits or accomplishments. Won't that be great? [*Beat.*] John?

JOHN: Wait: I'm trying to decide if this is a trick question.

[JACKIE *gives him a friendly hug and leads him to the door.*]

JACKIE: You don't know how much this means to me.

JOHN: [*Beat.*] Obviously.

[JOHN *exits.* JACKIE *goes to the answering machine.*]

LARRY'S VOICE: Hello, Jackie. This is Larry. I'm a Capricorn.

JACKIE: Aw, no . . .

LARRY: Wait, before you do anything, please just listen. I know you don't want to see me. I'm pretty empathic. I'm good at picking up all the subtle apprehensions in your demeanor. [*Beat.*] The restraining order was a pretty good one, too. Nobody's done that to me in years. I'm not going to bother you anymore. I just wanted somebody to talk to. [*Pause.*] You know all that stuff about Bangkok and everything? Well, I kind of was making that up. I guess I thought you would like it —

you know, the whole thing. I mean, who knows what women want these days, right? I thought you'd be different. I'll stop calling and writing, and I'll even stop driving by your apartment at three in the morning to see if any lights are on. [*Beat.*] Like my hero Nick Strathbourne says, "Sometimes you just gotta eat your love." I'd hate to think what my life'd be like without Nick. I'd be very, very angry.

[JACKIE *starts to collect leftover cups and dishes, and finds* JOHN'S *script that he left behind. She reads.*]

JACKIE: "Vanessa said to Nick, 'If you love me, let it be for nothing, but love's sake only...'"

[*Lights fade to black.*]

SCENE 2

A few days later. BETTY *and* JACKIE'S *apartment.* LOHMAN *comes out of the bedroom wearing a white V-neck T-shirt and boxer shorts. He scratches his belly, and sits in front of the TV. He opens a newspaper and turns to the sports section.* BETTY *enters from bedroom in a housedress. She goes to the kitchen nook and starts piling plates into the sink.*

BETTY: Hi, cutie.

LOHMAN: Hi.

BETTY: You know, sitting there like that, with your belly sticking out, do you know who you look like?

LOHMAN: Who?

BETTY: You look just like my — my — uhh...

LOHMAN: Like who?

BETTY: Never mind. What are you reading?

LOHMAN: Sports section.

BETTY: Oh. [*Pause.*] I saw John today. He's starting to really scare me, you know?

LOHMAN: Mm.

BETTY: He bought a cellular phone, did you know that? I kept asking myself, what does he need a cellular phone for? So I asked him. "John, who do you call on that piece of junk?" And he says to me, "My voice mail service." "My voice mail service!" Do you believe that?

LOHMAN: Mmm.

BETTY: Lohman, are you listening to me?

LOHMAN: Huh? Sure I am, honey. You saw John!

BETTY: [*Pause.*] Well, it's only ten-thirty. What'll we do for the rest of the evening?

LOHMAN: I dunno. What do you want to do tonight?

BETTY: I don't know. How about you?

LOHMAN: I dunno.

BETTY: Well, we could —

LOHMAN: I'm kind of tired.

BETTY: Oh.

LOHMAN: Why? Did you wanna do something?

BETTY: Well, no, not if you didn't.

LOHMAN: Oh. You sure? What about your friends who were going dancing?

BETTY: Oh, they left already.

LOHMAN: Hey, I'm sorry I was late. It's just John's been flaking on work and Norman wanted me to fill in for him for a while.

BETTY: It's all right.

LOHMAN: There's just so much stress at work, you know?

BETTY: I already forgave you.

LOHMAN: Cool. What's on TV tonight?

BETTY: But you really should've called to tell me you'd be late.

LOHMAN: I'm sorry. Okay? I didn't think it'd take so long. [*Under his breath.*] Geez, you're starting to act like my —

BETTY: What?

LOHMAN: Nothing, nothing. You have the remote control for the TV? I don't see 'em.

BETTY: They must be around here somewhere.

[LOHMAN *sulks in front of the TV.* BETTY *starts running the faucet in her kitchen sink. She slides on rubber gloves.*]

LOHMAN: Hey! What're those?

BETTY: What? These? These are dishwashing gloves.

LOHMAN: [*Beat.*] My mom used to wear those!

BETTY: Your mom?

LOHMAN: Yeah! All the time! Gardening, washing the car, shampooing my dad's hair . . .

BETTY: Lohman . . .

LOHMAN: Yeah?

BETTY: Do I . . .

LOHMAN: What?

BETTY: Do I remind you of your mother?

LOHMAN: [*Squints at her.*] Nah. Nah . . . they're just gloves, right?

BETTY: Right.

LOHMAN: Just gloves.

BETTY: Hey, why don't we just forget about going anywhere and just fool around.

LOHMAN: You mean goof off?

BETTY: I mean get serious.

[BETTY *kisses* LOHMAN. *She's still wearing the gloves.* LOHMAN'S *eyes fall on the gloves and he pulls away.*]

LOHMAN: Um . . . it's been a really long day. I've got all this new responsibility and stuff. Maybe I should just hit the sack.

BETTY: Don't you want to eat something before you go?

LOHMAN: Well, uh, what do you have?

BETTY: There's not much in the apartment. [*Goes through cabinets.*] Just some . . .

LOHMAN: Just some what?

BETTY: [*Holds up a package.*] Uh . . . Top ramen.

LOHMAN: I'm out of here!

BETTY: Lohman, what's wrong with you?

LOHMAN: Me? What's wrong with you?

BETTY: What'd I do?

LOHMAN: What did you — ?? You did everything! You made the bed, you cleaned the dishes, you let me sit in front of the TV in my underwear! And then — then, finally you did that . . . ramen thing!

[LOHMAN *puts on his pants, but has trouble zipping them up.*]

BETTY: Maybe if you button it first, then zip —

LOHMAN: I know how to put on my pants!

BETTY: Lohman, why don't we talk about this?

LOHMAN: No, I want to yell for a while!

BETTY: Fine, so yell!

LOHMAN: Stop letting me have my own way!!

[JACKIE *enters as* LOHMAN *storms out of the apartment.*]

JACKIE: Hey Lohman, your fly's open!

LOHMAN: What are you, my mother?

SCENE 3

At the restaurant. NORMAN *is chopping onions.* JOHN *rushes in, wearing his Armani suit, out of breath.*

JOHN: Norman . . . !

NORMAN: John.

JOHN: Norman . . .

NORMAN: John.

JOHN: Norman . . . I'm sorry, I'm late again.

NORMAN: John, my friend, there is no longer a reason to apologize.

JOHN: There isn't?

NORMAN: No. I'm letting you go.

JOHN: I'm . . . what?

NORMAN: I wish you much luck and happiness in your future vocation. [*Beat.*] Would you taste this sauce? Does it need basil?

JOHN: [*Tastes the sauce.*] More garlic. [*Beat.*] Hey, you're kidding me, aren't you! Ha ha! Yeah, right! For a second there —

NORMAN: John . . .

JOHN: You're the man, Norm! You're the man!

NORMAN: John!! [JOHN *freezes.*] I've warned you, John. You come in late and leave early. You're rude to the customers and to your co-workers, and lately you've been blaming others for your mistakes. You know it's true.

JOHN: But Norman...you don't understand...

NORMAN: Then enlighten me, John.

JOHN: It's not my fault! It's not me, it's —

NORMAN: Who?

JOHN: Nobody. It's nobody. [*Beat.*] I don't believe this. I can't lose this job!

NORMAN: Why not?

JOHN: Because — because —

NORMAN: [*Pause.*] Do you know why I cook spaghetti for five minutes exactly? Because overcooking it makes it soft, and I hate soft spaghetti. I hate it. Soft spaghetti sticks to the bottom of a pot like barnacles. John, it is the nature of pasta to be firm and alive, sleek and elegant.

JOHN: Am I still fired?

NORMAN: I watch you lately, and I see you beating food up, shoving dough into shape instead of massaging it. If you don't like working here anymore, John, that's fine. But don't take it out on the food. If you're going to be a cook, you've got to love food. You have to respect where it comes from, and what it becomes.

JOHN: Are you saying I'm not a cook anymore?

NORMAN: Hey, how can I say what you can or can't be? Maybe you're a cook, maybe you're a Chippendale's dancer! What do I know? [*Beat.*] But if after a while you find out that you are a cook after all, give me a call.

[NORMAN *exits;* LEONARD *enters.*]

LEONARD: Nick! I've been looking all over the place for you!

JOHN: Leonard, what're you doing here?

LEONARD: Nick, look at this and tell me it isn't what it looks like!

[JOHN *takes a sheaf of papers and looks through them.*]

JOHN: It's my pages for this month.

LEONARD: You're killing me, Nick! I'm bleeding!

JOHN: They're all there.

LEONARD: My lungs are filled with blood. My brain is splattered on the dashboard.

JOHN: What's wrong with it?

LEONARD: Wrong? Nothing's wrong if you enjoy reading crap!

JOHN: Hey, I've been saying it's crap all this time! What's so different now?

LEONARD: Up to now, you've been writing good crap! Now it's bad crap.

JOHN: What's the difference.

LEONARD: There's a difference. This stuff smells.

JOHN: What does it smell like?

LEONARD: It smells bad. It smells like politics.

JOHN: I'm going home, Leonard.

LEONARD: Look, you put this Japanese guy in here, and then you have a black woman over on this page.

JOHN: And . . . ?

LEONARD: That's it! What do you think you're doing?

JOHN: This is what you're paying me for. I'm making up characters!

LEONARD: You're making up politically loaded characters! Any time a white writer puts ethnic characters in a story, they become an issue!

JOHN: I'm not a white writer, Leonard.

LEONARD: [*Pause.*] I'm not racist or anything, Nick —

JOHN: John.

LEONARD: — John. It's just that *Blue Skies* isn't about Japanese people.

JOHN: What is it about?

LEONARD: It's about nothing. When you start putting ethnic people into it, it draws attention to itself. It has to become about something. And Meaning doesn't sell, John. This is an audience that is defined by its belief in pointless sensationalism. Are you going to deprive your audience?

JOHN: I'm not trying to do anything to my audience.

LEONARD: You don't understand *Blue Skies* at all, do you? In real life, white people get it from all sides. They have to feel bad about the African Americans, about the Native Americans, about the government, pollution, television, movies, and anything else with indoor plumbing. And nobody ever lets us have our own angst, because it's like we don't deserve it or something. Like we ought to direct all that depression into more guilt. Now *Blue Skies — Blue Skies* feels like home. We can relate to a character who feels alienated and isolated for no good reason at all.

JOHN: Leonard, what if I want to write about something I care about?

LEONARD: Just stop yourself! You've got a lot of people counting on your apathy.

JOHN: Nick Strathbourne is apathetic. Maybe that's not me anymore.

LEONARD: Come on! You've got to be Nick! The world needs a Nick.

JOHN: Fine, you be Nick! You deal with the fame and adulation!

LEONARD: [*Pause.*] This is a test, isn't it? I get it! You're trying to prove my loyalty, aren't you? Well, okay! I refuse! Now will you tell me what you're really thinking? God, it must be brilliant! Come on, Nick! Spill the beans! Don't be selfish!

[LEONARD *follows* JOHN *around the room, taunting him, until* JOHN *finally explodes and takes a swing at* LEONARD. *But it only lands badly on his shoulder.*]

JOHN: SHUT UP!

LEONARD: [*Honestly emotionally hurt.*] Why'd you do that?

JOHN: Come on, go ahead!

LEONARD: What?

JOHN: Take a shot! Hit me!

LEONARD: Why?

JOHN: I'm gonna punch your lights out! That's what Nick would do, isn't it?

LEONARD: I don't want to fight you!

JOHN: What, are you some kind of wimp? Hit me!

LEONARD: I'm sorry, Nick! I didn't mean to—I mean, I come on pretty strong sometimes, but I just—I'm just trying to help you! I'm on your side, really! [*Beat.*] You're not going to hit me again, are you?

JOHN: I can't do this anymore.

LEONARD: Ni—John, you can't do that, don't you realize? It's bigger than you. You're one of the greats, like Marilyn Monroe or James Dean! You can do anything you want—become a drug addict, date fifteen-year-olds...marry Elvis' daughter!

JOHN: That's crazy!

LEONARD: John, you're part of the American Dream! Here, see! [*Takes an* Independent *and flips to the personals.*] "S.W.F., "Vanessa" wants a Nick Strathbourne to take her from this awful world!" And look! "Seeking

Nick Strathbourne? He's really a Single Asian Male, and his real name is...John Hamabata..."

JOHN AND LEONARD: Oh, shit!

SCENE 4

JACKIE *and* BETTY's *apartment.* BETTY *is trying to work on her computer. There's a knock at the door, and she answers.* LOHMAN *is standing at the door.*

BETTY: What do you want?

LOHMAN: I had to tell you something.

BETTY: What?

LOHMAN: You're — you're not my mom.

BETTY: Thanks.

LOHMAN: So...what are you doing?

BETTY: I'm re-indexing the appendices to my thesis.

LOHMAN: You're doing homework? [*Short pause.*] Can I help?

BETTY: [*Short pause.*] Okay.

LOHMAN: All right! What can I do?

[LOHMAN *sits at* BETTY'S *desk.*]

BETTY: Why don't you check my spelling?

[LOHMAN *works intently while* BETTY *stands behind him. After a few moments,* BETTY *yawns.*]

BETTY: I'm tired; are you tired?

LOHMAN: Nah, I could go on for — Oh! Yeah, I'm real tired.

[*They exit into bedroom.*]

SCENE 5

JOHN'S *apartment.* JOHN *is wearing old comfortable clothing. As lights rise, we hear messages from his answering machine.*

VOICE 1: Hi John? Or should I call you "Nick?" This is Sheri. I don't know if you remember, but we were in Chem lab together. You know, I always knew you were special, even when you were a total geek! Call me! Beep!

VOICE 2: Hello, Mr. Hamabata? I represent an Asian American coalition group, and I want you to know that I am utterly appalled at the perverted role model you are giving to young men and women! Ah, would you be interested in participating in our annual fundraiser? BEEP!

VOICE 3: Mr. Strathbourne! God has instructed me to inform you that your days in this world are few, and you had better repent all your —

[JOHN *rips the cord out of the machine, and sits down again. There's a knock at the door; he ignores it. Another knock.*]

JACKIE: John? John, are you in there?

[JOHN *hesitates, then goes to the door and opens it.* JACKIE *stands there in a business suit, looking very formal.*]

JACKIE: Hi.

JOHN: Hi.

JACKIE: Can I come in?

[JOHN *motions in agreement. When she enters, she notices the pile of clothing.* JOHN *doesn't try to hide it.*]

JOHN: What's up?

JACKIE: You should really hang up your suit.

JOHN: I don't want it anymore. It's not me.

JACKIE: If I had something this nice, I wouldn't treat it so carelessly. Do you just toss away everything you're not comfortable with?

JOHN: If you like it, take it. I'm trying to simplify my life.

JACKIE: Maybe you should have thought more, before you bought it.

JOHN: [*Pause.*] You know, don't you?

JACKIE: Know what?

[JOHN *grabs a copy of the* Independent *and shows it to* JACKIE.]

JOHN: You've read this, haven't you?

JACKIE: Are you referring to any particular section?

JOHN: Why else would you be here? Of course you've seen it. That's it, isn't it? I'm done. I'm toast.

JACKIE: John, are you trying to tell me something?

JOHN: Okay, I'm sorry. I'm sorry it ever happened. It'll never happen again.

JACKIE: What won't happen again?

JOHN: You know it. You know I wrote those stories. You know I've been writing as Nick Strathbourne.

JACKIE: Yes, I know.

JOHN: Okay, then.

JACKIE: You were about to apologize.

JOHN: I just did! Why are you making this hard for me?

JACKIE: What were you expecting? Think about it!

JOHN: I'm trying to, all right?

JACKIE: Try this out, too, while you're at it. I did it! I wrote the ad! [*Short pause.*] I already knew, John! I found out a week ago and I wrote that announcement!

JOHN: No, you wouldn't!

JACKIE: Eye for an eye! Limb from limb!

JOHN: You mean limb for limb.

JACKIE: So what do you think of that? What do you say now?

JOHN: What, is this a pop quiz?

JACKIE: You had no right to do that to me! Did you think you were being funny? Was I supposed to laugh?

JOHN: [*Overlapping.*] No! No! You were supposed to give me a chance! Something I couldn't—John couldn't get! All I wanted was a date. Just a chance.

JACKIE: A date? You did all of this just because I wouldn't go out with you? You want me to believe that?

JOHN: Okay, don't believe me. You're real good at ignoring reality.

JACKIE: Oh, what's that supposed to mean?

JOHN: Think about it. No normal guy can get near you! You measure every man you meet up next to that actor Sam Shepard—another guy you've never met!

JACKIE: Sam is a playwright!

JOHN: The perfect guy...distant, inaccessible...

JACKIE: I was trying to meet Nick.

JOHN: And if you did, you would've been disappointed. Because he'd be human. He'd have flaws. Your ad didn't specify a flawed human be-ing.

JACKIE: I didn't specify a manipulating jerk either.

JOHN: And Nick succeeded where John failed. But John was almost the next best thing, wasn't he? Once he got the suit and car and contact lenses.

JACKIE: Well, John . . . I was starting to like John.

JOHN: But you still wouldn't go out with him.

JACKIE: I told you I wanted to, but —

JOHN: But what? It's not like I asked you for a kidney! I just wanted a date! And I was going to buy! Nothing was going to be good enough.

JACKIE: If I'm such a basket case, why couldn't you go harass someone else?

JOHN: I couldn't.

JACKIE: Why not?

JOHN: I just couldn't.

[*Pause.* JACKIE *goes to the pile of* NICK'S *belongings, touches the jacket, the phone.*]

JACKIE: I guess you wouldn't believe me if I said I wasn't just interested in the clothes and the car. I never said anything I didn't mean. Especially about the writing.

JOHN: The writing . . . right.

JACKIE: Nick — I mean, you have such a talent.

JOHN: Yeah, sure.

JACKIE: What? What's wrong? You're going to keep writing, aren't you? Aren't you?

JOHN: That was just to impress you. Nick isn't for real.

[JACKIE *takes a page of* NICK'S *novel from her purse and reads it.*]

JACKIE: "I understand life. Life is like an old novel you pick up in a musty, dimly-lit bookshop. You're not looking for anything, but as your hand runs along the rows of threadbare spines, one jumps up and grabs a hold of your hand. Open it, and you touch pages that haven't seen the brightness of light in so long they almost squint. And you keep it be-cause something catches your eye: a word, a phrase, an attractive set of semi-colons. Something on that page relates to you. There may be one word that describes you the way no other word describes you, or perhaps it says the exact thing you always wished someone would've said to you when you were young. If you're smart, you take that book with you. If you're really smart, you pay for it, too."

[*From outside, the noise of an angry mob rises.*]

JOHN: What's that noise?

[*The apartment door bursts open.* LOHMAN *is standing there, out of breath, clothing ruffled.* BETTY *stands behind him, a little more calm.*]

LOHMAN: John! Are you okay?

JOHN: Lohman, what's going on?

LOHMAN: It was crazy! We had to fight our way up here!

BETTY: We?

LOHMAN: Well, Betty had to fight, I sort of just ran alongside. All these people tried to grab at us and stop us, but Betty was a crazy woman, hitting them in the face and kicking them in the crotch! [*To* BETTY.] I'm so proud of you!

BETTY: What are they doing here, John? How did they find out you're Nick Strathbourne??

JOHN: Well —

JACKIE: Well —-

BETTY: You didn't!

JACKIE: Don't worry, I'll take care of it. I'll call the station. I'll say I made it all up.

JOHN: You'll get fired!

BETTY: They'd never believe you anyway.

LOHMAN: Yeah, it makes too much sense.

JACKIE: John, maybe you should tell them the truth.

JOHN: They don't want to hear the truth!

JACKIE: But what if they do?

JOHN: I'm not what they want! I'm not Nick Strathbourne! I'm — I'm not clever, or intellectual. I'm not confident like they want me to be! What am I supposed to tell them?

JACKIE: Why don't you just be honest with them?

JOHN: And tell them what? That all this time, the "voice of frustrated Caucasian Americans" is a Japanese cook?

JACKIE: They can't blame you for being yourself.

JOHN: They're trying to take it all away from me! They're telling me that the blue skies belong to them, not me! They want my life!

JACKIE: You wrote *Blue Skies*, John. It's yours. They can't take that away from you. I can't take that away from you.

[JACKIE *hands* JOHN *the sheet of paper with the* Blue Skies *monologue.* JOHN *gives* JACKIE *back the sheet of paper. He points to his head.*]

JOHN: The words are still in here.

LOHMAN: John, you going outside, or what?

BETTY: Shhh!

JACKIE: "If thou must love me, let it be for naught, but love's sake only."

JOHN: Jackie, I have to tell you something.

JACKIE: What now?

JOHN: That's the only Browning poem I know.

JACKIE: Nobody's perfect.

BETTY: I really hate to interrupt . . . but what are we going to do about Nick's fan club?

JOHN: I think it's about time I met my audience.

BETTY: Maybe now isn't the right time? Maybe we should concentrate on removing John from the apartment?

JOHN: I know where I should go.

[JOHN *exits out of the room. As the noise of the crowd increases, the lights fade in the apartment and in a far corner of the stage,* JOHN *appears. He waves his hand, trying to get attention. He is speaking to the crowd, pleading with them, but we don't hear his words. The noise of the crowd goes down slowly, and is replaced by a voiceover of* JOHN's *speech, spoken with calmness and softness. It is implied that however* JOHN *is speaking at the crowd, the essence of the voiceover is being conveyed. Slowly, the lights begin to dim until we can't see* JOHN *clearly.*]

JOHN: I'm going to tell the truth. I don't know any of you, and that scares me. Every time I meet someone new, I feel like I'm a stranger in somebody else's country. I've lived here all my life, yet still . . .

[*Beat.*]

I don't not want to be Japanese, I just don't want to be reminded of it like it's important. It's important to me, but it shouldn't be important to you. I want to love a beautiful woman, I want her to look at me with loving eyes. I want you all to like me, but from a distance, from a place that lets me breathe, that lets me walk unnoticed among you, and be lost the way so many of you seem to be, in your comfortable, recognized, lostness. I want you to want that for me too. I don't want you to resent me, just because my needs are written all over my face. [*Beat.*]

I don't know if I believe in anything, but I have faith. I have faith that everything I need and desire out of life is just like what anybody else in the world needs and desires. I have faith I am understandable, when I say that I'm Nick Strathbourne. I'm John Hamabata. I am a S.A.M., Single Asian Male. SAM I am.

[*Lights fade to black.*]

[JOHN *reappears in his apartment, supposedly at a much later date. He sits on his couch with a laptop computer and types. In her apartment,* JACKIE *enters. She sits on the couch and picks up a book. From across the gap,* JOHN *looks up at* JACKIE, *and they exchange a lingering glance.* JOHN *goes back to his computer and continues his work.*]

[*Lights dim.*]

THE END

Rob Shin

THE ART OF WAITING

The Art of Waiting by Rob Shin
© 1991 Rob Shin

Professionals and amateurs are hereby warned that *The Art of Waiting* is subject to royalty. It is fully protected under the copyright laws of the united States of America, and of all countries covered by the International Copyright Union (including the Dominion of Canada and the rest of the British Commonwealth) and of all countries covered by the Pan-American Copyright Conventions, and of all countries with which the United States has reciprocal copyright relations. All rights, including professional and amateur stage performing, video or sound taping, motion picture, recitation, lecturing, public reading, radio and television broadcasting, all other forms of mechanical or electronic reproduction, such as information storage and retrieval systems and photocopying, and the rights of translation into foreign languages, are strictly reserved. Particular emphasis is laid upon the question of readings, permission for which must be granted from the author or author's representative in writing. For performance of such songs and recordings mentioned in this play as are in copyright, the permission of the copyright owner must be obtained; or other music and recordings in the public domain substituted.

For performance rights and inquiries, contact: Rob Shin, 95 Second Avenue, #3, New York, NY 10003.

EDITOR'S NOTES

The social conflicts between African Americans and Koreans or Korean Americans have risen to the fore in recent years — but nearly every dramatic account about the situation seems to be offered by African American artists. There was Spike Lee's groundbreaking DO THE RIGHT THING. There was Anna Deavere Smith's unforgettable TWILIGHT — LOS ANGELES 1992. There was Silas Jones' surreal CANNED GOODS. And while Elizabeth Wong's KIMCHEE AND CHITLINS certainly addressed the subject, it did so through the character of a Chinese-American journalist trying to make sense of it all — even as Wong herself has been a Chinese-American journalist. One couldn't help wondering: where were the Korean American dramatists?

Though this is merely speculation, it seemed during my time at East West Players that Korean American writers might have been discouraged by the tendency for seemingly all Asian American theatres to be run by Japanese American artists. Though the conflicts between Japanese and Korean may originate on another continent, miles still separate the Little Tokyo and Koreatown sections of Los Angeles.

Whether for this or other reasons such as immigration patterns and history, many Korean American playwrights are only now making their voices heard. The haunting poetry of Sung J. Rno is on display in the apocalyptic CLEVELAND RAINING (in which a brother and sister reparent themselves in an unsettling duet that bears similarity to *As Sometimes in a Dead Man's Face*). Susan Kim is writing acidic comedies and dramas such as *The Arrangement*, in which a damaged man and woman substitute each other for the people they really love but can't have. Philip Chung straddles several media, writing one-acts like *Model Minority*, co-founding *Yolk Magazine* and providing stories for television's *Lois and Clark*. Each season seems to bring more Korean American writers into fresh view.

Among them, Rob Shin's brash, irreverent writing holds a special place of interest for its frank, uncompromising look at the mistrust between Korean Americans and African Americans, as well as Caucasians and Chinese. A winner of the American College Theatre Festival (and a natural for college productions because of a cast size few professional theaters can afford), *The Art of Waiting* looks at racism from every angle. Many writers are content to document the injuries done them by racism, or the injuries done to another group with which they sympathize. Few are as willing as Shin to indict themselves for the racist tendencies that sneak up, unwelcome, into one's own private thoughts.

The play is also striking in terms of its sheer theatricality. While Nicholson Baker's novel, *The Mezzanine*, explores every single thought and cross-reference to pass through its hero's mind during his lunch hour, rarely does a play attempt a similar narrative feat. Rob Shin focuses on an even tighter interval than Baker's lunch hour: the ten minutes he waits before going onstage to perform a stand-up act. The melange of daydreams and free associations brings a new meaning to the phrase "strange interlude." And the choral work that climaxes the play cannot help but have an effect on an audience (and uncannily echoes the climactic sequence of Chay Yew's *Porcelain*).

In one staged reading of the play, I was surprised to hear widely varying responses from women and men. Women were impressed by the candor of the play, by the extent to which Shin's character (himself) is willing to lay himself bare for the audience, warts and all. His honesty and vulnerability made a statement. Men, on the other hand, were disappointed. "When this play began," said one friend, "I thought he (the lead character) was going to be my hero. But all he did was explain the problem, he didn't triumph over it."

Maybe explaining the problem is triumph enough. But maybe Shin's character does triumph, depending on how the ending is staged. Shin leaves his ending ambiguous, as his character wonders whether to exploit an ethnic stereotype for laughs, or fall on his face in front of a live audience. The play looks like it's going to end with the old cliché, "Ah, so!" but instead ends with a final, flat "So." It's an ending that cries out for skillful direction, to explore what choice Shin's character finally makes.

British director Jonathan Miller, in *Subsequent Performances*, expresses consternation at how dramatists, as opposed to musicians, are so willing to leave their work open to interpretation by others. But writers whose work invites interpretation by actors and directors show an admirable artistic courage. It's a courage Rob Shin demonstrates in his ending — as well as throughout a play documenting the cruelties of ethnic humor, and implicating any audience member who's ever told — or laughed — at such jokes.

The Art of Waiting was first produced professionally at the Round House Theatre (Jerry Whiddon, Artistic Director), Silver Spring, Maryland, on March 20, 1993, with the following cast:

ROB	Ralph Pena
MR. SHOWBIZ	Michael Willis
THERAPIST/PROSECUTOR	Sadiqa P. Dailey
RADIO RAHEEM/JUDGE	D'Monroe
DANITA/GIRL AT TABLE	Toyin Fadope
GIRL AT TABLE	Sayla Godsey
MISS HARRISON/MRS. DUGAN	Marilyn Hausfield
SCOTTY/STEVE/WADE	Jason Kravitz
FATHER/DON	Ben Lin
MOMMY	Betty Manuar
WHITE CHILD	Joey Sorge
MISSY/WHITE CHILD	Kim Tuvin

Directed by Tom Prewitt. Set Design by Elizabeth Jenkins; Light Design by Daniel Schrader & Joseph B. Musumeci, Jr.; Costume Design by Rosemary Pardee; Sound Design by Neil McFadden; Properties by Kathleen Wolfrey; Production Stage Manager, Amy Vining; Stage Manager, Myles C. Hatch.

CHARACTERS

ASIAN AMERICAN:

BOBBY/ROB   a little boy; a nervous adolescent/post-adolescent
MOMMY/PERSON IN AUDIENCE
FATHER
DON
KOREAN MALE TAPE VOICE
KOREAN FEMALE TAPE VOICE
LITTLE ASIAN BOY

AFRICAN AMERICAN:

TABLE 4 WOMAN/PROSECUTOR
TABLE 1 MAN
TABLE 1 WOMAN
TABLE 3 GIRL A
TABLE 3 GIRL B
DANITA
RADIO RAHEEM

WHITE/CAUCASIAN:

DENISE
MR. SHOWBIZ
OLD WHITE GUY
LITTLE WHITE BOY
LITTLE WHITE GIRL
ADOLESCENT WHITE BOY
MISSY
WADE
SCOTT WHITEHEAD
TABLE 2 MAN
TABLE 2 WOMAN
STEVE
MRS. GARVEY
TEEN WITH TOO MUCH TIME TO KILL #1 AND TEEN WITH TOO MUCH
        TIME TO KILL #2
ACTOR
ACTRESS

RACIALLY NON-SPECIFIC:

AMERICAN MALE TAPE VOICE
AMERICAN FEMALE TAPE VOICE
"MISS AMERICA" TAPE VOICE
THERAPIST
TABLE 5 GUY A
TABLE 5 GUY B
TABLE 6 GIRL A
TABLE 6 GIRL B
STAGEHANDS
MISS HARRISON
MRS. DUGAN

> [*Previous productions have utilized an ensemble cast with each actor play-ing multiple roles. Many of the roles can (and should) be easily doubled/tripled/etc.*]

❖❖❖

> [*Darkness. The beginning of a foreign language tape. Traditional "Oriental" music plays. A bell rings.*]

> [*As the tape plays, lights slowly reveal the stage setting: four tables sur-rounding a central performance area. Eventually,* STAGEHANDS *enter and silently begin to set up the playing area: e.g., wipe tables, unstack chairs, set up microphones, etc.*]

AMERICAN MALE TAPE VOICE: Let's take a trip to Korea. Part II. If you have not listened to Part I, please flip the tape over and begin again.

[*A bell rings.*]

AMERICAN MALE TAPE VOICE: [*Cont'd.*] Your trip will be much more en-joyable when you can meet people and make yourself understood.

[*A bell rings.*]

AMERICAN MALE TAPE VOICE: [*Cont'd.*]Let's learn how to meet people on the trip.

[*A bell rings.*]

AMERICAN MALE TAPE VOICE: [*Cont'd.*]May I get you a drink?

KOREAN MALE TAPE VOICE: [*Exaggeratedly masculine.*] Hahn hun ha-shi-gae-ssum-nee-ka?

AMERICAN FEMALE TAPE VOICE: Do you have a light please?

KOREAN FEMALE TAPE VOICE: [*Exaggeratedly submissive.*] Bool-jum bil-lil-ka-yo?

AMERICAN MALE TAPE VOICE: Are you waiting for someone?

KOREAN MALE TAPE VOICE: Noo-goo-lil gee-da-ri-go gae-ssyn-nee-ka?

AMERICAN FEMALE TAPE VOICE: Would you like to dance?

KOREAN FEMALE TAPE VOICE: Choom-choo-roh ka-jee ahn-kae-ssum-nee-ka?

AMERICAN MALE TAPE VOICE: Would you like another drink?

KOREAN MALE TAPE VOICE: Han-jan ha-shee gae-ssum-nee-ka?

AMERICAN MALE TAPE VOICE: May I take you home?

KOREAN MALE TAPE VOICE: Taek-ka-jee tae-wuh-da du-ril ka-yo?

AMERICAN FEMALE TAPE VOICE: Thank you. It's been a wonderful evening.

KOREAN FEMALE TAPE VOICE: Ko-mahp-sup-nee-da. Ah-joo jul-goo-uhn jun-yuk-ee yus-uh-yo.

AMERICAN MALE TAPE VOICE: Do you live alone?

KOREAN MALE TAPE VOICE: Hohn-ja sah-shim-nee-ka?

[*A bell rings.*]

AMERICAN MALE TAPE VOICE: After so much travel, let's relax for a while and have some dinner.

[*A bell rings.*]

AMERICAN FEMALE TAPE VOICE: I'd like some...

KOREAN FEMALE TAPE VOICE: Johm joo-say-yo...

AMERICAN FEMALE TAPE VOICE: I'd like some beef.

KOREAN FEMALE TAPE VOICE: Sae-go-gee oiil joo-say-yo...

AMERICAN MALE TAPE VOICE: A beef steak.

KOREAN MALE TAPE VOICE: Beep-uh steak-uh.

AMERICAN FEMALE TAPE VOICE: Some roast beef.

KOREAN FEMALE TAPE VOICE: Lost-uh beep-uh.

AMERICAN MALE TAPE VOICE: Chicken.

KOREAN MALE TAPE VOICE: Tak-go-gee.

AMERICAN FEMALE TAPE VOICE: Duck.

KOREAN FEMALE TAPE VOICE: Rook-out-uh!

[*A loud crash.*]

AMERICAN FEMALE TAPE VOICE: Are you OK?

KOREAN FEMALE TAPE VOICE: Gaen cha-na you?

AMERICAN MALE TAPE VOICE: Clumsy waiter.

KOREAN MALE TAPE VOICE: Asshole.

[*A bell rings.*]

AMERICAN MALE TAPE VOICE: Now that we've had dinner, let's go see a show.

[*A bell rings.*]

AMERICAN FEMALE TAPE VOICE: What time does the play begin?

KOREAN FEMALE TAPE VOICE: Yun-gook nun maeh-shee-aeh shee-jak hap-nee-kah?

AMERICAN MALE TAPE VOICE: Are there any tickets for tonight?

KOREAN MALE TAPE VOICE: Ohn-ull jun-yuk pyo ga ip na yo?

AMERICAN FEMALE TAPE VOICE: What's the play about? Is it a comedy?

KOREAN FEMALE TAPE VOICE: Guh-guh-son uh-ton yun-gook ip-nee-ka? Juh un-gook nuhn hwee guk ip-nee-ka?

AMERICAN MALE TAPE VOICE: I hear the playwright's a real self-absorbed jerk.

KOREAN MALE TAPE VOICE: Jae ee-dum nuhn Robert Shin.

[*A bell rings.*]

✧✧✧

[*The sound of applause. Spotlight on an empty stage at Bob's Comedy Luau Hut. Enter* MR. SHOWBIZ. *He grasps the microphone.*]

MR. SHOWBIZ: Hey, how the fuck are ya? This is Bob coming at you from Bob's Comedy Luau Hut. How the hell you doin'. Thank you, thank you Mr. Joel Fontaine... He's a funny funny funny man. OK folks, just a little reminder. Tomorrow night is Back-to-the-Beach-with-the-Ladies Night... If you're a lady, you get in for half-price... and if you're a lady in Hawaiian beachwear, you get in for free... and for every three drinks you buy, you get a free lei—that's l-e-i. Y'know what I'm saying? ... Here's looking at ya... Heh-heh-heh... Alright, next up is a guy by the name of... [*He takes a piece of paper out of his pocket, reads.*] "Lu-cifer, the Prince of Darkness..." Ladies and gentlemen, LUCIFER, THE PRINCE OF DARKNESS. I'm kidding, I'm kidding…Heh-heh-heh…No, but seriously folks, next up is a kid with a whole heck of a lot of talent, making his sixth appearance on our All-Star Amateur Comedy Showcase…Scotty Whitehead…Scotty Whitehead, come up and make these people laugh…

VOICE OF SCOTT WHITEHEAD: So there's this Black guy, this Oriental guy, and this Iraqi guy, and they're stranded on this desert island. So they pull out their dicks and…

[*Laughter.* MR. SHOWBIZ *sees that all is going well, "exits" to…*]

❖❖❖

[*Backstage at Bob's Comedy Luau Hut where* ROB *is pacing nervously.*]

MR. SHOWBIZ: Alright, kid. You're up next.

ROB: Now? You want me up now?

MR. SHOWBIZ: No-no, ten minutes. After the Whitehead kid…

ROB: Ten minutes, OK, ten minutes, ten minutes…

MR. SHOWBIZ: Whatsamatter with you, Johnny? You look like you're gonna puke or something. Hey, you wanna know a little Showbiz trick? Take a towel, run it under some cold water, wrap it 'round your head…Yeah, wrap it around your head, always does the trick… Nothing to it, Johnny. [MR. SHOWBIZ *hands him a towel.*] You're gonna be fine, kid…Just remember. Chinese waiter. [*Giving the "thumbs up."*] Chinese Waiter, baby. If you're gonna puke, toilet's over there, don't miss.

[MR. SHOWBIZ *exits.* ROB *looks at his watch, begins to pace.*]

ROB: OK. Relax relax relax relax gotta relax relax…[*Takes a deep breath, counts to ten.*] Relax. [*Looks at his watch; pause.*] The Art of Waiting… [*Long pause.*] On Tables.
Hey, we're having fun now…[*Doing Steve Martin.*] Comedy Jokes.. . Alright, alright…if I had a wish and I wasn't allowed to wish for… world peace or…the end of suffering…or vast amounts of personal wealth, I'd wish…I would seriously consider wishing for…the ability to create time lapses…you know, be able to freeze things whenever you'd want to…so you'd have like three minutes to think of a really clever reply in any given situation…and then time would resume…and you'd be so fucking clever. [*Beat.*] Chinese Waiter. Chinese Waiter. [*Mimicking John Hughes'/Gedde Watanabe's "Long Duck Dong".*] "No more yankee my wankee. I never been so-uh hoppy in-uh mae-ee hole rife."

Acting: Difficult People Making Difficult Choices.

"To be or not to be."

Gel or paste.

Abbott or Costello.

MacNeil or Lehrer.

I'm in the moment. [*He jumps or poses/vogues.*] In the moment. [*He jumps or poses/vogues.*] In the moment. [*He jumps or poses/vogues. Then he begins to put on his apron, speaks directly to us.*]

I am a waiter. I wait on tables. In a restaurant. Downtown.

To be specific, it is a "Chinese" restaurant. Not that there's anything particularly "Chinese" about it. Except for the nature of its food and the nature of many of its employees. Such as myself.

I am a waiter. In a Chinese restaurant.

But I am not Chinese . . .

✧✧✧

[*On "Chinese," stereotypical "Oriental" music plays.*]

[*A Chinese restaurant. The events of an entire typical day in the restaurant — e.g.,* CUSTOMERS *being seated, served, receiving their checks, leaving, etc. — are compressed into and played out in one musical interlude — "Ode to Joy" from Beethoven's Ninth or "That Really Frenetic Music Whose Name I Can't Think of Right Now But Could Hum For You."*]

[*Activity in the restaurant ebbs and flows, but intensifies during the lunch and dinner rushes. During such periods, the place is a chaotic jumble of activity: many people "talk" simultaneously, making requests to the servers, talking amongst themselves, etc.* DON *moves about, showing people to their seats. His slow and steady demeanor contrasts sharply with the hectic manner of* ROB *and* DENISE, *who cope with this situation the best way they can — serving, busing, and cleaning their respective tables, all while — politely — trying to get people in and out as fast as possible . . .*]

[*After the lunch rush, as* ROB *and* DENISE *collapse to take their break, the music stops abruptly. A beat. They look at their watches. The music and activity start all over again for the dinner rush.*]

[*The intensity of the restaurant activity soon reaches a peak at which point the music suddenly stops and the actors freeze.*]

[*A bell rings here and there, the heretofore silent restaurant players burst into sound. For about fifteen seconds, the sound of restaurant activity intensifies, supplemented by additional (taped) restaurant noise, the volume of which slowly increases . . . activity and sound, both taped and "real," culminate in one intense blur, and then . . . Silence.*]

[NOTE: *The following scene is played in the midst of the above musical sequence/restaurant activity, and then replayed in isolation when the sequence is over. That is to say, it is played as one of many simultaneous silent scenes in the frenzy of restaurant activity, and then is replayed as a single scene by itself.*]

[*Lights up on the restaurant again . . . it is much quieter now. Everyone is gone except for* ROB *and* DENISE *and the customers at two tables:* TABLE 4 WOMAN *and* TABLE 3 GIRLS. ROB *is cleaning up.*]

TABLE 3 GIRL A: Hey mister . . .

ROB: Right. Can I get you anything else?

TABLE 3 GIRL A: We're all set.

ROB: OK, here you are. [*Rips off check.*] Thank you very much.

TABLE 3 GIRL A: [*To* TABLE 4 WOMAN.] OK, Mom. We'll see you when we get home.

TABLE 4 WOMAN: Now don't you forget about those clothes.

TABLE 3 GIRL A: OK, OK.

[ROB *sees that the* TABLE 3 GIRLS *have left, goes to clean table 3, finds no tip. He looks at* TABLE 4 WOMAN, *perhaps looks as if he wants to say something to her . . . but doesn't . . . Tableau. Lights fade on* TABLE 4 WOMAN *and rise on:*]

❖❖❖

[*A living room.* MOMMY *enters with a tape recorder.*]

MOMMY: Bobby, you see puh-rug ("plug")?

ROB: Mom . . . ?

MOMMY: [*Getting cord.*] Gaen-cha-nah. ["It's OK."] Mammy pah-eend. ["I found it."]

[MOMMY *plugs in the tape recorder, presses Play. She is listening to a language tape. The* VOICE *on the tape should probably sound like Miss America.*]

TAPE VOICE: How are you today?

MOMMY: [*Imitating tape voice, sounding out difficult sounds.*] How ahl yoo too-dae-ee?

TAPE VOICE: I'm fine. Thank you.

MOMMY: Ah-eem pine. Sank you.

TAPE VOICE: And you?

MOMMY: And-uh you?

TAPE VOICE: I'm well. Thank you.

MOMMY: Ah-eem hwell. Sank you.

TAPE VOICE: May I borrow some butter?

MOMMY: Mae-ee Ah-ee Bollow Sum-uh Buttuh?

TAPE VOICE: I'm making a casserole for my husband.

MOMMY: Ah-eem may-king casselole por mah-ee hus-bend-uh.

TAPE VOICE: There is a P.T.A. meeting Friday.

MOMMY: Sare ees Bee-Tee-Aeh-ee Mee-Ding Puh-rye-dae-ee.

TAPE VOICE: I'm going to the mall. Would you like to come?

MOMMY: Ah-eem go-ing to suh Marr. Ood...Ood...Ood...

TAPE VOICE: They are having a white sale.

MOMMY: Dae-ee arl hab-ing hwa-hwite sae-eel.

TAPE VOICE: I like being a housewife.

MOMMY: [Beat.] Aiy-goo. [Shuts off the tape recorder.] Bobby, how you sae-ee "ood?"

ROB/BOBBY: "Would," Mom, "would."

MOMMY: [Overlapping.] Oood.

ROB/BOBBY: Would.

MOMMY: Oood?

ROB/BOBBY: No, Mom. That's not right. "Would."

MOMMY: Oood.

ROB/BOBBY: "Wwwould." Watch me. Watch me.

BOBBY: "Wwwould."

MOMMY: [Imitates BOBBY's facial movements.] Oood.

BOBBY: No, Mommy, that's not right. "Wwould."

MOMMY: Oood.

BOBBY: "Wwould."

MOMMY: Oood.

BOBBY: Wwould.

MOMMY: Oood. Oh, Bobby, you know you Mommy no good Engrish-uh speak-uh.

BOBBY: Mommy, say "Volkswagen."

MOMMY: Pohkswagon.

BOBBY: Volkswagen, Mom.

MOMMY: Pohkwag—Bobby, why you rapp-uh? I caen not sae-ee "Pohkwagon."

BOBBY: Pokeswagon?

MOMMY: Pohkswagon. [*Pause.*] Oh Bobby, I sink it tah-eem yoo go bed.

BOBBY: Nooooo...I'm not tired.

MOMMY: You risten you Mommy. Be good boy.

BOBBY: I wuv you, Mommy.

MOMMY: I rub-uh you too, Bobby. But yoo bee good bo-eey. Now go.

BOBBY: But I didn't even get to see Daddy.

MOMMY: When Daddy come home, he see you. Now go. Be good boy.

BOBBY: OK...pboh-pbok joo-uh.

> [*She kisses him.*]

MOMMY: [*Cont'd.*] Don' foh-get blush you teess and say you plae-uh.

✧✧✧

> [BOBBY *alone with his teddy bear,* MR. BEAR. BOBBY *converses with* MR. BEAR *by making him move and talk.*]

BOBBY: Hi, Mr. Bear. How are you today?

MR. BEAR: I'm fine, Bobby. How are you.

BOBBY: I'm fine. How are you?

MR. BEAR: I'm fine. How are you?

BOBBY: I'm fine! How are you?!

MR. BEAR: I'm fine! How are you?!

BOBBY: I'm fine! How are you?!

> [MR. BEAR *"faints."*]

BOBBY: [*Cont'd.*] Hard day at the office, huh?

MR. BEAR: Yup, I'm pooped. But I've gotta work really hard so my baby bear...my cub can go to college someday.

BOBBY: OK, Mr. Bear. I'll see you later. I gotta go now. My wife's making me a casserole.

MR. BEAR: Mmmm...that sounds yummy.

BOBBY: Hey, you wanna eat at our house? We could play G.I. Joes and Six Million Dollar Man. Or we could go to Steve's house, and play with them in his sandbox.

MR. BEAR: Oooh, yeah?

BOBBY: Yeah, me and Steve have got all the Six Million Dollar Man stuff. We've got the dolls, we've got the game, and we've even got the coloring books. [*Pause.*] Steve always makes the Six Million Dollar Man's hair yellow.
It's not yellow.
It's brown.
I know.
'Cause I saw it on TV.

[*Enter* STEVE *and* MRS. GARVEY.]

STEVE: Uh-uuh . . . it's blond.

BOBBY: Nu-uuh.

STEVE: Oh yeah? Wanna bet? Go ask my Mom.

BOBBY: I asked Mrs. Garvey.

STEVE: No, Bobby, that's not right.
It's not brown.
It's dirty blond.

BOBBY: [*Simultaneously with "blond".*] Blond.
Dirty blond.
Whenever we play Six Million Dollar Man, Steve always gets to be Steve Austin . . . 'cause his hair is blond . . .

STEVE: Just like Steve Austin.

BOBBY: I always hafta be Oscar Goldman or Dr. Rudy Wells.
When I do my Six Million Dollar Man coloring book at my house with my crayons, my Six Million Dollar Man's gonna have black hair. Hey, guess what?

MR. BEAR: What?

BOBBY: [*Hitting* MR. BEAR.] That's what.

MR. BEAR: Ho-ho-ho-ho-ho-ho . . .

BOBBY: That's funny. Isn't it? That's a barrel of monkeys. I love you, Mr. Bear. You're better than Six Million Dollar Man. You're even better than Chewie the Wookiee. We had our Halloween parade at school today. Guess who I was?

MR. BEAR: Uh, Superman?

BOBBY: No, dummy, that was last year.

MR. BEAR: Not Superman? You were a great Superman. Hmmm...let me see. Oh, I know. You were...Duh-nuh-nuh-nuh-nuh-nuh-nuh...

BOBBY: [*Mimicking Michael Keaton.*] "I'm Batman." [*Shifting.*] Nope. Wrong again. Give up? [*Imitates the ominous wheezing of Darth Vader.*] I was Darth Vader. So was Scott Whitehead and Rick Wilson...and three other kids in the class. But my costume was better because my helmet was for real. Kim Lewis was Snow White. She said my costume was cool.
Scott Fernlund was a Chinaman.
His Mom painted his skin yellow...and he had one of those mustaches that hang off your chin. And he had one of those hats...you know, those hats...um, they're pointy on top...like the ones they were wearing at McDonald's when they had the Oriental Chicken McNuggets...
Scott won first prize, and he's getting his picture in the paper.
He kept coming up to me and bowing...saying Ah-so, Ah-so.
His costume wasn't that great.
My helmet was for real.

VOICE OF MOMMY: Bobby, what you doing? Stop tawking. Go to sreep.

◇◇◇

BOBBY: [*Perfunctorily.*] And Forgive Us Our Debts,
As We Forgive Our Debtors,
Lead us Not Into Temptation,
But Deliver Us From Evil,
For Thine Is the Kingdom, The Power, and The Glory Forever.
In Jesus' Name I Pray,
Amen. P.S.—
Dear God, Mr. Martin says that if we ask You for something with all our hearts, and all our might, and all our soul, You will give it to us. So God, three things...
First, please keep me and Mommy and Daddy and Cathy and Tiger and Mr. Bear and all the cousins and all the aunts and all the uncles and the two Grandmoms and the two Grandfathers and all my friends and all the good people in the world safe tonight and every night forever and ever...for infinity...for google...
Also, God, please make sure, um, Kim Lewis and I get married someday.
Also God...Please, please, please make me white. Amen.

✧✧✧

[The stage at Bob's Comedy Luau Hut. MR. SHOWBIZ enters, sits at one of the tables. A taped recording of his voice plays . . .]

MR. SHOWBIZ: Hey, hey, this is Bob coming at you from Bob's Hut of Comedy, the Comedy Luau Hut . . . I just wanna remind you folks . . . Tomorrow night is Salute the Troops Night . . . Anybody who gets up and tells an Iraqi joke wins a *free Operation Desert Storm T-Shirt* . . . and of course, all persons with military ID get in for free . . . *[Calling off-stage.]* Alright kid . . . I'm ready.

[ROB enters onstage, uncertain of himself, sees the microphone, adjusts it.]

ROB: Hey, how are ya? How are ya? Ah, it's great to be back. Actually, I've never been here before, but ah, it's great to be back . . .

Been a long time since I was last on stage, long time . . . Last time was third grade. It was the school pageant. The theme was Our Friend the Calendar, and all the kids were dressed up as different holidays. You know, the girl playing Valentine's Day wore this giant red cardboard heart and Thanksgiving wore a turkey outfit . . . and the guy playing Martin Luther King's birthday was dressed up as Bono.

New Year's was played by these twins — one of 'em was dressed as a giant martini and the other was dressed as a pool of vomit.

I played Easter, and I had fun, I did, but it was kinda hard trying to move around tied to that giant cross. *[He imitates a hopping third-grader tied to a giant cross.]* And you know, I'm all for realism, but the nails, I think, were just a little too much.

So I'm watching TV again the other night . . . real late and I'm sitting there and this Hair Club for Men thing comes on . . . "Not only am I the President . . . I'm also a client . . . " I'm watching this Hair Club for Men thing and it occurs to me . . . I see the image of Sy Sperling more often than I see my *father* . . . I mean, I haven't seen my father, I have not looked *on his face* in above five months . . . but I see this guy Sperling three, four, five times a day . . . it's sick . . . and the weird thing is .. *my hair is starting to fall out* . . . *[In a deadpan monotone, if not already.]* So anyway, I'm going blind . . . I have no sense of smell . . . my gums are rotting away . . . so, uh, the future's not looking too good . . . *[Cough, cough.]* I'm also kinda sick . . . the other day I woke up with a hangover and took a handful of aspirin tablets . . . but they weren't aspirin tablets . . . They were my roommate's girlfriend's birth control pills . . . So, uh, I've been feeling really weird . . .

And, uh, she's pregnant . . .

And, uh, she's suing me . . .

And her lawyer's my Dad . . .

And I asked my Dad why he's on her side and he said...
"Cause you're an asshole, Rob."
And speaking of litigation, my ex-wife calls me up the other day...

MR. SHOWBIZ: Hold it, hold it. Johnny, Johnny. What'd I tell you, huh? What is this? Whattaya call this? Huh? I tol' you. You wanna *work* in this business, you wanna get some*wheres*, make a *name* for yourself... You're gonna have to go with new material, baby. *This*. This is not funny, Johnny. I have seen funny, and this is not it. What-what-what is this shit? Huh? I'm gonna tell you something, Johnny —

ROB: Rob...

MR. SHOWBIZ: [*Ignoring him.*] You listen good. I like you. Y'know? You're a good kid. Y'know what I'm saying?
But you look at the greats. Y'know what I'm talking about? I'm talking Pryor. I'm talking Murphy...
Now, those guys. They got an identity. Y'know what I'm saying? They said "Hey, I'm Black So What Fuck You." Y'know what I'm saying? Listen to me, Johnny —

ROB: Rob.

MR. SHOWBIZ: [*Ignoring him.*] You're a lucky boy. Y'know why? Ask me why.

ROB: Why?

MR. SHOWBIZ: [*Immediately on "why."*] Now that I've taken you under my tutelage, I'm gonna give you some advice. You go back, go back rework this material. Give it an Oriental slant... Orien —
OK, you work on this, you come back, you see me. OK? We'll talk. Oh, and another thing, and don't get me wrong, 'cause I tell this to all the kids I teach, if you're gonna do a foreign accent on stage, decide whether you're going to be Italian or Jewish.

[*The spotlight begins to fade on* ROB.]

ROB: Uh, wait. Uh, sir? I have an ethnic joke.

MR. SHOWBIZ: You have an *ethnic* joke.

ROB: Uh, yes, sir.

MR. SHOWBIZ: Will you listen to this? Johnny has an "ethnic" joke. Johnny. Listen. One thing the world does not need is another Don Rickles. I don't want "*ethnic*." I want Oriental, baby.

ROB: No, sir, it's specifically an Asian joke...

MR. SHOWBIZ: Whazzat mean, Oriental?

ROB: Uh, yeah, sort of...

MR. SHOWBIZ: Alright, let's hear it.

ROB: [*Stumbling.*] Well, I come from a tough neighborhood, see? Uh, the San Francisco Bay Area...yeah, real tough neighborhood. In fact, it was so tough the guys down at the schoolyard would play hoops and the thing was...the nets were always getting stolen, so they had these metal nets instead, and every time someone would, uh, you know, swish the ball in, it would make this noise...(chink!). And, uh, this became part of the local playground jargon...uh, you know, they would refer to basketball as chink. And I knew it was a real tough neighborhood when I overheard some guys talking, and this one guy (big guy) says to the other: "what do you say we shoot some chink after school?" [*Long silence; maybe the sound of chirping crickets.*] No? OK, well, uh, I'll go home and work on it.
That's not — that's not actually my joke. I, uh, I stole it from some guy I saw on Star Search.

✧✧✧

[ROB *returns with a bag.*]

ROB: A brief history of the Asian American immigrant.
First, we were in the hot sun. [*He opens the bag, puts on a paper lamp-shade and puts in paper buckteeth.*] We toil and sweat in the rice paddies under the hot sun.
Then we went to America. [*He takes out an American flag, waves it.*] Oooohhh...Oooohhh...I predge arregiance to frag...United States Amelika.
And to repubric which it stand — one nation undel God.
Fol Justice and riberty for all.
Then we toil and sweat on the railroads...[*He puts on a metal lamp-shade.*]...under the hot sun.

MR. SHOWBIZ: OK, OK. Now we're getting somewhere.

ROB: You liked it?

MR. SHOWBIZ: No. No, I did not like it. But you're starting to listen to me. And that I like.
But this, this coolie stuff...I don't know. It's got the right tone, tone-wise it's very good...but, uh, you know, the average Joe, the average guy in the seats, he doesn't know that shit, he can't connect with that, know what I'm saying? Listen, listen, you work on this, OK? You work on this. Alright? You go home, you work on it...Listen, I got an idea...can you do a Chinese Waiter?

ROB: Chinese waiter?

MR. SHOWBIZ: Yeah, yeah, Chinese Waiter.

ROB: Are you serious?

MR. SHOWBIZ: Yeah, you know, like, uh ... "That's one flied lice, one egg drop soup-uh."

ROB: Chinese Waiter.
Uh, OK, I'll — I'll work on it.

MR. SHOWBIZ: [*Starts to leave.*] OK, you work on it. You work on it, you talk to me. OK?

ROB: Yessir.

MR. SHOWBIZ: Alright good.

ROB: Chinese Waiter ... [*Calling after him.*] Yeah, I'll — I'll work on it.

MR. SHOWBIZ: You do that.

ROB: I'll work on it.

[MR. SHOWBIZ *exits.*]

❖❖❖

ROB: [*To us.*] I *am* a waiter. I wait on tables. In a restaurant. Downtown. I am a waiter. In a Chinese restaurant. But I am *not* Chinese.

❖❖❖

[*The Chinese restaurant.* DON, *a small elderly Asian gentleman, is sweeping the floor.* ROB *enters.*]

ROB: Morning, Don.

DON: Morning, Bop. How you today?

ROB: Tired. Very tired.

DON: You wan' coppee?

ROB: Naw, I don't want any coffee. Thanks though. Does Edwin know I'm late?

DON: Yes, he know you rate. Edwin alway know you rate.

ROB: Was he mad?

DON: I don' know. He say nossing to me.

[*Enter* DENISE.]

ROB: Hey Denise. Listen, thanks for doing my soy sauces.

DENISE: Don't worry 'bout it.

ROB: You do the waters too?

DENISE: Yep.

DON: Going be busy day today.

[DENISE *exits*.]

DON: [*Cont'd.*] Today Welpare day. Bery busy.

ROB: Aw no . . . it's today? You're sure it's today?

DON: Today pipteenth-uh. Yeah, today Welpare day.

ROB: Oh shit. You sure it's today? Oh yeah, it's gotta be today. Look at 'em, swarming out there. Straight from the bank.

[*The customers have accumulated at the door.*]

DENISE: [*To the customers.*] Excuse me. We're closed. We'll be opening shortly. [*Pause.*] Well, it's not eleven o'clock yet.

ROB: [*To customers.*] Well, you see, the cooks have to make extensive preparations before they're able to provide you with the fine cuisine we all know and love.

DENISE: Yes, yes, eleven o'clock.

ROB: [*To us.*] The first and fifteenth of every month is known at the restaurant as Welfare Day. Apparently, people receive their biweekly welfare checks and for some reason, the first thing they wanna spend it on is greasy Chinese food . . .
Oh fuck, why delay the inevitable? Don, Don, you gonna open? OK, let's go.

[DON *slowly files through his enormous keyring. Finally, he unlocks the front door. A stream of people come in.* DON *seats them at various tables and gives them lunch menus while* ROB *speaks to the audience. When* ROB *speaks, the customers "freeze."*]

ROB: [*To us.*] The cooks here have stubbly facial hair, wear dirty white T-shirts, speak little English and smoke Winstons while tending to the spitting, hissing wok-mass of beef shards and broccoli cuts . . . later to become "Beef and Broccoli Combo with Spring Roll." The spring roll costs an extra 79 cents. The cigarette ash does not.

[*A customer gags on his food.*]

ROB: [*Cont'd.*] The head cook Al is a nice man. Or at least, he is nice to me. On his breaks, he sits on a fifty pound barrel of monosodium glutamate, smokes like a fiend, and complains to me about his general lack of respect in the kitchen—a kitchen which would, after all, be nowhere today without his culinary and organizational skills.

During their breaks, the cooks sit around smoking, yakking rapidly in this only half-intelligible hybrid of English and Chinese.

I thought of the Boneless Chicken Combo.

You see, with Boneless Chicken and gravy, you get fried rice and egg roll.

TABLE 1 MAN: Alright, give me that. And she'll have—

TABLE 1 WOMAN: I'll have the—have you got the whattaya-call-it? Those Chinese Chicken Wings.

ROB: Well, there's nothing particularly Chinese about them, but...

[TABLE 1 WOMAN *is not laughing.*]

ROB: [*Cont'd.*] And, would you like the Combo or a regular order?

TABLE 1 WOMAN: Combo.

ROB: Would you like bread with your order?

TABLE 1 MAN: How much is the bread?

ROB: Well, uh, it's free with the meal.

TABLE 1 MAN: Shit, in that case, bring it on.

ROB: Right, right.
I'll be back with your order as soon as I can. Just let me know if you need anything. [ROB *moves to Table 2.*] Hi, how are you?
Are you ready to order?

TABLE 2 MAN: OK, I think I'll just start off with a Mai Tai. [*To his companion.*] You want anything, schnookums?

TABLE 2 WOMAN: Just a diet coke.

ROB: Would you like anything to eat?

TABLE 2 WOMAN: Uh, could you give us a little more time please?

ROB: OK, I'll be back in a bit. [*To Table 6.*] Everything OK here?

TABLE 6 GIRL A: Duck sauce.

TABLE 6 GIRL B: Yeah, duck sauce.

ROB: Right.

TABLE 2 MAN: Hey, could you get me one of those little Chinese umbrellas? You know, for your drink, those little Chinese umbrellas—are they Japanese?

ROB: Ordering one Kung Pao Gai Ding combo, one shrimp fried rice, shrimp fried rice, two won ton bowls, not cups, bowls.

TABLE 6 GIRL A: What're you talking about?
Duck sauce has nothing to do with ducks.
Nowhere is waterfowl involved here.
Duck sauce is duck sauce.
Ask the waiter.

TABLE 6 GIRL B: Then why do they call it duck sauce?

TABLE 6 GIRL A: What kind of question is that?
Duck-duck-duck sauce. I don't know why they call it that.
Who knows why we call it that?
Why do we call pepper "pepper?" Why do we call salt "salt?"

TABLE 6 GIRL B: So you know ... what's what.

TABLE 6 GIRL A: Hey, hey, what's the matter with you?
It's a seasoning.
We're talking seasonings here.

ROB: Bowls.
I didn't say cups. I said bowls.

TABLE 2 WOMAN: Yes, could I get some chopsticks and a gin and tonic please?

ROB: Bowls, yes, bowls.
Won-ton. Right.

TABLE 1 WOMAN: Could we get our bread before the meal?

ROB: Also ordering: two chicken wing combos, three boneless chicken combos, one sweet and sour pork dinner.

TABLE 1 MAN: Hey, can I get an eggroll with that too?

ROB: Dinner. No combo.
Dinner.
No combo.
No.

TABLE 5 GUY B: Oh yeah?
You know what they say ...

TABLE 5 GUY A: No, what do they say and shit?

TABLE 5 GUY B: "The meek shall inherit the earth ... "

ROB: That's a double fried rice.

TABLE 5 GUY A: Meek?

Who the hell wants to be meek and shit?

ROB: Is this my order?
I ordered pork.

TABLE 5 GUY A: You know what's really weird, man?
Who invented food and shit?
I mean, that's weird.

ROB: That's not pork.
Believe me, "I've seen pork, and this is not it."

TABLE 5 GUY B: I don't know who invented food.
But it was probably the same guy who invented shit.

ROB: OK, OK, I know. I know.
Thank you. Thank you. [*To us.*] The owner does not speak English
very well.
His English is broken.
It needs to be fixed.

TABLE 5 GUY B: Hey waiter.
Waiter.

ROB: Yeah?

TABLE 5 GUY B: Where are you, uh, where are you *from*?

ROB: Uh, where am I from? New Jersey.

TABLE 5 GUY B: No, no, no, what I mean is . . . where are you, you know,
"from" from?

ROB: New Jersey.

TABLE 5 GUY B: No, no, what I'm asking you is where are you from . . . ?

ROB: Uh, which part don't you understand?
New.
Jersey. [*To us.*] The owner will yell at you if he misunderstands your
order.
If he misunderstands your order, it means the food has to be thrown
away.
All the food ends up in one of two places:

TABLE 5 GUY A: In someone's stomach or in the trash.
Yeah, yeah, yeah . . . [*To his companion.*] This guy sucks. His jokes suck,
and his service . . . Jesus, I've waited longer to die.

ROB: During my time here, I only learned one word of Chinese —
Malacha. [*To* TABLE 5 GUYS.] Malacha. [*To us.*] It means "Fuck You."

The owner is impossible to understand. Not just because he doesn't speak much English, but also because he stutters:
A Chinese stutterer. You can imagine ... it's like Richard Lewis or Woody Allen trying to speak in sign language. [ROB *imitates this*.] The owner was not given the gift of verbal expression, so he chooses to express himself physically ... with the waitresses.
He would flirt with them ... making lewd suggestions and gestures that would later go into the Kung Pao Gai Ding (Dinner $8.95, Combo $5.95).
And then ... if he thought he could get away with it, he would touch them, put his hands on them.
I tried to get the women to take legal action against the owner.
Socially conscious Ivy League semi-liberal educating the oppressed to take action against the oppressor? I would like to think so.
No, more like semi-conscious Ivy League socially-liberal educating the oppressed to enact my own personal revenge against the owner.
I was getting paid $2.65/hour + tips.
With tips, I could make ... oh, eight, nine, ten dollars an hour.
Without tips, I could make ... oh, $2.65.
I was not in college.
I was in the school of life, as Dad would say.
After I was stoned at graduation of high school, Dad said to me ...
Dad said to me ... "Someday, someday you're going to learn how life really is, how it really works."
This was a threat.

✧✧✧

[*Back at the restaurant — though we've never left.* DENISE *is attending to her duties.* ROB *is holding a check.*]

DENISE: Rob. Table 2.

ROB: Denise.
You see this? You see this?
Look at this. Hundred dollars in tips.
What is this?

DENISE: [*Looking at his check.*] Hundred dollars in tips.

ROB: [*Overlapping.*] Bullshit.
I wish I could make *fifty* in tips.
Fucking fifty per week, I'd be writhing in ecstasy for that kind of money. That's bullshit, man. He can't fucking estimate. I'm telling you, I know I don't make 8%. Fuck this. This is bullshit. I work my ass off ...

DENISE: [*Overlapping.*] I'm working my ass off...

ROB: We work our asses off, and this is what we get?
He's taxing us for money we're not making. You can not fucking estimate.
Look Denise, it's very simple.
If for every three tables you have, two tables stiff (and as we know, this
is not a conservative figure. Right?). If two tables stiff, and one table
gives you 15%. You're dealing with 5%. Fucking 5%. This is not to
mention hauling your ass for three tables and the sheer disappoint-
ment — the fucking *emotional pain* — of cleaning two tables and not
finding anything there.

DENISE: [*Baby-talk.*] Aww, poor baby.

ROB: Are you listening to me on this?
I mean, I'm not alone in this, am I? [*Rapidly, animated.*] Look, it's very
simple. You get a table with three people.
Average lunch order per person is what? You got entree, drink —
that's what? Ten.

DENISE: [*Simultaneous with "ten."*] Eight.

ROB: Ten.

DENISE: Nine.

ROB: *Drinks.*
Ten bucks.
OK. Say you have three tables of three, average order, and (this is a
conservative estimate) — you get ninety bucks in merchandise. Now,
if one table tips you even 15% (and this, as we know, is a *generous* estimate) — and the others stiff you. You've got $4.50 in tips total for
ninety bucks of merchandise. You're dealing with what? Five percent.

DENISE: Rob, you're in the country, speak the language.

ROB: Denise, what I'm saying here is *we are being exploited.*

[*A pause.* DENISE *looks at* ROB, *removes his glasses, fiddles with his collar.*]

ROB: [*Cont'd.*] What? What are you — ?

DENISE: Now. Can you speak Chinese?

ROB: What-what-what does that have to do with anything?
Why do you think — ? What does that — ?
No, I can't speak Chinese.
I'm not — I'm not Chinese.

DENISE: Well, what are you then?

ROB: What am I?
Uhhh...

✧✧✧

[*Nightclub stage. The Restaurant customers are now an audience at a nightclub.* ROB *stands onstage with a microphone.*]

ROB: Once...I was walking down the street.
No, not "once." I walk down the street many times (ha ha ha), but this particular time, I was walking. It was dark.
Down the street. Very dark.
This car pulls up behind me. *Crawls* behind me.
Like it was *stalking* me.
No, it wasn't that dramatic. But it was a little unsettling — this car following me.
So I stop. I turn. I look.
A window starts to roll down.
I look for a gun. Anticipate a threat.
My cat-like reflexes ready to spring at the first sign of danger.
I hear a voice.
It is friendly.
"John Kim."
Again.
"John Kim."
My name
is *not*
John Kim.
There were two people in this car — a man and a woman, a boy and a girl, a boy and a woman, a guy — they were college students.
And they were calling out "John Kim."
And I just shook my head... "No, no."
And kept walking, but they must have thought it was some kind of a game, because they kept following me...
"John Kim."
"John Kim." (OR "John-a-rooney," "the Johnster," et al.)
"John Kim."
And finally, I thought to myself, you've got the wrong guy and went up to the window and said...
"Right race, wrong face."
Actually, I didn't say that.
But I thought of it like three minutes later.
And uh, what happened?

Oh, the woman who was in the front seat was really embarrassed. She was like "Oh, God. Oh, God." and like the guy...
I was like, "I totally understand."
It was *dark*.
And it's a *fact*, a lot of Asian males have black hair and wear glasses.
And the ones that don't are probably wearing contacts.
Yes, this is a fact; it's been scientifically proven. There have been studies—which I've read, and I can show you.
In fact, I happen to have the most recent study right here. [*Pulls out a thick, official-looking folder.*] This is the Holman-Weller Report done in 1987, and it concludes that: [*Reading.*] "91% of Asian Males have black hair and require the use of corrective lenses."
Why don't I pass this around? [*Hands the folder to an audience member.*] Yes, it's true, they tend to look alike. Especially in the dark. And their names: John Kim, Vincent Chin, Ho Chi Minh. I mean, who can tell the difference?
In fact, I was in downtown Seoul a couple of years ago, and I was on this balcony not too far from the street, and I was just sitting there looking at all the people walking by, walking by, and you know, if I were stoned or something and somebody said "Invasion of the Body Snatchers," I probably would've freaked out.
And it's not just because of the black hair or the—what's the euphemism?—almond-shaped eyes...or even the glasses, but it's also the haircuts.
The haircuts tend to be the same.
Apparently, there's the one barber who does everybody's hair.
Everybody knows him.
His name is John Kim.
And I'll tell you something, during my adolescence when I would, uh, choke the chicken...

PERSON IN AUDIENCE (ACTUALLY ROB'S MOTHER): I'm sorry. I didn't catch that.

ROB: What's that?

PERSON IN AUDIENCE (MOMMY): I couldn't hear you. Could you repeat that last line?

ROB: Uh, OK.
During my adolescence, when I would jerk the gherkin...

MOMMY (IN AUDIENCE): I'm sorry. You're going to have to speak more clearly.

ROB: Oh man...

Uh, OK. I'm sorry.

During my adolescence, when I would...During my adolescence, when I would ma—ma—masturbate. Not that I don't, *you know*... now.

I mean, you know what they used to *say*...if you keep on doing it, you're gonna...go blind. [ROB *wiggles his glasses at a male member of the ensemble/audience who is also wearing glasses.*]

So anyway, there seemed to be this direct scientific correlation between the frequency of my...you know, afterschool job and the severity of my near-sightedness.

Why am I talking about this?

Oh, yes, well, there are ethnic and/or racial stereotypes of a sexual nature, obviously...

Uh, for example, has anyone heard the Rolling Stones song "Some Girls?" Well, part of it goes:

"White girls, they're pretty funny
Sometimes they drive me mad
Black girls just wanna get fucked all night
I just don't have that much jam
Chinese girls are so gentle
They're really such a tease
You never know quite what they're cookin'
Inside those silky sleeves."

And that's a shame because I...I used to like the Rolling Stones a lot ...Uh, what I'm trying to say here is there are sexual stereotypes of Asian males having to do with, uh, body and facial hair and — [*Clears throat.*] — penis size...specifically, the lack thereof.

Now, I don't know how this particular stereotype got started, but I know it exists from smart remarks made in high school insinuating a certain...lack of manhood...not through direct observation of course... [*Lounge lizard-like.*] Thank you.

Uh, this has been a great night for me. I mean, here I am...in a roomful of strangers, talking about masturbation and penis length. *Wow.*

I've got to get a real job.

❖❖❖

[THERAPIST *and* ROB. THERAPIST *has a notebook.*]

THERAPIST: So tell me your earliest childhood memory.

ROB: My earliest childhood memory.

THERAPIST: Yes.

ROB: You're serious.

You're really asking me this?

OK, OK, fine. Uh, let's see . . .

OK, when I was little, I would crawl into our dryer and try to shut the door, but uh, I could never get it closed because you know, there are no handles in there . . .

THERAPIST: And where was your mother during all this?

ROB: My mother? [*Laughs.*] What are you, kidding me? My mother? What-what is this?

Oh, right—mother, the dryer, the womb, blah, blah, blah.

Uh, no. That's not really my earliest childhood memory.

Alright, fine. Uh, my earliest childhood memory . . .

[*The following is acted out by* BOBBY, OLD WHITE GUY, *and his two grandchildren*—LITTLE WHITE BOY *and* LITTLE WHITE GIRL.]

ROB: [*Cont'd.*] We were on a family trip.

We were coming back from the beach, and we had to stop someplace to eat, and we came upon this great cheesy little place. It was a, uh, combination gas station, diner, gift shop. Uh, and we went in to eat. And while our food was getting ready, my parents let me look around the gift shop. There were no walls, you know, between the diner and the gift shop. And uh . . .

ROB/BOBBY: I was in there checking out the plastic dinosaurs and the $1.99 sculptures paying homage to the American Indian.

And all of a sudden . . .

OLD WHITE GUY: Kaneecheewa.

ROB: And you know, this kind of scared me, this big old white guy comes up to you and says . . .

OLD WHITE GUY: Kaneecheewa.

ROB: So I put the dinosaur back and went to check out something in the other aisle . . . but sure enough, there he was again.

OLD WHITE GUY: Kaneecheewa.

Kaneecheewa.

Do you know what that means?

[BOBBY *shakes his head.*]

OLD WHITE GUY: [*Cont'd.*] You don't know what that means?

That's Japanese for hello.

Kaneecheewa.

You know, I used to be in the service, and I went to Japan.

That's how I learned to say
Kaneecheewa.
Paulie, Maria, come over here.
Say hello to the little Japanese boy.
Say "Kaneecheewa."

LITTLE WHITE BOY AND LITTLE WHITE GIRL: Kaneecheewa.

❖❖❖

[*The Chinese restaurant.* ROB *and* DENISE *exactly as we left them.*]

DENISE: So do you speak any Chinese?

ROB: No, I can't speak Chinese.
I mean, I don't speak Chinese.
I'm not Chinese.

DENISE: Well, what are you then?

ROB: What am I? [*Pause.*] Does it matter?

DENISE: I was just wondering.

ROB: OK.

DENISE: Uh-oh, here comes Mrs. Dugan.

ROB: That's alright. I'll get it.
I already owe you one.

MRS. DUGAN: Good morning, Denise-ileh.

DENISE: You know, sometimes people come in here, they wanna talk to you . . . And it's not like they talk about the menu or today's special. They wanna talk about their lives.

ROB: That's alright. Don't worry about it. [*To* MRS. DUGAN.] Hi, how are you today? Are you ready to order?

MRS. DUGAN: I am fine. Thank you.
That is a beautiful shirt you're wearing there. Just beautiful. You know, my daughter-in-law bought it for my son and I didn't think (She's not Jewish) and the goyim, they don't have such good taste but she bought him that shirt and it is just beautiful. I love it, and it looks beautiful on you.

ROB: Uh, why don't I give you a few more minutes?

DENISE: I told you.
If you let them, they'll talk to you and talk to you and keep talking to you like they have no one else to talk to.

ROB: I bussed tables at this expensive French restaurant once.

I don't know what's worse — I mean which would you rather have? A Fifty-year-old Businessman talking about golf and wine and treating you like the nameless, faceless economic pawn that you are...or a Not-So-Wealthy Seventy-year-old Woman with Woolworth shopping bag and dog-eared romance novel...

DENISE: My God, the businessman. No doubt about it. 'Cause you see, with the businessman, you can make jokes in the kitchen behind his back...I mean, what the hell? He's rich and he thinks the tan he got like marlin-fishing in the Florida Keys makes him look really good. Mrs. Dugan has no one else to talk to.

I mean, don't get me wrong. It's good to establish a rapport with the customers. Talk about the weather, talk about...talk about the earthquake in California, talk about their kids, tell jokes, remember their names and how they like their chop suey...

The usual: Extra noodles on the side, Robileh.

ROB: The usual, Mrs. Dugan? Extra noodles on the side...

MRS. DUGAN: [*Simultaneously.*] Extra noodles on the side, Robileh. You know what else? Bring me a fork...'cause I can not eat with that sticks. My husband Morris (rest his soul) told me that: Always ask for a fork in a Chinese restaurant.

DENISE: If you do this well, you'll find your tips will grow larger and larger.

ROB: [*To us.*] Sometimes I think I am an emotional whore.

This is not to say I am a whore who gets emotional.

I am a whore who deals in emotions.

There was this one guy who would come in every Sunday night, and he was just the sweetest, saddest guy. He was kind of oafish, and I don't mean that in a bad way, (well, how can that be positive?) but this guy was just the sweetest, saddest guy...he reminded me of Willard Scott with a speech impediment but with none of the money. This is not to say Willard Scott is a sweet man, or that a lot of money will make a person happy obviously, but anyway...

When it wasn't busy, I would talk to this guy.

He had just been transferred back to Providence, and he wanted to know if Haven Brothers was still around 'cause he always used to eat there. He had this limp, because he used to referee in the NHL, twenty-twenty-five years ago, but he hurt his leg, and he couldn't skate and when he couldn't skate, he couldn't ref anymore.

And I just remember, this one night we were closing, and I let him out and he said goodbye, and I said goodbye, and he said goodbye, and he was walking down the street, and I was just standing there watching him through the window. It was snowing, and he was walking, limping down the street, and he kind of weaved to the left, then he weaved to the right, and he was just wobbling down the middle of the street, and that's when I realized he didn't really have any place else to go.

But tell me something, would I have felt that badly for him, would I have thought about him, would he have broken a part of my heart, if I hadn't just picked up the five dollar rip he left on his table for his ten dollar meal?

I mean, if he weren't such a great tipper?

I don't know.

MRS. DUGAN: Robileh, which way to the bathroom? I got some schmutzig on my hands I got to wash off.

[ROB *tries to assist her.*]

MRS. DUGAN: [*Cont'd.*] No, I'm fine. Thank you.

[*She exits.*]

ROB: And that's what I hate about waiting on tables.

[ROB *proceeds to clean up in the restaurant. He does not see . . .*]

◇◇◇

[FATHER *sits at a side table, drinking whiskey.* FATHER'*s speech should be fully converted to dialect.*]

FATHER: Hey, Rober, come here. Come here.
Daddy wanna talk you.

ROB: Dad?
Is that you?
What-what're you doing here?

FATHER: Whass-a-mattah, Rober?
I can not come talk my own son?

ROB: [*Embarrassed.*] Dad, I'm . . . I'm uh . . . in the middle of a play here.

FATHER: You in middre what?

ROB: A, uh, play.

FATHER: Come on, Rober.
Be serious.
You risten you Daddy.
I wanna talk you.
Come sit you Daddy.
We talk.

I tell you something Rober, I tell you. When Daddy first come America . . . twenty-two year ago, I so poor . . . so poor I quit smoking I so poor. I know, I know, "you know, you know."
Come on, Rober, you risten you Daddy.
Be selious. I wan' talk you.
I work hard, work two jobs, so you and Mommy come here. I work hard you go school. When I you age, after war, I have nothing eat. We hab no food. I eat weeds I so hungry. You think that funny? That not funny. You don't know what hungry is.
OK.
I take examination . . . school examination. I make good grade, I can go good school, number one school. You grandfather, I lob him, but he bery poor. He school teacher. Yeah, school teacher. He can no afford put me school.
So I sell pencil — *pencil*, shoerace, try make money. I even take examination for rich boy. I make good grade, he gib me money.
I teach karate American soldier, American soldier love learn Karate. American soldier — they tell me about America. They help you Daddy come here.
So I work hard, work two job, so you and Mommy come here. You know, when you little baby, I no see you. My son.
I so poor, I quit smoking, I so poor.
Your Uncle Mike, he help me. I become cop. I work hard, save money, and so you come.
When you and mom come, I so happy. So happy. You know, when I first see you, you cry. You don't know I you Daddy. And when I try hug Mom, you fight me. Yeah, fight me.
But I hurt. I hurt, you don't know me.
Of course, you don't know me. Not your fault. I just strange *ajeshi*. You never see me.
You know, Rober, I know you don't want be doctor, businessman, OK. I rearn. You do what you want. But you know my dream, dream I hab Rober? I want you become first PHD in family. First PHD. That's my dream.

✧✧✧

ROB: [*To us.*] When I was less than now, my Dad had a big bicep.
He could beat up anybody else's Dad — even Scott Sanders' Dad who played for the Giants.
For some reason, this made me proud.
Now, of course, I think this is just silly.

Now, of course, I know he can't beat up Scott Sanders' Dad who played for the Giants.

When I was less than now, when my Dad came home, I would make him kiss my mother because my best friend Steve's parents would always kiss when Mr. Garvey came home.

Mommy and Daddy would look at each other funny, and then they would kiss.

My mother grew up on a farm in Korea.

She was a Korean Farm Girl.

She was not a French City Man.

She was a Korean Farm Girl.

My mother owns a store.

A store in an urban neighborhood.

My mother owns a store not unlike the store owned by the Koreans in the movie *Do The Right Thing*.

When my sister saw the battery scene...

[*Enter* TABLE 1 MAN *as* RADIO RAHEEM, *carrying a boom box blaring Public Enemy's "Burn Hollywood Burn." The boom box dies.*]

TABLE 1 MAN/RADIO RAHEEM: Give me twenty "D" batteries.
"D," not "C," "D," you stupid motherfucker. Why don't you learn how to speak the goddamn language?

ROB: When my sister saw the battery scene, she laughed so hard she had to put her face on her blond boyfriend's shoulder.
"That's just like Mom," she said. "That's just like Mom."
When my mother was a little girl, she dreamt about who she was going to marry.
She did *not* dream about what she was going to be when she grew up.
She did *not* dream of selling unlicensed Batman T-shirts and inch-think plastic gold ropes.
My mother responds to her customers' requests for special merchandise.
She does not respond to customers' requests to fix her broken English.
It was right around Christmas.
I was standing at the door.
The door of the store.
I was looking for people who had come in to do some last-minute Christmas shoplifting.

[*Enter* TEENS WITH TOO MUCH TIME TO KILL, *both played by white actors.*]

TEEN WITH TOO MUCH TIME TO KILL #2: Hey, look who it is, Moo Goo Gai Man.

ROB: Teen With Too Much Time To Kill #1 left Teen With Too Much Time To Kill #2 by me, after making a request to my mother to fix her broken English.

TEEN WITH TOO MUCH TIME TO KILL #1: Ah-so, Charlie Wong.

ROB: Now, I don't know Charlie Wong, but I'm sure he's a very nice man... But this case of mistaken identity combined with their request for my mother to fix her broken English combined with their relatively small size made me (for some reason) think of my SAT Verbal score... But instead of letting them know exactly what that happened to be, I just... [*To* TEEN WITH TOO MUCH TIME TO KILL #1.] Fuck You.
My mother soothed, not my temper, but that of Teen With Too Much Time To Kill #1, who despite his smaller size, was not about to let this challenge to his honor go unanswered.
But I went back to school and therefore missed the possible appearance of Older, Much Larger Teen With Too Much Time To Kill, brother of Teen With Too Much Time To Kill #1.

[*Both* TEENS WITH TOO MUCH TIME TO KILL *exit.*]

ROB: [*Cont'd.*] And, uh, not that this makes any difference, but both Teens With Too Much Time To Kill were Black Teens With Too Much Time To Kill.

◇◇◇

[*The Chinese restaurant.* ROB *and* DENISE.]

DENISE: Now, I don't wanna get you alarmed or anything, but sometimes... Sometimes we get some customers in here who, you know, are not exactly of the desirable sort.
Well, sometimes they're drunk.
Sometimes they're violent.
Sometimes they're trying to show off for their girlfriends...
And sometimes (hey, what do you know) they're drunk, violent, and trying to show off for their girlfriends.
So... if you get some customers who are making trouble, and they look like they're gonna start breaking shit, go get Al.
Oh, and another thing... if you see a roach, do not let the customers catch on to the fact you've seen it...
And whatever you do, do not yell "OMIGAWD, A ROACH!"

ROB: I won't do it again.

DENISE: And this is just a personal thing...
I will not clean vomit.
I will not clean drool. OK?

ROB: OK.

DENISE: Oh, a customer gets on your nerves, and you'll see, this happens all the time, customer gets on your nerves...don't yell at them. Count to 10 slowly and breathe deeply. This is good for stress. And it clears the pores.
And if that doesn't work.
Spit in their food.

ROB: Hey, what about tips?

DENISE: Most old people tip OK.
Cops tip pretty well.
And Black people don't tip.

ROB: What?

DENISE: Black people don't tip.

ROB: [*To us.*] Some faults of mine:
1) I don't always cap the toothpaste tube.
2) I smoke too much.
3) I often put things off until the last minute.
4) I don't always stand up for what I believe in when someone makes a racist remark.

DENISE: No, seriously, I'm telling you...they don't tip.

ROB: So what you're saying is...
Some customers...who happen to be black...never tip you.

DENISE: No, what I'm saying is...they don't tip.

ROB: Well...

DENISE: Look, I'm not prejudiced.
It's true.
Black people don't tip.

❖❖❖

[*A school assembly.*]

MISS HARRISON: And now...parents, teachers, and children...
I want to welcome all of you to our special assembly today.
As we know, Dr. Martin Luther King, Jr. was a great, great man. A man whose achievements should not be forgotten.
A man who gave us the name for our school.
A man who provided hope and inspiration for Americans everywhere.
And in honor of his birthday, today Missy Harper, Danita Wright, and Johnny Kim...

BOBBY: [*Whispering.*] Bobby.

MISS HARRISON: . . . will recite from Dr. King's famous "I Have A Dream" speech.

[*Her nose held high,* MISSY *moves to the microphone.*]

MISSY: "I say to you today my friends even though we face the difficulties of today and tomorrow I still have a dream It is a dream deeply rooted in the American dream I have a dream that one day this nation will rise up and live out the true meaning of its creed 'We hold these Truths to be self-evident that all Men are created equal.'"

DANITA: [*Loudly and flatly.*] "I have a dream that one day on the red hills of Georgia sons of former slaves and sons of former slave-owners will be able to sit down together at the table of brotherhood I have a dream that one day even the state of Mississippi a state swel-tering with the heat of injustice swel-tering with the heat of oppression will be transformed into an o-a-sis of freedom and justice . . . "

BOBBY: "I have a dream that my four little children will one day live in a nation where they will not be judged by the color of their skin but by the content of their character I have a dream . . . I have a dream that one day . . . little black boys and little black girls will be able to join hands with little white boys and little white girls as sisters and brothers I have a dream today . . . "

DANITA: "This will be the day when all of God's children will be able to sing with new meaning 'My country 'tis of thee sweet land of liberty of thee I sing Land where my fathers died land of the Pilgrim's pride from every mountainside let freedom ring' And if America is to be a great nation this must become true . . . "

MISSY: "When we allow freedom to ring when we let it ring from every village and every hamlet from every state and every city we will be able to speed up that day when all of God's children black men and white men Jews and — [*Mispronounces.*] Gentles Pro-testants and Catholics will be able to join hands and sing in the words of the old Negro spiritual 'Free at last free at last thank God almighty we are free at last.'"

✧✧✧

[*A high school locker room.* ADOLESCENT WHITE BOY (WADE) *and* ROB.]

ROB: OK, so my Dad catches me jerking off the other day. Right?

WADE: Dude, that *sucks*.

ROB: It's a joke, Wade. So my Dad catches me jerking off the other day. Right?

WADE: Right.

ROB: And he goes "Rob, if you keep doing that, you're gonna go blind."
And I say... "Uh, Dad...
I'm over here."

WADE: OK, OK, I've got a new one, I've got a new one.
Alright. This guy walks into this taxidermist office, right? He's got these two dead rabbits. So he goes up to the guy at the desk and he's like: "I'd like to have these stuffed, please..."
So the guy's like "Sure, sure...would you like them mounted?"
The guy thinks for a minute and says..."No, holding hands is fine."
Alright.
OK, OK, what'd the Polish guy do when his wife had triplets?

ROB: I don't know, Wade. What?

WADE: He went out looking for the other two fathers.
You get it?

ROB: [*Giving him the buzzer.*] I don't know, man.

WADE: Alright, alright.
You hear the one about the Jewish Ethiopian?

ROB: No.

WADE: He's the guy with the Rolex around his waist.
You get it?
Come on, Man. Alright, OK...
This black woman walks into a drugstore. Right? And she's, you know, having her period. So she goes up to the guy at the counter and says: "'Scuse me suh, I'm having my period, but I don't know what to use." Guy goes, "OK, ma'am, I can help you. What's your flow like?"
She thinks for a minute and says...
"*Linoleum.*"

ROB: Wade.
Babe.
Keep the day job.

WADE: So funny, Rob.

ROB: [*Mimicking* WADE.] Funnier than you, Wade.

WADE: Alright, alright...
What do you call one white guy with ten thousand black guys?

Warden. [*Laughing to himself,* WADE *puts on his Dartmouth "Review"* *sweatshirt.*] What're you looking at, you fucking homo?

ROB: Well, Wade, I was just looking at your cute little ass and I figured since it was just you and me in the locker —
Actually, Wade, I was looking at your neck...
I wasn't sure if it was really red...but, you know, upon further inspection I see that it is...

WADE: [*Inspecting his neck in a "mirror."*] Where?

ROB: Your neck is red.
You have a red —
I've got a joke for you, Wade.
There's this white guy, this black guy, this Mexican guy, and this Oriental guy...right?

WADE: [*Like he's heard this one before.*] Oh yeah, yeah, yeah...they're at the gates of heaven and along comes St. Peter...right?

ROB: No, no, that's not it.

WADE: Oh, no, no, no...they're in the middle of the desert. Right? And one's got a fan, one's got a bucket of water, and one's got a car door...

ROB: No, that's not it either. You gonna let me finish?
OK, so there's this white guy, this black guy, this Mexican guy, and this Oriental guy, right? And they're like stranded on this island. And they're like totally shitting their pants, because they don't have any water, and they don't know where the fuck they are...
So naturally the black guy pulls out his twelve-inch dick and a bucket of fried chicken...

WADE: Right...

ROB: And the Oriental guy pulls out his one-inch dick.
Did I say one inch?
I meant fifteen *feet.*
Alright.
So the Oriental guy pulls out his fifteen foot penis and bowl of chop suey.
And the Mexican guy pulls out his seven-inch dick and beef burrito...

WADE: Yeah?

ROB: [*Relishing the delivery.*] And the black guy and the Oriental guy and the Mexican guy proceed to beat the living shit out of the white guy.

WADE: Yeah? And then what?

ROB: What?

WADE: What's the punchline?

ROB: That's it.

WADE: That's it?

ROB: Yeah.

WADE: I don't — I don't get it.

ROB: No.
     You don't.
     I'll see you around, man.

WADE: Later, Rob.

> [ROB *exits.* WADE *sits for a moment, still trying to figure out the joke.*]

❖❖❖

[*The Chinese restaurant.*]

TABLE 3 GIRL A: Hey, mister . . .

ROB: Right. [*Moves to Table 3.*] Can I get you anything else?

TABLE 3 GIRL A: We're all set.

ROB: OK, here you are. [*Rips off the check.*] Thank you.

TABLE 3 GIRL A: [*To* TABLE 4 WOMAN.] OK, Mom. We'll see you when we get home.

TABLE 4 WOMAN: Now, don't forget to pick up those clothes.

TABLE 3 GIRL A: I won't.

> [*When the* TABLE 3 GIRLS *have exited,* ROB *goes to clean Table 3 and finds no tip.*]

ROB: The Art of Waiting on Tables.
     The basic idea is that you have a certain amount of tables and you have a certain amount of customers, and you have a limited amount of resources — the resources being your ability to serve them. And the idea is that you distribute your resources accordingly, because there's a limited amount and you do it according to — I mean, why are you doing it? To make money, to make a living, to accumulate capital. So you have to decide which customers to wait on, which customers will be more likely to reward you for your efforts. When the number of customers exceeds the capacity of your resources to serve all of them equally, a decision has to be made.
     A customer walks in. You judge him/her according to how well you

think they're going to tip. So when a customer walks in, you're gonna be looking at what distinguishes her or him from other customers — usually, that's dress and sad to say it, it is also race.

Obviously, this is one restaurant, in one city, in one part of America, and this does not speak for everybody, but as a waiter, there's a certain degree of scientific method utilized, and all the data (limited as it is) all the data does tend to indicate that sure enough, black customers do not tend to tip as often as other customers.

This is not to say this is true of every black customer — there are plenty of exceptions to the rule. However...

❖❖❖

TABLE 4 WOMAN: The Art of Waiting For My Food.

The basic idea is that you have a certain amount of hunger and you have a certain number of places to eat, and you have a limited amount of resources — the resources being the money you have to pay for the food. And the idea is that you distribute your resources accordingly, because there's a limited amount, and you do it according to — I mean, why are you doing it? To eat, to fill your stomach, to satisfy your hunger. So you have to decide which restaurants to eat at, which restaurants are most likely to best serve your need for nourishment.

Now a waitron walks in. You judge him/her according to how well you think they are going to serve you. You're gonna be looking at what distinguishes him or her from other waitrons — usually, that's dress and sad to say, it is also racism.

Obviously, this is one restaurant, in one city, in one part of America, and this does not speak for everybody, but as a black customer, there's a certain degree of scientific method utilized, and all the data (limited as it is) all the data does tend to indicate that sure enough, waiters in Chinese restaurants do not tend to provide equal service to black customers.

This is not to say this is true of every waiter in Chinese restaurants — there are plenty of exceptions to the rule. However —

❖❖❖

ROB: [*To* TABLE 4 WOMAN.] Uh, excuse me.

Uh, I don't mean to disturb you, but that... that girl who was just sitting here...

You're her mother, right?

TABLE 4 WOMAN: [*Slightly defensive.*] Yes, I am.

ROB: [*Delicately, gently.*] Well, uh, you know, she comes in here a lot. And, uh, well...

You know, I don't know how to put this, but...

Your daughter, she didn't — she didn't tip me, and you know, I don't understand it, 'cause every time she's come in here and uh, I've waited on her...I, you know, I've always done the best I can, and uh, you know, I mean that sincerely, but...she never tips, and you know...I don't mean to offend you or anything...

I just thought she might not know about tipping, and well, you know, I have to...make a living.

TABLE 4 WOMAN: Well, I don't even know if I have enough to tip you today.

ROB: [*Delicately, gently.*] Ma'am, no, no, Ma'am.

I'm not...I'm not asking for money.

I mean, if you don't tip me, I don't care.

Just...

I don't know.

If you could just...maybe *talk* to your daughter, so next time maybe, you know...

You know, I'll tell you something, I'm just like you.

I have to work for a living.

'Cause I'll tell you the truth.

I mean, if it's not busy, I will wait on anybody.

But there are other waiters here who remember you when you don't tip, and you know...

TABLE 4 WOMAN: [*Miffed.*] So next time I come in here, you're not going to wait on me.

ROB: No, no, I didn't say that.

I'm just saying there are waiters here...

I mean, people who don't tip and come back — we tend to remember who they are, and when they come back, you know, they...

If you find yourself being ignored, if the waiter goes to all the other tables and ignores you, well, I mean, there's a reason for that.

TABLE 4 WOMAN: [*Getting angry.*] You know, I've been coming in here fifteen years, and no one has ever talked to me like that. You ask Don. He knows me. I've been coming in here every week for fifteen years...

ROB: [*Overlapping.*] I'm not, I'm not...

Ma'am...

I'm not...

Alright, I was out of line, I'm sorry...

TABLE 4 WOMAN: Well, you can just forget about your tip.

ROB: [*Getting angry, restraining himself.*] Ma'am, I don't expect you to tip me.
In fact, I know you're not going to tip me.

TABLE 4 WOMAN: You're right.

ROB: Ma'am, I don't want your money...
I just...
I just want...
Please don't...

❖❖❖

[*Note: italicized text/plain text = "interior"/exterior.*]

ROB: OK, here we are pupu platter for two, boneless chicken combo, chicken wing combo, coke and diet coke. If there's anything else I can get you, please let me know.
smile will-tip suits move move stay up up order in
what
Duck sauce. Right. Duck sauce.
messy mouths fucking Duck sauce
move move order in
tables tables messy tables choking
Don Don the piper's son
Don, Don.
grandfather hair-dye grease
Don, listen to me. You've gotta ease up.
I've got too many tables.
door fidgeting hungry winter coats
Hey man, I know there are people waiting.
time energy sweat money
I can only do so much. I've got sixteen tables.
nod nod
move kitchen door light watch carpet trip hiss spit wok light
Ordering one Moo Shi Pork...two boneless chicken combos...
FLIP...one chicken broccoli combo, two...TWO sweet-sour chicken combos...*FLIP*...three...THREE regular order chicken wings...*FLIP*...two BOWLS won-ton...three CUPS won-ton...
FLIP one Moo Goo Gai Pan Special...One Cashew Chicken Dinner ...*FLIP* two Pupu Platters For Two...Three Kung Pao Gai Ding Combos...
ARE YOU LISTENING
OK?...You got all that?...
Fuck-up's not my fault not my fault no English

Is that mine?
OK, here you are.
chicken man beef lady rice hot coke straw diet lady
Anything else I can get you?
Say no
smile
Great.
If you need anything just let me know.
order check tax cleaning time tip tip tip
what
stiffer
I'll be right with you.
what
what
what
I said I'll be right with you.
fucking nerve stiffer stiffer fucking nerve
Can I take your order?
not even ready
tap
tap
tap
Alright.
SHRIMP FLY LICE
And would you like something to drink?
battery acid
OK. Thank you.
Business Suits table 3 hand tap waiting
shit pen pen pen
I'm sorry. I'll be right with you.
move it move it patience edge
pen pen
ah
I'm sorry.
white working mother office buddy dines aesthetically
Are you ready to order?
Moo Shi Chicken — two, tea for two you for me me for you
OK, thank you. I'll be with you as soon as I can.
Just let me know if you need anything else.
order move do checks do checks
wipe rag clean table
do checks do checks

what
shit forgot sorry
Duck sauce. Right. Duck sauce.
dirty table empty get sauce sticky dollar tip
Here you are.
more tables more tips
mark stiffers
"7 out of 20 tip, 13 out of 20 stiff"
Welfare Day
fuck
9.66 + .57 = 10.23 black? check
yes please remember to tip your host
12.99 + .78 = 13.77 black? no
circle
8.15 + .49 = 8.64 black? yes BUT SUIT
no
circle
get em out go go go
Here you are. Thank you very much.
rip
Was everything alright?
Good.
Thank you very much.
rip
Was everything alright over here?
OK, here you are. Thank you very much.
table 9 left table 15 leaving check
tip run run for tips
over under clear here
fuck
fuck
check 15
bowl bones sweet sour sticky sauce
no tip
fuck fuck FUCK
7 for 22
Don. Don.
Come here. Listen.
When you're giving us tables, when you're dividing up tables...you gotta be fair...y'know what I'm saying? You gotta divide 'em up equally. Y'know what I'm saying?
Look at Denise's section. Look at Denise's section.

She's got more wh—
What I'm saying is... don't just give us an equal *number*.
Give us an equal number of *types*.
Don, for every two suits you give Denise, give me two suits.
Is everything alright over here?
Great, thank you very much.
How's everything over here?
Just let me know if you need anything else.
Is everything alright over here?
Great, thank you very much.

❖❖❖

[*Back to* TABLE 4 WOMAN *and* ROB *as they were at the restaurant.*]

ROB: [*Delicately, gently.*] Ma'am, no, no, Ma'am.
I'm not... I'm not asking for money.
I mean, if you don't tip me, I don't care.
Just...
I don't know.
If you could just... maybe *talk* to your daughter, so next time maybe, you know...
You know, I'll tell you something, I'm just like you.
I have to work for a living.
'Cause I'll tell you the truth.
I mean, if it's not busy, I will wait on anybody.
But there are other waiters here who remember you when you don't tip, and you know...

TABLE 4 WOMAN: [*Miffed.*] So next time I come in here, you're not going to wait on me.

ROB: No, no, I didn't say that.
I'm just saying there are waiters here...
I mean, people who don't tip and come back — we tend to remember who they are, and when they come back, you know, they...
If you find yourself being ignored, if the waiter goes to all the other tables and ignores you, well, I mean, there's a reason for that.

TABLE 4 WOMAN: [*Getting angry.*] You know, I've been coming in here fifteen years, and no one has ever talked to me like that. You ask Don. He knows me. I've been coming in here every week for fifteen years...

❖❖❖

TABLE 4 WOMAN: I've been coming here for fifteen years. Every week fifteen years.

I like this place.
The food is cheap.
You don't know me?
Yes, you do.
I know your mother.
Yes, your mother and I—we go way back.
Every week I go into her store—her store that you hate so much. Her store with the fake Gucci sweatshirts, the Mercedes Benz T-shirts, the imitation gold ropes with their plastic BMW charms.

[TABLE 3 GIRLS *enter the "store."*]

TABLE 4 WOMAN: [*Cont'd.*] My children have quite a thing for earrings, a fascination for ear-wear, and your mother has quite a collection: bangles and beads and hoops and chains and squares and circles—every shape and every possible cheap mass-producible material you could think of.
All "Made in Taiwan."
And all only a dollar a pair.
My children love those earrings. They stand at the counter, and they spend hours looking sometimes, deciding which earrings would go best with one of their three dresses.
They look and they look and they look.
Not that earrings are so terribly important.
But when they're looking at your mother's collage of pretty plastic and bent metal, when they've got those quarters and dimes and nickels in their hands, they know they are going to get something...
And they want to make that feeling last...
So they look and they look and they look.
And when they've finally decided, when you clear your throat because too many customers are coming in the store and it's getting too crowded, my children put it all on the table.
They slide their coins across the glass...

TABLE 3 GIRL A: A dollar twenty-five... thirty-five... forty-five... fifty-five...

TABLE 3 GIRL B: Sixty... seventy... seventy-five... eighty... ninety... ninety-five... *two* ...

TABLE 3 GIRL A: Two dollars.

ROB: I'm sorry, but it's two dollars and twelve cents.

[*The* TABLE 3 GIRLS *look at each other.*]

TABLE 4 WOMAN: My children always forget about the tax.

So now all that stands between them and the brass hoops and the red teddy bears is twelve cents.

And you, in your infinite Ivy League generosity, think what the heck it's only twelve cents and shrug your shoulders, and soon the earrings are in a bag and in my children's hands and they're running to meet me at the Woolworth's at 6:30 just like we agreed upon at lunch.

[*The* TABLE 3 GIRLS *have exited.*]

TABLE 4 WOMAN: [*Cont'd.*] And you feel, for a brief flash of less than a thought, almost good about yourself.

[*The following text can be re-cut/re-divided according to the number of cast members in the ensemble. Each character enters on his/her line and speaks completely out of character.*]

STEVE: When you used to pass a homeless person on the street, you used to give up your spare change — not much to pay for penance...

MRS. DUGAN: But now you look straight ahead, hoping they will not say anything, force you to answer them...

OLD WHITE GUY: Because after all, they're always there and there's nothing anybody can do about it and ah, they'll probably just buy drugs with it anyway.

TABLE 4 WOMAN: Right?

MISS HARRISON: And when you were in Washington, you were amazed by the people you saw...

ADOLESCENT WHITE BOY: Not by how terribly sad their lives were, but how they got even you to notice them... a drooling man with no legs...

LITTLE WHITE GIRL: A black man in a wheelchair with some sort of nerve disorder sipping a Roy Rogers cup of coke through a straw...

LITTLE BLACK GIRL: A sleeping woman using the *Washington Post* as a pillow on the concrete...

DENISE: Next to the ATM machine where you went to get more money... so you could go back to the bar and buy more beer...

RADIO RAHEEM: You didn't give then.

TABLE 4 WOMAN: But somehow it's easier for you to give two small black children twelve cents.

And it's even easier when you already have two of their dollars in your hand.

MOMMY: And when your mother scolds you for giving them the twelve cents (because sometimes kids will fake that they don't have enough money so they won't have to pay...)

ROB: [*Overlapping.*] I know...

MOMMY: And don't you remember the time you weren't paying attention and that little kid swiped the whole display board of sterling silver chains...

ROB: [*Overlapping.*] I know...

FATHER: You feel uncontrollably sad that your mother is like this, and you think of her face — her constant grimace and that you have not heard her laugh in two years, and you remember the picture you saw of your parents at your grandparents' house and how your father's slicked-back haircut made him look like the Asian James Dean and your mother's bouffant made her look like the Korean Jackie Kennedy, and how they actually used to be quite attractive, and how your mother never laughs anymore and how you love her and maybe, just maybe she wouldn't be like this, quibbling over twelve cents if you didn't go to your goddamn $20,000-a-year school.

TABLE 4 WOMAN: You don't know me?
Yes, you do.
I know your mother.
Your mother, and I — we go way back.
Her labor, my children's earrings.
We put you through school.

❖❖❖

[TABLE 4 WOMAN *and* ROB *circle each other, no longer in the restaurant.*]

TABLE 4 WOMAN: Well, you can just forget about your tip.

ROB: [*Getting angry.*] Ma'am, I don't expect you to tip me. In fact, I know you're not going to tip me.

TABLE 4 WOMAN: You're right.

ROB: Ma'am, I don't want your money...
I JUST WANT TO STOP THINKING THE THINGS I AM THINKING ABOUT YOU RIGHT NOW.

❖❖❖

[*During the following, as each member of the ensemble speaks his/her line, he/she moves upstage behind* ROB. *They eventually form a chorus. Again, each individual is not in character and again, the text may be re-cut/re-divided according to the number of individuals in the ensemble.*]

ROB: One word...

OLD WHITE GUY: Nigger.

ROB: Loaded words...

MRS. DUGAN: Chink.

ROB: One word...
Brings back every time as a kid I was called that...

MISS HARRISON: [*Overlapping.*] Nigger.

ROB: ...and all that pain from your childhood is in that one word...

LITTLE BLACK GIRL: [*Overlapping.*] Chink.

ROB: To be pointed out...

STEVE: [*Overlapping.*] Nigger.

ROB: ...singled out because you're different...

MOMMY: [*Overlapping.*] Chink.

ROB: You start hating yourself for that.

RADIO RAHEEM: [*Overlapping.*] Nigger.

ROB: You start hating yourself because...

FATHER: [*Overlapping.*] Chink.

ROB: You start hating that because it causes you so much hurt...

DENISE: [*Overlapping.*] Nigger.

ROB: 'Cause when you're in grade school...

ADOLESCENT WHITE BOY: [*Overlapping.*] Chink.

ROB: When you're going to school...

LITTLE WHITE GIRL: Nigger.

ROB: You don't wanna be different... you just wanna be the same. You just
wanna fit in...
"Forgive me, Father, for... "

ENSEMBLE: [*To* ROB.] Chink.

ROB: [*To* TABLE 4 WOMAN.] Nigger.
...I have sinned.

❖❖❖

[*A trial.* TABLE 4 WOMAN *plays the* PROSECUTOR. *The ensemble/chorus
is now a* JURY. RADIO RAHEEM *sits centerstage, apparently on trial.*]

PROSECUTOR: You have been charged with some very serious crimes. How do you plead?

ROB: What are the charges?

PROSECUTOR: Greed.

ROB: He's guilty.

PROSECUTOR: Jealousy.

ROB: Guilty.

PROSECUTOR: Selfishness.

ROB: Guilty.

PROSECUTOR: Lust.

ROB: Very guilty.

PROSECUTOR: Envy.

ROB: Guilty.

PROSECUTOR: Sloth.

ROB: Guilty.

PROSECUTOR: Self-indulgence.

ROB: Very, very guilty.

PROSECUTOR: The renunciation of your ethnic heritage.

ROB: What?
    What're you talking about?

PROSECUTOR: The subconscious desire to become a white male. How do you plead?

[RADIO RAHEEM *stands. He puts on the* JUDGE's *robes.*]

ROB: Now wait a second...

PROSECUTOR: Remember...
    You're under oath.

ROB: I don't know what you're talking about.

PROSECUTOR: Really?
    Then how do you explain this?
    I have here a voucher made out in your name requesting $350.00 worth of merchandise from the J. Crew company.
    I submit this to the court as Exhibit 1A.
    Now, is it not true, that in the spring of '79 you consulted a certain Dr. Richard Wilson — a noted plastic surgeon —

ROB: [*Overlapping.*] Whoa, whoa, wait a second here...

PROSECUTOR: Regarding the possibility of an "eye" job?

ROB: [*Overlapping.*] I was a kid...

PROSECUTOR: [*Grilling him.*] And isn't it true that in the summer of 1981, you considered the possibility of bleaching your hair...but only stopped yourself when you realized you would look *really silly.*

ROB: This is ridiculous.

PROSECUTOR: Yes, Rob, the truth is rather ugly. Isn't it?

ROB: I didn't...
I don't...
I don't know what you're talking about.

PROSECUTOR: Now, please answer for the court (and remember, you're under oath): haven't you always...always wanted to be white?

ROB: [*A pause.*] Yes, yes, I have.

JUDGE: [*Banging gavel.*] Order.
I say Order in the Court.
Order in the Court.

PROSECUTOR: And finally...during your employment at the Shanghai House of Food, you entertained certain thoughts...

ROB: Thoughts?
Yes, I thought frequently...
I thought —

PROSECUTOR: [*Overlapping.*] Yes, certain thoughts...
Certain ugly thoughts...
Racist thoughts...

ROB: [*A pause.*] Yes, yes, I did.
But — but I can explain.
It was temporary insanity.
I was under a lot of pressure at work...
I - I wasn't getting money from home...
No, I can't explain.

JUDGE: Mr. Kim, don't you think it's time you stopped shifting the blame onto external factors? Don't you think it's time you took a little personal responsibility for your actions?

[*A pause.*]

ROB: You're right. [*A pause.*] I'm guilty.

JUDGE: Very well.

Step forward and receive your sentence.

[ROB *does so.*]

JUDGE: [*Cont'd.*] I've gone over the evidence, and I have no choice but to hereby denounce you as a racist.

Racist.

[*The ensemble creates an aural tapestry of different voices, pitches, etc., entirely composed of the word "racist."*

ENSEMBLE: Racist.
Racist.
Racist.
Racist.
Racist.
Racist.

[*Lights fade and shift, leaving a single spotlight on* ROB. *Then slow fade to black . . . .*]

[*In the darkness, the ensemble's chorus of "racist" slowly evolves into a unified chant.*]

[*Lights up. The ensemble/jury are now patrons at Bob's Comedy Luau Hut. They rhythmically strike the tables and chant "racist" . . . the lighting should not suggest reality. The ensemble's chanting is interrupted by the voice of* MR. SHOWBIZ. *However, they continue to mime striking the tables.*]

VOICE OF MR. SHOWBIZ: Johnny, Johnny . . . what-what-what the hell is this? You're on in *two* minutes, baby . . .

✧✧✧

[*Backstage at Bob's Comedy Luau Hut.* ROB *has a wet towel wrapped around his head. Enter* MR. SHOWBIZ. *Faint bursts of canned laughter can be heard periodically during the following.*]

MR. SHOWBIZ: Johnny, Johnny . . . what-what-what the hell is this? You're on in *two* minutes, baby . . .

ROB: I can't . . .
I can't go out there . . .

MR. SHOWBIZ: What are you, fucking kidding me?
Listen to 'em, bunch of live ones out there, they're eating Scotty's shit up . . .
Hey, hey, kid, don't worry 'bout a thing.
They're gonna love you, baby. [MR. SHOWBIZ *looks in "onstage" direc-*

tion.] When Scotty's done, he'll come back, give you your cue...I'll introduce you and wham-bam-look it's Japan! You're on, baby, you're *on*...*Two* minutes.

[MR. SHOWBIZ *exits.*]

ROB: Oh God...

[*Nauseated,* ROB *looks "onstage" at the comedy club patrons. They resume thumping the tables.*]

ROB: [*Cont'd.*] OK, relax relax relax gotta relax relax gotta relax...

[*Pacing,* ROB *recites the words "relax" and "gotta relax" over and over again, until they attain an almost mantric quality for him. He begins to repeat the words in synch with the sound of the thumping tables...the thumping increases in intensity as he regains his confidence...and then, the sound of thumping is overcome by the sound of massive applause.* ROB *watches the following transpire on the comedy club stage:.*]

❖❖❖

[*A tuxedo-clad* ACTOR *and evening gown-clad* ACTRESS *enter "onstage." They are both white.*]

ACTOR: And now for the moment we've all been waiting for.
We've been told we're running a little late, so we're just going to cut right to the chase.

ACTRESS: This year's nominees for Best Verbal Harassment of an Asian-American Child are:

ACTOR: This Old Man. Scott Whitehead, producer.

[LITTLE WHITE BOY *approaches* LITTLE ASIAN BOY, *acts out the following:*]

LITTLE WHITE BOY: Hey Johnny.
See the refrigerator? Open it up.

[LITTLE ASIAN BOY *does so.*]

LITTLE WHITE BOY: [*Cont'd.*] Take out the coke.

[LITTLE ASIAN BOY *does so.*]

LITTLE WHITE BOY: [*Cont'd.*] Drink the coke.

[LITTLE ASIAN BOY *does so.*]

LITTLE WHITE BOY: [*Cont'd.*] Ha-ha. [*Singing to the tune of "This Old Man".*] Me Chinese, Me Play Joke,
Me put pee-pee in your coke.

[LITTLE WHITE BOY *clasps his hands together and bows "like a*

Chinaman." *Thunderous applause.* LITTLE WHITE BOY *and* LITTLE ASIAN BOY *take a bow.*]

ACTRESS: Great. Thank you.
Our second nominee is "Chinese, Japanese." Missy Harper, Alan Parker and John Hughes, producers.

[LITTLE WHITE GIRL *approaches* LITTLE ASIAN BOY, *acts out the following:*]

LITTLE WHITE GIRL: Hey Johnny. [*Slants her eyes up.*] Chinese. [*Slants her eyes down.*] Japanese. [*Points to* LITTLE ASIAN BOY'S *knees.*] Dirty knees. Look at these.

[*She pulls* LITTLE ASIAN BOY'S *shorts down. Thunderous applause. Little White Girl curtsies,* LITTLE ASIAN BOY *bows.*]

ACTRESS: Great. That was wonderful.

ACTOR: And our final nominee is "Cultural Interchange." Trip McDonald, Dolph Lundgren and Michael Cimino, producers.

[ADOLESCENT WHITE BOY *approaches* LITTLE ASIAN BOY, *acts out the following:.*]

ADOLESCENT WHITE BOY: Ahh-so. [*Makes various sounds mimicking Chinese language and noises made by actors on Kung Fu Theatre.*] Hey, what's your name?
What's your name, Chinese Boy?
Hey, I'm talking to you.
Where you from?
Bangkok?

[*He knees* LITTLE ASIAN BOY *in the groin, laughs. Thunderous applause.* ADOLESCENT WHITE BOY *and* LITTLE ASIAN BOY *take a bow.*]

ACTRESS: And the winner is... [*Starts to open the envelope.*] Oh, this is so exciting. [*Reads.*] "This Old Man," Scott Whitehead, producer.

[*A very triumphant* SCOTT WHITEHEAD *descends from the audience, approaches the microphone. Celebratory music plays: a fanfare/orchestration of "This Old Man"/theme music from "Superman.".*]

SCOTT WHITEHEAD: They told me to keep this brief, but...
This is...
I can't even begin to express... what I'm feeling tonight.
I'm incredibly grateful for this honor, and I can't thank you all enough. This one is by far the sweetest.
I want to thank Doug Morgan and Dave Collins for believing in us and supporting the project. Barry Fox and Peter Johns for having the courage and the vision to dare to believe in miracles. Stephen for pro-

viding invaluable guidance and love...Oh God, I know I'm gonna forget somebody. John and Tommy and Ollie and Chris and Sutherland...Thank you. And God bless...

[*Applause. He looks at the audience for a moment, raises his hand for silence.*]

SCOTT WHITEHEAD: [*Cont'd.*] Uh...
As I said...I am incredibly grateful for this honor, but I cannot...I cannot accept this in good conscience...
For there is someone here tonight, who is far more worthy, far more *deserving* of this award...
Someone who showed the courage, the vision and the sheer talent...that make me very, very proud to be a part of this industry...
I must say that his Trial Scene was perhaps the most moving and brilliant piece of filmmaking I have seen in the last ten years and that is why...if this award is to truly mean what it is supposed to mean...I must give this award to...Rob Shin...

[SCOTT *thrusts the Oscar in the air. "Offstage," as if in a dream,* ROB *slowly raises his hand as if it were he who were holding the award in the air. Thunderous applause.* MR. SHOWBIZ *enters "onstage."*]

MR. SHOWBIZ: I'm sorry Johnny couldn't be here this night to accept this award for which I am sure he is very grateful...
What can I say?
You know, I tol' him, tol' him when he was just starting out, when he was just a kid...
Johnny, you wanna *work* in this business, get somewheres, make a name for yourself...you gotta go with the Chinese Waiter, baby...
Chinese Waiter...
I made this kid...he was nowhere, nowhere without me...

[*He holds up and waves the Oscar for the television cameras.* MR. SHOWBIZ *continues to mime a celebratory speech as his voice can be heard elsewhere:*]

VOICE OF MR. SHOWBIZ: [*Taped.*] Thank you Scott Whitehead...he's a funny funny funny man.
Next up is a guy, young kid, by the name of Johnny Kim. Johnny Kim come and make these people laugh...[*Pause.*] Ladies and gentlemen, *Johnny Kim.* [*Pause.*] Johnny Kim, ladies and gentlemen. [*Pause.*] Johnny Kim...

❖❖❖

[*Backstage.* ROB *is pacing, clutching the towel. Enter* SCOTT WHITEHEAD, *undoing his bowtie.*]

SCOTT WHITEHEAD: Rob.

Yo Rob, what the fuck you doing? You're on, man, you're on, get out
there...

◆◆◆

[*Onstage again at Bob's Comedy Luau Hut.* MR. SHOWBIZ *is at the microphone.*]

MR. SHOWBIZ: Uh, well folks...I don't know what to say...during the
day, Johnny's a waiter at the Shanghai House of Food...maybe he
went out to get everybody some eggrolls...heh-heh-heh...And
speaking of eggrolls, how about those little Japanese imports—

[ROB *enters, out of breath.*]

MR. SHOWBIZ: [*Cont'd.*] Oh, there he is...Ladies and Gentlemen,
heeeere's Johnny Kim...

[*Spotlight on the microphone.* ROB *takes the microphone, looks out at the
audience. A pause.*]

ROB: Ah...
Ahhh...
So.

◆◆◆

CURTAIN.

VOICE OF BOB: Hey Susan, did you see that?

VOICE OF SUSAN: I sure did, Bob, and that means it's time for a game.

VOICE OF BOB: Right. So everybody look very carefully and you can play
the game right along with us.

VOICE OF SUSAN: OK.

VOICE OF BOB: Ready?

[*Music begins to play: Sesame Street's "One of These Things Is Not Like
The Other." As the music plays, the cast appears for the curtain call.*]

VOICES OF SUSAN AND BOB: [*Singing.*] One of these things is not like the
other
One of these things is not like the other
Can you tell which thing is not like the other
By the time we finish our song?
Doo Doo Doo De-Doo-Doo-De-Doo-Doo
Doo Doo Doo Doo-Doo-Duh-Do
Doo Doo Doo De-Doo-Doo-De-Doo-Do
Doo Doo Doo Doo-Doo-Duh-Doo
Did you guess which thing is not like the others?

Did you guess which thing doesn't belong?
If you guessed this thing is not like the others . . .
Then you're absolutely . . . Right.

VOICE OF SUSAN: Because three of them were coconuts.

VOICE OF BOB: And the other one was Ernie's rubber duckie.

[*They laugh.*]

END OF PLAY

Denise Uyehara

HIRO

EDITOR'S NOTES

Denise Uyehara comes to theatre from the same performance art background as Sandra Tsing Loh, but her performance style is remarkably different. Her smooth and understated voice plays in effective contrast to her severe crewcut (Fearless Hair is the name of her production company). Whether in solo pieces such as *Headless Turtleneck Relatives*, or in concert with a group called Sacred Naked Nature Girls, Denise explodes preconceptions about Asian women and sexuality with a quiet self-assurance. One of her earliest theatre scripts was a one-act entitled *Hobbies*, about an Asian college girl who is totally absorbed with European culture, and her difficulties in fending off a Caucasian suitor fascinated by all things Asian. More than simply an indictment of sinophiles, it was a wry portrait of people who look outside their culture for a validation they haven't found from their own upbringing.

Perhaps *Hobbies* would have been the more natural selection for a volume about multiethnic issues. But I have included *Hiro* in this volume instead, because it's a type of multicultural play that seems remarkably rare: a play about people of color, in which their color is not a plot point. While Caucasian protagonists routinely drive stories in which race is not a factor, the vast majority of plays about ethnic characters pivot on that very ethnicity. Either the events in the play happened to the characters because of their color, or are of note because of the same reason.

All of the characters in *Hiro* are clearly Asian American. But their cultural references draw from three continents, Europe, Asia and North America. They are neither fully of the East nor fully of the West –but rather, they are fully comfortable in that space between East and West. Unlike the characters of *As Sometimes in a Dead Man's Face*, who are so tired of being asked to choose between red and blue when they're really violet, the characters of *Hiro* seamlessly blend together the colors of different worlds.

The rarity of this situation cannot be stated strongly enough. How often does one see a play like, say, *All My Sons* or *The Odd Couple*, say, that just happens to be about Asians? Caucasian characters are free to operate without concern about their ethnicity. Caucasian writers are free to operate without addressing racial politics. But Asian writers who write plays that have nothing to do with Asian politics (James Yoshimura's *Ohio Pick-Up*, Susan Kim's *The Arrangement*, Rosanna Yamagiwa Alfaro's *Pablo and Cleopatra*) will rarely find those plays produced at Asian theatres, or at mainstream theatres looking for "this season's ethnic statement."

Director Des McAnuff once remarked, "I'm Canadian — but if that meant I could only direct plays about hockey, that would be a dreadful fate." Yet that fate is sealed for the majority of Asian American writers. In the Asian American works that reach the widest audience, be they *M. Butterfly* or *Tea* or even Margaret Cho's television series *All-American Girl*, race matters. This is not an indictment of those works: race must matter, given the ceaseless controversy about the topic in our society. At least in Denise Uyehara's *Hiro*, however, we can anticipate a day when more and more plays will be written in which the ethnicity of the characters, while a valued part of their identity, is simply background instead of the motor of the plot. The story will matter more than the race of the heroes; the play will be the thing. In this sense, although alphabetical order determined the arrangement of this anthology, it feels particularly fitting that this volume closes with *Hiro*.

Hiro is also uniquely theatrical in that it's about a woman who flies, yet it specifically asks producers not to go out and rent flying apparatus. The flying is to be created by the actress and the lighting, the language and the mood. In an era where the biggest stage events seem to be about replicating sensations (the chandelier in *The Phantom of the Opera*, the helicopter in *Miss Saigon*), it's refreshing to be reminded that the theatrical event really takes place in the minds of the audience. You'll believe a woman can fly.

Hiro was first produced at East West Players (Tim Dang, Artistic Director) in association with AT&T: On Stage, in Los Angeles, California, on July 7, 1994, with the following cast:

HIRO	Jeanne Sakata
SHELL	Freda Foh Shen
QUEEN T	Amy Hill
ACE	Darrell Kunitomi

Directed by Roxanne Rogers. Dramaturg, Brian Nelson; Set Design by Devin Meadows; Light and Sound Design by Keith Endo; Costume Design by Lydia Tanji and Dori Quan; Fight Choreography by Bob Goodwin; Production Manager, Dena Paponis.

Hiro was developed in the David Henry Hwang Writers Institute and the Mark Taper Forum Mentor Playwrights Project.

CHARACTERS

SHELL   31. A rather attractive woman who feels life has moved on without her. Her mode of survival is to drink and keep a sense of humor and practicality whenever possible. Speaks with an acquired Southern accent.

HIRO   Her older sister. 35. Has the ability to levitate and fly. Rather juvenile with a fast, dark energy to her.

QUEEN T   Their mother. About to turn 50. Glamorous and selectively telepathic. Often focused in an entirely different reality.

ACE   Shell's separated husband. A well-read, philosophical man who drives a truck. Visits Shell and her mother on occasion. Late 30s.

RADIO VOICE   Male. (Can be played by the actor who plays Ace.)

SHELL, HIRO, QUEEN T and ACE are Asian American and require Asian American actors.

TIME: *The present. Summer.*

PLACE: *A small coastal town.*

SETTING: *A water tower. The front porch of* SHELL'S *weathered home, in front of which is a dying lawn and dried tall grass, and beyond that, the sea.*

NOTE:

This play is real, magical and metaphorical. Like flight itself, the words have an inherent lightness and darkness to them. HIRO'S *levitation should be achieved with the actors' movement, dialogue and light changes. No cables or other technical distractions are to be used.*

ACT I

SCENE 1

In spotlight, HIRO *stands in a royal blue bodysuit, moving her arms slowly, like a bird.*

HIRO: There's a stage you reach in deep sleep, when your mind becomes your perfect friend, when you catch the sun in flight, embrace winds and cross rushing wheat fields. For some it is dreaming, for others more lucid. Their dreams become real. All I know is, one morning while I slept, I dreamed I was flying. I woke up and I was.

[*She stretches her arms up like an eagle in flight. As she lifts from the ground, lights simultaneously crossfade to:*]

SCENE 2

A woman with arms outstretched in the same manner as HIRO. *It is* SHELL. *She stands on top of a dangerously high water tower. She has been drinking whisky. It is late afternoon in the summer.* SHELL *is considering jumping to her death. She stands near the edge with her arms out, then stops, moves back. She repeats this several times.* HIRO *enters from around the back of the tower, sits against the ledge, takes off her helmet, admiring her reflection in its face shield. She has a fast-paced energy and is oblivious to* SHELL'S *attempts.* SHELL *attempts again.*

SHELL: I'm going this time.

HIRO: Where are you going, Shell? [*No answer.*] Are you going out?

SHELL: Yes.

HIRO: Wow. Things have really changed since I've been around. You come up here to practice flying, right? Just like before, except back then you used to watch me. I'd float in the air and turn around and you'd be standing on the ledge, waving to me. Waving.

SHELL: I'm going down.

HIRO: Down? No, you gotta reach out. [*She shows* SHELL *how.*] Come on just reach, and breathe.

SHELL: Hiro. Stop it, I'm doing something.

HIRO: OK. So go ahead. [SHELL *looks at her closely.*] What's wrong?

SHELL: I . . . just never thought I'd see you again, that's all. You've been away so long.

HIRO: I've been real busy. I've got this new governmental flying thing. I've been preparing for Guinea Bissau.

SHELL: [*Beat.*] What?

HIRO: That's my next assignment. [*Pulls out a map.*] See? Guinea Bissau. A French colony in Africa. It's a lot like Chile. Lots of desaparecidos there. It's very top secret, but you're family. It's OK, I know I can trust you.

SHELL: [*Reading map.*] Guinea . . . Bissoh.

HIRO: Bissau.

SHELL: Jesus Christ. That's the middle of nowhere. Guinea Bissoh. More like Guinea Pig. After all these years you come back and tell me you were in Guinea Pig?

HIRO: No, I'm going there. Next assignment.

SHELL: Oh. OK. You're on your way to the middle of nowhere. Hah. Pretty sad you've been gone fifteen years and you still end up in the middle of nowhere. Guinea Pig. Hah. You might as well've stayed here, Hiro. 'Cause see, this is the middle of nowhere, too. Fifteen goddamn years in the middle of nowhere.

HIRO: Have I been gone that long? I feel like Moses. Or Odysseus. I should write a book, like Odysseus did. *The Odysseusey!* Dad's favorite book. All those pictures of the mermaids and the one-eyed giant. And the chariots. Those were fun. [*Pretends to ride a chariot.*] The god of the sun rides his flaming chariot across the sky — "Go, boy, yah! Yah!"

SHELL: Hiro.

HIRO: [*Involved in her chariot.*] Yeah? Yah!

SHELL: What do you want?

HIRO: [*Pacing.*] Hmmm. . .what do I want? That's a good question. An enchilada pie! I'd like that. I'm hungry, Shell, are you hungry? Just like Queen T used to make. I miss her. It's so good to be back home. Gee, I was a legend in my own time. I am a legend in my own time. A phenomenon! I amaze myself in overcoming my own inertia. Inertia's the stuff that keeps you in old habits. But see? I overcame my inertia!

SHELL: Hiro. Please. I'm doing something.

HIRO: OK. I'll be quiet.

SHELL: I'd like to be alone.

HIRO: — enchilada pie! Yeah. How is Queen T? I think about her all the time. You think she remembers me? I mean after Dad died I had to leave so quickly — she's here, right?

SHELL: I'm really going now. 'Cause this is nowhere. And up there, behind the sky, is somewhere.

[SHELL *attempts to jump again.*]

HIRO: Now we can travel together, all over the state. The nation! The world! You're a phenomenon! Well, second phenomenon. I'm the original, but you're following in my footsteps. Against inertia. Go ahead. That's right. Think of deep water. Rise up. [SHELL *falls off the edge of the tower, more out of drunkenness than true death wish.* HIRO *grabs her by the arm as* SHELL *dangles with one leg and arm over the edge.* SHELL *yells in horror.*] What's wrong with you? No! Flap! You gotta flap! Concentrate!

SHELL: Jesus! Help! Help me!

HIRO: Concentrate, Shell!

SHELL: I can't concentrate when you're pulling my arm out of its socket!

HIRO: Put your mind into it![HIRO *pulls* SHELL *away from the edge. They collapse on the ledge. Long pause as they recuperate.*] You have to follow through. You could've gotten yourself killed. The most important part is setting your sights on flight. The sun. The clouds. The birds. And flap your arms. Concentrate. [SHELL *is in a state of shock. She sits cross-legged with her head in between her knees.*] Come on Shell, just take on the air. The air is clean. Cheer up. Better than living in dirt and smog on the ground. [*Pause; she points.*] What's that?

SHELL: [*Barely looking up.*] Rock refinery.

HIRO: I know that. But what's it for?

SHELL: [*Head still down.*] Refining rocks.

HIRO: [*Watches.*] That's really odd. I never thought I'd see rocks on a conveyor belt. You know. It seems slow. The conveyor belt.

SHELL: Sometimes it's slow.

HIRO: You think she'll recognize me, in my new apparel?

[SHELL *lays on her stomach and lets her head dangle over the edge as she looks down.*]

SHELL: Oh God. I almost did it.

HIRO: Yeah, see? You were almost there. [*Pause.*] I bet she'll be really surprised. Queen T used to send me messages. You know — [*Puts the back of her hand to her forehead.*] Head messages. But then she stopped. About two years ago. Just ended. I sent a letter here once, but you know what? It came back about a month later with cancellation marks from Austin and Eureka. As if the post office was looking for my own family. Spy Headquarters thought I was sending messages in and out. A code. Isn't that intriguing? Thought I better look for my family myself. [*Beat.*] Rocks on a conveyor belt. Little rocks. [*Beat.*] You know what this place reminds me of? Hell.

SHELL: [*Not moving from her place.*] It's hot, that's all.

HIRO: No. Because it's boring. Too quiet. Listen. [*They listen; fifteen seconds of absolute silence.*] That annoys me.

SHELL: Not talking.

HIRO: What?

SHELL: Not talking.

HIRO: What? [*Beat.*] Shell, I can't hear you when you have your head over the side like that.

SHELL: [*Doesn't get up.*] It's too quiet because we're not talking.

HIRO: Yeah. Whatever it is. I hate it. If you're bad, you go to a place like this. You get condemned to putting rocks on a conveyor belt. Boring. It's a good thing you have yourself a home. It's nice you have a home. And a job. Well, you had a job. What was it you used to do? Pharmacy? Pills. [*Pause.*] Shell. [*Beat.*] Hey. Shell.

SHELL: [*Sitting up.*] I quit.

HIRO: I thought you were fired.

SHELL: No. I quit. They didn't have enough work, so I decided to quit. [*Beat.*] And the term is "laid off." Nobody gets fired anymore, it's too harsh. In between jobs.

HIRO: Can I see her?

SHELL: [*Standing.*] —And I can change my mind anytime I want. About anything. My job. My life. [*Beat.*] My death . . . my non-life . . . my afterlife—

HIRO: I need to see Queen T.

SHELL: —and all the little life moments in between that make up life. Little life moments. [*Beat.*] God I almost did it. [*Beat.*] Why don't you call her Mom like everyone else?

HIRO: Who calls her that?

SHELL: I do for starters.

HIRO: Oh, normal people do. You think she remembers about what happened to Dad?

SHELL: I reckon so. She's not the type to forget things like that. Maybe she don't want to see you.

HIRO: I could cheer her up, you know that. Come on. Take me to see Queen T. Maybe you could help ease me in again. I don't wanna bring back bad—I don't wanna shock her, it's been so long. I could stay a while, since you're going away—

SHELL: I've changed my mind.

HIRO: Come on, Shell. Sis. What do you say. Come on, come on, come on.

SHELL: No.

HIRO: Come on.

SHELL: No.

HIRO: Yes.

SHELL: No.

HIRO: [*Beat.*] OK. OK.

SHELL: [*As* HIRO *begins to leave.*] Where are you going? Hiro? Here. Have a drink.

HIRO: [*Still with back to* SHELL.] I don't drink.

SHELL: We're in hell, remember? You can do anything you want. [*Beat.*] She's not much at conversation. Ever since you . . . She's been worse. She wanders, all over in her mind. I'm thinkin' if you come back, you're gonna bring back bad memories, that's all. I'm tired of it. You promise you'll be leavin' shortly afterwards?

HIRO: [*Turning to face her.*] Sure. I'm only here for a short visit.

SHELL: So you'll be leaving shortly afterwards?

HIRO: That's a short visit, right?

SHELL: Promise.

HIRO: I promise. Cross my heart and hope to die. Stick a needle in my mother's eye.

SHELL: Religious? [*Looks out at the orange grove.*] Get a load of those trees in the grove. See 'em? Look. Each one of those trees is special. A single orange tree. I never thought of that. An orange tree. Always thought of it as one big mass. Ain't that a sight.

HIRO: I could use a place to rest my head.

SHELL: Her Semi-centurian, that's why you're here, because she's turning fifty. Because she's getting old. She's really lost it. Sad to say. [*Looks out at the grove.*] Ain't that a beautiful sight? A single orange tree. Change my mind, anytime I want. [*Pause.*] If you're religious, Hiro, then when I take you to see her, you could get down on your knees and pray for her. For us. God bless it. Pray for us.

HIRO: Thank you, Shell. You're a saint.

SHELL: She's dying.

SCENE 3

That evening. RADIO ANNOUNCER *speaks, lights slowly rise.*

RADIO: — the Open Market continues throughout the summer months, every second and fourth weekend. And bring the children! Come out to support your local farming community and remember: family farmers are "Turning Water Into Food."

[*We see the front porch of* SHELL'S *home.* QUEEN T *sits on the porch in a chair facing upstage, so that only her back is visible. She sips a drink from a straw. She is listening to the news on the radio.*]

RADIO: Now the weather: was sunny again today, in case you didn't notice, with lows in the lower 80s and highs, well it was up there, Southland weather broke 100 in some parts, right now the Santa Ana Civic Center checks in at a mild 76 degrees . . .

QUEEN T: Then, my good man, the lows are in the 70s.

RADIO: . . . uh . . . then, I suppose we should say they'll be lows in the 70s . . . uh . . . tomorrow looks like a carbon copy of today, breaking 90 in some parts, some smog in the Inland Empire, but clear in Orange County —

[QUEEN T *turns off the radio. She picks up the glass, sucks noisily through the straw until every drop is gone, turning downstage so she is in full view. She examines the bottom of the glass.* SHELL *enters.*]

SHELL: Mom.

QUEEN T: This glass, Shell, the bottom needs cleaning. Look at these abominable white deposits. Perhaps a stronger detergent.

SHELL: They're frosted.

QUEEN T: . . . where is that store? A stronger detergent.

SHELL: [*Looking offstage.*] Mom. You remember Hiro?

QUEEN T: [*Vaguely.*] Hiro. [*Beat.*] Oh! How silly of me, of course, Hiro-chan, I miss her so much, do you think Daddy is taking good care of her?

SHELL: I suppose. [SHELL *looks at* HIRO, *offstage, and motions for her to keep back.*] 'Cause what if she . . . what if I was able to bring her here for a visit, wouldn't that be somethin'?

QUEEN T: [*Lightly.*] I think that would be quite an accomplishment, considering she's dead.

SHELL: Aw, maybe everyone's been too harsh on her leaving, maybe she's still around —

QUEEN T: No, she's gone to the Elysians, I can feel it. She and I have always been close, in our minds, you understand. [HIRO *walks onto the porch as quietly as she can, until* QUEEN T *sees her.*] Oh, Hiro, there you are! I was just talking about you, I'm so glad you came to see me!

HIRO: Queen T!

[HIRO *is about to hug her, but* QUEEN T *stands straighter, draws back a bit.* HIRO *keeps her place.* QUEEN T *extends her hand, elegantly.* HIRO *takes it and puts it to her own forehead, bowing a bit.*]

QUEEN T: How good to see you. Did you vacuum under the credenza?

HIRO: Uh. Yes. Yes I did.

QUEEN T: Because there was some dust under that credenza. That is your chore. I do believe you have been slightly delinquent on vacuuming, Hiro-chan.

SHELL: I've been cleaning everywhere else.

QUEEN T: Of course, dear. You see, Hiro, your sister has had to do so much of your burden while —

[QUEEN T *stops mid-sentence, motionless, as if listening to something. Long pause.*]

SHELL: [*To* HIRO.] She's thinking.

HIRO: I can see that.

SHELL: Oh, that foolish radio announcer. Lows are in the 70s. [*Sings.*] Lavender blue, dilly, dilly . . .

HIRO: Queen T.

QUEEN T: Oh, forgive me. As I was saying it's such a burden your sister carries for you, I'm glad you have finally decided to return.

SHELL: I knew you'd like to see her.

HIRO: I have a job. I'm a special flying agent with the government. My next assignment is in Guinea Bissau . . .

QUEEN T: Really? That's like Chile, where the desaparecidos are.

SHELL: So we should all sit down and have a nice, cool, mint julep, or lemonade, don't you think? I'm so glad I could get you to visit us, Hiro. I was worried when we didn't see you for such a long time, but I reckon that's all part of the business you're in .. how long you say you had this governmental spy thing? How about some orange?

QUEEN T: That would be splendid, Shell.

HIRO: Oh, yeah, I'd like one. Please.

SHELL: [*Points to the orange grove.*] There they are, Hiro. Some real ripe ones right there, see 'em? Mr. Johnson doesn't mind, I go pick 'em all the time. Thanks Hiro, I'd be much obliged if you —

HIRO: "Obliged." Isn't that a little Southern?

SHELL: Well, I suppose so.

HIRO: "Reckon so."

SHELL: [*As* HIRO *laughs.*] What's wrong with the way I talk?

HIRO: Nothing.

QUEEN T: Now, now, that is simply a dialect Shell has acquired. Like tofu, one must acquire a taste for differences.

HIRO: Reckon so.

SHELL: Stop it, Hiro. The oranges, if you would be so kind.

HIRO: In a minute, Shell. [*To* QUEEN T.] The mission is top-top — [*Leans closer.*] — secret. Secret stuff.

QUEEN T: Your daddy must be so proud, did he come with you this time?

HIRO: Oh, no. But he's fine.

QUEEN T: You know, Hiro-chan, he may look average, but he's an intellectual, they always look that way. [*Beat.*] I must say, I've been a tad preoccupied recently, preparing for this Semi-centurian, this "pilgrimage" which is rather absurd since I'm already in my home town. But you know our omniscient Committee — of mystics, druids, merlins and people like you and I — the Committee insists I "celebrate" my 50th. I wonder what exactly this celebration will entail. In any case, you know how rituals are, they just get in the way of living. I have a date with my age, so to speak. But in my opinion, a woman should never reveal her true age or bust size. It's quite against my standards. And the Committee implying that I'm half a century old. A lie. I'm 50 in human years only. Otherwise, I'm content with . . . 43.

HIRO: You look about 40, Queen T.

QUEEN T: Thank you, Hiro-chan, my darling.

HIRO: I missed you.

QUEEN T: I sent you messages almost every day.

HIRO: I stopped getting your messages about two years ago—I thought . . .

QUEEN T: Oh, it must have slipped my mind. I do apologize. Recently things have eluded me like soap bubbles. Fleeting. Your daddy understands this. My mind was superior and . . . fleeting at the same time.

SHELL: I've been helping her memory some.

QUEEN T: My memory is just a little selective.

SHELL: Her doctor said some things she remembers very clearly. Particular, traumatic events.

[HIRO *looks up at* SHELL.]

QUEEN T: I can't imagine what is keeping him.

HIRO: Who?

QUEEN T: Your daddy.

HIRO: He said he can't make it this time, maybe later. He . . . sends his regrets for not attending your Semi-centurian. He says you're too beautiful for such an artificial landmark age.

QUEEN T: Oh, sweet David. [*Beat.*] Oh. Another royal flush. Put down the one-eyed Jack. Yes, the Jack. Yes, that one. No, the other Jack. You fool: the Jack of Spades!

SHELL: Now, mother, remember to stay here with us. I'm here. Stay here.

QUEEN T: [*Becoming more lucid.*] Shell.

SHELL: I'm here, Mom.

QUEEN T: Ah, yes. You are, Shell. My dear. [*Puts her hand to* SHELL'S *cheek.*] Now, what was I going . . . oh, yes. A celebration is in order. For Hiro's return—we should bring out the best champagne, or the fatted calf—it is almost Biblical. And also in a dubious toast to my 50th birthday.

HIRO: Human years.

QUEEN T: Yes, in human years. Guests. That's it, lots of guests.

HIRO: Maybe just a family thing. You know, I'm very top, top secret.

QUEEN T: Oh, yes. Well, then, just family. [*Pause.*] Andrew.

HIRO: Who?

SHELL: No. I told you that's over.

QUEEN T: Ah, but you're still legally wed. He is family. I believe Andrew should be notified by me personally.

[QUEEN T *holds her finger to her forehead, concentrating, then points her finger in the direction of the front door.*]

HIRO: You were married, Shell?

SHELL: It's unimportant now —

HIRO: My sister, married. [*Beat.*] Here? Did you have it here, the wedding?

SHELL: Yeah.

HIRO: Just like we used to talk.

QUEEN T: [*Breaking from her telepathy.*] She wore lace. White as a tsuru. An elegant bird dancing in the snow performing the nuptial mating dance.

HIRO: You were gonna have lots of white roses, on the trellis, an outdoor wedding. And tiny babies' breath in your hair. And candles, all along the aisle in the grass. Where's the lawn?

SHELL: It died. We've had a drought. It'll grow back.

HIRO: [*Beat.*] I was supposed to be the maid of honor.

SHELL: It was a small wedding, Hiro.

HIRO: Why didn't you tell me?

SHELL: Why do you think?

HIRO: I don't know, you could have looked me up, or something. It was a mistake. Dad just slipped!

SHELL: People don't just let go at 100 feet up!

HIRO: I swear, he did. [*Beat.*] So that's what this is about. Shell, I thought you were having a bad day.

SHELL: That's 'cause you interrupted me! I was trying to jump to my death and you interrupted me!

QUEEN T: What are you two quarreling about?

[HIRO *runs inside the house. We can see her levitating about in the living room.* SHELL *chases her and yells at her from outside on the porch.*]

HIRO: It wasn't my fault, you know it.

QUEEN T: What . . . what . . . ?

SHELL: [*To* QUEEN T.] It's alright, Mom. [*To* HIRO.] Jus' couldn't stick around for Dad's funeral.

QUEEN T: Daddy, what . . . what has happened?

SHELL: [*Running between her sister and mother.*] You just flew away . . . it's OK, Mom . . . just like now, like you always do, ain't that so? Stop it! Damn it, Hiro!

[*Sound of a truck pulling into driveway.*]

HIRO: [*Levitating.*] No, no, I had to leave, they were gonna come after me.

SHELL: — but ain't that so?

QUEEN T: Shell. Hiro-chan. What has happened to your Daddy?

SHELL: Hiro, come down from there.

[HIRO *comes back on the porch.* ACE *enters.*]

QUEEN T: Ah, Andrew.

[ACE *holds a large bundle of logs. He drops them heavily near the chopping block in front of the porch.*]

ACE: Greetings from the Sierras.

SHELL: Hi.

[*He kisses* SHELL *and* QUEEN T *on the cheek. He puts a piece of wood on a cutting stump and chops the wood with an ax. The others watch.*]

HIRO: [*Surprised that Andrew is actually someone she knew by another name.*] Ace!

[*He does not respond to her.*]

QUEEN T: You will always be Andrew to me. I'm so glad you've come. I thought we'd have a little something to celebrate my 50th.

SHELL: She doesn't look 50, does she?

ACE: No, not at all.

QUEEN T: Some say I'm 50. And what a swift repondez s'il vous plait.

ACE: [*As he chops.*] Happened I was coming back from my brother's new place. I heard this voice way, way back in my head. Scared me near to death. Almost hit a possum, I was so distracted. You know Rusty's got a house the size of Riverside, and another five acres for his backyard, stretches as far as you can see. Some fellas have all the good fortune.

He's living like Thoreau. Except he's a fishery ranger. And he doesn't read.

QUEEN T: We must celebrate the return of the Prodigal Daughter.

ACE: [*To* SHELL.] Were you away?

QUEEN T: No. Hiro is the Prodigal Daughter.

HIRO: Ace, remember me?

ACE: [*Stops chopping.*] Hiro . . .

SHELL: Just for a short visit.

ACE: Hiro's dead.

[*Beat. He chops.*]

QUEEN T: My good man, this is Hiro, right here.

[*She goes behind* HIRO *and puts her hands on her shoulders. Beat.*]

ACE: There's no one there.

QUEEN T: Andrew, dear, right here.

ACE: No, I don't think there's anyone there, ma'am.

HIRO: Ace, don't you remember me? High school.

SHELL: Right there. In the blue suit.

ACE: The blue suit.

SHELL: Yeah. Don't you see her?

HIRO: [*Waving her arms at* ACE.] Hello, Ace. Andrew.

ACE: OH, OK, OK, yeah, I see her. The suit. A corporate look. [*To the air in front of him.*] I never thought I'd see you in a suit, Hiro. It's. Neat.

SHELL: In the blue bodysuit.

HIRO: Spandex.

SHELL: Are you OK?

ACE: You've been drinking.

SHELL: Not since this afternoon.

ACE: Long dry spell, wasn't it?

SHELL: Mom sees her just fine.

ACE: OK you two. Remember. Sometimes what you want to see, you see. I'm taking this with a grain of salt. You two see plenty of things.

SHELL: Andrew, she's right here.

[SHELL *points to* HIRO. ACE *tests the area in front of him with his hand, but* HIRO *dodges him, making it a game.*]

HIRO: Marco! Polo! Marco! Polo!

SHELL: Come on, Hiro.

ACE: A large grain of salt.

HIRO: Fish outta water! Fish outta water!

SHELL: I'm not making this up.

ACE: All right. We shall see.

[*He holds a small log of wood vertically in front of him. Beat. He drops the wood. It hits the ground. He shrugs. Beat.*]

SHELL: What does that prove?

ACE: If she were here, she would've snatched it up before it hit the ground.

HIRO: Come on, Ace, you have to tell me when the game starts.

SHELL: You just think you're always right, don't you, Mr. Philosopher. She doesn't need to dance for you.

HIRO: Yeah, that's right—

SHELL: She's here—

HIRO: Clear as day—

SHELL: You can't see the log in your own eye—

QUEEN T: That is a Biblical allusion—

HIRO: I'm a holy fish outta water!

ACE: Now ladies, hold your pouncing horses, I'm not accusing you of anything. [*Beat.*] OK. Platonically speaking. Yes. She could be real.

SHELL: What's that supposed to mean?

ACE: Platonically, as "in or relating to the theories of Plato."

HIRO: Platonically . . . where did you learn to use words like platonically?

QUEEN T: Plato, one of the late philosophers—

ACE: —you see, Plato theorized that even ideas are real. If you can conceive in your mind the idea of triangle, then it exists.

SHELL: She's not just something in my mind.

HIRO: I am not a triangle.

ACE: Platonically speaking, Hiro exists.

QUEEN T: That's right. Andrew, you always had the power of intellect. St. Augustine and Descartes. But you see Hiro, don't you?

ACE: Ma'am, I'm sorry I don't. Platonically, yes. Or spiritually. I can accept that Hiro's spirit is here.

HIRO: I'm dead to you?

QUEEN T: Her spirit has always transcended our plane, our atmosphere —

ACE: And a spirit cannot catch wood.

[ACE *picks up the wood again, drops it.* HIRO *tries to catch the wood. She misses.*]

HIRO: Ace, what's happened to you?

SHELL: She's a ghost?

ACE: Perhaps, or an idea.

[ACE *drops log.* HIRO *misses.*]

QUEEN T: — her ability to be light as feathers. Like Icarus, embracing the sun. You remember Icarus, don't you, Andrew?

ACE: His old man warned him the wax on his wings —

QUEEN T: — would melt. And he flew closer —

ACE: — to the sun. He wanted to feel the heat on his body. The sun's rays. [*He drops wood;* HIRO *misses.*] His wings deteriorated.

QUEEN T: Icarus was young.

ACE: — spiraled down, into the sea.

HIRO: What did you do to him, Shell?

ACE: The moral being: you should — [*About to drop wood, stops;* HIRO *snatches at nothing.*] — well, we all have memories of Hiro. I sometimes think about her.

SHELL: You do?

ACE: Here and there.

HIRO: Really?

ACE: [*Drops wood;* HIRO *misses.*] But she's gone. I thought we had discussed this before. She's passed on.

[ACE *crosses himself with the wood.*]

SHELL: Biblical?

ACE: [*To* SHELL.] Covering my ass. Never know. Shelly. I know you miss her, but you see things. The fishing boat in your bathtub. Little samurai with toothpicks that they pierced back in the mattress in the evening — [*About to drop wood, stops.*] — just like that Japanese fairy tale.

HIRO: Shell, don't listen to him.

ACE: She's dead, I'm sorry, ma'am.

QUEEN T: Hiro-chan? No.

ACE: If she were here she couldn't resist a challenge.

[ACE *is so confident he simply holds his arm out as he drops the wood, not even watching it fall.* HIRO *misses.*]

HIRO: [*In frustration and panic.*] I'm here!

ACE: She's a visage. [*Drops wood;* HIRO *misses.*] A visage of those we wish were still with us. [*Drops wood;* HIRO *misses.*] A mere visage.

[*He drops the wood; this time* HIRO *catches it in mid-fall and holds it there.* ACE *turns when he doesn't hear the wood hit the ground and sees a log floating in mid-air.*]

HIRO: I'll play your silly game. [*She smashes it on the ground in front of them.* ACE *is astonished, still cannot see her.*] I'm right in front of your eyes.

SCENE 4

Sometime that evening. SHELL *in spot on porch, holding a paring knife.* ACE *in spot near the chopping block.*

SHELL: And what am I to this family? There was a time when Little Shelly was miraculously pretty. But now . . .

ACE: There's a spirit in our house. A ghost. Moves like the air, the way she always did.

SHELL: I swear, I can feel her, taking her place again — center of attention — as soon as I turn my back. My sister. The miraculous one.

ACE: At first it was just Queen T. I'd be reading, Mishima or Kant, and my mother-in-law's voice would get inside my head, as if she were right over my shoulder. A constant party line: me, Mishima and my mother-in-law.

SHELL: I'm backed against the steps of my own front porch. Did I ask for this? Now she's crept under my skin —

ACE: Shell used to get jealous, complained she could never receive messages from her own mother. It's no privilege. Once I ran out in the field and read to the fading sunlight: hues of sunflower. I couldn't hear her. Found out that was the only time my mother-in-law couldn't talk to me. But now this spirit brings back memories.

SHELL: Someday Mom's gonna be sitting there holding a cup of mineral water and she'll just expire.

ACE: Was I searching for her?

SHELL: I'm looking for something I dropped in the street drain, and when I reach between the bars with a stick, I can hear something metal dragging along the concrete, but I can't seem to snag it up. [*Cuts herself.*] Of course I bleed. Who am I kiddin'?

ACE: Someone who is not real, your fingers pass right through —

[ACE *reaches out with his hand.*]

SHELL: But where can I go to find my own miraculous?

ACE: [*Draws back hand and wrings it.*] — or shall I leave the past well enough alone?

SHELL: Where does the miraculous lie?

SCENE 5

Later that same evening. HIRO *levitates inside the house. We can see her through the window.* QUEEN T *sits in her porch chair with a glass of mineral water.*

QUEEN T: [*Hearing a message.*] . . . a flying woman in a cycling outfit. [HIRO *turns to her.*] . . . blue cycling outfit. White helmet . . . why, that's you, Hiro.

[QUEEN T *turns on the radio. First there is static and then the news.*]

RADIO: — but witnesses say they did see a figure, probably female, floating along the Santa Ana River bank, a few feet above the ground.

[*The two talk over the radio announcer, who continues.*]

HIRO: A few feet?

[HIRO *stops levitating, comes over and holds* QUEEN T*'s hand to her forehead.*]

QUEEN T: They love you, Hiro.

HIRO: I can't let them know. Tell them . . . my levitation was a mirage caused by the heat from the riverbed.

QUEEN T: Of course, dear. Her levitation has the lightness of a mirage, rising as easily as heat from the riverbed —

RADIO: — at first spectators thought she was a mirage, but found she was indeed flying, perhaps energized by the heat from the riverbed.

HIRO: I'm really just a normal citizen in my cycling gear who stopped to admire the view. Just a blue-collar worker — [*She can't resist:*] — turned Olympic biker.

QUEEN T: She's really half an Olympian citizen in full gear — [*to* HIRO.] Hiro, we're not blue-collar —

RADIO: — with real Olympian strength she apprehended two white-collar criminals —

HIRO: I'm just a cyclist tired of home. Home prevents me from seeing the geography of the sky.

QUEEN T: She just flew to the sky, but remembered the sacred mother of the earth, Geo.

RADIO: — who just flew from authorities in a compact car. A Geo.

HIRO: And traumatic events, maybe a death in the family, make me wish I could touch the clouds —

QUEEN T: — and traumatic events became clouds at her touch —

RADIO: — unfortunately the dramatic events were clouded —

HIRO: So I could keep up hope —

QUEEN T: A mother can only hope —

RADIO: — and we hope — Jim, I know this is an incredible story, but —

HIRO: If you could conjure up the energy —

QUEEN T: She conjures up the energy —

RADIO: — she conjures up the energy to defy gravity —

[SHELL *enters, turns the radio off and attends to* QUEEN T *who rests, exhausted from the telepathy, in her chair.* HIRO *continues, thinking* QUEEN T *and the radio announcer are still listening, but soon begins to talk to her sister.*]

HIRO: . . . if you could will it to happen, pretty soon you'd be flying. You'd look down, and your house would be so small. You'd realize you don't need home anymore. You wouldn't need a father preaching philosophy and a mother talking ethereal sense to you. You could leave it all! A long time ago I took to the sky and I never looked back. Never. It gets you nowhere, Shell. You gotta seize the day! That's what Dad used to say. Funny thing was, he lived too much in his head. Always quoting and analyzing. I took him up and let him go. I thought he'd soar, but he fell like a withering lizard dropped from an eagle's beak. [*Beat.*] I was in trouble, they were gonna blame me and I needed your help. But you just stood there, yelling at me, saying I killed him. I gave him his chance, I can't coddle my own father. I don't coddle anyone. Now you hate me for it, don't you? Go ahead, say it: I killed our father. Say it all you want. 'Cause I know he just had no followthrough. He was soft, Shell! Just like you. Soft! And he got exactly what he deserved!

QUEEN T: [*Weary, speaks to the air.*] There you are, Hiro . . . [HIRO *turns at her mother's voice to see* SHELL. *The two look at each other.* HIRO *exits quickly.*] Hiro . . . I'm so glad you've come to see us. Why have you returned? . . . Hiro . . . Hiro-chan?

ACT II

SCENE 1

The next afternoon. QUEEN T *and* SHELL *on the porch.* ACE *sits on his wood-chopping stump, reading.*

SHELL: And tomorrow we'll have a party for you.

QUEEN T: A splendid celebration. We could cast flowers along the lawn.

SHELL: OK.

ACE: [*To* SHELL.] We don't have a lawn.

SHELL: Don't worry about that, it'll grow back.

QUEEN T: What I would like is an elixir that could forestall my age. Do you see any grey, Andrew?

ACE: [*Looks back and points.*] There's one.

QUEEN T: Really? Pluck it.

SHELL: [*As* ACE *hesitates.*] It's safe to come near the house, Andrew.

ACE: I'm not afraid of spirits, I'm just saying she should keep what's natural.

QUEEN T: I cannot be seen with grey hair. It's premature grey. Just one?

ACE: Uh huh.

SHELL: We could invite your friends, have a small dinner reception.

QUEEN T: The house must be very exquisite. Yes, pull it out, that one, dear.

ACE: Shell, tell your mother I don't pull grey hair.

QUEEN T: I do believe it's white. My . . . [*Pulls it out herself.*] I wonder where she's gone to. Didn't Hiro pay us a brief visit yesterday? Where did she go? [ACE *walks tentatively upstage to the porch, then picks up his ax and chops wood on the cutting block.*]

SHELL: I don't really care this time. Maybe to check the winds up on the tower, that's where she usually goes. [*Watches* ACE.] Andrew, why do you chop so much wood?

ACE: I get immediate results.

QUEEN T: She went to test the winds. [*Singing.*]

If your dilly, dilly heart
Feels a dilly, dilly way

[*Recovers.*]

QUEEN T: [*Cont'd.*]Oh, you must pardon me when I do that. Andrew looks so handsome today, doesn't he, Shell?

SHELL: Yeah, I reckon so.

QUEEN T: He looks like a prince.

SHELL: I wouldn't go that far . . .

ACE: [*Stops chopping.*] I would.

QUEEN T: Sweet as David.

SHELL: [*Pause, takes glass.*] Are you finished there, Mom?

QUEEN T: You could wash the bottoms a little better.

SHELL: They're frosted.

QUEEN T: Do you think she'll be back later?

SHELL: I hope not.

QUEEN T: What a terrible thing to say, Shell.

SHELL: Now don't worry, she'll be back soon. She's family. She's here for your party. She would never miss a decent party, just would miss cleaning the house when it was over. Well, time for a nap, OK? [*Beat.*] Mom. OK?

QUEEN T: Yes darling I'm here. [*Beat.*] Where is it?

SHELL: Come on. I'll show you.

QUEEN T: [*Walks toward the porch stairs which lead to the field.*] Here?

[*As if from many years of practice,* SHELL *and* ACE *quickly move closer to prevent her from possibly falling off the porch. They wait, frozen.*]

SHELL: No.

QUEEN T: [*Points to front door.*] Oh. This.

SHELL: [*Relieved.*] Uh huh. Come on.

QUEEN T: Has the sun gone down yet?

SHELL: No. Later.

[SHELL *helps her mother into the house. They exit.* ACE *is left sitting on the porch. He checks to make sure he is alone. Then he walks over to the log of wood, which is still on the ground from the evening before, picks it up tentatively, holding it vertically. Beat. He lets it fall to the ground. Nothing.*]

[HIRO *enters quietly and stands at foot of porch, watching him.* ACE *lights up a cigarette.*]

ACE: I bet you're surprised — that is, if you're really here — the way I've become more of a thinker. But really, it's not too great a distance between long-haired delinquent and a philosopher. Back then, I was drifting. About fifty miles out to sea, it was a black sea. The wind was high. I'd walk around the school, jumping out of my mind. I was setting lockers on fire. I'd see the girls in their new spring outfits. Lisa Wang, Debbie O'Brien, and Shawna . . . Yasugi, yeah Shawna. But whenever I'd look at them, they'd look away, laugh with their friends. I knew they saw me. It's because I look somber. That scared them. [*Beat.*] I started letting my stubble build until it looked like something, that took near a week, but it was worth it every time. My mother would complain, "Andrew, you need a shave, you look like a bum!" And then I'd shave. I looked forward to it. Usually on Sunday morning. Early. With the light from the small window shining down on the bathroom sink. I'd lather up and feel the roughness through the cream. Carve a fine, clean new face. Some go to church. Some read the funnies over coffee. I shave. You know, we became friends because we didn't have any. And friends are hard to come by. Just ask any somber kid. We were the outcast twosome, huh? We'd sit in the field after school. You'd smoke and I'd draw. I could whip out a samurai in full armor in a minute and fifteen seconds. Yeah, Ace was fast. I still have that drawing of you as a superhero. Hiro, the superhero. With a cape. I even drew you a helmet, because you were afraid you'd konk your head and have amnesia for the rest of your life. That distressed you, huh? Seeing people lose their memory. [*He pulls a small, worn drawing from his wallet and examines it. In the following exchange while* HIRO *speaks,* ACE *senses her presence and cannot hear her.*] Do you still look like this?

HIRO: [*Peers over his shoulder.*] That's why I made you keep it. I thought you'd forget me, someday.

ACE: I can't imagine.

HIRO: All the time I was flying to Eureka I thought of you.

ACE: I'm older now. Can you believe it? Jesus, you'd think I was an old man the way I talk. I thought I'd have done more by this time, but all I've acquired is age.

HIRO: I don't have a cape.

ACE: I thought you were dead. But . . . then . . . why did you leave like that?

HIRO: An essential accessory, my instructor told me. But what the hell did he know? He couldn't fly.

ACE: Why did you leave? Just took off like that.

HIRO: I'm sorry.

ACE: After you left I had a long, dry spell. No ocean. No black sea. A desert. I started getting crazy because of the void. I read all I could about life. Still do. It helps fill the desert. Then I met her one day, at the pharmacy of all places. Shell's good-looking and she stayed in one place. I needed that. A place. I was in love, or lust. I can't remember. It's the same thing. After a while, if you stay long enough, you grow to love someone even if it began as lust. Before I was only thinking of superheroes and burning things to the ground, but I was ready when I met her.

HIRO: I should've said goodbye.

ACE: I wish you'd stuck around, Hiro. Maybe things would be different.

[HIRO *steps closer to him. She kisses him. Then they embrace in a long kiss.* ACE *stops and backs away, not in fear but in reservation.* HIRO, *resonating more from the kiss than the rejection, exits.*]

SCENE 2

Later that day. SHELL *sits on the water tower, drinking.* HIRO *sits beside her.*

HIRO: Reminds me of school.

SHELL: Reminds me of the sea.

HIRO: [*Beat.*] It's boring up here.

SHELL: Then go away.

HIRO: I hate boring. Is this what home is like? It's more interesting to be distracted. Or in love.

SHELL: You're bored because you don't do it enough. You gotta experience boring for a long time, then it's not anymore.

HIRO: That's backwards, Shell.

SHELL: Oh? Is it? [*Pause.*] It's Zen.

HIRO: I've been interested in basket weaving. I want to basket weave, is that Zen? Do all those family things. I could even collect pills in bottles, like you did. [*Drinks.*] What is this?

SHELL: I made it up. Distillate hops. Wheat. Steeping for 21 days. Zen. Very Zen. I've recently become Zen. Just now. As I said it. I became Zen. That's Zen in itself. One man's boring is another man's Zen. Your problem is you're too active.

HIRO: [*Stands, prepares to fly.*] No. I'm too proud. I learned that from our royal mother. Pride. Because if you don't speak up, your own family will eat you for breakfast, like oatmeal. Pride. I've used it to overcome this inertia. But we could be both, Shell. You could teach me basket weaving, enchilada pies, all those house and home things. And then we could go flying. Flyers with enchiladas. Come on, let's get out of here. Let's go. You can do it, Shell. Mom's telepathic, I fly, so you must do something.

SHELL: Like what? Name it. I can do nothing. It's very Zen.

HIRO: You can tend to plants. All those plants around the house.

SHELL: Plants! Goddamn, I knew there was something! Well, at least plants make good companions. You water, they grow. Water. Grow. Water. Grow. Water—

HIRO: Ace thinks I'm dead.

SHELL: Everyone does.

HIRO: You told him I was going to Eureka, right? [*Beat.*] Right? That's what you told him? [*Beat.*] You told him I was dead?

SHELL: Everyone thought you were, the way you disappeared. It was better that way, if Ace, Mom and everyone had the same story. My story would have no holes. You know if Mom knew the truth, that you'd killed Dad and ran away like that, she'd be heartbroken —

HIRO: We were flying and he let go. There's a reason why we do everything.

SHELL: No one lets go at 100 feet up.

HIRO: But I had a good reason. I had this dream the day I first flew —

SHELL: I don't want to hear this —

HIRO: Oh, come on, we used to always tell each other our dreams. In fact, you made me make mine up when I couldn't remember the whole thing.

SHELL: That was kid stuff.

HIRO: I was a kid when I dreamed this. OK. The first day I flew, I dreamed I was in a desert in a dust storm with about 20 tourists, and we were all climbing to the top of a large metal Egyptian pyramid. The dust kept flying in my mouth. Everyone crawls and struggles to get to this small shack on the top of the pyramid, but the tourists keep taking pictures: click, click, click, click —

SHELL: I know there's a good point to this, tell me when you get there.

HIRO: And I realize, "Hey, I'm having a dream. But I won't remember this when I wake up," and then your voice comes out of nowhere and you say, "Make it up, then." So I do. I want to lift up, so I do! I want to fly past the tourists, so I do. I crash through the straw roof of the shack and you know who's inside?

[She pauses dramatically.]

SHELL: Me.

HIRO: Dad. Dad's standing there with a glass of water and he's drinking it and floating in the air, just like me. Then all the tourists look through the windows and take pictures of us. We're famous!

SHELL: [Beat.] I know there's a good point to all this.

HIRO: The point is I knew he had potential. I was careful with him, Shell. I waited until I could levitate without a flaw, without tipping to one side or the other and I made sure I could carry his weight. I practiced with a sack of potatoes and then a tire strapped on my back.

SHELL: Dad is not a sack of potatoes.

HIRO: People don't understand. The air is like water for me. With a little arm movement — [She flaps, gracefully.] I can tread the air, like treading water in a swimming pool, it's that easy. It carries me, I don't have to fight it. So in the air, a heavy object was half its weight, a ten pound sack of potatoes was five, and a 50-pound tire was 25, and a 135-pound cow —

SHELL: A cow?

HIRO: Was half that in the air.

SHELL: You mean a 135-pound calf.

HIRO: A cow. A baby cow.

SHELL: OK. Where did you find a baby cow? A dead baby cow?

HIRO: No, I'm not gonna lift some cow corpse into the air. A live cow. From a field. Mr. Johnson's field.

SHELL: Did you drop it?

HIRO: Of course not.

SHELL: A flying cow?

HIRO: So, I knew if I could lift a cow that weighed what Dad weighed, I could lift Dad. I put the cow down and I turned around in the field and there was Dad, standing there, waiting for his turn, with this part smile on his face. And I asked him if he wanted to try it out, that I was ready now. And I had him get on my back, piggy-back style. I'll show you.

SHELL: Just tell me.

HIRO: I'll show you, Shell. [HIRO *stands in front of ledge on a lower platform.* SHELL *gets on* HIRO'S *back, one leg still on the ground supporting her.*] See? It's very secure. He was on my back, his arms wrapped around my shoulders, I said, "Look at the clouds, Dad, see, we're almost in the clouds!" And he said, "That's fine, honey, I've always wondered what it was like up here, almost like heaven." Like heaven. Then, I felt his hands slip from my shoulders and I turned around and he was gone. [*Beat.*] I was trying to be careful, he just slipped away.

SHELL: Guess you thought all it took was a little bit of concentration. Well, Hiro, it takes a little gift from above, too. And some of us didn't have that. [*Beat.*] We're not leaving the ground, you got it?

HIRO: OK, OK. I promise. Just put your other leg up so you can see how stable we were. [SHELL *puts her other leg around* HIRO'S *waist.*] See? Now, what you have to do is concentrate — that's what I told Dad, I mean — just think of breathing steady, think of when you're at the bottom of a pool and you can see the sun in the water sparkling above you and you just rise up. It just happens, right? It takes very little ef-fort.

SHELL: [*Tries to concentrate.*] Hiro, Dad couldn't swim.

HIRO: I know, but he could imagine it.

SHELL: No wonder he fell, Dad's never been in the ocean in his life.

HIRO: But we live right next to it, he had an imagination. [SHELL *starts to get down from* HIRO'S *back.*] What are you doing? Wait!

SHELL: You told him to swim and he doesn't.

HIRO: Wait! Will you concentrate or this isn't gonna work.

SHELL: I ain't gonna concentrate because I'm not gonna go up in the air with you. I'm sure it's fine and thrilling, but I'm too old for this and so are you.

HIRO: You're just afraid. Just concentrate, Shell, or this isn't gonna work right.

SHELL: It's not gonna work at all. Hiro, if you weren't so reckless we'd still have an entire family! I was the one who held the scraps of this fam-ily together, patching up for your errors because you were so god-damn irresponsible. Just. Let. Me. Go!

[*Suddenly their bodies take a deep breath and hold in complete silence as they rise up.* SHELL *is in awe,* HIRO *is focused, almost trance-like. They whisper.*]

SHELL: Jesus Christ.

HIRO: Like heaven.

[*Blackout.*]

SCENE 3

The porch. ACE *is combing* QUEEN T*'s hair.*

ACE: It's an intriguing question: is man naturally good and society makes him bad? Or is man naturally evil and society makes him good?

QUEEN T: Man is naturally good, of course, what sort of world would this be if men were evil? How could women trust them? Ah, but to con-tinue.

ACE: Rousseau believed man was naturally good and that man would put others before himself. For example, let's say there is a bag of potato chips in a room and two people in the room want it.

QUEEN T: Oh, raise the stakes.

ACE: Two people starving —

QUEEN T: A desert island, and they have no food —

ACE: — of course they don't have any food —

QUEEN T: — because they're starving.

ACE: Except for a bag of potato chips —

QUEEN T: Which they both desire —

ACE: What will win out? Survival or sympathy? Will they fight for the potato chips —

QUEEN T: Or will they give it to the other, as common courtesy.

ACE: — although this is not even courtesy, it's human nature.

QUEEN T: Really? But it's also etiquette. Who's older?

ACE: Who?

QUEEN T: Of the two starving men, who's older?

ACE: It doesn't make a difference, this is a closed environment, an ideal setting, no race, no age —

QUEEN T: Ah, but you see, in today's world, it would make a difference, about age.

ACE: True, but this is talking about the origin before social norms.

QUEEN T: What would we do if the youth did not respect their elders?

ACE: And ideally they would share the bag of chips and both survive. They would be a little hungry, but it would hold them over until something better came along.

QUEEN T: That is fascinating. The seed of humankind's actions and folly. When I talk to you it seems very clear.

ACE: Thank you.

QUEEN T: You're welcome. [*He finishes and hands her the brush; pause.*] You help ease my mind while my husband is away.

ACE: I'm sure he'd be here if he could.

QUEEN T: Sometimes I think I hear him calling my name, from very far away, but recently I've been disappointed it's only Shell calling me to dinner. Sometimes when you talk, you sound like my husband. Say my name. My real name.

ACE: Tsuruko.

QUEEN T: Yes, yes, it does sound similar. In any case, David used to explain these things to me, philosophy . . . I'm surprised how I can still follow theory quickly . . . I do miss you. When will we see each other again?

ACE: [*Hearing her telepathy, slightly entranced.*] My dear Queen T, very soon, as sure as there is water in the sea. For time often calls mystics and philosophers early in their season. Alas, my time came suddenly. But soon we shall meet again.

QUEEN T: My sweet David, even as you are a philosopher, you speak with poetry. You have grown to understand my heart.

ACE: Philosophy and poetry are simply where the sky and water touch.

QUEEN T: Even as you are an intellectual, and although at times a skeptic, you did marry me. That, dear, was the most skeptical thing you could have done.

ACE: I'm skeptical only that I may find purity, Queen T. For we are an unusual match, but the purity comes through waiting for the clearest water to rise above the sediment.

QUEEN T: A Biblical allusion?

ACE: No. One that is real, Tsuruko. Real with a long life.

QUEEN T: Sweet King David.
[*Sings.*]

I'll be your queen
Who told you so, dilly dilly
Who told you so?
I told myself . . .

ACE: [*Breaking the telepathy.*] Real with a long life . . . Ma'am. I'm not David.

QUEEN T: [*Lightly.*] Of course not, Andrew. I was just reminiscing.

SCENE 4

In spotlight. SHELL *on* HIRO'S *back. They are flying. Wind blows in their faces. Wagner plays.*

HIRO: The flying sisters! Yah, boy! Yah! Come on, help me fly the chariot. Yah!

SHELL: Yah. Yah!

HIRO: Yah! Come on boy!

SHELL: Come on boy! [*Beat.*] I can do this. I can do this.

HIRO: Yes!

SHELL: I'm doing this!

HIRO: Just flap! We're gonna be famous. Look. Cameras. Pose for them.

[*They strike a pose for an invisible camera.*]

SHELL: Twin flyers!

HIRO: Flying sisters!

SHELL: Seize the day! Come on, yah! Yah! [*She rides* HIRO *like a horse.*] Seize the day!

HIRO: Yah! Woooweeee! Yah!

SHELL: Seize the day!

HIRO: Fight for those wings! [SHELL *quietly disappears behind* HIRO'S *shoulders;* HIRO *looks around, then calls down.*] That's right, Shell! Concentrate! And flap your arms. Flap your arms! [*Beat.*] Hey, Shell. Shell!

[*Music soars as lights fade.*]

SCENE 5

Ten minutes later. ACE *chops wood while he hums a tune.* SHELL *stomps up to porch. Her hair and clothes are drenched. She sits. She wrings out the front of her shirt as she wears it.* ACE *looks at it, then checks the sky for evidence of rain clouds. He's about to ask her why she is wet, but instead shakes his head and exits.* HIRO *enters, panicked. She sees* SHELL *and is overcome with relief.*

HIRO: See? That wasn't so bad, huh? You did it! The famous flyer! Sure ended with a splash. Hey. You just got to go up there more often, to practice. We could go up on the tower every day. I could coach you. [*Smells her clothes.*] You better wash the chlorine out, Shell, otherwise your clothes will be all bleached and your hair —

SHELL: You dropped me.

HIRO: You were flying. You just landed awkward.

SHELL: I wasn't flying, I was on your back and you tried to drop me!

HIRO: I knew we were over a pool, OK?

SHELL: You aimed for the concrete.

HIRO: [*Puts hand on her shoulder.*] Come on, Shell, why would I do that, what would I possibly gain from killing my little—[SHELL *pulls* HIRO'S *hand away and shoves her.*] Hey, watch it! Jesus. I take her up in the air and she becomes a bitch.

SHELL: Flying my ass! You keep your great ideas to yourself. In fact keep your whole life outta this house.

HIRO: Hey, this is my house too, as long as I'm family—

SHELL: You're not family, I just disowned you. You want to knock me off and waltz right on in. This is not espionage, this is family. Not I Spy, not Guinea Bissoh, or whatever you call that place.

HIRO: You were the one who let go.

SHELL: Bullshit! You're all bullshit. You're trying to wipe me out. It's not that easy.

HIRO: You let go.

SHELL: Why would I do that, huh? Tell me. Why would anyone let go at 100 feet up? No one does. You threw me off your back. Hell, even if you killed me in your sleep, at least I have the satisfaction to know that you'll be all alone soon. You're picking off your family, one by one.

HIRO: Queen T will always be here. We're gonna have a whole life together.

SHELL: Oh, yeah, and how long do you think she's gonna last? You're back too late. Ain't that a fucking shame. Little Hiro-chan, the only one left!

HIRO: She'll be around another 50 years. That's a long time. We're special, better than normal.

SHELL: Besides, you couldn't take care of her, you don't know how. [*Beat.*] You don't know how to sit still, that's the problem here.

HIRO: Shut up.

SHELL: You can't sit still.

HIRO: Shut up. [*Makes a fist by her side.*] Don't make me do it.

SHELL: No one makes you do anything. You can't sit still!

[SHELL *shoves* HIRO. HIRO *hits* SHELL *hard on the jaw.* SHELL *stumbles back onto the porch.* HIRO *turns away confidently.* SHELL *grabs a log of wood from the porch basket as she recovers, and as she comes up, she hits* HIRO *on the side of the head.* HIRO *staggers, disoriented.*]

HIRO: Oh come off it, Shell. Fuck. [*Staggers back.*] Stop it. Just calm down!

SHELL: Don't tell me to fucking calm down!

HIRO: Ace!

[SHELL *drops log to search for a better weapon and finds the paring knife on the porch table.* ACE *returns to the porch, sensing* HIRO.]

SHELL: [*To* ACE.] Stay out of my business!

[*She comes up behind* HIRO *and pulls her by the neck to the ground, knife to* HIRO'S *cheek.* SHELL *makes a cut in* HIRO'S *cheek. There is no blood.*]

HIRO: Help me, Ace!

ACE: [*Senses her.*] Hiro?

SHELL: [*To* ACE.] Stay the fuck away.

HIRO: Ace! Help me, Ace!

SHELL: Come on, bleed!

ACE: Shell, she's not real.

HIRO: [*Looks at* ACE, *astonished.*] Mom! Help!

SHELL: [*Standing.*] She's my mother. I earned her.

HIRO: I'm her daughter. Mom! Help!

SHELL: I hurt you? Let's see you bleed! Don't move, I'll take it right through to your heart. You have it coming to you, Hiro. Little Hiro-chan. Tried to kill me. Dropped me just like Dad. Ain't that so?

HIRO: I didn't do anything!

SHELL: I'm not such a fucking pushover. Hear me? Hear me?

HIRO: Yes.

ACE: Shell. Leave Hiro alone. She's not real.

SHELL: [*Looks up at him, then to* HIRO.] It doesn't really matter. Do ghosts bleed? Are you a spirit? Whatever you are. You owe me, Hiro. Give me back my life! Come on. You owe me fifteen years of blood. You owe me fifteen lonely years! Say it!

HIRO: Fuck you!

SHELL: [*Pushes her to ground, gets on top, shaking her.*] Say it! I owe you –

HIRO: I owe you . . .

SHELL: — fifteen lonely years.

ACE: Shell. Shelly—

HIRO: . . . lonely . . .

SHELL: — fifteen lonely years.

ACE: Shell.

[HIRO, *dizzy, touches her hand to her own cheek. Blood appears.* SHELL *holds her sister's bloody hand for an instant, then lets go, turns away.*]

HIRO: I'm bleeding. Fifteen . . . I owe . . .

SHELL: All my youth, wasted on my fucking family. My tired fucking family.

HIRO: [*Looks up, calmly realizing.*] No. You owe you. You stayed here. I asked you to come, but you just stood there yelling at me. [*Smiles weakly.*] Shell, you let go, didn't you? You can fly.

[HIRO *gets up.*]

SHELL: No.

HIRO: So, this is life without a helmet? I just needed a place to rest my head. I don't owe you. You owe you. [*Laughs quietly.*] I never knew my sister was so violent.

SHELL: I don't have a sister. Get out of my life.

[HIRO *exits.*]

SCENE 6

Early the next morning, just before sunrise. Faint sound of seagulls. QUEEN T *stands on porch in spotlight. She has aged suddenly overnight. She talks as if to* HIRO.

QUEEN T: Ah, you're here, Hiro-chan. I'm afraid I'm a little under the weather, and here it is my birthday. I'm up before the sun, but it's better I depart while things are quiet. Quiet takes many forms nowadays. You see where the water ends there? I'm taking a boat out to sea. Some say the sea doesn't really end, because the closer you are, the more the horizon jumps forward. You see, there comes a point when we are not mother and daughter anymore, but two people who know each other. That's when we can talk of important things. [*Beat.*] When I was very young, my mother gave me a present: a globe of the world, the kind that spun on a metal axis. I put it on my desk and held my finger on it lightly and spun it around and around until it stopped. I landed in Brasilia, or Dharmasala, or in Austin, but never once did I land in my own home town. [*Beat.*] Oh, my dear Hiro, I wish we could have discussed geography longer, but it seems we've been apart for some time. Well. be a good girl now and stay here. Yes, stay right here. I promise to send you messages every day. I promise.

[QUEEN T *walks offstage into the sea. Distant clang of a boat bell, growing fainter.*]

[HIRO *enters, holding her hand to her wounded cheek. She stands to the side of the porch, looking out to sea, watching something. She lowers her hand to reveal a reddish scar, then holds her hand to her forehead, waiting for a message. But she receives none. She begins to cry silently.*]

[SHELL *comes out onto the porch. She has just woken up.* ACE *follows her out. They do not touch but are hopefully gentle in each other's presence. They look out at the ocean.*]

[HIRO *looks at* SHELL.]

SHELL: [*She has lost her Southern accent.*] I was thinking of swimming in a vast lake. I could dive in and feel the underwater plants brushing around me. You know, I haven't gone swimming like that in a long time.

ACE: Is this a dream you had?

[SHELL *sees* HIRO *for a brief moment, and then calmly distracted, looks out to sea.*]

SHELL: Nah, it wasn't a dream. Something I was thinking of this morning, after I woke up. [HIRO *exits quickly. The sunrise casts an orange hue across* ACE *and* SHELL'S *faces.*] Isn't that a sight?

ACE: Hues of sunflower.

SHELL: [*Calling.*] Mom! Mom, wake up. Come see the sunrise.

[*Calling, calmly.*]

SHELL: [*Cont'd.*] Mom?

[*Beat.*]

SHELL: [*Cont'd.*] Mom.

[*Lights fade as they watch the sunrise.*]

END OF PLAY

ABOUT THE EDITOR

During his tenure as Literary Manager and Dramaturg at East West Players, Brian Nelson inaugurated the David Henry Hwang Writers Institute, and created and curated The Writers Gallery, a new works series for both established and developing playwrights. As a theatre director, his credits include his own adaptation of *The Joy Luck Club* for the Mark Taper Forum Literary Cabaret, productions at East West of *The Rising Tide of Color* and *Twelf Nite O Wateva!* (for which he received an Ovation Award nomination), and Texas Shakespeare Festival productions of *King Lear* and *Cyrano de Bergerac*. His television writing includes - stories for *Lois and Clark*, *Jag* and *Vanishing Son*, as well as the ABC miniseries adaptation of *20,000 Leagues Under the Sea*; he is currently adapting Tom Robbins' *Jitterbug Perfume* for Universal Pictures. His critical writing has been published in On-Stage Studies and the Los Angeles Reader. He holds degrees in literature and theatre, respectively, from Yale University and UCLA, where he was the recipient of the first Michael Peretzian Directing Award. He lives in Southern California with stunning redhead Barbara Calvi and their daughter, Madeleine.

WOMENSWORK
Five new Plays from the Women's Project
Edited by Julia Miles

The voices of five major playwrights offering a vibrant range of styles and themes can be heard here as they resound from the stage of The Women's Project. The dramas which converge here from Maria Irene Fornes, Cassandra Medley, Marlane Meyer, Lavonne Mueller and Sally Nemeth emanate with international character and universal allure.

MA ROSE Cassandra Medley
FIVE IN THE KILLING ZONE Lavonne Mueller
ETTA JENKS Marlane Meyer
ABINGDON SQUARE Maria Irene Fornes
MILL FIRE Sally Nemeth

paper • ISBN: 1-55783-029-0

WOMEN ON THE VERGE:
7 Avant-Garde American Plays
Edited by Rosette C. Lamont

This APPLAUSE anthology gathers together recent work by the finest and most controversial contemporary American women dramatists. Collectively, this Magnificent Seven seeks to break the mold of the well-wrought psychological play and its rigid emphasis on realistic socio-political drama. The reader will imbibe the joyous poetry flowing in these uncharted streams of dramatic expression, a restless search that comes in the wake of European explorations of Dada, Surrealism and the Absurd.

THE PLAYS:

Rosalyn Drexler Occupational Hazard

Tina Howe Birth and After Birth

Karen Malpede Us

Maria Irene Fornes What of the Night?

Suzan-Lori Parks The Death of the Last Black Man in the Whole Entire World

Elizabeth Wong Letters to a Student Revolutionary

Joan M. Schenkar The Universal Wolf

paper • ISBN: 1-55783-148-3

The Scarlet Letter

by Nathaniel Hawthorne

Adapted for the stage by

James F. DeMaiolo

Leslie Fiedler pronounced it the first American tragedy. F.O. Mathiessen considered it the "Puritan Faust." Richard B. Sewall compared its inexorable dramatic force to King Lear. These chieftains of American literature were not, as one might suspect referring to a play by O'Neill. They are not in fact, referring to a play at all, but to a masterpiece of nineteenth century fiction. Until now, it appeared that Nathaniel Hawthorne's haunting drama of judgment, alienation and redemption would be forever confined to the page. The Scarlet Letter continues to be the most frequently read novel in American high schools today as well as one of the most widely circulated novels in the American library system. And now comes the stage version to do it justice.

A century and a half after its first incarnation, James DeMaiolo has forged an alliance of craft and spirit so potent in its own right and so faithful to Hawthorne's original that his stage version is certain to compel all non-believers to recant and take heed. The audience joins the chorus as they weigh the American contract of freedom against the fine print of convention and taboo.

Paper•ISBN 1-55783-243-9 • $6.95

Performance rights available from APPLAUSE

APPLAUSE

Bunny, Bunny
Gilda Radner,
A Sort of Love Story
by
Alan Zweibel

"Very rarely when reading a book do I find myself actually laughing out loud, but it happened very often in Alan Zweibel's hilarious account of his adventures with Gilda Radner. **I MUST ADMIT, THERE WERE ALSO A FEW MOMENTS WHEN I FOUND MYSELF FIGHTING BACK TEARS.**"
— MEL BROOKS

" ... AN INTIMATE ANDFASCINATING LOOK AT A VERY FUNNY, VERY COURAGEOUS, VERY LOVED WOMAN." — JOAN RIVERS

"AFFECTIONATE, FUNNY, and at times actually well written. Just a joke, Alan." — CHEVY CHASE

"TRANSFORMS HISTORY INTO SOMETHING LIKE ART ... CHARMING, FUNNY, POIGNANT." — PHILADELPHIA INQUIRER

Paper•ISBN 1-55783-276-5 • $12.95
Performance rights available from APPLAUSE

NEW BROADWAYS

THEATRE ACROSS AMERICA AS THE MILLENIUM APPROACHES
by Gerald M. Berkowitz

"AN OUTSTANDINGBOOK OF THE YEAR ...
HIGHLY RECOMMENDED"— CHOICE

"THE MOSTCOMPLETE GUIDE YETCOMPILED"
— AMERICAN THEATRE

In 1950, the terms "American theatre" and "Broadway" were virtually synonymous. As the century ends, Broadway is only a small part of a vital, creative, and varied national theatrical scene. A thorough revision and expansion of the award–winning 1982 book, *NEW BROADWAYS: THEATRE ACROSS AMERICA* treats such subjects as the contributions of the Ford Foundation, the importance of pioneers such as Joseph Papp, the checkered history of Lincoln Center, the evolution of the Broadway musical, and the experimental companies of the 1960s. As the American theatre faces the new millennium, Berkowitz draws on interviews with artistic directors of leading theatres around the country to offer predictions — and some warnings — for the future.

$24.95 • cloth
1-55783-257-9

PLAYS BY AMERICAN WOMEN: 1930-1960

Edited by Judith E. Barlow

Sequel to the acclaimed *Plays by American Women: 1900-1930* (now in its fifth printing!), this new anthology reveals the depth and scope of women's dramatic voices during the middle years of this century. The extensive introduction traces the many contributions of women playwrights to our theatre from the beginning of the Depression to the dawn of the contemporary women's movement. Among the eight plays in the volume are smart comedies and poignant tragedies, political agitprop and surrealist fantasies, established classics and neglected treasures.

THE WOMEN Clare Boothe

THE LITTLE FOXES Lillian Hellman

IT'S MORNING Shirley Graham

THE MOTHER OF US ALL Gertrude Stein

GOODBYE, MY FANCY Fay Kanin

IN THE SUMMER HOUSE Jane Bowles

TROUBLE IN MIND Alice Childress

CAN YOU HEAR THEIR VOICES? Hallie Flanagan and Margaret Ellen Clifford

paper • ISBN: 1-55783-164-5

APPLAUSE

PLAYS BY AMERICAN WOMEN: 1900-1930

Edited by Judith E. Barlow

These important dramatists did more than write significant new plays; they introduced to the American stage a new and vital character—the modern American woman in her quest for a forceful role in a changing American scene. It will be hard to remember that these women playwrights were ever forgotten.

A MAN'S WORLD Rachel Crothers
TRIFLES Susan Glaspell
PLUMES Georgia Douglas Johnson
MACHINAL Sophie Treadwell
MISS LULU BETT Zona Gale

paper • ISBN: 1-55783-008-X

APPLAUSE

THE MUSICAL

A LOOK AT THE AMERICAN MUSICAL THEATER
by Richard Kislan
New, Revised, Expanded Edition

Richard Kislan examines the history, the creators, and the vital components that make up a musical and demonstrates as never before how musicals are made.

From its beginnings in colonial America, the musical theater has matured into an impressive art and business, one that has brought millions the experience that director-choreographer Bob Fosse describes as when "everybody has a good time even in the crying scenes."

Kislan traces the musical's evolution through the colorful eras of minstrels, vaudeville, burlesque, revue, and comic opera up to the present day. You'll learn about the lives, techniques, and contributions of such great 20th-century composers and lyricists as Jerome Kern, Rodgers an d Hammerstein, Stephen Sondheim and others. Kislan explains all the basic principles, materials and techniques that go into the major elements of a musical production—the book, lyrics, score, dance and set design.

Richard Kislan's acclaimed study of America's musical theatre has been updated to bring it up to the cutting edge of today's musicals. A new section entitled: Recent Musical Theater: Issues and Problems includes chapters on **The British Invasion • Competition from the Electronic Media • Escalating Costs • The Power of the Critics • The Depletion of Creative Forces • Multiculturalism • The Decline of the Broadway Neighborhood*** **Stephen Sondheim** and his influence on the present day musical theater.

Paper $16.95 • ISBN 1-55783-217-X

❦APPLAUSE❦

THE END OF ACTING
by Richard Hornby

Acting in America has staggered to a dead end. Every year, tens of thousands of aspiring actors pursue the Hollywood grail and chant the familiar strains of the Stanislavski "Method" in classrooms and studios across the nation. The initial liberating spirit of Stanislavski's experiments long ago withered into rigid patterns of inhibitions and emotional introspection. Hornby urges the American theatre artist to emulate the average British actor who, he writes, is "more flexible, has a broader range, is more imaginative, and even has more emotional intensity than his American counterpart."

"**Passionate...provocative**...A clear, comprehensive book bound to be read with great interest by anyone concerned with the future of American acting ..."
—VARIETY

"**Few theorists are this brave; even fewer are this able**."
—William Oliver, CRITICISM

"This very important work is **an essential purchase**..."
—LIBRARY JOURNAL

"**Theatre lovers will find much to ponder** in his zingy restatement of a central argument about American acting."
—PUBLISHERS WEEKLY

paper • ISBN: 1-55783-213-7

APPLAUSE

The Day the Bronx Died

A Play

by Michael Henry Brown

"THE DAY THE BRONX DIED COMES ON LIKE GANGBUSTERS...LIKE A CAREENING SUBWAY TRAIN spewing its points in a series of breathless controntations"

—MICHAEL MUSTO, *The New York Daily News*

"Michael Henry Brown is A SMOKING VOLCANO OF A WRITER...THE DAY THE BRONX DIED is an engrossin drama… the danger exceeds our expectations"

—JAN STUART, *New York Newsday*

Two childhood friends—one black, the other white—struggle to live in a racist world.

Michael Henry Brown wrote the screenplay, DEAD PRESIDENTS directed by the Hughes brothers. He is the author of the HBO Mini-series LAUREL AVENUE. Among his other plays is GENERATION OF THE DEAD IN THE ABYSS OF CONEY ISLAND MADNESS which was produced to great acclaim at the Long Wharf Theatre in New Haven and the Penumbra Theatre in St. Paul

Paper•ISBN 1-55783-229-3 • $6.95
Performance rights available from APPLAUSE

THE REDUCED SHAKESPEARE COMPANY'S

COMPLEAT WORKS OF WLLM SHKSPR
(abridged)

by JESS BORGESON, ADAM LONG, and DANIEL SINGER

"ABSL HLRS." —*The Independent* (London)

"Shakespeare writ small, as you might like it!... Pithier-than-Python parodies...not to be confused with that august English company with the same initials. This iconoclastic American Troupe does more with less."

— *The New York Times*

"Shakespeare as written by *Reader's Digest*, acted by Monty Python, and performed at the speed of the Minute Waltz. So Forsooth! Get thee to the RSC's delightfully fractured *Compleat Works*."

— *Los Angeles Herald*

$8.95 • PAPER • ISBN 1-55783-157-2

THEATRE FOR YOUNG AUDIENCES:

AROUND THE WORLD IN 21 PLAYS
Edited by Lowell Swortzell

See the world through the ages in this international volume of classic, modern, and contemporary plays. Heading the expedition is Lowell Swortzell, whose compelling introductions propel the reader into the historical and social background of each play. Journey into myth, fantasy, and folklore, and inevitably, back home into everyday life.
Among the selections:

Jack Juggler • MOLIERE The Flying Doctor • CARLO GOZZI The Love of Three Oranges • Punch and Judy • AUGUST STRINDBERG Lucky Peter's Journey • STANISLAW WITKIEWICZ Childhood Plays • GERTRUDE STEIN Three Sisters who are not Sisters • LANGSTON HUGHES Soul Gone Home • WENDY KESSELMAN Maggie Magalita • JOANNA HALPERT KRAUS The Ice Wolf • PER LYSADER AND SUSAN OLSEN Medea's Children

$29.95 • cloth
1-55783-263-3